TEACHING MATHEMATICS TO ALL CHILDREN

Designing and Adapting Instruction to Meet the Needs of Diverse Learners

BENNY F. TUCKER

ANN H. SINGLETON

TERRY L. WEAVER

Merrill
Prentice Hall

Upper Saddle River, New Jersey
Columbus, Ohio

Library of Congress Cataloging-in-Publication Data

Tucker, Benny F.
  Teaching mathematics to all children: designing and adapting instruction to meet the needs of diverse learners /
by Benny F. Tucker, Ann H. Singleton, Terry L. Weaver.
    p. cm.
  Includes index.
  ISBN 0-13-027021-0
  1. Mathematics--Study and teaching (Elementary)   I. Singleton, Ann H.   II. Weaver, Terry L.   III. Title.

QA135.5 .T83 2002
372.7'044--dc21   2001021909

Vice President and Publisher: Jeffery W. Johnston
Executive Editor: Ann Castel Davis
Editorial Assistant: Keli Gemrich
Production Editor: Sheryl Glicker Langner
Production Coordination: Roark Mitzell, York Production Services
Design Coordinator: Diane C. Lorenzo
Photo Coordinator: Sandy Lenahan
Cover Designer: Thomas Borah
Cover Photo: The Stock Market
Production Manager: Laura Messerly
Director of Marketing: Kevin Flanagan
Marketing Manager: Amy June
Marketing Coordinator: Barbara Koontz

This book was set in Novarese Book by York Graphic Services, Inc. It was printed and bound by Courier Kendallville, Inc.
This cover was printed by Phoenix Color Corp.

Photo Credits: pp. 4, 38 by Todd Yarrington/Merrill; pp.6, 20, 71, 76, 165, 205, 252, 342 by Barbara Schwartz/Merrill;
pp.18, 22, 34, 50, 286, 317 by Scott Cunningham/Merrill; p. 56 by Sandy Lenahan/Merrill; p. 99 by Anthony
Magnacca/Merrill; p. 123 by Silver Burdett Ginn Needham; p.143 by Ken Karp/Prentice Hall College; p. 233 by Silver
Burdett Ginn; p. 273 by Barbara Hadley/U.S. Department of Health and Human Services; p. 341 by Pearson
Learning; p. 364 by Michael Provost/Silver Burdett Ginn; p. 373 by Anne Vega/Merrill.

Prentice-Hall International (UK) Limited, *London*
Prentice-Hall of Australia Pty. Limited, *Sydney*
Prentice-Hall Canada, Inc., *Toronto*
Prentice-Hall Hispanoamericana, S.A., *Mexico*
Prentice-Hall of India Private Limited, *New Delhi*
Prentice-Hall of Japan, Inc., *Tokyo*
Prentice-Hall Singapore Pte. Ltd.
Editora Prentice-Hall do Brasil, Ltda., *Rio de Janeiro*

10 9 8 7 6 5 4 3 2 1
ISBN: 0-13-027021-0

PREFACE

Why This Book?

Recently, elementary classrooms have become increasingly diverse. This diversity includes differences in gender, race and ethnicity, religion, culture, ability and interest, learning styles, family background and support, and availability of resources such as books and technology. Furthermore, there is a current trend toward inclusion of special needs children in the regular classroom, a trend unlikely to be reversed in the foreseeable future. Typical preparation of special education teachers and regular classroom teachers does not equip either group to operate effectively in the kind of inclusion settings that they are now likely to see. In this text, we provide an approach to the planning and teaching of elementary school mathematics that will better equip teachers to be successful with diverse groups of students and in inclusion classrooms. We hope the teaching suggestions in this text will help teachers be more effective as they attempt to *teach mathematics to all children*.

Structure of the Book

The text begins with three introductory chapters that provide a basic understanding of instructional activities, diversity, and lesson planning. Then there are eight chapters devoted to teaching the content that most commonly appears in elementary school mathematics textbooks. The final chapter is devoted to practice activities that can be adapted to a wide variety of content.

We have not attempted to provide comprehensive coverage of every mathematics topic that might appear in an elementary school mathematics textbook. Rather, our intent has been to emphasize a way of teaching effectively that will result in learning, understanding, retention of important concepts and skills, and ability to apply those concepts and skills to solve problems. An important part of that way of teaching is effective planning. Therefore, we have made planning for effective teaching an important part of this text.

Emphasis on Concept and Skill Development

Based on findings of educational research that support more complete development of concepts and skills, calls from the National Council of Teachers of Mathematics for more effective development in lessons, and our personal experiences, we have chosen to make more effective development of mathematical concepts and skills a major emphasis. As a result of that emphasis, virtually all activities suggested in the chapters related to specific mathematics content are developmental activities. Since we made a conscious choice not to include practice activities in those chapters, the final chapter is devoted to effective practice. In that chapter, we present a selection of practice activities that can be used after the concepts and skills have been taught.

Basic Philosophy

We believe that successful teaching results in understanding, that understanding provides the most sound basis for skill development, and that understanding results in better retention of what is learned. We believe that the best way to help students understand mathematical ideas is to lead them to connect those ideas to other ideas that they already understand. We believe that, for elementary children, understanding of mathematical concepts and skills depends on the development of appropriate mental imagery for those concepts and skills. And, we believe that *all children* should be given the opportunity to develop that kind of understanding of mathematics.

Acknowledgments

This book evolved over several years from informal conversations with many colleagues about how teachers could plan to teach more effectively, from preservice and inservice teachers who responded to our ideas before they were fully formed, and from reactions of children who demonstrated that the more fully evolved teaching methods really worked. And, of course, invaluable assistance was provided by these professionals, whose reviews of the preliminary manuscript helped to direct the text into its final form: Bruce F. Godsave, SUNY Genesco; Dennis Munk, Northern Illinois University; Ann L. Lee, Bloomsburg University of PA; Thomasenia Lott Adams, University of Florida; and Dorothy Spethman, Dakota State University.

Benny F. Tucker
Ann H. Singleton
Terry L. Weaver

DISCOVER THE COMPANION WEBSITE ACCOMPANYING THIS BOOK

The Prentice Hall Companion Website: A Virtual Learning Environment

Technology is a constantly growing and changing aspect of our field that is creating a need for content and resources. To address this emerging need, Prentice Hall has developed an online learning environment for students and professors alike—Companion Websites—to support our textbooks.

In creating a Companion Website, our goal is to build on and enhance what the textbook already offers. For this reason, the content for each user-friendly website is organized by topic and provides the professor and student with a variety of meaningful resources. Common features of a Companion Website include:

For the Professor—

Every Companion Website integrates **Syllabus Manager™,** an online syllabus creation and management utility.

- **Syllabus Manager™** provides you, the instructor, with an easy, step-by-step process to create and revise syllabi, with direct links into Companion Website and other online content without having to learn HTML.

- Students may log on to your syllabus during any study session. All they need to know is the web address for the Companion Website and the password you've assigned to your syllabus.

- After you have created a syllabus using **Syllabus Manager™,** students may enter the syllabus for their course section from any point in the Companion Website.

- Clicking on a date, the student is shown the list of activities for the assignment. The activities for each assignment are linked directly to actual content, saving time for students.

- Adding assignments consists of clicking on the desired due date, then filling in the details of the assignment—name of the assignment, instructions, and whether or not it is a one-time or repeating assignment.

- In addition, links to other activities can be created easily. If the activity is online, a URL can be entered in the space provided, and it will be linked automatically in the final syllabus.

- Your completed syllabus is hosted on our servers, allowing convenient updates from any computer on the internet. Changes you make to your syllabus are immediately available to your students at their next logon.

For the Student—

- **Chapter Objectives**—outline key concepts from the text

- **Interactive Self–quizzes**—complete with hints and automatic grading that provide immediate feedback for students

  After students submit their answers for the interactive self–quizzes, the Companion Website **Results Reporter** computes a percentage grade, provides a graphic representation of how many questions were answered correctly and incorrectly, and gives a question by question analysis to the quiz. Students are given the option to send their quiz to up to four email addresses (professor, teaching assistant, study partner, etc.).

- **Message Board**—serves as a virtual bulletin to post–or respond to–questions or comments to/from a national audience

- **Net Searches**—Offer links by key terms form each chapter to related Internet content

- **Web Destinations**—links to www sites that relate to chapter content

To take advantage of these and other resources, please visit the *Teaching Mathematics to All Children: Designing and Adapting Instruction to Meet the Needs of Diverse Learners* Companion Website at

www.prenhall.com/tucker

CONTENTS

7   MULTIPLYING AND DIVIDING WHOLE NUMBERS: Combining Equal-Sized Groups and Separating Quantities into Equal-Sized Groups   139

8   FRACTIONS: Working with Units Smaller Than One   199

9   DECIMALS AND PERCENTS:
Working with Base-Ten Units Smaller Than One and Using Hundredths as a Common Denominator   245

10   MEASUREMENT:
Assigning a Number to a Quantity   281

NOTE: Every effort has been made to provide accurate and current Internet information in this book. However, the Internet and information posted on it are constantly changing, so it is inevitable that some of the Internet addresses listed in this textbook will change.

TEACHING MATHEMATICS TO **ALL** CHILDREN

CHAPTER 1

INSTRUCTIONAL ACTIVITIES:

The Building Blocks for Effective Instruction

THE LEARNING PRINCIPLE

Students must learn mathematics with understanding, actively building new knowledge from experience and old knowledge (National Council of Teachers of Mathematics, 2000, p. 20).

THE ASSESSMENT PRINCIPLE

Assessment should support the learning of important mathematics and furnish useful information to both teachers and students (NCTM, 2000, p. 22).

Basics for the Effective Use of Activities, the Building Blocks for Construction of Effective Lessons

What Are the Students Learning?

A common pitfall for teachers who use an activity-based program of instruction is to focus on the procedures of the activity and to judge its instructional value primarily on how fun it is, on how much the pupils like it, or on how "neat" it is. Certainly, we want learning to be fun. We want our pupils to like learning, and we want to do things with them that are "really neat." However, really neat isn't enough. The primary criterion for judging an instructional activity is, *what are the pupils learning during the activity*? It follows, then, that the first step in selection of an instructional activity must be identification of the learning objective. But the type of activity that is appropriate depends on the nature of the objective. The kind of activity that should be used depends on whether the objective is for students to learn something new, to become proficient with something that they have already learned, to be able to use what they have already learned to solve problems, or whether the objective is for the teacher to find out what level of mastery the pupil has achieved. For our purposes in this book, we will classify activities into four types:

- Developmental (for new learning)
- Practice (for development of proficiency with material already learned)
- Application (for problem solving using concepts and skills already learned)
- Assessment (for demonstration of level of learning)

Developmental Activities

Developmental activities are activities that teach something new. If students have to already know the target concept or skill in order to do the activity, then the activity is not developmental. There are two distinct levels of developmental activities: **exploratory** and **consolidating.**

The purpose of **exploratory developmental activities** is to provide a core of experiences that will form the basis for generalization of concepts or skills. Sometimes the student's previous life experiences are an adequate basis for the needed generalizations. But more frequently, it is necessary to create opportunities for students (at least some of them) to have the needed experiences. This necessity arises out of the obvious fact that, before student experiences can be used by the teacher to develop a new idea, the students must have had those experiences.

The purpose of **consolidating developmental activities** is to help students to identify patterns and recognize relationships; to hypothesize and test those relationships; to clarify concepts; to develop procedures; and to learn terminology and notation with which to communicate about those patterns, relationships, concepts, and procedures.

Practice Activities

Practice activities are activities that help students to become proficient in the use of concepts and skills that have already been developed. While the emphasis of developmental activities is to develop comprehension or understanding, the emphasis of practice activities is to develop skill. As a general rule, students do not learn new things from practice. However, through practice, they may very well get more proficient with what they have already learned. Appropriate practice may also help to add more permanence to that learning. As is true with developmental activities, there are two distinct types of practice activities: **think-time** and **speed-drill.**

Think-time practice activities place the emphasis on accuracy. The student has adequate time to think carefully about concepts and connections, and plenty of time to think carefully through each step of a procedure. The student may even be allowed time to look up things that need clarification. Students are told, *there is no hurry, but be sure you are right*.

Speed-drill practice activities place the emphasis on quick answers. Some teachers feel that speed drill can contribute to memorization and to the ability to habituate procedures. Other teachers point out that, under speed-drill conditions, answers come only from those who already have quick recall of the facts or who can already quickly apply the procedure. These are, of course, precisely the ones who do not need this practice. On the other hand, those who cannot respond quickly are encouraged to make a wild guess or simply say, "I don't know," and then stop thinking about it.

One must seriously consider whether the overall effect of speed drill is negative rather than positive. Indeed, with a very few exceptions, very little is accomplished with speed-drill practice that would not be accomplished more effectively with appropriate think-time practice. Speed-drill practice activities will, therefore, receive limited attention in this book.

Application Activities

Application activities are activities that help students learn to use concepts and skills in settings that are different from the settings in which those concepts and skills were learned. Application activities allow them to use the concepts and skills that they understand and are proficient with to solve a variety of problems. Application activities can be categorized into two groups: **classroom applications** and **real-world problems.**

Classroom applications include instructional activities that require students to build on already learned concepts and skills, using them to develop new ones. Since an activity may involve application of old ideas to develop new ones, it follows that a single activity could be application with respect to one topic and also developmental with respect to another topic. Classroom applications also include contrived examples such as textbook problems that require pupils to use recently learned concepts and skills. A thin line separates this kind of classroom application from practice. The difference is that practice typically requires the student to use the new concept or skill more or less like they used it when it was being learned. On the other hand, contrived examples used as classroom application typically require the student to use the new concept or skill in ways that are, to some degree, different from the ways the concept or skill was used when it was being learned.

Real-world problems are problems like those students will encounter outside the classroom. To devise a real-world problem that applies a particular concept or skill, it is necessary to first determine how that concept or skill is used outside the classroom, i.e., in the real world. The next step is to create an activity that will require the student to use the concept or skill in exactly that way.

Assessment Activities

Assessment activities are activities that require students to demonstrate, in an observable way, their depth of learning of concepts and skills. There are two big ideas of assessment. These two big ideas guide the selection of or development of specific types of assessment. The first of the two big ideas is **validity.** Although there are actually several different types of validity, all of them assure that the assessment measures what it is supposed to measure. An assessment is invalid if it does not measure what it is supposed to measure. The second big idea of assessment is **reliability.** An assessment instrument is reliable if it produces dependable results—if those results are consistent. As with validity, there are several types of reliability. But every type of reliability assures that the results produced by the assessment are consistent, stable, or dependable. We always want the assessment to be both valid and reliable. If an assessment is not valid, the information produced is meaningless. If it is not reliable, then the information produced is not dependable.

If learning has taken place, there will be tasks that the child can do as a result. Tasks that depend on the learning are observable. If we observe to determine whether or not the child can perform these tasks, then they are **assessment tasks.** The child's success with these tasks can help indicate whether or not the child has met the learning objective. For each learning objective, we would expect there to be many potential assessment tasks.

There are three types of assessment tasks that we will consider here. They are objective assessment tasks, subjective assessment tasks, and performance assessment tasks.

Contrary to common belief, whether tasks are objective or subjective is not determined by the kind of thinking that the student will be required to use. Rather, these

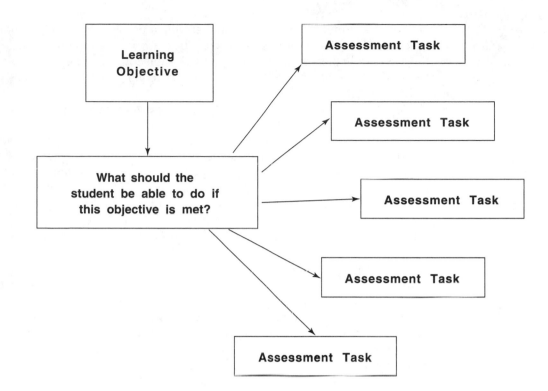

two types are distinguished by what the scorer of the assessment task is required to do. An assessment task is *objective if the scorer is not required to make a value judgment* about the response. The response is either correct or incorrect, either acceptable or unacceptable. The scorer is not required to make a value judgment about how correct or how acceptable the response is.

Some examples of objective assessment tasks are completing a true–false test item, completing a multiple-choice test item, completing a matching exercise, giving a short answer, completing a statement with a missing word, arranging a series of items in order, solving a problem, using a skill to produce a result, and representing a number with a base-ten model. These assessment tasks are **objective** because the scorer can determine whether the response is correct without making a value judgment.

Each of these assessment tasks requires the person being assessed to either select or supply a response. The response will either be correct or incorrect. They are not objective because they are easy or because they require only low-level thinking. Indeed, it is possible to design objective tasks that require any level of thinking to get the correct answer. They are objective because the scorer is not required to make a value judgment about whether the response is right or wrong.

An assessment task is *subjective if the scorer is required to make a value judgment about the quality of the response.* A response may have degrees of correctness, and the scorer must determine how correct it is. Subjective tasks are not necessarily more difficult than objective tasks, nor do they necessarily require more complex thinking. Subjective tasks may require *any* level of thinking—knowledge, comprehension, application, analysis, synthesis, or evaluation. They are not subjective because of what the person being assessed is required to do, but because of what the scorer must do. They are **subjective** because the scorer is required to make a value judgment about the quality of the response.

Some examples of subjective tasks are explaining why a statement is or is not correct, describing the relationship between two variables, drawing a diagram to show a relationship, showing several ways to find the area of a composite shape, completing a proof of a theorem, explaining why the area formula for parallelograms is the same as the area formula for rectangles, and solving a problem for which partial credit may be given. These tasks are not subjective because they are more difficult or because they require higher-level thinking. They are subjective because the scorer is required to make a value judgment. What the scorer is required to do determines whether the task is subjective.

The third category of assessment tasks is **performance tasks**. Performance tasks *may be* either objective or subjective. Performance tasks are generally not completed with pencil and paper. Although the performance task may not require more complex thinking than other objective or subjective tasks, the performance itself is generally more complex. Performance tasks generally require the integrated application of many previously learned concepts and skills. Some examples of performance tasks are gathering and analyzing data, demonstrating a proof of a theorem before the class, creating a poster that presents the results of a project, planning the route for a family vacation, and planning a balanced meal containing fewer than 1000 calories.

Performance tasks are an excellent way to determine whether students are able to apply concepts and skills in a meaningful way. Because of the integrated nature of performance tasks, a weakness in any of those integrated concepts and skills could result in an unsuccessful performance. When a student is unsuccessful in a performance task, it is often difficult to determine the specific cause of the failure.

People normally think of assessment as giving tests or quizzes, usually after the teacher has completed instruction. However, a recent trend in the field of assessment is the movement toward nontraditional assessment. Nontraditional assessment uses a variety of ways to determine the depth of a student's learning, often including the use of a combination of objective, subjective, and performance tasks. One of the nontraditional assessment techniques commonly recommended is to devise activities that do not seem, to the student, to be a test, but that require students to demonstrate their learning.

The significant characteristic that differentiates such assessment activities from other instructional activities is that *the teacher must pay attention*. The teacher must take note of who knows and who does not know. The teacher must take note of what each student does know and does not know and the contexts in which each student can do what is required as well as those in which the student cannot do what is required. This information can provide a clear understanding of the student's level of learning. If the teacher is observing and gathering this kind of information, then every instructional activity—developmental, practice, application—can also be an assessment activity.

Level of Involvement

A key factor in the selection of instructional activities is the level of student involvement that will occur during the activity. The teacher always has a limited amount of time to teach, and the student always has a limited amount of time to learn. It is reasonable, then, to want to maximize the student's involvement in learning.

If the teacher teaches for 10 minutes but the student only pays attention for 2 minutes, that is a 20% level of involvement. We would certainly hope for better. If six students are playing a game where the players take turns and are not required to participate in any way when it is not their turn, that is 16.7% involvement. That is not good. If the teacher has an activity that requires virtually 100% involvement of one student while 23 other students wait, that is 4.2% involvement, a deplorable level of involvement.

When the level of student involvement is low, students learn less because less time is spent in learning and opportunities for behavior problems to occur become more frequent. Anyone who has spent a lot of time around children and young people will tell you that they do not like to be left waiting with nothing to do; they want to be mentally stimulated. If teachers allow "dead time," time when students are not involved, those students will find something to do, and more often than not, the teacher will dislike what they find to do. Indeed, behavior problems are often a direct result of the teacher employing learning activities with a low level of student involvement.

Perhaps a word of caution would be appropriate here. Increasing the level of involvement *will* improve and maintain attention. However, it is essential that the teacher keep in mind that student involvement in useless activity has little value. What we should always be after is a high level of involvement in activities *that are purposeful— activities that will help move the child toward achievement of the learning objectives.*

It is impossible to achieve 100% involvement for any group of students and virtually impossible to reach that goal with a single student. But invariably, teachers can improve the level of student involvement—first, by being aware of its importance, and second, by constantly searching for ways to adjust procedures to increase the level of student involvement. We feel that all the activities that have been included in this book are effective for learning, but they vary in expected level of student involvement. Level of involvement is not the only consideration, but it is an important one. Therefore, as you consider the activities presented, apply the level-of-involvement test. Is the level of involvement high? Is it high enough for your situation?

Flexibility

Webs of Activities

In order to develop an activity-based system of instruction, it is useful to first identify content topics, and second to develop a web of instructional activities for each of those topics. For each topic, the web should include developmental activities, practice activities, application activities, and assessment activities. The web may include pencil-paper activities, physically active activities, whole class activities, small group activities, or individual/partner activities. To illustrate such an activity web, we have arbitrarily chosen the topic, *similarity*. We will illustrate activities of each type.

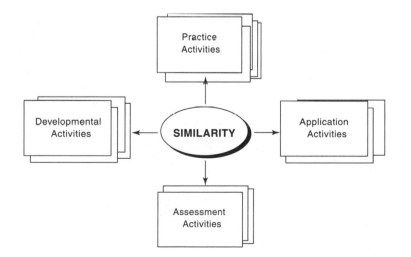

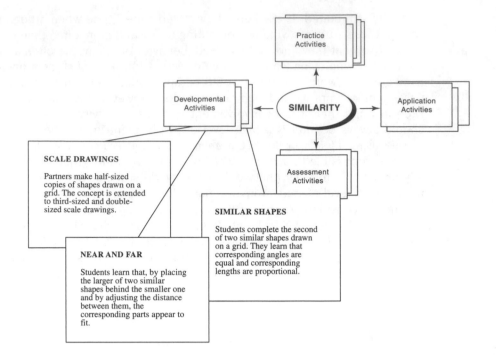

SCALE DRAWINGS

Partners make half-sized copies of shapes drawn on a grid. The concept is extended to third-sized and double-sized scale drawings.

SIMILAR SHAPES

Students complete the second of two similar shapes drawn on a grid. They learn that corresponding angles are equal and corresponding lengths are proportional.

NEAR AND FAR

Students learn that, by placing the larger of two similar shapes behind the smaller one and by adjusting the distance between them, the corresponding parts appear to fit.

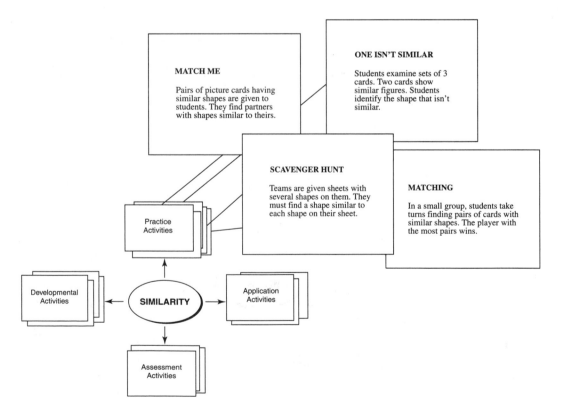

MATCH ME

Pairs of picture cards having similar shapes are given to students. They find partners with shapes similar to theirs.

ONE ISN'T SIMILAR

Students examine sets of 3 cards. Two cards show similar figures. Students identify the shape that isn't similar.

SCAVENGER HUNT

Teams are given sheets with several shapes on them. They must find a shape similar to each shape on their sheet.

MATCHING

In a small group, students take turns finding pairs of cards with similar shapes. The player with the most pairs wins.

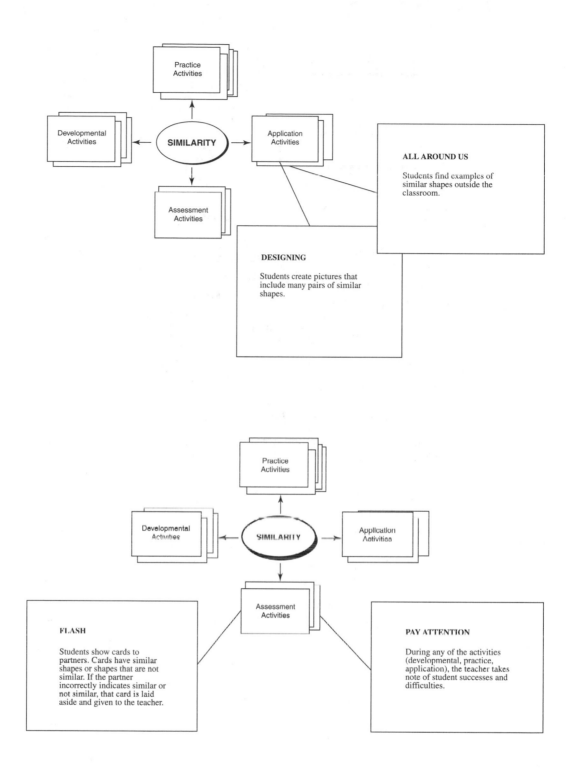

Content Flexibility Webs

Almost any effective instructional activity or game can be adapted and used in other content areas and at other levels. When a game or activity that works well has been developed or discovered, it is useful to develop a content flexibility web for that game or activity. The following is a content flexibility web that helps us see how to use an activity with a variety of content.

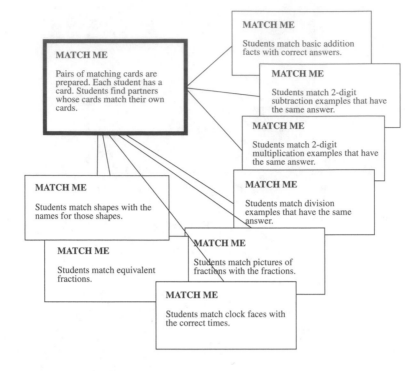

MATCH ME

Pairs of matching cards are prepared. Each student has a card. Students find partners whose cards match their own cards.

MATCH ME

Students match basic addition facts with correct answers.

MATCH ME

Students match 2-digit subtraction examples that have the same answer.

MATCH ME

Students match 2-digit multiplication examples that have the same answer.

MATCH ME

Students match division examples that have the same answer.

MATCH ME

Students match shapes with the names for those shapes.

MATCH ME

Students match equivalent fractions.

MATCH ME

Students match pictures of fractions with the fractions.

MATCH ME

Students match clock faces with the correct times.

Procedure Flexibility Webs

When a teacher has found a particularly nice set of materials or has spent time and effort to develop such materials, it is useful to consider the many ways that they might be used. The following is an example of a procedure flexibility web. A procedure flexibility web shows how we might adapt the procedures used with a set of materials to meet a variety of instructional needs.

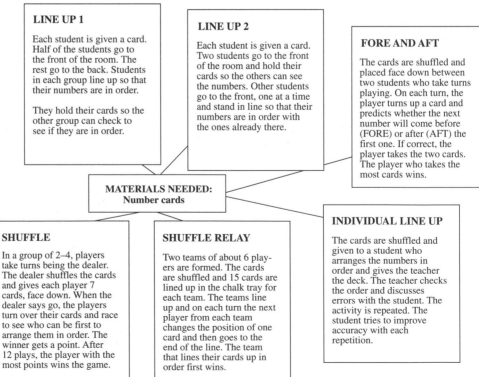

LINE UP 1

Each student is given a card. Half of the students go to the front of the room. The rest go to the back. Students in each group line up so that their numbers are in order.

They hold their cards so the other group can check to see if they are in order.

LINE UP 2

Each student is given a card. Two students go to the front of the room and hold their cards so the others can see the numbers. Other students go to the front, one at a time and stand in line so that their numbers are in order with the ones already there.

FORE AND AFT

The cards are shuffled and placed face down between two students who take turns playing. On each turn, the player turns up a card and predicts whether the next number will come before (FORE) or after (AFT) the first one. If correct, the player takes the two cards. The player who takes the most cards wins.

MATERIALS NEEDED:
Number cards

INDIVIDUAL LINE UP

The cards are shuffled and given to a student who arranges the numbers in order and gives the teacher the deck. The teacher checks the order and discusses errors with the student. The activity is repeated. The student tries to improve accuracy with each repetition.

SHUFFLE

In a group of 2–4, players take turns being the dealer. The dealer shuffles the cards and gives each player 7 cards, face down. When the dealer says go, the players turn over their cards and race to see who can be first to arrange them in order. The winner gets a point. After 12 plays, the player with the most points wins the game.

SHUFFLE RELAY

Two teams of about 6 players are formed. The cards are shuffled and 15 cards are lined up in the chalk tray for each team. The teams line up and on each turn the next player from each team changes the position of one card and then goes to the end of the line. The team that lines their cards up in order first wins.

Exercises and Activities

1. Suppose you are preparing to teach first-grade children to add two- and three-digit numbers with regrouping (renaming, carrying). Describe an exploratory developmental activity that will give the children preliminary experience with regrouping outside of the context of addition. To build mental imagery for the regrouping process, use bundled sticks in the activity.

    For example, the number represented here.

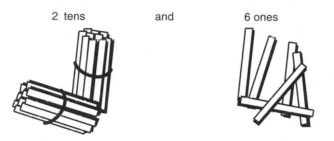

    is the same as the number represented here.

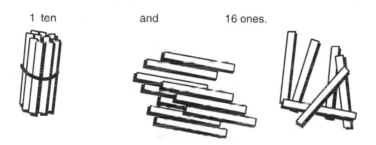

2. Suppose you are preparing to teach a measurement lesson to third-grade students on the customary units of length (inches, feet, and yards). Before teaching the lesson you want to establish the need for standard units. Describe an exploratory developmental activity that will give the children an understanding of why we need standard units of length.

3. Consider the following instructional activity for teaching finding area of rectangles. Decide whether the activity is a developmental activity or a practice activity. Explain your reasons.

    Display, on the walls of the classroom, about 20 rectangles cut from colored construction paper. Write the length and width in inches on each rectangle. Have the children work with partners. Each pair of partners should choose and find the areas of two rectangles.

4. It has been said that whenever teachers evaluate the work of their students, they are also evaluating the work of their students' teacher. Explain what you think this statement means. If this statement is true, why is it important to include assessment activities in your lessons?

5. Standard 6: Analysis of Teaching and Learning in *Professional Standards for Teaching Mathematics*, published in 1981 by the National Council of Teachers of Mathematics, states:

    "The teacher should engage in ongoing analysis of teaching and learning by—observing, listening to, and gathering other information about students to assess what they are learning; examining effects of the tasks, discourse, and learning environment on students' mathematical knowledge, skills, and dispositions; In order to—

- ensure that every student is learning sound and significant mathematics and is developing a positive disposition toward mathematics;
- challenge and extend students' ideas;
- adapt or change activities while teaching;
- make plans, both short- and long-range;
- describe and comment on each student's learning to parents and administrators, as well as to the students themselves."

In your own words, explain what each point of this standard says about assessment activities.

6. Choose any lesson from a commercially published elementary school mathematics textbook. Analyze the lesson plan that is presented in the teacher's guide. With respect to its contribution to learning of the stated lesson objective, identify and label each part of the suggested lesson plan as development, practice, application, or assessment.

7. This game is a practice activity for *hard basic addition facts*:

Prepare a set of 24 cards, each showing a hard basic addition fact with the answer missing. Give the cards to 2 children and have them play this game. After the cards are shuffled, the dealer gives each player 4 cards, face down. When the dealer says start, the players race to arrange their cards in order, from smallest answer to largest answer. If the first player to finish is correct, that player gets one point. If the other player challenges the result, the first player must prove the answers. The players repeat the process until all the cards have been played. The player who scored the most points is the winner.

Adapt this game for the topic, *area of triangles*.

8. This activity is a developmental activity for teaching *triangles*.

Display about 5 triangles, all with different shapes. Explain that these shapes are all triangles. Ask the children to tell you what is the same for all triangles. (Answers may vary. For example the children may point out that all the triangles have 3 sides. Or, they may say that all the triangles have straight sides. Or, they may notice that all the triangles are closed figures.) If they indicate that all the triangles have 3 sides, agree with them that all triangles have 3 sides, then draw a counter example like the one on the right. Ask if this is a triangle. Ask why not. Repeat this process with counter examples that do not have other required characteristics of triangles.

Adapt this activity for teaching *rectangles*.

9. Find an article in a recent issue of *Teaching Children Mathematics* that describes a learning activity or game. Analyze the activity or game and decide whether it is development, practice, application, or assessment.

References and Related Readings

Baker, J. M., & Zigmond, N. (1990). Are regular education classes equipped to accommodate students with learning disabilities? *Exceptional Children, 56*, 515–526.

Bransford, J. D., Brown, A. L., & Cocking, R. R. (1999). *How people learn: Brain, mind, experience, and school.* Washington, DC: National Academy Press.

National Council of Teachers of Mathematics. (1989). *Curriculum and evaluation standards for school mathematics.* Reston, VA: NCTM.

National Council of Teachers of Mathematics. (2000). *Principles and standards for school mathematics*. Reston, VA: NCTM.

Popham, J., & Baker, E. (1970). *Systematic instruction*. Upper Saddle River, NJ: Prentice Hall.

Web Sites

http://www.ed.gov/pubs/EarlyMath/
(A site targeted at parents. Good parental involvement ideas.)

http://www.nctm.org/tcm/1999/11/doingmath.htm
(Article with good parental involvement ideas.)

http://www.nctm/org/tcm/1999/04/home.htm
(Article with good parental involvement ideas.)

http://www.ed.gov/pubs/parents/Math/index.html
(What parents can do at home.)

http://npin.org/library/pre1998/n00280/n00280.html
(Targeted at parents. Good parent resources.)

http://www.coled.umn.edu/nceo/OnlinePubs/Synthesis28.htm
(Alternative assessment for children with disabilities. Article with references.)

http://www.nwrel.org/msec/mpm/developing.html
(Developing performance assessment tasks.)

http://www.nwrel.org/msec/mpm/scoregrid.html
(Scoring guide for performance.)

http://www.sedl.org/scimath/compass/v02n02/scored.html
(Scoring rubric for discussions.)

http://forum.swarthmore.edu/mathed/assessment.html
(Links to articles.)

http:/www.sedl.org/scimath/compass/v02n02/
(Links to articles.)

http://www4.nas.edu/csmee/mseb.nsf/79ef91b52c61d434852566900077f071/37e0908b222 22be38525645f0059fa37
(Assessment issues.)

http://www.nwrel.org/psc/bestofnw/singleprac.asp?id=74&phrase=mathematics
(Report on school that used a visual hands-on approach.)

http://www.learner.org/exhibits/dailymath/
(Applications of math in daily life.)

CHAPTER

DIVERSITY IN THE CLASSROOM:

Variations of Individual Needs

THE EQUITY PRINCIPLE

Excellence in mathematics education requires equity—high expectations and strong support for all students (National Council of Teachers of Mathematics, 2000, p. 12).

THE ASSESSMENT PRINCIPLE

Assessment should support the learning of important mathematics and furnish useful information to both teachers and students (NCTM, 2000, p 22).

Why Diverse Classrooms?

The emphasis in this text on planning for diverse student populations comes as a result of the reality that already exists. Historically, "normal" classrooms have always been diverse. Among the students in the classroom, there has always been a range of capability. There has always been a range of maturity. There has always been a range of experiences. There has always been a range of interests. There has always been a range of parental support. There has always been a range in the economic background of students.

In the 20th century other kinds of diversity have become prevalent. Classrooms have gender, racial, ethnic, religious, and cultural diversity. They may have language diversity. In the introduction of *Curriculum and Evaluation Standards for School Mathematics*, published in 1989 by the National Council of Teachers of Mathematics, the writers referred to the necessity of *teaching mathematics to all children* in diverse classrooms.

The social injustices of past schooling practices can no longer be tolerated. Current statistics indicate that those who study advanced mathematics are most often

white males. Women and most minorities study less mathematics and are seriously under-represented in careers using science and technology. Creating a just society in which women and various ethnic groups enjoy equal opportunities and equitable treatment is no longer an issue. Mathematics has become a critical filter for employment and full participation in our society (p. 4).

In *Principles and Standards for School Mathematics*, published by the National Council of Teachers of Mathematics in 2000, when discussing the Equity Principle, the writers point out that

> All students, regardless of their personal characteristics, backgrounds, or physical challenges, must have opportunities to study—and support to learn—mathematics. Equity does not mean that every student should receive identical instruction; instead, it demands that reasonable and appropriate accommodations be made as needed to promote access and attainment for all students (p. 12).

Recently, there has been a movement away from special services for students with handicapping conditions offered in separate settings toward the inclusion of these students in regular classrooms (see U.S. Department of Education, 1996). Teachers can no longer rely on the truly different student being placed in a separate class. Indeed, teachers should expect to encounter diversity of every kind in the classroom. Coupled with this new diversity are debates in methodology (e.g., constructivism, cooperative learning, democratic classrooms, diagnostic/prescriptive teaching, direct instruction, holistic learning, and reductionism). Trying to master the best practices from those currently in use is challenging. The skepticism exhibited by teachers when faced with challenges to their ways of doing things points to a need for truly workable solutions, rather than theoretical and idealistic notions (Scruggs & Mastropieri, 1996). Teachers are beginning to understand that teaching to the average or middle group does not answer the needs of students in today's diverse classroom.

Students have many characteristics that were usually never considered in the past (Dunn & Dunn, 1992; Hall, 1980), such as learning styles, modality preferences for learning, and performance preferences for showing what has been learned. In addition, many students do not come to school adequately prepared. Others cannot keep up with the curricular demands and time frames as they occur in the regular classroom. Students with special needs have been denied access to the regular curriculum for a variety of reasons, sometimes because they did not exhibit the prerequisite skills needed for the different academic lessons being presented. Others were denied access due to the structure and content of the curriculum (e.g., cognitive levels/demands were too high, or assumed knowledge was not present, or abstract concepts or analytic skills were absent). The special educator was assigned responsibility for the learning of these students.

Today, these special-needs students are being reassigned to the regular classroom. The courts have determined that they have the right to learn in the "least restrictive environment." In response to such judicial mandates, we have seen the broad implementation of mainstreaming and are now seeing the movement toward a more extreme practice of inclusion. Since these children are returning to the regular classroom, there is a growing need for teachers to rethink what they are asking their students to do and whether those things are appropriate given the students' unique developmental learning and behavioral characteristics.

Racial, Linguistic, and Cultural Diversity

More and more commonly, elementary teachers are faced with groups of students that are racially, linguistically, and culturally diverse. As the National Association for the Education of Young Children (NAEYC) points out,

> Parents and educators must recognize that children actively attempt to understand their world through their own language and culture. For this reason, children learn best when they acquire skills in a meaningful context. Identifying what children already know and building on their prior learning, regardless of language, will help promote an environment that engages all children in learning.
>
> NAEYC's position statement acknowledges the challenges facing early childhood educators who may not be adequately trained to work with children whose home language is not English. Even though an educator may not be familiar with a child's language and culture, the educator has a responsibility to respect the child and family. Encouraging dialogue, play and projects that promote social interaction and first-hand experiences are the best ways to facilitate second language learning among preschoolers (National Association, 1999).

The recommendations that will be made in this text for designing instruction are particularly effective for racially, linguistically, or culturally diverse student groups. The NAEYC calls for development of skills in a meaningful context, for building on prior learning, first-hand experiences, and social interaction. In this text we, too, will encourage more thorough development of concepts and skills. We, too, will propose that development be done in a meaningful context and include building on prior experiences. We, too, will call for more social interaction.

Perhaps the most important caution that we offer for dealing effectively with student groups with racial, linguistic, and cultural diversity relates to the "first-hand experiences," the "prior experiences" of these students. The teacher must be particularly aware that where there is cultural diversity, the prior experiences of the students will also be diverse. If the development of a concept or skill is to build on particular prior experiences, more time must be spent in exploratory development to assure that all students have had those necessary prior experiences.

Learning Style Preferences

Although the descriptions of the preferences and special needs may be familiar, a brief review can help in understanding the adaptations, modifications, and accommodations being presented. All students have a learning style, which according to Sternberg (1998), is a preferred way of using one's abilities. First, all students have one sensory input and output modality that is stronger or more dominant than their other sensory input and output modalities and hence, is preferred. Some have an auditory input dominance and prefer listening over watching or doing while others have a visual input dominance and prefer watching over listening and doing. A great many have a kinesthetic or tactile input dominance and prefer doing over watching, listening, and speaking. Teachers must remember that while there are preferred input and output modalities, all children still need to develop their nonpreferred ones. All these modes of input and output need to be used during lessons so that each child has the opportunity to use his or her strength and modality.

To better illustrate these preferences, consider the following set of activities. All are practice activities, so we are assuming that the concept has already been adequately developed. All these activities have the same learning objective, but they differ in the input/output modality that the student is required to use.

An Activity for the Auditory Learner.

> **Objective:**
> The student will compare decimals and determine which is greater.
>
> **Required Input/Output Modality:**
> Auditory
>
> **Procedures:**
> The teacher will read two decimals aloud. The student will listen carefully and then respond by telling whether the first decimal or the second decimal is greater.

An Activity for the Visual Learner.

Objective:
The student will compare decimals and determine which is greater.

Required Input/Output Modality:
Visual

Procedures:
The teacher will hold up two cards, each with a decimal printed on it. The student will point to the card with the decimal that is greater.

An Activity for the Tactile Learner. You should note that this version of the activity requires the child to already have mastered the names and values of coins and one dollar bills. Before using this activity, the teacher should assure that this prior learning is present.

Objective:
The student will compare decimals and determine which is greater.

Required Input/Output Modality:
Tactile

Procedures:
The teacher will use dollars, dimes, and pennies to represent ones, tenths, and hundredths. Two decimals will be represented using the money. Each will be placed inside a paper bag. The student will feel the money and tell which decimal is greater.

An Activity for the Kinesthetic Learner.

Objective:
The student will compare decimals and determine which is greater.

Required Input/Output Modality:
Kinesthetic

Procedures:
The teacher will draw a number line on the chalkboard about 12 inches above the chalk tray. Then the teacher hands the student two cards, each with a decimal printed on it. The student will go to the chalkboard and place the cards in the chalk tray beneath the number line to show the approximate location of the numbers on the number line. Then the student will tell which decimal is greater.

Kinds of Intelligence

Another kind of diversity relates to the student's intellectual abilities as seen in Gardner's (1983) multiple intelligences: spatial, bodily-kinesthetic, musical, linguistic, logical-mathematical, interpersonal, intrapersonal. Extending Gardner's contention that there are many varying types of intelligence, Levine (1996) recognizes that students who are very "average" or even "below average" with respect to some types of intelligence are "above average" with respect to other types. There is, therefore, a preference for learning activities that make use of one's intellectual strengths.

Some prefer to express themselves and their ideas using oral and written language while others prefer to construct things. Still others prefer expressing themselves and their ideas through sounds, pitch, and tones and others through numbers and reasoning. Some focus on self-discipline and internal changes while some focus on others and their actions. Many prefer to focus on visual-spatial aspects of their learning world. When a teacher teaches as if there is only verbal intelligence, the strengths of many students are ignored. They are not allowed to use their real abilities. They are viewed as dull students because their teachers do not recognize that they have a bright side. These students are often doomed to mediocrity or even dismal failure, not by their own inability, but by the teacher's.

Low Cognitive Ability

Students vary in their cognitive abilities. Low cognitive ability may be exhibited in any number of different ways. For example, students with low cognitive abilities may have difficulties with language development (Polloway, Patton, Payne, & Payne, 1989) including reduced vocabulary levels and difficulties with reasoning, especially conceptual abstractions. These students also may have difficulties with memory, usually exhibiting a smaller capacity for processing of information and recall. Moreover, difficulties across academic areas such as reading or mathematics may occur due to cognitive limitations. Among techniques that are often successful with low-cognitive functioning students are the following.

Use More Developmental Activities. A far greater portion of the lesson should be devoted to developmental activities. Developmental activities provide connections to what the child already knows. These connections make it easier to understand new concepts and remember newly learned material. Because these connections help the student to see how new material is related to material that is already understood, the new material has a familiar, comfortable feel to it. Connections make it easier to use what has been learned in new settings.

Developmental activities provide mental imagery for mathematical ideas. This mental imagery allows the student to "see what the teacher is saying." Mental imagery helps mathematics to make sense to the student because the student can "see" that "that's the way the world is." Mental imagery facilitates concrete thinking, even when the concrete materials are not available.

Expanded use of developmental activities increases retention, improves problem-solving ability, reduces the amount of practice needed, and consequently decreases the overall time required to master content. Increasing the portion of the lesson devoted to developmental work effectively improves learning for the low-cognitive functioning student, and for all other students as well.

Organize Material Into Smaller, More Manageable Units. It is always easier for the low-cognitive functioning student to master smaller rather than larger amounts of new material. Furthermore, when the teacher is able to celebrate success in many small things, an atmosphere of success is established. When a child's experiences have taught him that he is able to learn, then that child will want to learn more. A teacher is always more successful with a cooperative student. And, of course, success does breed success for the low-cognitive functioning student, as well as for all other students (Leverett & Diefendorf, 1992).

Simplify Vocabulary or Provide Vocabulary Aids. Low-cognitive functioning students generally possess a more limited vocabulary than do other students. As a result, they are at a disadvantage when it comes to understanding directions. Teachers can revise directions for low-cognitive functioning students to assure that they are more likely to understand the assigned task. The revisions should eliminate words that the student will have difficulty understanding. If the difficult word is absolutely necessary to the directions, marginal helps can increase the likelihood of understanding (Leverett & Diefendorf, 1992). For example, the margin might contain a simpler word with the same meaning with a line connecting the two words.

Students who have difficulty reading often find text printed in a larger size is easier to read. They also find it easier to read several short lines rather than a few long lines of type. Consequently, printed directions will typically be easier for the low-cognitive functioning student if they use a large size type and if the printed lines are short.

Consider the directions in the following two examples and the illustrated revisions:

Problem Solving

Chess was first played in Asia centuries ago. Later variations were played in Arabia, Spain, Europe, and Persia (Iran). Today chess masters from all countries compete in international tournaments. Solve each of these problems.

Problem Solving

Long ago in Asia, people played a game like chess.

Later, chess was played in the rest of the world.

Today, chess players from

Determine how many objects in the photographs are shaped like rectangles.

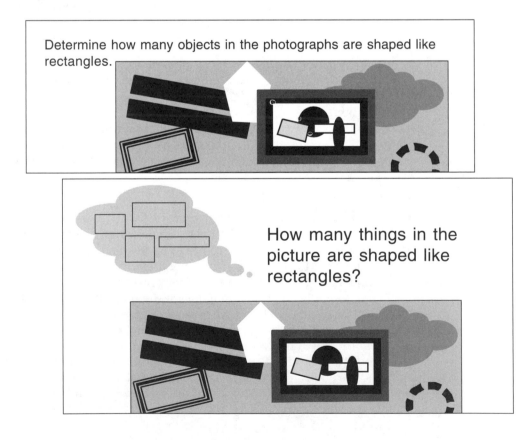

How many things in the picture are shaped like rectangles?

Where Appropriate, Allow Work to Be Completed by Partners.   When low-cognitive functioning students are partnered with more capable students for the completion of a task, the natural discussion that results will help to clarify concepts and improve skills (Slavin, 1988). Both partners receive more immediate reinforcement when things work as they should, and the more capable student is often able to provide immediate correction of errors made by the low-cognitive functioning student. The process of explaining to the low-cognitive student results in clearer understanding for the more capable student. Partnering improves learning for the low-cognitive functioning student, and for all other students as well.

Learning Disabilities

Having a learning disability is not the same as having low intelligence. Indeed, it is not at all uncommon for learning disabled children to have high intelligence. They may even be gifted, and at the same time, learning disabled. They tend to be strong in some areas and weak in others. The variance in their attentional, perceptual, cognitive, and memory abilities is often striking. They may exhibit a puzzling combination of strengths and weaknesses. Although some students have disabilities exhibited primarily in one subject area, learning disabilities generally cross academic content lines due to:

- **Perceptual difficulties such as:**

  Figure-ground confusion, which is difficulty in separating irrelevant background stimuli from the important details, particularly as they are found on the printed page

  Difficulties with spatial awareness, including positional relationships between objects and themselves and positional relationships among objects—either real or on the printed page

  Visual or auditory distractibility, resulting in the inability to ignore irrelevant visual or auditory stimuli and focus on an assigned task

- **Difficulties with listening or attending,** including what to attend to, sustaining attention, sharing and changing that attention, and ignoring or dealing with other demands on their attention. These same attentional difficulties are found in children with attention deficit disorder (ADD) or attention deficit hyperactivity disorder (ADHD).

- **Difficulties with remembering,** including organization of information for storage, capacity of short-term memory, and strategies for moving information into and out of long-term memory. Some children have particular difficulty with visual memory, that is, the ability to visualize or revisualize things that they have seen. However, it is far more common for children to have difficulty with auditory memory, that is, the ability to remember things that they have heard.

- **Difficulties with thinking or understanding,** that become apparent when the child needs to abstract, generalize, or conceptualize

Visual or Auditory Impairments

Students who have visual or auditory impairments may exhibit total loss or partial loss. Their difficulties seem apparent given common classroom structure and instructional methodology (difficulty in understanding written or oral directions and missing important information that is provided visually or orally). The solution is equally apparent. The directions and the information must be provided using modes that do not require use of the impaired sense. However, students with visual or auditory impairments may also exhibit overlapping disabilities including a combination of those already mentioned.

Physical Impairments

Teachers should not be surprised to find that students with other physical impairments are in the classroom. For these children, the primary concern is often mobility and flexibility. The physical impairment may limit the child's ability to perform a variety of tasks without special equipment. The teacher should remember that in addition to the more obvious physical impairment, these children will also have the same variety of learning problems, disabilities, preferred learning styles, and preferred ways of expressing themselves as seen in other children.

Summary

Meeting the diversity demands of today's classroom begins with an analysis of the learning characteristics of the students. Student learning styles, modality preferences, preferred abilities, disabilities if any, and interests must be determined on an individual basis if student progress (i.e., gains in learning) is to be made. Teachers must also examine their own learning and teaching styles, preferred abilities, and interests. Along these same lines state curricular demands, textbook demands, and individual lesson demands need to be analyzed to determine the types of adaptations, modifications, and accommodations to incorporate. In particular, given the increasing numbers of students labeled with learning disabilities and with attention deficit disorders, lesson requirements must be examined and academically appropriate alternatives created.

This text directly addresses how well instruction that meets individual needs and preferences meshes with regular curriculum and traditional methods. Most teachers tend to plan for the class as a whole and not for individual students. For such teachers, adaptations, modifications, or accommodations to meet individual students' needs must start with the class plan. For example, part of the lesson may become a movement activity rather than a seat activity to better meet the needs of kinesthetic/tactile learners and others with high energy levels. Or a class activity may become an individual activity or a group-based activity so each individual's preferences or strengths can be used. While modifications like these help to accommodate special needs, they do not have any detrimental effect on the majority or the average learners.

Other adaptations focus on a particular need or disability and involve a more specific change in order to accommodate the particular problem so that a single child may participate successfully, for example, the adaptation may provide for the use of both oral directions and written directions to accommodate a hearing-impaired student. Again, these changes do not have any detrimental effect on other students.

Still other adaptations focus on providing for the needs of several students who have problems of a similar type, allowing all of them to participate more fully. These include separating parts of a worksheet so that a student who is spatially impaired or a student whose visual field is limited can both have success. These adaptations may also be beneficial to those whose strength lies in spatial abilities or to those who have low cognitive abilities and a sense of being overwhelmed when presented with the typical type-filled page.

Exercises and Activities

1. Read the discussion of "Standard 3: Knowing Students as Learners of Mathematics," on pages 144–150 of *Professional Standards for Teaching Mathematics*, published by the National Council of Teachers of Mathematics in 1991. Compare and contrast the recommendations in this chapter with those included in the discussion of this standard.

2. Consider activities 2.01 and 2.02. They have the same learning objective: The student will match the correct number with quantity.

   a. Which activity would be more appropriate for a visual learner?

   b. What learning style preference would the other activity appeal to?

   c. Adapt the activity so that it would be appropriate for a tactile learner.

x + 4 **ACTIVITY 2.01   How Many Bounces?**

Have the children turn around and face the back of the room. Tell them to listen carefully. Bounce a basketball 3 times. Ask them to tell you how many times you bounced the ball. Repeat with other numbers.

x + 4 **ACTIVITY 2.02   How Many Chips?**

Tell the children to watch the overhead projector screen. Place 3 counting chips on the projector. Ask them to tell you how many chips they see. Repeat with other numbers.

3. Consider activities 2.03 and 2.04. They have the same learning objective: The student will use customary units to measure the length of objects.
   a. Which activity would be more appropriate for a kinesthetic learner?
   b. Which activity would be most appropriate for an auditory learner?

x + 4 **ACTIVITY 2.03   How Many Feet?**

Prepare about 100 strips of cardboard that are all 12 inches long. Place them in a box at the front of the room. Assign the children to partners. Identify something in the room for each pair of partners to measure (a table, a shelf, the chalkboard, the teacher's desk, etc.). Have the partners get enough "feet" from the box to measure the length of their assigned object.

x + 4 **ACTIVITY 2.04   How Many Feet?**

Cut a 1" x 1" board into 6 pieces that are all 1 foot long. Show the board pieces to the children. Tell them that each piece is 1 foot long. Tell the children to watch and listen to see how long your desk is. Place the pieces of board end to end across the length of your desk. Slap each "foot" onto the desk so the children can hear each piece being put into place. Ask the children how long the desk is.

4. Consider activities 2.05 and 2.06. They have the same learning objective. Which of them would be more appropriate for a child with a hearing impairment?

x + 4 **ACTIVITY 2.05   Give Me a Fraction**

Prepare pairs of cards showing fractions. The fractions on each pair of cards should be equal. Also prepare a list of all the fractions on the cards. Give each child one card. Give the list of fractions to one child. This child is to choose any fraction on the list and ask for the fraction that is equal to that one. (For example, "Bring me the fraction that is equal to one half.") When the equal fraction is brought forward, the child must decide if it is correct. Have the child repeat the process with another fraction. Let several children have a turn asking for fractions.

×÷ **ACTIVITY 2.06** **Equal or Not?**

Prepare pairs of cards showing fractions. The fractions on each pair of cards should be equal. Write "Are These Fractions Equal?" on the chalkboard. Place two cards in the chalk tray, under the question. Read the question and call on a child to answer. Repeat the process, sometimes with fractions that are equal and sometimes with fractions that are not equal.

5. Consider activities 2.07 and 2.08. They have the same learning objective. Which of them would be more appropriate for a low-cognitive functioning student?

×÷ **ACTIVITY 2.07** **Same Shape, But Bigger**

Redraw the shape so that the lengths are twice as long.

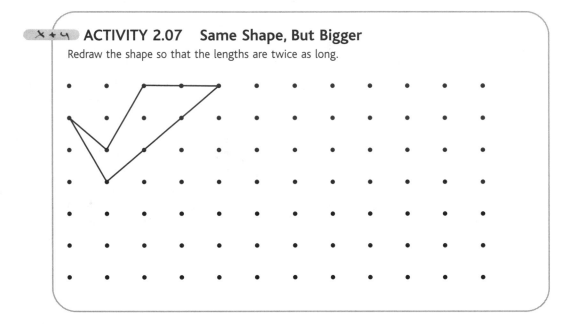

×÷ **ACTIVITY 2.08** **Same Shape, But Bigger**

Redraw the shape so that the lengths are twice as long.

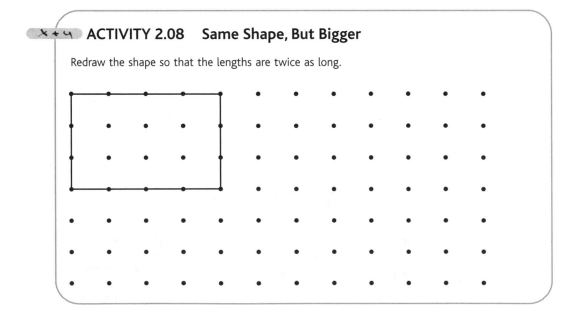

6. Consider activities 2.09 and 2.10. They have the same learning objective. Which of them would be more appropriate for a child with a visual impairment?

x + y   ACTIVITY 2.09   What's in the Bag?

Place a penny, a nickel, a dime, and a quarter in a paper bag. Have a child reach into the bag and, without looking, take out the quarter. Ask how the child could tell it was the quarter. Repeat the procedure with each of the other coins.

x + y   ACTIVITY 2.10   What's the Difference?

Place a penny, a nickel, a dime, and a quarter on a table. Have a child look at two of the coins and tell the ways that they are different. Repeat this procedure with each of the possible pairs of coins.

7. Consider activities 2.11 and 2.12. They have the same learning objective. Which of them would be more appropriate for a child with a hearing impairment?

x + y   ACTIVITY 2.11   Give Me a Fraction

Prepare pairs of cards showing fractions. The fractions on each pair of cards should be equal. Also prepare a list of all the fractions on the cards. Give each child one card. Give the list of fractions to one child. This child is to choose any fraction on the list and ask for the fraction that is equal to that one. (For example, "Bring me the fraction that is equal to one half.") When the equal fraction is brought forward, the child must decide if it is correct. Have the child repeat the process with another fraction. Let several children have a turn asking for fractions.

x + y   ACTIVITY 2.12   Equal or Not?

Prepare pairs of cards showing fractions. The fractions on each pair of cards should be equal. Write, "Are These Fractions Equal?" on the chalkboard. Place two cards in the chalk tray, under the question. Read the question and call on a child to answer. Repeat the process, sometimes with fractions that are equal and sometimes with fractions that are not equal.

8. Consider activity 2.13. Adapt the activity so that it provides more visual input.

x + y   ACTIVITY 2.13   What Are Parallelograms Like?

Ask the children if they know what parallelograms are. Ask them to describe what parallelograms are like. If an important characteristic is omitted, ask leading questions to get the children to describe that characteristic. (For example, you might need to ask, "Are the sides curved?")

9. Consider activity 2.14. Adapt the activity so that it will be more kinesthetic.

---

x + y **ACTIVITY 2.14   More or Less?**

Prepare about twenty cards with a decimal written on each. Also prepare a card with the word "More" on it and another card with the word "Less" on it. Use a piece of yarn to divide the bulletin board into two sections. Use a thumb tack to place "More" on one side of the yarn and "Less" on the other side of the yarn. Place one of the decimal cards right on the line. Then, one at a time, hold up the other decimals and have the class tell whether the decimal that you are showing is more or less than the one on the yarn. Use thumb tacks to place the decimals on the correct side of the yarn.

---

10. Read the following two articles that are found in the March/April 1997 issue of the *Journal on Learning Disabilities*:

"Instructional Design in Mathematics for Students with Learning Disabilities," by Douglas Carnine, pp. 130–141.

"Mathematics Instruction for Elementary Students with Learning Disabilities," by Carol A. Thornton, Cynthia W. Langrall, and Graham A. Jones, pp. 142–150.

Write a two-page reaction to the articles, comparing and contrasting them with ideas presented in this chapter.

References and Related Readings

Bransford, J. D., Brown, A. L., & Cocking, R. R. (1999). *How people learn: Brain, mind, experience, and school*. Washington, DC: National Academy Press.

Carnine, D. (1997). Instructional design in mathematics for students with learning disabilities. *Journal on Learning Disabilities, 30*, 130–141.

Delquadri, J., Greenwood, C. R., Whorton, D., Carta, J. J., & Hall, R. V. (1986). Classwide peer tutoring. *Exceptional Children, 52*, 535–542.

Dunn, R., & Dunn, K. (1992). *Teaching elementary students through their learning styles*. Boston: Allyn & Bacon.

Gardner, H. (1983). *Frames of mind: The theory of multiple intelligences*. New York: Basic Books.

Hall, R. J. (1980). Cognitive behavior modification and information processing skills of exceptional children. *Exceptional Education Quarterly, 1*, 9–15.

Lerner, J. W. (2000). *Learning disabilities: Theories, diagnosis, and teaching strategies*. Boston: Houghton Mifflin.

Leverett, R. G., & Diefendorf, A. O. (1992). Students with language deficiencies: Suggestions for frustrated teachers. *Teaching Exceptional Children 25*(4), 30–35.

Levine, H. M. (1996). Accelerated schools: The background. In C. Finnan, E. P. St. John, J. McCarthy, & S. P. Slovacek (Eds.), *Accelerated schools in action: Lessons from the field* (pp. 3–23). Thousand Oaks, CA: Corwin Press.

National Association for the Education of Young Children. (1999). Linguistic and cultural diversity—Building on America's strengths [On-line]. Available: http://www.pbs.org/kcts/preciouschildren/diversity/read_linguistic.html.

National Council of Teachers of Mathematics. (1989). *Curriculum and evaluation standards for school mathematics*. Reston, VA: NCTM.

National Council of Teachers of Mathematics. (2000). *Principles and standards for school mathematics*. Reston, VA: NCTM.

Polloway, E. A., Patton, J. R., Payne, J. S., & Payne, R. A. (1989). *Strategies for teaching learners with special needs* (4th ed.). Upper Saddle River, NJ: Merrill Prentice Hall.

Scruggs, T. E., & Mastropieri, M. A. (1996). Teacher perceptions of mainstreaming/inclusion, 1958–1995: A research synthesis. *Exceptional Children*, 63(1), 59–74.

Slavin, R. E. (1988). Synthesis of research on grouping in elementary and secondary schools. *Educational Leadership*, (Sept.), 67–77.

Sternberg, R. (1998). *Thinking styles*. New York: Cambridge University Press.

Thornton, C. A., Langrall, C. W., & Jones, G. A. (1997). Mathematics instruction for elementary students with learning disabilities. *Journal on Learning Disabilities*, 30, 142–150.

U.S. Department of Education. (1996). *Eighteenth annual report to Congress on the implementation of the individuals with disabilities act*. Washington, DC: U.S. Department of Education.

Web Sites

http://www.ldonline.org/
(Your guide to LD Online.)

http://www.ldonline.org/ld_indepth/math_skills/math_skills.html
(Internal links to articles about math learning disabilities. The following links seemed interesting.)

    http://www.ldonline.org/ld_indepth/math_skills/garnett_ldrp.html
    (This article presents assessment guidelines and specific teaching considerations for increasing number-fact fluency in students with learning disabilities.)

    http://www.ldonline.org/ld_indepth/math_skills/adapt_cld.html
    (This article provides information on how to adapt and modify mathematics instruction to promote success and understanding in the areas of mathematical readiness, computation, and problem solving for students with math disabilities.)

    http://www.ldonline.org/ld_indepth/math_skills/coopmath.html
    (This article discusses the components of cooperative learning and presents an example of how cooperative learning can be used to teach mathematics skills.)

http://adhd.mentalhelp.net/
(Good first site—symptoms, treatment, online resources, organizations, online support, research.)

http://www.ldonline.org/ld_indepth/add_adhd/ael_firststeps.html
(Article dealing with ADHD.)

http://www.shianet.org/~reneenew/calc.html
(Links to articles and other information on Dyscalculia.)

http://www.addclinic.com/
(Attention Deficit Disorder (ADD), Attention Deficit Hyperactivity Disorder (ADHD), Obsessive Compulsive Disorder (OCD), Tourette Syndrome (TS).)

http://www.aos-jax.com/capd.htm
(CAPD. National Institute of Mental Health site.)

http://www.ldonline.org/ld_indepth/process_deficit/living_working.html
(Living and working with a central auditory processing disorder (CAPD).)

http://www.theshop.net/campbell/central.htm
(Central auditory processing disorders web pages.)

http://www.tsbvi.edu/math/
(Teaching math to visually impaired students.)

http://www.ncrel.org/sdrs/pathwayg.htm
(Links to assessment, at-risk, curriculum, early childhood, goals and standards, governance, instruction, integrated services, leadership, learning, literacy, math, parent and family involvement, preservice education, professional development, safe and drug-free, school-to-work, science, technology.)

http://www.ldonline.org/ld_indepth/add_adhd/eric522.html
(This fact sheet summarizes for parents and teachers information on children who have an attention deficit disorder with hyperactivity (ADHD), are gifted, or are both ADHD and gifted.)

http://www.people.memphis.edu/~coe_rise/
(Inclusion ideas.)

LESSON DESIGN:

Creating Lessons that Meet the Needs of a Diverse Classroom

THE EQUITY PRINCIPLE

Excellence in mathematics education requires equity—high expectations and strong support for all students (National Council of Teachers of Mathematics, 2000, p. 12).

THE CURRICULUM PRINCIPLE

A curriculum is more than a collection of activities: It must be coherent, focused on important mathematics, and well articulated across the grades (NCTM, 2000, p. 14).

THE TEACHING PRINCIPLE

Effective mathematics teaching requires understanding what students know and need to learn and then challenging and supporting them to learn it well (NCTM, 2000, p. 16).

THE LEARNING PRINCIPLE

Students must learn mathematics with understanding, actively building new knowledge from experience and prior knowledge (NCTM, 2000, p. 20).

THE ASSESSMENT PRINCIPLE

Assessment should support the learning of important mathematics and furnish useful information to both teachers and students (NCTM, 2000, p. 22).

Combining Activities into a Lesson

What Is a Lesson?

A lesson is a related set of instructional and learning activities organized in a coherent manner. A lesson is generally organized in parts, each of which is designed to accomplish some part of the process needed to meet the learning objectives. For our purposes, we will organize our lessons to include the following parts. Although other components may also be included, most lessons would include these:

Lesson Opener. This part of the lesson should provide context for the concept or skill being developed. It draws the attention of the student and smoothly leads into the lesson.

Development. This part of the lesson provides the experiences that help the student to learn the new concept or skill. Development should smoothly build on what the student already knows. Students progress from not knowing to knowing the new material. Development leads to their being able to do the independent practice exercises.

Monitoring Learning. Ideally this part of the lesson is not separated from the other parts of the lesson. When learning is constantly monitored, the teacher will be aware of who understands and who does not, of when teaching is being understood and when it is not, of what needs to be retaught, and of what needs to be taught differently.

Practice. Practice provides reinforcement of what has been learned in the development part of the lesson and should not begin until the teacher is sure that understanding of the concept or skill has been accomplished. If the students do not yet understand, then more development is needed before the practice.

A Traditional Lesson Plan

We begin by examining a plan for a mathematics lesson that was developed by following the kind of suggestions that are typically provided in the teacher's guide. This lesson plan is very traditional. It calls for the teacher to teach the textbook pages in the way that most teachers would teach them. The lesson plan is actually a pretty good one.

LESSON OBJECTIVE

The student will recognize symmetric shapes and lines of symmetry.

Lesson Opener

State the following: "We have already learned to recognize congruent figures. Today, we will learn to identify figures that are symmetric."

Development

Begin by showing half of each of the following shapes: heart, circle, star. Have students identify the shapes by looking at the half-shapes.

Next, direct students' attention to the first teaching example in the student book. Ask students how they could check to be sure that the two halves of the triangle are congruent. Point out that if the triangle were folded along the dotted line, the two halves of the triangle would match exactly. They would be congruent.

Tell the students that when a shape can be folded in half like this so that the two halves match exactly, then the shape is **symmetric.** We call the line along which the shape was folded the **line of symmetry.**

Tell the students that some shapes have more than one line of symmetry. Direct their attention to the second shape on the page. This shape could be folded in two ways so that the two halves match exactly. This shape has two lines of symmetry.

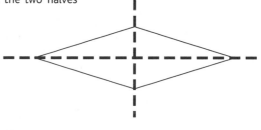

Monitor Learning

Lead students through the *Check Understanding* examples in the student book. Based on student responses to the *Check Understanding* examples, identify those students who have difficulty understanding.

Practice

Assign the *Reteaching Worksheet* to those who would benefit from reteaching. Assign the practice exercises from the student book to the rest of the students.

Closure

As math time is ending, remind the children that:

1. A symmetric shape is one that can be folded so that the two halves match exactly.
2. The fold line for symmetric shapes is called the line of symmetry.

The Nature of Standard Traditional Lessons

As mentioned earlier, traditional lessons that follow suggestions in the teacher's edition are usually good lessons. Traditional lessons normally have two common characteristics. First, they are designed to teach the textbook pages. Second, they are aimed at the average child. On the average, they serve their purpose well. The difficulty, of course, is that very few students fit that "average mold." Such lessons usually do not allow for the diverse learning preferences of children. Moreover, such lessons typically do not take into consideration the diverse learning needs of most children.

Adapting Lessons for Diverse Learning Needs

Rather than attempt to provide separate adaptations of these lessons for every child's learning needs, we will adapt the lessons by expanding the types of activity that appeal to most learning-style preferences and that provide for most learning needs. It is understood, of course, that even after these suggested changes are made, additional adaptations may very well be needed to provide for some children. Traditional lesson plans will be adapted in the following ways.

First, the developmental part of the lessons will be expanded. This is the most important thing that can be done to make lessons more effective—if we equate effectiveness with students' learning of concepts and skills. More thorough development of concepts and skills can be accomplished in several ways. Understanding must develop out of personal experiences with real things. Those experiences should be designed to allow the children to "see" important relationships and procedures. The nature of what we help them to see should provide them with useful mental imagery for the concepts and skills being learned.

Understanding must be developed by helping the children to see and understand how what is being learned is related to other things that they already know (Ginsburg, 1989; Carpenter, 1986). These interrelationships should have an almost constant emphasis. Whenever a teacher is trying to help a child understand something new, a common approach should be, "Let's think about what we already know that can help us here." This will tap into the child's previous learning and encourage many more natural interconnections which enhance memory and recall.

In the development of concepts, a wide variety of examples and nonexamples should be examined. For every example of the concept, the children should discuss why it is an example. For every nonexample that is identified, the children should discuss why it is not an example. The why and why-not questions keep a constant focus on the essential characteristics of the concepts being learned.

The children should continually search for patterns and learn to generalize concepts and procedures from those patterns. Their ability to test those generalizations by trying them out to verify whether or not the generalization is correct helps develop students' confidence.

An excellent developmental teaching method is one called the laboratory approach. In the laboratory approach, the students are led through a series of steps.

1. **Explore (or experiment).** In this step, the student explores the topic under the guidance of the teacher using a physical or pictorial model. Usually, the student is led to use the model to find a variety of results (answers). If the process is modeled effectively, the student will believe that the results are correct. Since the student can see where the answer came from, common sense will tell the student whether the answer is correct.

2. **Keep an organized record of results.** The teacher leads the student to record the results achieved with the model. The recording is done in a way that will facilitate recognition of the patterns that the teacher wants the student to notice.

3. **Identify patterns.** The patterns should be stated in the language of the student. "Every time we did this, the answer turned out to be. . . ." The patterns will suggest ways to get the result (answer) without using the model.

4. **Hypothesize (or generalize) how to get results without the model.** "We can get the answer by. . . ."

5. **Test the hypothesis (the generalization).** Complete an example using the hypothesized procedure. Then redo the example using the model to verify that the result is correct.

This instructional process, which is an inductive process, is utterly convincing to students. Students have discovered a way to get answers that are believable, because they can literally see where those answers come from. Students will believe that the procedure is correct because they have seen the procedure working.

There is, however, one real danger in the use of inductive teaching. The results are derived from experience with a series of examples. If the examples are not sufficiently varied and are only examples of some special case, it may be possible to find a pattern that is consistent for the examples used but not consistent for all examples. It is possible for patterns drawn from special cases to lead to procedures that are true of those special cases, but not true in general. For example, suppose you used a model to discover that

$$\frac{1}{3} + \frac{1}{5} = \frac{8}{15}, \quad \frac{1}{3} + \frac{1}{6} = \frac{9}{18}, \quad \frac{1}{2} + \frac{1}{3} = \frac{5}{6}, \quad \frac{1}{4} + \frac{1}{3} = \frac{7}{12}, \quad \text{and} \quad \frac{1}{5} + \frac{1}{2} = \frac{7}{10}.$$

The children might see that, in every case, the numerator of the answer is the sum of the denominators of the fractions being added, and the denominator is the product of the denominators of the fractions being added. Although this "rule" is true whenever you are adding unit fractions, it is not true when you are adding other kinds of fractions. During instruction, the teacher should avoid making generalizations based on special cases, because children tend to apply those generalizations in settings for which they are not appropriate.

More thorough development of concepts and skills accomplishes several important things. Development results in more complete understanding, a common result when interconnections with other things that students know are emphasized. Because of those interconnections, retention of what is learned is better. Because of improved retention, much less time needs to be spent on review and practice. Because of the interconnections and better understanding, students are better able to apply what they have learned to solve problems.

Second, the lessons will be adapted to provide more visual input. In most lessons there is more than enough auditory information; however, students nearly always need more visual information. Procedures are described, but students need to have them demonstrated. Teachers tell students rules and directions, but students need to see them written down and demonstrated. Teachers tell students what a rectangle is, but they need to be shown. Teachers explain how to borrow in subtraction, but students need to see a ten being traded for 10 ones.

Third, the lessons will be adapted to include more kinesthetic activity. Children are not passive creatures. Motion is an integral part of what they are. They fidget, wriggle, and squirm. They like to interact actively with things. They like to try things and do things. Teachers can wear themselves out trying to make children sit still. Lessons that place a high premium on sitting still and listening go against the nature of children. Kinesthetic learning activities, on the other hand, encourage children to move. They use the child's natural tendency toward movement for learning. Fewer behavior problems result because the child is able to do what is natural without getting into trouble. Because the child is involved both physically and cognitively in the learning activity, attention problems are reduced. It should be noted that kinesthetic learning activities are particularly effective for students with ADD or ADHD.

Fourth, the lessons will be adapted to encourage more communication from and among the students. The classroom should be viewed as a community of learning. All members of that community should be a part of an intellectual exchange about mathematics (Baroody, 1996). Together, they should explore ideas, gather information, look for patterns, generalize concepts and procedures, and try out those generalizations and adjust them based on their experiences. All of this requires constant communication within the learning community. One benefit of increased communication is a deeper sense of involvement on the students' part. Learning activities should be planned that encourage—and even require—communication from and among the students, as well as from the students to the parents (Escalante & Dirmann, 1990).

Fifth, the lessons will be adapted to make monitoring of learning more continuous throughout the lesson. Too often, learning is monitored only after the lesson has been taught. An after-the-fact check on learning can inform the teacher whether or not the lesson has been effective. However, if the lesson has failed with the whole class, or even with individual children, the teacher must wait until next time to clarify unclear ideas, correct skills that are full of errors, or straighten out misconceptions. By then, those unclear ideas, error-filled skills, and misconceptions will have been practiced and will be more difficult to undo. Rather, the teacher must monitor learning while it is happening. In the midst of the lesson, understanding must constantly be checked so the teacher has a strong sense of what is understood and what is not, of what the students can do and what they cannot, of who is learning and who is not. The teacher should know when the teaching is being effective and when it is not, when another teaching example is needed, when a different approach is needed, when students are interested and when they are not, when instruction is working and when it needs to be changed.

To summarize, lesson planning that is more likely to be appropriate for all children in a diverse classroom includes accomplishing the following:

Expanding development
Increasing visual input
Increasing kinesthetic activity
Increasing student communication
Monitoring learning continually

Adapting a lesson in this way makes it appropriate for a diverse group of children. However, you should also bear in mind that further adaptations may still be necessary to provide for specific needs of some children.

A Lesson Adapted for Diverse Learners

On the following pages is a lesson plan adapted from the traditional lesson plan on symmetry that we have already seen. As you consider this adapted plan, note how much more time is devoted to development. Also note how visual input has been increased, how kinesthetic activity has been added, how more opportunities for student communication are included, and how learning is monitored during all the major activities of the lesson.

LESSON OBJECTIVE

The student will recognize symmetric shapes and lines of symmetry.

Lesson Opener

Cut symmetric figures in half along their lines of symmetry and pass out the picture-halves to the children.

Explain that you have cut some pictures in half and each person has half of a picture. Have all the students find the ones who have the other half of their pictures. Ask what they can say about the two halves of a picture when the halves are an exact match. [Remind them if necessary of previous learning. They are congruent.] **Monitor understanding.** Identify students who do not understand or who are having difficulty. Provide assistance to these students.

State the following: "We already know what congruent figures are. Today we will learn to identify symmetric figures."

Development
Prepare 8 sheets of tracing paper with large letters on them. Prepare two copies of each of the letters F, O, S, and Y. Show the letters to the students.

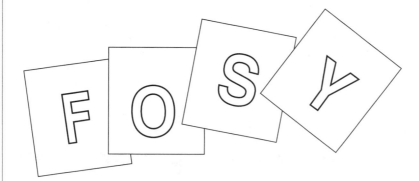

Ask which of the letters could be cut into halves so that the two halves would be an exact match. Allow children to come to the front and cut the sheets.

Ask how we could check to make sure before cutting. [We could fold the paper.] Fold the Y to see if the two parts will be an exact match. Have children come to the front to see if they can fold the other letters to get an exact match.

Group the students with partners. Hand out to each pair of partners a shape that has been cut from paper. Some shapes should be symmetric and others should not be symmetric.

Give simpler shapes like the ones below to low-cognitive functioning students.

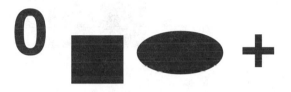

Tell the students to work with their partners to try to fold the shape so that the two parts are an exact match. When everyone is finished, have them show what they found out. **Monitor learning.**

Identify students who are having difficulty and provide assistance.

Tell the students that when a shape can be folded in half like this so that the two halves match exactly, the shape is **symmetric.** Write "symmetric" on the chalkboard. Tell the students that the line along which the shape is folded is the **line of symmetry.** Write "line of symmetry" on the chalkboard.

Have everyone with a symmetric shape hold it up for the class to see. Have those with shapes that are not symmetric hold them up for the class to see. **Monitor learning.** Identify students who do not understand and, at the first opportunity, provide assistance.

Next, direct students' attention to the first teaching example in the student book. Point out that If the triangle were folded along the dotted line, the two halves of the triangle would match exactly. The shape is **symmetric.** The dotted line is the **line of symmetry.**

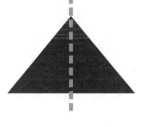

Tell the students that some shapes have more than one line of symmetry. Direct their attention to the second shape on the page. This shape could be folded in two ways so that the two halves match exactly. This shape has two lines of symmetry.

Hold up a square. Tell the students that a square also has several lines of symmetry. Have a student come to the front and fold the square to show one line of symmetry. Have another student try to fold the square to show a different line of symmetry. Continue until all four lines of symmetry have been found.

Show the students a shape like the one pictured at the right. Have students come forward and fold the shape to find lines of symmetry. Ask how many lines of symmetry the shape has. [3]

Use the third example on the student page to demonstrate how to use scissors to cut a symmetric shape from a folded sheet of paper. Have two students come to the front and cut out other symmetric shapes.

Lead students through the *Check Understanding* examples, in the student book.

Monitor Learning

Based on student responses to the *Check Understanding* examples, identify those students who are having difficulty understanding.

Practice

Group the students with partners. Have them work with their partners to complete the practice examples in the student book. **Monitor learning.** Pay extra attention to the students who have been having difficulty and their partners. If their difficulties continue provide help and/or reteaching.

Closure

As math time is ending, ask what kind of shapes we have learned about today. [symmetric shapes] Ask how we can tell if a shape is symmetric. [Symmetric shapes can be folded so that the two halves match exactly.] Ask what we call the fold line in a symmetric shape. [The fold line is the line of symmetry.]

Follow Up

Tell the children to explain to their parents what a symmetric shape is. Have them, with the help of their parents, make a list of symmetric things that they see at home.

Adapting Another Lesson

Now we will adapt another lesson, this time, a lesson on regrouping in addition. Again, we will begin with a traditional plan that follows suggestions like those found in a teacher's guide. As was true of the previous lesson, this is not a bad lesson. But notice that there is very little time spent developing understanding of the concepts and skills of the lesson.

LESSON OBJECTIVE

The student will add a 2-digit number to a 1-digit number and regroup ones to tens.

Lesson Opener

Choose students to give answers to the following facts: 2 + 5, 6 + 7, 4 + 6, 5 + 7, 8 + 5, 5 + 4. Ask why 2 + 5 and 5 + 4 are different from the other facts. State the following: "Sometimes when you add, you have fewer than 10 ones and sometimes you have 10 or more ones. Today we will learn to regroup ones to tens."

Development

Begin by having a child read the sentence at the top of the page [If I join these two groups, I can make another group of ten]. Have the children point out the numbers 25 and 7. Ask: How many ones are in the first number? How many ones are in the second number? How many ones are there altogether? Are there enough ones to circle ten? How many tens are there altogether? How many ones are left?

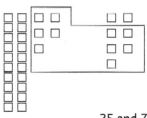

25 and 7
<u>32</u> in all

Have the children write 32 in the answer blank.

Monitor Learning

Lead students through the *Check Understanding* examples in the student book. Based on student responses, identify those students who have difficulty understanding.

Practice

Assign the *Reteaching Worksheet* to those who would benefit from reteaching. Assign the practice exercises from the student book to the rest of the students.

Closure

As math time is ending, remind the children that, when you have ten or more ones after adding, you must group 10 ones to make another ten.

Adapting the Lesson for a Diverse Group of Students. As you consider the adaptations to this lesson plan, notice the increase in the quantity of developmental instruction. Notice also the shift in instructional emphasis from teaching the pages of the student book toward an emphasis on teaching the concept. As before, we will increase visual input, kinesthetic activity, student communication, and monitoring of learning.

LESSON OBJECTIVE

The student will add a 2-digit number to a 1-digit number and regroup ones to tens.

Lesson Opener

Write 25 on the chalkboard. Have a child come forward to represent that number using base-10 blocks. Have the student place the blocks in a box. Ask other students, "How many ones are in the box?" "How many tens?" Tell them to watch carefully. Drop 2 more ones into the box, one at a time. "Now what number is in the box? How many tens? How many ones?" Complete the addition sentence, 25 + 2 = 27, on the board. Have a child look in the box to check the answer. Repeat the process with 32 + 4, and then with 46 + 3, except write the addition in vertical form.

$$\begin{array}{r} 32 \\ + \ 4 \\ \hline 36 \end{array} \qquad \begin{array}{r} 46 \\ + \ 3 \\ \hline 49 \end{array}$$

Repeat the process with 28 + 5. After the 5 ones have been added to the box, ask how many tens are in the box and record the 2 tens in the answer. Next ask how many ones are in the box and record the 13 ones after the 2 tens.

$$\begin{array}{r} 28 \\ + \ 5 \\ \hline 213 \end{array}$$

Ask the children if that answer looks right. Ask what is wrong. [It looks like we have 2 hundreds, 1 ten, and 3 ones.] Point out that we only have room to write one digit in each place. So if we have 10 or more ones, that is too many to write.

Monitor Understanding

Use these examples as an opportunity to be sure that all the children understand how to represent numbers with the base-10 blocks. Take note of those having difficulty and provide extra help.

State the following: "Today we will learn that, when we have too many ones to write, we trade 10 ones for a ten."

Development

Begin by writing 43 on the chalkboard and labeling the tens and ones. Have a child come to the front and choose the base-10 blocks to represent that number. Pick up one of the tens. Ask how many ones you could trade the ten for. Have a child come forward to make the trade. After the trade is completed, ask "How many tens are there now?" "How many ones?" Record this new result. Point out that this is still the same amount, but is just shown in two ways. Repeat the process, starting out with 64 and trading a ten for 10 ones.

tens	ones
4	3
3	13

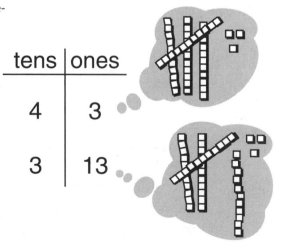

Monitor Understanding

Observe carefully to be sure that all the children understand that after the trade you still have the same amount. You may need to show both forms of the number side by side so that the children can see that they are the same amount.

Next, reverse the process. Start with 5 tens and 18 ones. Trade 10 ones for a ten and record the number in its new form. How many tens are there altogether? How many ones are left? Repeat with 3 tens and 13 ones and then with 4 tens and 12 ones.

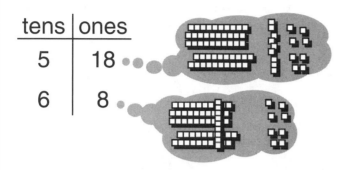

Write 28 + 5 on the chalkboard and remind the children that this is the example that they looked at earlier. Remind them that when you added 5 to 28 you ended up with 2 tens and 13 ones. Record this example on the board, labeling the tens and ones.

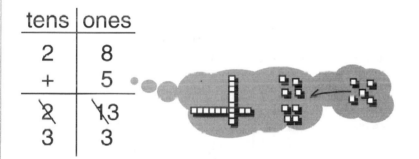

Point out that we now know how to make a trade to get an answer that can be written in standard form. Using base-10 blocks, have a child trade 10 ones for a ten and record this result. Repeat the process with 46 + 5 and with 39 + 6.

Monitor Understanding

Observe carefully to be sure that all the children understand.

Lead the children through the teaching examples on the student page. Point out that the pictures on the page are showing base-10 blocks like the ones that they have been using. Also point out that they are to draw a ring around the ones that they would trade.

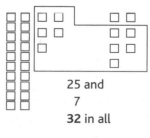

25 and

7

32 in all

Monitor Understanding

Observe carefully to be sure that all the children understand how to ring 10 ones and how to record their answers.

Practice

Assign the practice exercises from the student book.

Monitor Understanding

Observe the children to identify those who are having difficulties. Provide individual assistance to them. If lower-ability children have trouble with the pictured base-10 blocks, allow them to use real base-10 blocks. If you have low-vision children, it may help them if you provide them with enlarged pictures from the textbook.

Closure

As math time is ending, ask if someone can tell the class what we learned today.

Follow Up

Write 34 + 8 on the chalkboard and have the children copy the problem. Have them take this problem home and explain to their parents how to get the answer.

Exercises and Activities

1. Choose a lesson from any published elementary school mathematics program. Identify procedures that the authors suggest that provide information to the students visually. Describe ways that additional visual input could be provided.

2. Choose a lesson from any published elementary school mathematics program. Identify the developmental part of the lesson. Describe how to expand the developmental part of the lesson.

3. Choose a lesson from any published elementary school mathematics program. Identify the ways that the children are involved. Describe how you could involve the children in more kinesthetic activity.

4. Choose a lesson from any published elementary school mathematics program. Describe how you could provide more opportunities for the children to communicate among themselves and to the teacher about the concepts or skills being learned.

5. Choose a lesson from any published elementary school mathematics program. Identify the parts of the lesson in which the teacher should monitor learning. In each case, what should the teacher be looking for?

6. Choose a lesson from any published elementary school mathematics program. Adapt the lesson by expanding the developmental part of the lesson, providing for more visual input, adding more kinesthetic activity, increasing opportunities for student communication, and calling for continual monitoring of learning.

7. A teacher has enlarged pictures of base-10 blocks from the textbook to help a child with low vision, but she would also like to add texture to the pictures to provide tactile information for the child. List several ways that the teacher might add texture to the pictures.

8. Read Assumption 1 on page 17 of *Curriculum and Evaluation Standards for School Mathematics*, published by the National Council of Teachers of Mathematics. How does this assumption relate to the recommendation in this chapter that the developmental part of lessons be expanded?

9. Read the discussion of Standard 2, Mathematics as Communication that is found on pages 26–28 of *Curriculum and Evaluation Standards for School Mathematics*, published by the National Council of Teachers of Mathematics. How does this standard relate to the recommendation in this chapter that the lessons should include more communication from and among children?

10. Read "Preparing Teachers to Teach Mathematics to Students with Learning Disabilities," by Rene S. Parmar and John F. Cawley. The article is found on pp. 188–197 of the March/April 1997 issue of the *Journal of Learning Disabilities*. Write a one-page reaction to the article, comparing and contrasting it with the ideas presented in this chapter.

References and Related Readings

Baroody, A. J. (1996). An investigative approach to the mathematics instruction of children classified as learning disabled. In D. K. Reid, W. P. Hresko, & H. L. Swanson (Eds.), *Cognitive approaches to learning disabilities* (pp. 545–615. Austin), TX: PRO-ED.

Carnine, D. (1997). Instructional design in mathematics for students with learning disabilities. *Journal of Learning Disabilities*, 30(2), 134–141.

Carpenter, T. P. (1986). Conceptual knowledge as a foundation for procedural knowledge: Implications from research in the initial learning of arithmetic. In J. Hiebert (Ed.), *Conceptual and procedural knowledge: The case of mathematics* (pp. 113–132). Hillsdale, NJ: Erlbaum.

Cawley, J. F. & Reines, R. (1996). Mathematics as communication. *Teaching Exceptional Children*, 28(2), 29–34.

Escalante, J., & Dirmann, J. (1990). *The Jaime Escalante Math Program*. Washington, DC: NEA.

Ginsburg, H. P. (1989). *Children's arithmetic* (2nd ed.). Austin, TX: PRO-ED

Hunter, M. (1982). *Mastery teaching*. El Segundo, CA: Tip Publications.

National Council of Teachers of Mathematics. (1989). *Curriculum and evaluation standards for school mathematics*. Reston, VA: NCTM.

National Council of Teachers of Mathematics. (2000). *Principles and standards for school mathematics*. Reston, VA: NCTM.

Stein, M., & Davis, C.A. (2000). Direct instruction as a positive behavioral support. *Beyond Behavior*, 10(1), 7–12.

Thomlinson, C. A. (1995). *How to differentiate instruction in mixed-ability classrooms*. Alexandria, VA: Association for Supervision and Curriculum Development.

Zahoric, J. A. (1995). *Constructivist teaching*. Bloomington, IN: Phi Delta Kappa Educational Foundation.

Web Sites

http://www.uni.edu/coe/inclusion/strategies/types_adaptation.html
(Nine adaptations for successful inclusion.)
http://www.nctm.org/standards/
(Principles and Standards for School Mathematics.)
http://nctm.org/about/
(About NCTM.)
http://www.mcrel.org/standardsbenchmarks/docs/chapter7.html
(Identifies several sources of standards for school math.)
http://www.nwrel.org/psc/bestofnw/singleprac.asp?id=74&phrase=mathematics
(Report on exemplary school program that used a visual hands-on approach.)
http://teachers.net/lessons/
(Lesson plans from teachers.)
http://www.studyweb.com/Mathematics/toc.htm
(Lesson plans for content areas.)
http://www.proteacher.com/100000.shtml
(Lesson plans for content areas.)

CHAPTER 4

BEGINNINGS:

Mathematics Learning in Early Childhood

THE LEARNING PRINCIPLE

Students must learn mathematics with understanding, actively building new knowledge from experience and prior knowledge (National Council of Teachers of Mathematics, 2000, p. 20-21)

THE ALGEBRA STANDARD

"Even before formal schooling, children develop beginning concepts related to patterns, functions, and algebra" (NCTM, 2000, p. 91).

THE GEOMETRY STANDARD

"The geometric and spatial knowledge children bring to school should be expanded by explorations, investigations, and discussions . . ." (NCTM, 2000, p. 97).

THE MEASUREMENT STANDARD

"Children should begin to develop an understanding of attributes by looking at, touching, or directly comparing objects" (NCTM, 2000, p. 103).

THE REASONING AND PROOF STANDARD

"Two important elements of reasoning for students in the early grades are pattern-recognition and classification skills" (NCTM, 2000, p. 122).

THE COMMUNICATION STANDARD

"Throughout the early years, students should have daily opportunities to talk and write about mathematics" (NCTM, 2000, p. 128).

THE CONNECTIONS STANDARD

"Young children often connect new mathematical ideas with old ones by using concrete objects" (NCTM, 2000, p. 132).

A Common Misconception

People who have not studied child development often think that very young children do not have previously learned concepts and skills to build upon. But in fact, the opposite of this is true (Baroody, 1987; Court, 1920). Prekindergarten and kindergarten children are nearing the end of a period of extremely rapid intellectual growth. They are normally excellent problem solvers. They are very intuitive, in that they use their past experiences to make sense of new experiences. They are concrete thinkers, basing new ideas on their physical experiences.

About Young Children

Because young children learn new things in context rather than in isolation, it is generally agreed that the best approach to the teaching of early childhood mathematics is to keep the mathematical ideas in natural contexts. For example, if the child is learning about one-to-one matching, then one-to-one matching should be examined in the contexts where the child will see one-to-one matching naturally. The child might place one plate on the table for each person in the family—one for Mommy, one for Daddy, and one for me. The child might then place one napkin at each plate, and so on. Or, in another context, the child might experience one-to-one matching by placing one toy with each of five dolls.

A common phenomenon is a situation in which a child does some task in an orderly way and with apparent purpose to produce a result that makes absolutely no sense to the teacher. For example, suppose a child is given an assortment of geometric shapes and asked which shapes go together. (The teacher obviously expects the child to choose the circular shapes, or the square shapes, or perhaps the shapes with some other common attribute.) The child might choose a large triangle and a small square. Although we do not believe those two shapes go together, the child might choose them because, as they were presented, these two shapes together reminded the child of a tree.

When shown a set of large and small red and blue circles and squares and told to pick out the ones that are alike, another young child might select the large red square, then select the large blue square, then select the large blue circle, then select the small blue circle.

We might not understand the criteria the child has used to select the shapes. However, among young children criteria for classification often do not remain constant. For example, after the first shape was chosen, this child may have chosen a shape that was like the last one selected. The first shape was a large square (a large red square) so another large square was selected (a large blue square). The second shape was a large blue shape so another large blue shape was selected (a large blue circle). The third shape was a blue circle so another blue circle was selected (a small blue circle). The child was selecting shapes with the same characteristics, but the common characteristics were constantly changing.

In both of these cases, many teachers would be tempted to conclude that the child has simply given a wrong answer. However, when working with a young child, it is almost always more productive to assume that the answer is correct and then try to figure out what question the child has answered. The teacher needs to work hard to "get inside the child's head" to understand how the child is thinking. Encourage the child to talk about the choices that have been made (Baroody, 1996). When the teacher understands why the child thinks those shapes go together, it is relatively easy for the teacher to rephrase the question to channel the child's thinking toward the geometric attributes of shapes. When the teacher understands how young children think, then it is easier to communicate ideas clearly and effectively.

There are three things to remember then, that will help the teacher of young children to be more successful in the teaching of mathematics.

1. Develop new ideas within contexts that are familiar to the children, building on their own experiences.
2. Encourage the children to communicate about mathematics in their own words.
3. Get "inside the heads" of the children. Learn how they think. Learn to think like they do.

Teaching Classification

Concept development is based on classification, so helping children develop this skill is an important responsibility of a teacher of young children. When children are learning to classify, their thinking should be focused first on this question: What are characteristics of the included objects? Later, the focus should shift to a second question: Why were other objects not included? We will examine one classification example, considering each of these two questions. Suppose we are thinking about dogs.

If we placed all dogs together, we would have large, short-haired, black dogs with four legs, short tails, pointed ears, and a deep rumbling bark. We would have large, long-haired, brown dogs with four legs, long bushy tails, big floppy ears, and a strong bark. We would have tiny, short-haired, gray dogs with four legs, long skinny tails, pointed ears, and a high pitched yelping bark. We would have large, white dogs with medium-length hair, four legs, long thin tails, pointed ears, and a bark that sounds like a wailing child. We would have a continuing long list of dogs with widely varied characteristics. These animals are all examples of dogs. What characteristics are allowed? What characteristics do all dogs have in common?

But now, let's think about some animals that are not included. Here is a small, brown, short-haired monkey with a long thin tail. Why is it not included with the dogs? Here is a large, short-haired, brown calf with four legs, large ears, and a long tail. Why is the calf not included with the dogs? Here is a small, black cat with short hair, four legs, a long thin tail, and a howl that sounds like a wailing child. Why is it not included with the dogs? These animals are nonexamples of dogs. What characteristics of dogs do these animals not have? What characteristics do these animals have that dogs do not have? Why are these animals not dogs?

What are the essential characteristics that make an animal a dog? What essential "dog characteristic" is not present in a monkey? *Dogs have four legs. Dogs cannot grasp things with their tails.* These are essential characteristics of dogs. What essential "dog characteristic" is not present in a calf? *Dogs have soft padded feet. Dogs can bark.* These are essential characteristics of dogs. What essential "dog characteristic" is not present in a cat? *Dogs can bark.* This is an essential characteristic of dogs.

In classification, the variety of included *examples lets us see what is allowed* in the class, but the variety of *nonexamples lets us see the essential characteristics* of the members of the class. It is important that we deal with both examples (why they were included) and nonexamples (why they were not included).

The attributes that distinguish learning classifications in an early childhood classroom are typically less complex than the characteristics of dogs. But little children learn to tell the difference between cats and dogs even though they have so many common attributes. Little children are able to classify. They have been engaged in informal classification all their lives. We will now consider some classification activities that are fairly typical in the early childhood classroom.

A Simple Classification Activity

✕ + ◠ ACTIVITY 4.01   Buttons and Boys

Ask all the boys who are wearing shirts with buttons to come to the front of the class. Discuss characteristics of the children in this group. Point out ways that members of this group are different and ask why they are in the same group. [They are boys wearing shirts with buttons.]

Point out a boy who is not in the group. Say, "He is a boy. Why isn't he in this group? [He is not wearing a shirt with buttons.] Point out a girl who is wearing a shirt with buttons and ask why she is not in the group. [She is not a boy.]

A Classification Activity Related to a Story

x + 4 ACTIVITY 4.02   Three Bears

Prepare flannelboard cutouts of three bears—one large, one medium, and one small. Also prepare large, medium, and small cutouts of bowls, spoons, chairs, and beds.

Read the story, *Goldilocks and the Three Bears*, to the class.

Ask the children to tell what bears were in the story. As the father bear, the mother bear, and the baby bear are mentioned, place the large, medium, and small bear cutouts on the flannel board. Point out that these are the bears in the story. Ask if a large hare is part of this group. [No.] Why not? [It is not a bear.] Ask if Winnie-the-Pooh should be in this group. [No. Winnie-the-Pooh was not in the story.]

Show all the other cutouts (the bowls, spoons, chairs, and beds). Ask which of these things belong to baby bear. After all the small-sized objects are placed on the flannel board, ask why these things were chosen. [They are baby-bear sized. They are small.] Point out the large bed. Ask if it belongs in this group. Why not? [It is big. It is Father Bear's bed.]

Continue by classifying different groups of objects. Ask why they are included. Ask why other objects are not included.

Classification activities for early childhood might be teacher-directed, as were the two preceding examples, or they might be self-directed. They could be activities for individual children, partners, groups, or the whole class. The classification activities included in this text include examples of all these types.

Teaching Comparison and Seriation

Comparison

Objects are compared by relating them with respect to some attribute. For example, if you are comparing two runners to see which one is faster, the attribute you are interested in is speed. One runner has more speed than the other runner. If you are comparing two pencils to see which is longer, the attribute you are interested in is length. One pencil has more length.

When some things are compared, the comparison could be made with respect to a variety of attributes. For example if a male college student is comparing two female college students, a number of attributes might be the focus of the comparison, and the result of the comparison will vary depending upon the attribute. One of the female students might be taller (more height). The other one might be prettier (more beauty). One might be smarter (intelligence). The other might be older (more age). One might be more popular. The other might be more wealthy. One might be heavier. The other might be more talented. Notice that some comparison attributes are objective (comparing height, age, or weight does not require a value judgment), while others are subjective (comparing beauty, popularity, or talent does require a value judgment). A comparison of intelligence or wealth may be either objective or subjective, depending on how it is done.

Before a child can make any comparison, he or she must have developed a sense of the attribute being compared. For example, a child cannot decide which of two objects is longer until a sense of length has been developed. Virtually all instruction to develop the ability to make comparisons centers around developing a sense of the comparison attribute. This instruction must use both examples and nonexamples to focus on what the attribute is and what the attribute is not. Size comparisons can be confusing to the child because there are so many different kinds of size—length, area, volume, mass (weight).

When the teacher says "longer," the child often thinks "bigger." So, for clarification, comparison *examples* must include both of these types.

Which is longer?   ### Which is longer?

The second example above helps the child to understand that we are not talking about thickness. We should also include each of the following types of examples.

Which is longer?   ### Which is longer?

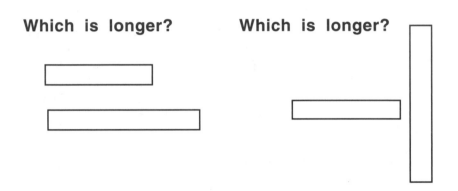

This second example helps the child to see that length does not depend on direction. We should also include each of the following types of examples.

Which is longer?   ### Which is longer?

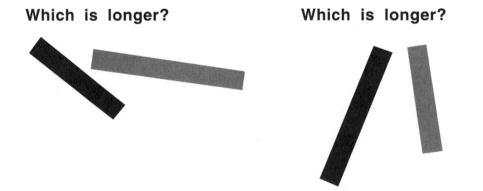

These examples help the child to understand that the concept of length is different from the concept of color. The following example would help the child separate the kind of bigness that we call area from the notion of length.

Which is longer?

The child should also compare lengths of long objects that are very light and short objects that are very heavy to separate the concept of length from that of heaviness.

We see that in the development of understanding the attribute length, our examples must be varied enough to help the child to rule out all the other attributes that might be confused with the one being learned. Also, our examples should begin with gross comparisons in which a child who already understands the comparison attribute is easily able to tell which object has more of the comparison attribute. For example, if we want children to decide which child is taller, then we might begin by having them compare the shortest child and the tallest child. Or, if we place objects of varying weights in bags and want the child to decide which of two bags is heavier, we would begin by comparing a very heavy bag with a very light bag.

After the child is able to make gross comparisons of obviously different objects, the examples should include more difficult comparisons (finer discriminations)—where the objects being compared are more nearly the same with respect to the comparison attribute. For example, if the lengths of objects are being compared, the objects might need to be placed side by side to see the difference. Or, if the weights of objects are being compared, a balance device might be needed to see the difference.

Two Simple Comparison Activities

ACTIVITY 4.03 Long and Short Shoes

Choose the tallest child, the shortest child, and three other children of varying sizes. Ask all five children to remove a shoe and then have them bring the shoes to the front of the room. Hold up the longest shoe and the shortest shoe so that they are about three feet apart. Ask which shoe is longer. Next, hold up two shoes that are about the same length. Ask which shoe is shorter.

Ask what could be done to make it easier to tell which is shorter. [Hold them next to each other.]

ACTIVITY 4.04   Stretch

Spread your hands as far apart as you can. Say, "See how far I can reach." Have all the children stand up and spread their hands out to see how far they can reach.

Have one child guess which child in the class can reach the farthest. Have that child come to the front and show everyone how far he or she can reach. Choose a second child to come forward and stand in front of the first child so the class can see who can reach farther.

If any children think they can reach farther than the first child, have them come forward so the class can make the comparison and decide.

Seriation

Seriation is the ordering of objects according to some consistent criterion. For example, words might be arranged in order so that the number of letters in every word is less than or equal to the number of letters in the next word. Using this criterion, these six words,

zero three ten eleven seventeen ninety

would be arranged like this,

ten zero three eleven ninety seventeen

or like this.

ten zero three ninety eleven seventeen

In mathematics, seriation is normally concerned with examples in which the ordering criterion is based on some mathematical attribute such as size or numerical quantity. Indeed, seriation is in fact an extension of comparison. Comparison orders two objects while seriation orders more than two objects.

The process of seriation can be thought of as a series of comparisons. This is both the most obvious and most productive way to teach seriation. The following activity illustrates this process.

x + 4   ACTIVITY 4.05   Tallest and Tallest and Tallest

Choose five children who have different heights, and have them come to the front of the room.

Have the class identify the tallest child in this group. Direct this child to stand next to every other child to verify that he or she is tallest. In other words, compare the height of this child to each of the other children. When the class is sure that the tallest child has been identified, have this tallest child stand to one side. Tell the class that this child is first in line. Follow the same process to identify the tallest child in the group that remains. Have this child stand second in line with the first tallest child.

Continue this process until all the children in the group have been lined up according to height.

This same process is illustrated in each of the following activities.

A Group Seriation Activity

ACTIVITY 4.06   Shorter than a Yardstick

Hold up a yardstick. Tell the class that you want everyone to find a stick that is shorter than the yardstick and bring it to class tomorrow. You should bring several sticks the next day for those who forgot their sticks.

Form groups of four or five children. Direct them to compare sticks and identify the longest one. Then have them compare the remaining sticks to find the second longest one. Have them continue this process until they have arranged their sticks in order.

Have each group show their result to the rest of the class.

Ask questions. Use in context, appropriate length comparison terminology: long, short, longer, shorter, longest, and shortest.

A Partner Seriation Activity

ACTIVITY 4.07   Up and Down

Have two children experiment with a balance, placing different weights in the pans.

After sufficient time has been allowed for experimentation, ask them why one side goes down and the other side goes up. Have them take turns holding two objects, one that is heavy and the other light. Show them that you are going to place one object on each side of the balance. Have them predict which object will go down and which will go up.

Give them three objects to arrange in order from heaviest to lightest. Monitor their work to be sure that they understand.

Have them show and tell the class what they did.

An Individual Seriation Activity

ACTIVITY 4.08   Ordering the Rods

Give an individual child a set of colored number rods.

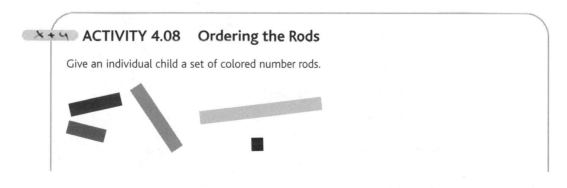

Have the child make comparisons to arrange the rods in order.

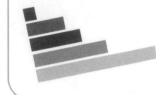

Matching and Prenumber Comparisons

Another type of comparison involves early notions related to number. With these comparisons, the focus is not on size of the objects, but is on whether one group has more objects. The comparison is made by matching objects of one set with objects of the other set, one-by-one. When you run out of objects in one of the sets, then the other set has more. Two examples of this type of comparison follow.

x + y ACTIVITY 4.09   More or Fewer

Form two groups of children, one with six children and the other with seven children. Ask the rest of the children how we could decide which group has more. If someone suggests a way to decide, try it to see if it works. If no one suggests the following method, demonstrate it.

Have each child from one group go hold hands with one person from the other group. One child will be left over. Point out that this child makes the difference between the two groups. The group with the extra child has *more* children. This group has *one more* than the other group. The other group has *fewer* children.

Repeat the activity with groups of other sizes.

x + y ACTIVITY 4.10   Birds and Nests

Make cut-outs of 12 birds and 12 nests.

Place seven nests on the bulletin board where they can be reached by the children. Place eight birds on a table where the children can see them. Ask the children whether there are more birds or more nests.

Have children one at a time, place the birds on nests. When there are no more nests, ask again whether there are more birds or more nests.

Repeat with different numbers of birds and nests.

Matching and Prenumber Seriation

A natural extension of using one-to-one matching to compare the numbers of objects in sets is using one-to-one matching to order three sets of objects according to the numbers of objects in the sets. The procedure for doing this is illustrated in the activity that follows.

ACTIVITY 4.11   The Most Pennies

Choose three children. Give each child a different number of pennies. Ask them who has the most pennies. The child who thinks he or she has the most must use matching to show that he or she does have more pennies than each of the other children.

Then ask the remaining two children who has the most pennies. Have that child use matching to show that he or she has more.

Have the children line up in order according to the number of pennies they have.

The Beginning of Geometric Concepts: Relative Position

Relative position concepts (above, below, between, near, far, inside, outside) build spatial awareness and lay the groundwork for many mathematical concepts, particularly in the area of geometry. An effective way to develop relative position concepts and vocabulary is illustrated in the activities that follow. First, set up a situation where the concept is inherently present. Next, introduce the concept and the vocabulary. Then use, and have the children use, the vocabulary in a natural context (Tucker, Weaver, & Singleton, 2000).

Above

ACTIVITY 4.12   Hold Up?

Give sheets of colored construction paper to four children. One child should have yellow. Another should have green. The others should have orange and purple. Have them hold the papers as pictured. Tell the children that the purple paper is above the orange one. Point to the green paper. Tell the children that the purple paper and the orange paper are both above the green one. Ask the children what colors are above the yellow. Have the children rearrange the papers. Point to a paper. Ask what colors are above the one that you point to. Repeat with other arrangements.

Below

ACTIVITY 4.13   What Colors Are Below?

Give sheets of colored construction paper to four children. One child should have yellow. Another should have green. The others should have orange and purple. Have them hold the papers as pictured. Tell the children that the yellow paper is below the green one. Point to the green paper. Tell the children that the green paper is below the orange paper and also below the purple one. Ask the children what colors are below the purple. Have the children rearrange the papers. Point to a paper. Ask what colors are below the one that you point to. Repeat with other arrangements.

Above and Below

✕ ➕ ╺ ACTIVITY 4.14   Things Above, Things Below

Have four children bring objects such as a baseball cap, a shoe, a picture, a mug, or a book to the front of the room. Have them hold the objects in a vertical arrangement. Name any of the objects and have the children tell which ones are above and below the one you named.

Between

✕ ➕ ╺ ACTIVITY 4.15   Stuff Between

Have children cut out pictures of objects such as a baseball cap, a shoe, a dog, a tree, or a book and place them on the bulletin board in a vertical arrangement.

Point out two pictures that have another picture between them. Then point to the picture between them. Name the object in the picture and tell the children that it is between the others. Choose two other pictures that have another between them. Have the children tell what is between the ones you identified. Have the children move the objects into a horizontal arrangement and repeat the activity.

✕ ➕ ╺ ACTIVITY 4.16   People Between

When the children are lined up to go to recess, art, or music, name two children and ask who is between the ones that you named.

Near and Far.   Near and far are relative terms. Objects are considered near to us or far from us only relative to other objects. For example, if you are considering people in a room, a person who is 30 feet away might be considered far away, while at a football game, another spectator who is 30 feet away would probably be considered near to you. Because of their relative nature, the "near" and "far" concepts are almost always dealt with together. Often we would ask a child to decide which of two (or more) objects is near (compared to the other objects) and which is far (compared to the other objects). The next activities demonstrate how a teacher can help children to develop these concepts.

✕ ➕ ╺ ACTIVITY 4.17   People Near and Far

When the children are lined up to go to recess, art, or music, identify two children and have them hold their hands up. Ask another child which of them is near and which is far away. Repeat with other children.

✕ ✦ ५ ACTIVITY 4.18   Table Shapes

Cut out three shapes, a square, a circle, and a triangle. Line them up on a table so that they are about 24 inches apart. Identify the first shape on the children's left. Ask which of the other shapes is near to the one you identified. Ask which shape is far from it. Rearrange the shapes and repeat the activity.

Move the middle shape so that it is near the one on the children's right. Call the attention of the class to the middle shape and ask the children which of the other shapes is near to it and which is far from it.

Inside and Outside

✕ ✦ ५ ACTIVITY 4.19   It's in the Box!

Stick a strip of masking tape on the floor. Place an open-topped box (about 12-inches wide by 18-inches long) about 7 feet from the line. Stand behind the line and toss a block into the box. Tell the children that the block is inside the box. Toss the block again and miss the box. Tell the children that now the block is outside the box.

Toss the block several more times. After each toss, have the children tell if the block is inside or outside the box.

Have children take turns tossing the block. After each toss, have the class tell if the block is inside or outside the box.

✕ ✦ ५ ACTIVITY 4.20   In the Circle

Have about nine children hold hands in a circle. Have two children stand inside the circle and have two stand outside the circle. Have the class tell who is inside and who is outside.

Choose another group to form a circle. Call on other children to go stand either inside or outside the circle.

Open and Closed.   In young children development of the geometric notion of open or closed nearly always makes use of the concept of inside or outside. We might talk about a dog being able to get outside of the yard if the gate is left open. We can tell if the fence is open or closed by whether or not the dog can get out.

ACTIVITY 4.21   Can the Dog Get Out?

Open or Closed?

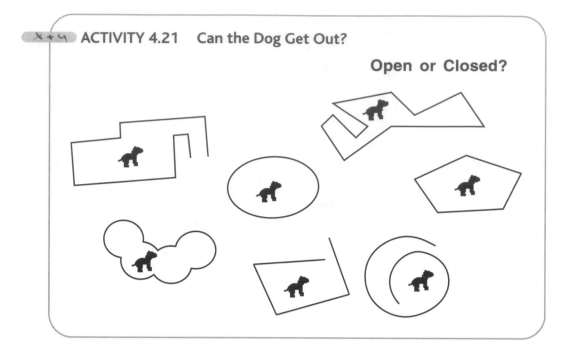

Straight or Crooked.   There are three simple and easy-to-use tools for checking whether things are in a straight line: a stretched string, a sight line, and a folded sheet of paper. The following activities develop these tools and use them to check for straightness.

ACTIVITY 4.22   Straight as a String

Lay a 36-inch string on a table so that the string is crooked. Ask the children if the string is crooked or straight.

Pick up the string by its ends and stretch it out until it is straight. Explain to the children that a stretched string is straight.

Draw a freehand line that is about 24-inches long on the chalkboard. Ask if it is crooked or straight. Hold the stretched string next to the line to check whether it is straight.

Check some other things for straightness.

ACTIVITY 4.23   Make a Straight Edge

Form an odd-shaped sheet of paper by cutting away the corners and straight edges from a large sheet of paper.

Show the resulting shape to the children. Point out that there are no straight sides. Tell them that you can make a straight side by folding the paper. Fold the paper and show the folded edge to the children. Stretch a length of string next to the folded edge to check its straightness.

Use the folded edge of the paper to check several things for straightness.

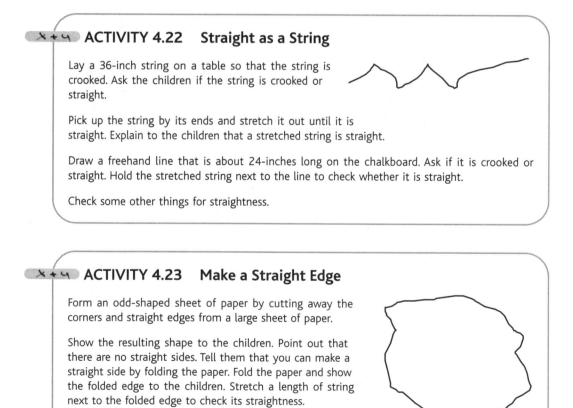

✕ + ◥ ACTIVITY 4.24 Looks Straight

Place three blocks on the table so that they are not in a straight line.

Have a child look along the line of blocks. Ask if the middle block is in line with the others or if it sticks out. Have several others also look.

Have a child look along the line of blocks while you slowly push the middle block into line. Have the child stop you when all three blocks are lined up. Have another child look also to check.

Stretch a length of string next to the blocks to check whether they are in a straight line.

Then use a folded edge of paper to check the line of blocks for straightness.

Have five children stand in a line. Have another child look down the line and move children until the line is straight.

A Revised Lesson

The following example of a lesson plan is similar to one that is based entirely on the suggestions provided in the teacher's guide of a kindergarten-level textbook. It is a good plan; however, its focus is on using the textbook pages and the developmental part of the lesson is minimal. The example lesson plan is followed by a revised plan that expands the amount of developmental activity, increases the amount of kinesthetic activity, provides for increased communication among and from children, and makes monitoring the learning a more continuous process. Remember that these adaptations will make the lesson appropriate for virtually all students. But, remember also that some students with severe needs may require further instructional adaptations.

LESSON OBJECTIVE

The student will identify objects in specified positions: above, below, and between.

Lesson Opener

Ask children to raise their hands based on criteria such as color of clothing or eye color. Have them raise one hand above their heads and hold the other hand below their chins. Have them wiggle the fingers of the hands that are below their chins. Have them wiggle the fingers of the hands that are above their heads.

Development

Direct the attention of the class to the first example on the first page of the lesson. Point out that one cat is above the table and the other cat is below the table. Have the children trace the ring around the cat that is above the table. Have them trace the X that marks the cat below the table. Direct the attention of the children to the first example on the second page. Point out that the yellow toy is between the other two toys.

Monitor Learning

Have the children look at the second example on the first page. Have them name the things that they see. [A dog in a dog house and a cat on top of the dog house.] Have them draw a ring around the animal that is above the other one. Have them mark an X on the animal that is below the other one. Have them complete the third example on the page. Provide individual help for children who do not understand. On the second page, have the children color the middle object yellow on the remaining two examples. Provide individual help for children who do not understand.

Practice

Assign the *Shape Reteaching Worksheet* to those who would benefit from reteaching. Assign the practice worksheet to the rest of the students.

We will now revise the lesson to make it more appropriate for diverse learners.

LESSON OBJECTIVE

The student will identify objects in specified positions: above, below, and between.

Lesson Opener

You will need a step ladder and three dolls. Choose three children to come to the front. Give each of them a doll to place on different steps of the ladder. Ask other children to tell which doll is highest, which doll is lowest, and which doll is in the middle on the ladder.

Repeat the activity with different children.

Tell the class that today we are going to learn to use the words above, below, and between to describe how things are arranged.

Development

Call on three new children to place the dolls on the ladder. Ask how many children have heard the word **above.** Explain that the doll that is highest on the ladder is above the others. Have someone identify the doll that is above the others. Rearrange the dolls. Ask which doll is above the others.

Monitor Learning

Take note of any children who seem to have trouble understanding. Involve them as the activity is repeated.

Ask how many children have heard the word **below.** Ask who knows which doll is below the others. Rearrange the dolls several times and have someone tell which doll is below the others.

Monitor Learning

Take note of any children who seem to have trouble understanding. Involve them as the activity is repeated.

Point to the doll in the middle. Ask if anyone knows a word that tells this doll's position. After children have had a chance to respond, tell them that this doll is **between** the others. Rearrange the dolls and ask which doll is between the others.

Place the dolls side by side on top of a table. Ask if any of the dolls is above the others. [No.] Ask if any of the dolls is below the others. [No.] Point out that the doll in the middle is still between the others.

Place three different-colored blocks in a line on the table. Ask which block is below the others. [None of them is below the others.] Ask which block is between the others.

Monitor Learning

Some children may be confused by the change from a vertical arrangement of objects to a horizontal arrangement. Take note of any children who seem to have trouble understanding. Involve them as the activity is repeated.

Place three objects on the bulletin board in a diagonal arrangement. Ask which of these objects is between the others.

Choose two children to come forward. Have one of them lie on top of the table and have the other lie under the table. Ask who is above? Who is below? Is anyone between them?

Place four objects in a vertical arrangement on the bulletin board. Ask which object is above the others. Which is below the others? Point out that now there are *two things between* the top one and the bottom one.

Draw three objects on the chalkboard in a vertical arrangement. Have a child draw a ring around the one that is above the others. Have another child mark an X on the one that is below the others. Have a third child point to the one that is between the others. Repeat this with four objects. [Now there will be two things between.] Draw two objects and have a child draw an object between them.

Have the children work with partners. Give partners four different-colored blocks. Have them take turns stacking the blocks. The other child says which blocks are above, below, and between the others.

Monitor Learning

Take note of any children are having trouble. Provide individual assistance as it is needed.

Closure and Follow-Up

Ask if someone can tell what three words we learned to use today. Have different children tell in their own words what each of these three words means. Have the children look at the pages from the textbook. Explain how to complete the pages. Have the children take the pages home and use them to explain to their parents about above, below, and between.

Exercises and Activities

1. Describe a classification activity for young children. Have them form two groups, one consisting of familiar objects with some specified attribute, the other consisting of familiar objects without that specified attribute.
2. Develop a classification activity based on a children's story like the one described in Activity 4.02 on page 53.
3. Develop a developmental length comparison activity that uses objects familiar to young children.
4. Develop a practice activity on seriation that uses objects familiar to young children.
5. Develop a partner activity in which children use one-to-one matching to compare the size of two groups of objects familiar to young children.
6. Develop an outdoor activity that helps develop the concepts of near and far (developmental, not practice).
7. Study the traditional and adapted lesson plans on pages 63–65. Identify the changes in the adapted plan that increase the development of the concepts taught in the lesson.

8. Study the traditional and adapted lesson plans on pages 63–65. Identify the changes in the adapted plan that increase the student communication about the concepts taught in the lesson.

9. Study the traditional and adapted lesson plans on pages 63–65. Identify the changes in the adapted plan that increase the visual information about the concepts taught in the lesson.

10. Study the traditional and adapted lesson plans on pages 63–65. Identify the changes in the adapted plan that provide for more kinesthetic activity.

11. Write a complete lesson plan to teach the concepts of open and closed. Place heavy emphasis on development activity and kinesthetic activity.

12. Consider the following situation: The teacher showed some young children a doll, a book, a baseball, a toy car, a football, and some doll clothes, and then asked them to choose some things that go together. The teacher expected the children to choose the doll and the doll clothes or perhaps the two balls. However, the teacher was surprised when one child selected the baseball, the book, and the toy car.

    (a) What do you think the child was thinking? Why do you think the child answered the way he or she did?

    (b) What follow-up question might allow the teacher to understand what the child is thinking?

13. Consider the following situation: The teacher showed three things and the children decided which one was different from the others. However, when showing a donut, a bagel, and a carrot, the teacher was surprised when one child said the donut was the one that was different.

    (a) What do you think the child was thinking? Why do you think the child answered the way he or she did?

    (b) What follow-up question might allow the teacher to understand what the child is thinking?

References and Related Readings

Andrews, A. G. (1996). Developing spatial sense—A moving experience. *Teaching Children Mathematics*, 2, 290–293.

Baroody, A. J. (1987). *Children's mathematical thinking: A developmental framework for preschool, primary and special education teachers.* New York: Teachers College Press.

Baroody, A. J. (1996). An investigative approach to the mathematics instruction of children classified as learning disabled. In D. K. Reid, W. P. Hresko, & H. L. Swanson (Eds.), *Cognitive approaches to learning disabilities* (pp. 545–615). Austin, TX: PRO-ED.

Court, S. R. A. (1920). Numbers, time, and space in the first five years of a child's life. *Pedagogical Seminary*, 27, 71–89.

Dunn, R., & Dunn, K. (1992). *Teaching elementary students through their individual learning styles: Practical approaches for grades 3–6.* Needham Heights, MA: Allyn & Bacon.

Freed, J., & Parsons, L. (1997). *Right-brained children in a left-brained world: Unlocking the potential of your ADD child.* New York: Simon & Schuster.

Linksman, R. (1997). *The fine line between ADHD and kinesthetic learners* [On-line]. Available: http://www.latitudes.org/learn01.html.

National Council of Teachers of Mathematics. (1989). *Curriculum and evaluation standards for school mathematics.* Reston, VA: NCTM.

National Council of Teachers of Mathematics. (2000). *Principles and standards for school mathematics.* Reston, VA: NCTM.

Tucker, B. F., Weaver, T. L., & Singleton, A. (2000). Relative position concepts are whole-body concepts. *The Journal of Early Education and Family Review*, 8(1), 23–28.

Web Sites

http://npin.org/library/pre1998/n00170/n00170.html
(Parents' and teachers' suggestions for transition to school.)

http://www.ldonline.org/ld_indepth/parenting/johnson_helping.html
(Help for parents of children with LD. Links, links, links...)

http://www.ed.gov/databases/ERIC_Digests/ed380308.html
(Making mathematical connections in the early grades. ERIC D*igest*.)

http://www.circleofinclusion.org/pim/five/adaptations.html
(Excellent early childhood site, also addresses mathematical concepts.)

http://www.pbs.org/kcts/preciouschildren/diversity/read_linguistic.html
(Language and cultural diversity in early childhood.)

CHAPTER

WHOLE NUMBERS AND NUMERATION:

Naming and Writing Quantity

THE LEARNING PRINCIPLE

Students must learn mathematics with understanding, actively building new knowledge from experience and prior knowledge (National Council of Teachers of Mathematics, 2000, pp. 20–21).

THE NUMBER AND OPERATIONS STANDARD

"As students work with numbers, they gradually develop flexibility in thinking about numbers, which is the hallmark of number sense" (NCTM, 2000, p. 80).

THE COMMUNICATION STANDARD

"Building a community of learners, where students exchange mathematical ideas not only with the teacher but also with one another, should be a goal in every classroom" (NCTM, 2000, p. 131).

THE CONNECTIONS STANDARD

"Teachers... should make explicit the connections between and among the mathematical ideas students are developing..." (NCTM, 2000, p. 132).

THE REPRESENTATION STANDARD

"They use physical objects such as their own fingers, natural language, drawings, diagrams, physical gestures, and symbols. Through interactions with these representations, other students, and the teacher, students develop their own mental images of mathematical ideas" (NCTM, 2000, p. 136).

Building on What Children Already Know

Before learning to name and write numbers, children will already have developed considerable "number sense" (National Council, 1989; Greenes, Schulman, & Spungin, 1993) that can be used as a foundation for new learning about numbers. Good teaching invariably builds on existing knowledge so smoothly that nothing seems new to the child. Rather, each concept or skill that is taught seems merely to be an extension of what is already known. Not only is this good teaching, but it is also efficient teaching, because more is learned, and it is learned more quickly. In addition to being good and efficient teaching, it is also effective teaching, because what is learned is better understood, more likely to remembered, and easier to apply in varied settings.

Before working on number concepts, children will have been encouraged to use prenumber quantitative vocabulary to describe their environment. For example, they have had a lifetime of experiences with the number one.

"I have some cookies. You only have one."

"Here is one of your shoes. Where is the other one?"

"There are some pencils on the desk. Will you bring me one?"

"No, you can't have a piece of candy. You've already had one."

Children also have a strong sense of the meaning of "more." They have had years of experience with this concept. Often the word more is in the form "one more."

"I have more than you have."

"Share with your sister. You have more than she has."

"I want you to eat one more bite of carrots."

"I'll read you one more book. Then you have to go to sleep."

"If you do that one more time, you'll be in big trouble!"

"All right, you may hit the ball one more time. Then your turn will be over."

Other examples of prenumber quantitative vocabulary can be developed using one-to-one correspondence, a skill already emphasized. Using one-to-one correspondence children are able to continue their development of prenumber quantitative vocabulary. "As many as," "more than," and "less than" can describe many situations as the following illustrate:

"There are just as many desks in the room as there are children."

"There are as many cartons of milk as there are children."

"I have a lot more crayons than he does."

"There are more girls than boys here today at school."

"There are more chairs in the room than there are children."

"I have no more cookies."

Therefore, as we examine each topic we consider what the child already knows that can serve as the basis for building the new idea. We then explore how that already available knowledge can be extended to include the new idea.

Students need to make the connection that the language they use to describe natural activities in their lives and the language used to describe mathematical activities in the classroom are the same. The following activity describes how this natural connection can be made.

ACTIVITY 5.01   M&Ms

Give the following directions to your students: "When I give you a bag of M&Ms, carefully put them into groups and be ready to describe your bag of M&Ms without using numbers."

Discuss the students' bags of M&Ms by encouraging them to use prenumber quantitative vocabulary as:

"I have more brown M&Ms than any other color."
"I have the same amount of red M&Ms as I do yellow M&Ms."
"Some of my M&Ms have chipped edges."
"All of my M&Ms are chocolate."

Use food very cautiously when planning activities to develop mathematical concepts. A compelling reason for this caution is the high prevalence of children with food allergies, and at best, candy is not conducive to good dental hygiene and encourages poor food choices so prevalent in today's world. The M&M activity is described here because it is a natural connection between the language students use when they are describing the real world in which they interact and the language we use in describing the mathematical world in which they participate in the classroom. This activity can easily be adapted by using bags of small toys or cutouts from a die-cut machine.

As students become proficient in describing relationships between quantities, they are ready to describe their surroundings in more detail. They should be led to discover the importance of using quantitative concepts in their descriptions. To do this, they must understand whole numbers.

The Big Picture

Children should understand the concept of the quantitative value before the written expression is introduced. Unfortunately, if the number 2 is the topic of the day, often teachers will begin their lesson by showing the children the numeral 2 on the board first, and then they will begin the developmental activities. A teacher should provide many examples of "2" before introducing the written numeral. For example:

"I have two eyes."
"I have two hands."
"I have two ears."
"Here are two books."
"Here are two crayons."

These examples demonstrate the quantitative concept to the child. After the teacher has identified the quantity two for the children, that knowledge should be reinforced by having them show the quantity two. For example:

"Show me two crayons."
"Show me two fingers."
"Clap two times."

After the child has learned the concept of "twoness" and then demonstrated the quantity of "twoness," nonexamples should be included with examples to ensure complete understanding. For example:

"Do I have two noses?"
"Do I have two feet?"
"Do I have two necks?"
"Do I have two fingers?"
"Do I have two desks in this room?"

After children have fully developed this concept of "twoness," they are ready to learn the symbolic notation for this number. It is important to remember that the language used in writing 2 must match the model it describes.

Development of Numbers and Numeration

The activities described in this chapter promote the children's ability to attain these goals. First, they will be able to identify the quantity that is named by the number. Second, they will be able to name the number or say it. Third, they will be able to write the number clearly using standard notation. The following objectives convey these important abilities:

1. When children are shown a quantity (that is, some number of objects), they will be able to say the number that names the quantity.
2. When children are shown a quantity, they will be able to write the numeral that names the quantity.
3. Shown a numeral (a written number), children will be able to show that quantity (that many objects).
4. Shown a numeral, children will be able to say the number.
5. Given a number orally, children will be able to show that quantity.
6. Given a number orally, children will be able to write that quantity.

Counting is an important skill in the development of children's knowledge of numbers. However, it is important to remember that the ability to say the numbers in their correct order does not ensure an understanding of the process of counting. For example, a very young child can say the numbers 1 to 5 in a rote fashion. Yet, when a key ring with three keys on it is presented, the child might "count to five" while touching the three keys.

The ability to assign a number for each unit added when counting is related to one-to-one correspondence. Because using one-to-one correspondence is important in counting, teachers should physically count as well as verbally count in order to demonstrate this concept. For example, the teacher should touch each pencil as they are counted or touch each child as they are counted. After children have fully understood the concept of one-to-one correspondence, the teacher could stand close to each student as they are counted. Eventually the teacher will be able to simply point to each student as they are counted. The important thing for the children to understand is that something is being counted instead of just hearing numbers recited orally.

One-Digit Numbers

The meaning that a child attaches to a number depends on the mental image that he or she associates with that number. Young children think concretely, that is, in terms of mental images of things existing in their world. Therefore, the mental image for the number three, or any number, should not be an abstract symbol.

Rather, the image should be of three objects. And, often, the child will place those three objects in some particular arrangement.

Remembering that one goal is to establish mental imagery for numbers, we must be aware of a problem related to establishing that mental imagery. To illustrate this problem with a rather extreme example, we show three numbers represented below by linear arrangements of objects. At a glance, it is nearly impossible to recognize the numbers being represented.

After rearranging the objects to "organize" the mental imagery, notice how much easier it is to recognize the numbers.

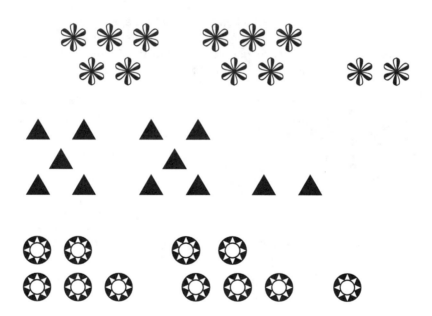

Linear arrangements of objects for numbers greater than three should be avoided. Rather, use arrangements that help the child recognize quantity without counting.

When teaching the numbers 1 to 9, take the time to develop each number thoroughly before another number is introduced. In other words, if a teacher uses the following scope and sequence for teaching one-digit numbers: 1, 2, 3, 4, 0, 5, 6, 7, 8, and 9, the number 2 needs to be fully developed before progressing to the number 3.

What is meant by full development? As already mentioned, the students should have many opportunities to see the concept. For example, students can be taught to see the number 7 by using concrete or pictorial examples. Students also need to express orally that what they are being shown is "seven." Then they should be given opportunities to show "seven." When children have had sufficient opportunities in experiencing "seven," then, and only then, should they be shown how to write the numeral 7. For a smooth transition it is important to use the same language when describing concrete situations, pictorial situations, and symbolic situations of the number.

For example, the teacher can demonstrate "seven" by counting seven books and saying, "Here are seven books." The teacher could also draw seven books on the board and say, "Here are seven books." Then the teacher writes on the board "7 books" and says, "this says seven books." With consistent language, students will be able to understand that all three representations describe the same situation, seven books.

When students fully understand the concept of seven and have been taught to write the number 7, the teacher introduces the next concept. Full attention should be given to the development of the new concept using the same types of activities described in the development of the concept of 7. Again, make sure that the students know what this new concept looks like, know how to say the number when they see it described, know how to model it, and then know how to write its corresponding numeral.

Numbers will be meaningful for children when they are connected to what the children already know and when they are developed out of experiences that provide mental images for numbers. For example, building on the concept of one more, children should understand 7 and be able to visualize 7 as 6 and one more.

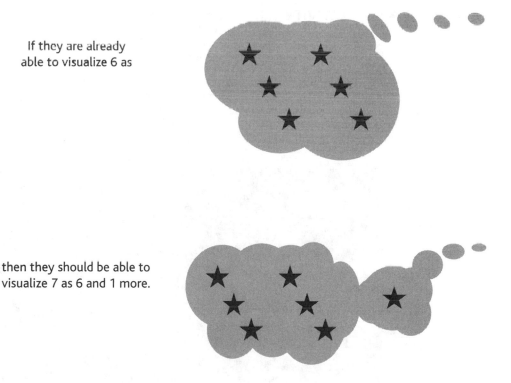

If they are already able to visualize 6 as

then they should be able to visualize 7 as 6 and 1 more.

The children should see and understand 7 as a composition of many combinations of numbers that they already know.

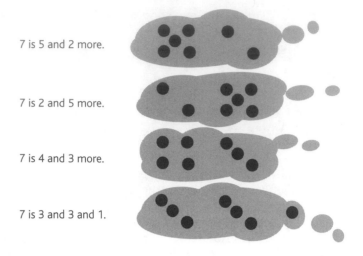

7 is 5 and 2 more.

7 is 2 and 5 more.

7 is 4 and 3 more.

7 is 3 and 3 and 1.

Domino patterns provide efficient and easily recalled mental images for small numbers. There are, in fact, a number of effective instructional activities using dominoes.

Two activities that help children learn to combine numbers to form a larger number are described below.

ACTIVITY 5.02   Domino Match

Form a group of 2 or 3 children. Place a set of dominoes, face up, on the table. One of them starts by choosing a domino and places it to the side. They count to see how many dots are on that domino.

Then they take turns finding another domino with the same number of dots. When they cannot find any more dominoes with that many dots, another child selects a domino and they start over.

x + 4 ACTIVITY 5.03   And One More

Form a group of 2 or 3 children. Place a set of dominoes, face up, on the table. One of them starts by choosing a domino and places it to the side. They count to see how many dots are on that domino.

Then they take turns finding another domino with one more dot than that one. When they cannot find any more dominoes with one more dot, another child selects a domino and they start over.

Is it not important to follow the preceding instructional sequence exactly. What is important is that each number is given full attention and the students completely understand each number's meaning before they are introduced to and taught how to write its symbol. The concept of 0 should be taught only after several numbers, because it is easier to understand "nothing" after the concept of "something" has been taught.

The use of nonexamples is as important in developing number sense as it is in the development of any concept (Ehrenburg, 1981). After the students have been given ample experience with a particular concept, they should be shown examples that do not contain the concept being studied, emphasizing that this is *not* an example of the concept. As more and more numbers are learned, these nonexamples could be previously learned numbers, and therefore, meaningful review of past numbers becomes a natural part of the day's math lesson.

One structured format for ensuring long-term retention is to plan a review lesson following each newly learned concept. For example, after the students have learned about the number 2 and are currently learning the number 3, a review lesson emphasizing both numbers 2 and 3 should follow. The number 4 is taught next. A review lesson emphasizing the numbers 3 and 4 follows and then a review lesson emphasizing the numbers 2, 3, and 4. Numbers 1 through 9 are taught in this format. Even though it may seem as if a large proportion of the math lessons consists of review, the more time spent developing these important basic concepts, the less time is needed to remediate later. The following activities illustrate how a teacher might develop the concept of four

x + 4 ACTIVITY 5.04   I Have Four

Fill a box with various school supplies, including four of each of the items. For example, four pencils, four erasers, four boxes of crayons, four bottles of glue, and so on.

Tell the students that you have a box of school supplies. You need to know what's in it. Ask them to help you figure out exactly what is in the box.

First, let the students help you group each kind of item together. Then, count each group and announce each time that you have four of these. After counting each group, ask the students to count with you. As a closing activity, ask the students how these groups are alike? [Each group has four in it.]

x + 4 ACTIVITY 5.05   Move and Count

Fill a baggie with various counters, including four of each of the counters. Before you give each student his baggie, tell your students as soon as they get their baggies, they should put the counters into groups. After distributing the baggies, use an overhead projector to demonstrate the grouping. As you arrange each group on one side, ask your students to put their groups on one side. Now you are ready to move and count. Ask your students to slide each counter over to the other side as they count. Count each group of counters in this fashion emphasizing that each group has four in it.

ACTIVITY 5.06 Four-Leaf Clovers

Draw several stems for four-leaf clovers on a piece of drawing paper, or make them using brown yarn. Cut out the leaves for the students to use, or let them cut the leaves out if time permits.

Tell the students that today they will make four-leaf clovers. Ask if anyone has ever seen a four-leaf clover. Have a short discussion about what a four-leaf clover looks like. Emphasize that each four-leaf clover has four leaves. Using an overhead projector, demonstrate how they can make their own four-leaf clovers. Have the class count with you each time you make one. Ask how many leaves their four-leaf clovers will have.

ACTIVITY 5.07 Four or Not Four

Make a work sheet by drawing several flowers, some having four petals, some having fewer than four petals, and some having more than four petals. Tell the students they are going to color only the flowers with four petals.

Use an overhead projector to show and discuss each flower and have the students count with you to decide if it should be colored. Remember the emphasis is on whether the flowers have exactly four petals or not. It is all right to name the numbers already learned, but the emphasis is on the development of the concept of four.

ACTIVITY 5.08 Simon Says

Plan for a game of Simon Says by having directions use the concept of four, for example, Simon says to clap four times. Simon says to hop four times on one foot. Cough four times.

Review the rules for playing Simon Says. Play the game as planned. After the game is finished, ask if anyone noticed something about the things Simon asked them to do. Help your students to remember the particular moves Simon requested. As your students respond with statements like. "We clapped four times," write the statements on the board. After all the directions using four have been written on the board, ask a student to point to the symbol that says four.

Two-Digit Numbers

The previously discussed instructional sequence for teaching one-digit numbers is also followed when teaching two-digit numbers. The numbers are introduced as quantities and are related to already learned numbers (quantities) before the written notation is taught. We want the child to know what the number (the quantity) "looks like" before learning to write the number. The mental image for the number twelve, for example, should not be an abstract symbol. Rather, the mental image should be of twelve objects. Unfortunately, when the number is greater than 10, that many objects often appears to the child as a "bunch." Groups of 11, or 12, or 13 objects are virtually indistinguishable.

The mental image may be "organized" by helping the child to see 12 as an easily recognizable arrangement of that many objects (Schram, Feiman-Nemser, & Ball, 1990). When this is done, the new number is represented as some combination of already recognizable quantities. For example, 12 could be shown in many ways.

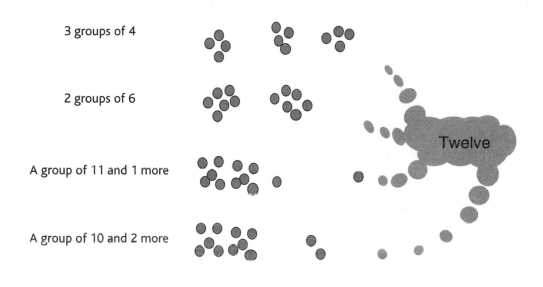

3 groups of 4

2 groups of 6

A group of 11 and 1 more

A group of 10 and 2 more

Twelve

Since numbers greater than 10 are named as a combination of tens and ones, the last of the images shown for twelve (10 and 2 more) is an important one. A device called the ten-frame is an effective way to structure the mental image for numbers in the teens. The ten-frame helps the child see the number as tens and ones.

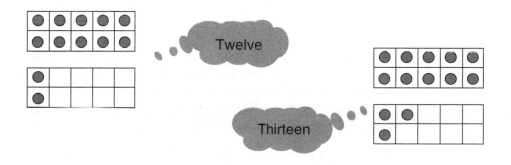

Bundled sticks are another excellent model for helping children develop mental imagery for two-digit numbers. Twelve sticks in a pile just looks like a bunch of sticks, but when 10 of them are bundled together, it is easy to see 12 as 10 and 2 more.

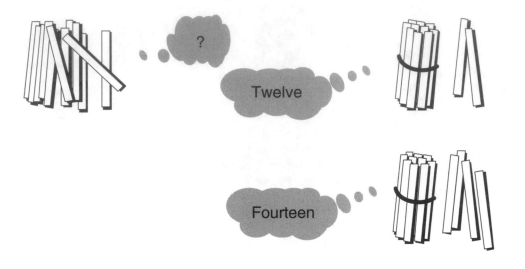

Base-ten blocks are another effective model for two-digit numbers. Base-ten blocks consist of small cubes, rods (sometimes called longs), flats, and large cubes. The small cubes represent ones. Rods are equal in length to 10 small cubes and represent tens. Flats, which are the equivalent of 10 longs, represent hundreds. Large cubes, 10 flats in size, represent thousands.

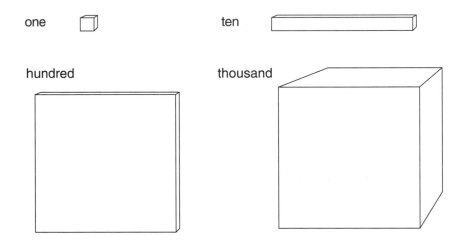

When introducing the base-ten blocks, the teacher should build on the one-digit-number concepts that the students already know. The teacher usually begins by representing one-digit numbers with the small cubes. Then the teacher shows the children the 10-rod and asks what number it represents. By lining up 1-cubes alongside the rod, children can understand that the rod is the same amount as 10 ones, so they must be equal.

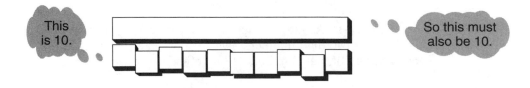

The student can see that there are two ways to represent 10, with 10 1-cubes or with 1 10-rod. Similarly, other numbers can be represented in two ways, as ones or as ten and ones.

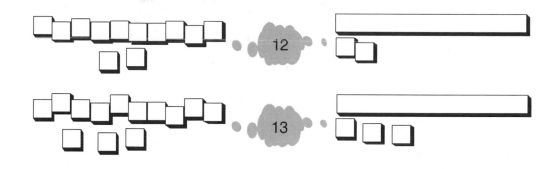

The children should have many experiences representing teen numbers using tens and ones. In each example, the teacher emphasizes, so the children understand, that using tens and ones is just another way to show the same amount. But, the children should also understand that it is easier to recognize the number at sight when tens and ones are used, because the mental imagery is better.

As the children visualize the teens as ten and ones, written notation should be introduced. Although many children are already able to write 10, 11, and 12, and possibly other two-digit numbers, it is important that the teacher emphasize that the written symbol actually indicates the one ten and the number of ones.

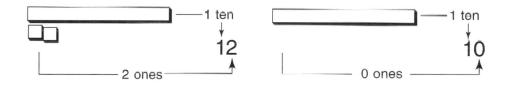

When the child is thinking of the teen numbers as tens and ones, it is easy to move on to understanding other two-digit numbers. Nineteen is 10 and 9 ones. One more than 19 is 20, so 20 is 10 and 10 ones, or 2 tens and no ones.

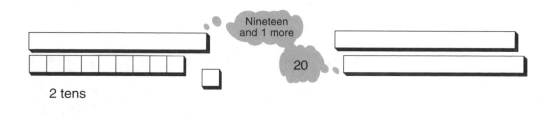

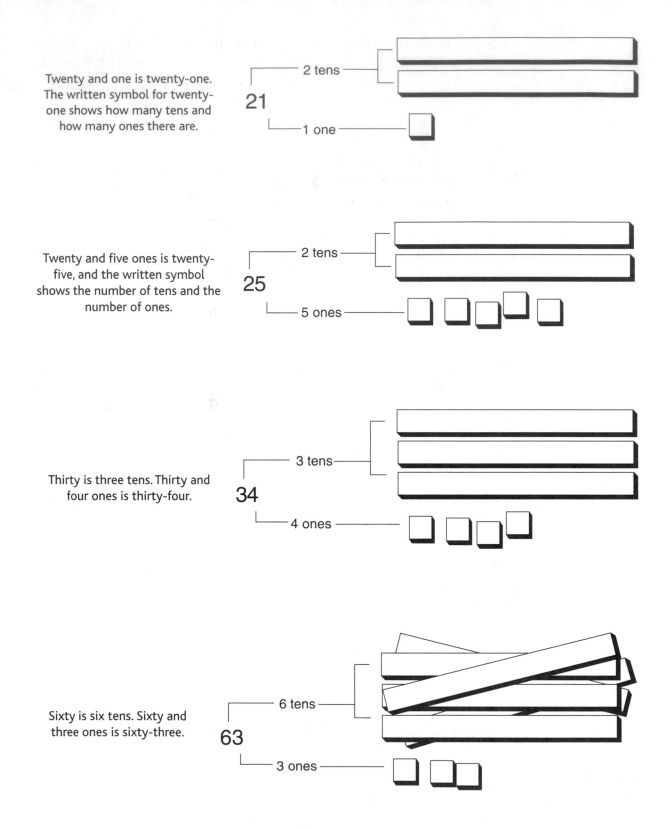

Twenty and one is twenty-one. The written symbol for twenty-one shows how many tens and how many ones there are.

21   2 tens
      1 one

Twenty and five ones is twenty-five, and the written symbol shows the number of tens and the number of ones.

25   2 tens
      5 ones

Thirty is three tens. Thirty and four ones is thirty-four.

34   3 tens
      4 ones

Sixty is six tens. Sixty and three ones is sixty-three.

63   6 tens
      3 ones

The following activities illustrate how a teacher might develop the concepts of two-digit numbers.

ACTIVITY 5.09 Bundle Them Up

Place 20 popsicle sticks in a bag for each student. Keep 20 sticks for your own use.

Tell the students that you have some sticks and that you need to know how many you have. Have them count with you as you count 20 sticks. Count 10 sticks and place a rubber band around them. Ask how many are in the bundle. Do the same thing to form another bundle of 10.

Ask how many bundles of 10 you have. [2] Remind them that there were 20 sticks altogether, so two tens must be the same as twenty. Remove the rubber bands and count out 12 sticks. Then bundle 10 of them so that you have one group of 10 and 2 single sticks.

Pass out the bags of sticks. Have everyone count out 15 sticks and lay the extra sticks aside. Then have them bundle 10 of the 15 sticks. Ask how many sticks they have altogether. [15] Ask how many bundles of ten there are and how many other sticks there are. [1 ten and 5 single sticks.]

Lead the class to show all of the teen numbers.

ACTIVITY 5.10 Let's Trade

From a set of base-10 blocks, place one 10-rod and 19 1-cubes in a bag for each student. Keep a set for your own use.

Show six cubes and ask how many there are. Do the same for three cubes and nine cubes. Allow someone to count them if necessary. Show 10 cubes and have someone count them. Line up the 10 cubes beside a 10-rod so that the children can see that they equal the same amount. Ask what number name should be given to the rod. [10] Ask how many cubes you should trade for one rod if it is an even trade. [10] Show 12 cubes. Ask if there are enough to trade for a 10. Do that and point out that 12 is the same as 10 and 2.

Pass out the bags of base-10 blocks. Have everyone count out 15 cubes. Then have them trade 10 cubes for a 10-rod. Ask the students to tell another name for 15.

Repeat with all of the teen numbers.

ACTIVITY 5.11 Match

Using base-10 blocks, place representations of two-digit numbers in paper bags. Represent each number two or three different ways. For example, 27 might be represented as 27 ones, as 1 ten and 17 ones, and as 2 tens and 7 ones.

Hand out the bags to the children. Have them look at the numbers in their bags and write the numbers that they have on the outside of the bags.

Then have them move around the room and get together with everyone else with the same number. Finally, have each group look at the numbers in the bags to make sure the same number is in all the bags in the group.

Have each group report to the class the different names that they have for the different representations of the same number.

ACTIVITY 5.12   See and Say

Have sets of nine 10-rods and 30 1-cubes ready for groups of students. Keep a set for your own use.

Form groups of 2 or 3 children. Give each group a set of base-10 blocks.

Write 23 on the chalkboard. Have the groups figure out how to show the numbers using the fewest pieces from the base-10 blocks. After checking to see that everyone understood and that they represented 23 as 2 tens and 3 ones, write several other two-digit numbers on the board and have the groups represent them as tens and ones.

ACTIVITY 5.13   Too Many

Have each child draw and cut out a picture of a boy.

Read the poem "Too Many Daves" by Dr. Seuss. Using 23 of the boys that were drawn by the children, group the boys into groups of ten as the story of Mrs. McCave's dilemma of having 23 sons, all with the name of Dave, unfolds with alternative names.

ACTIVITY 5.14   *Moria's Birthday*

Moria's Birthday by Robert Munsch is a delightful children's book that uses numbers in a variety of ways, for example, the number of children to be invited to a party, the number of pizzas ordered for the party, and the number of presents brought to the party. Resolution of the chaos also presents and uses numbers. Read the book and discuss the ways that numbers are used. Emphasize how numbers are used to help us understand how much.

Three or More Digits

The introduction and development of three-digit numbers, as well as numbers with more than three digits, can easily be connected to the children's knowledge of two-digit numbers. The mental imagery previously developed for two-digit numbers can be extended using any of the models that allow the child to see the basic units: base-10 blocks (add the hundreds-block and, later, the thousands-block); bundled sticks (add bundles consisting of 10 tens); play money (add hundred-dollar bills and thousand-dollar bills).

It is still important that the child see numbers visually represented before they learn the number names or write the numerals. If base-10 blocks are being used, the teacher might have the children combine 10 tens and show that they are the same amount as the larger block. If the children can count rationally to 100, they might also combine 100 ones to see that they are also the same amount as the larger block. Then, the number name for the larger block (one hundred) can be introduced with meaning.

We call this
one hundred

10 tens

100 ones

If bundled sticks are used, 10 bundles of 10 can be combined into a larger bundle. The number name for this larger quantity is one hundred. The individual sticks can then be counted to verify that the large bundle does contain 100 sticks.

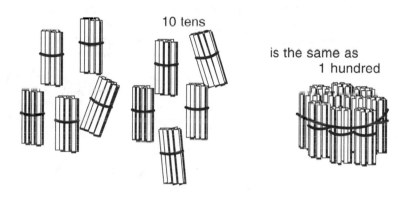

10 tens

is the same as
1 hundred

Children need to visualize and think of these new numbers in terms of their basic units. For example, we do not want the child to think of 247 as two hundred forty-seven of something. Rather, the child should think of this number as two of something (hundreds), and four of another thing (tens), and seven of still another thing (ones). They should be able to recognize these numbers, write these numbers, and read or say these numbers. When children are presented with a three- or four-digit number in any of these forms, they should be able to respond by giving that same number back in each of the other two forms.

As the children use these larger numbers, they should not only be taught to write them using standard notation, but also to read them in the standard way. It is correct to think of the number 384 as three hundred and eighty-four. It is equally correct to think of 384 as three hundred and eighty and four. However, the standard way to read and write this number is "three hundred eighty-four."

Children should be encouraged and led by the teacher to use the standard language. The teacher should consistently use standard mathematical language. However, the teacher should not overreact when an occasional "and" creeps into the reading and writing of multi-digit whole numbers. A gentle correction followed by moving on to more important things is generally the most productive way to bring the children to consistent standard language. The following sequence of activities illustrates how a teacher might develop three-digit numbers.

✕ ✦ ᴄ ACTIVITY 5.15   Too Many to Write? Make a Bundle

Have a child come forward and use bundled sticks to represent 35. Have the child place the number in a box. Ask how many bundles of 10 are in the box. [3] How many extra sticks? [5]

Have the children watch as you drop three more sticks into the box. Ask how many tens are in the box. [3] How many ones are in the box? [8] What number is in the box? [38]

Drop five more sticks into the box. Ask how many tens are in the box. [3] How many ones are in the box? [13] Ask what we need to do before we can write the new number. [Make a trade, or make a new bundle.] Take 10 sticks out of the box and use a rubber band to bundle them together. Drop the new bundle into the box. Ask what is in the box now. [4 tens and 3 ones]

Do another similar example. Place 58 in the box, then add six more sticks. Make a new bundle and name the new number. Emphasize that when you have too many ones to write the number, make a bundle.

✕ ✦ ᴄ ACTIVITY 5.16   Too Many to Write? Make a Big Bundle

Have a child come forward and use bundled sticks to represent 85. Have the child place the number in a box. Ask how many bundles of 10 are in the box. [8] How many extra sticks? [5] Have the children watch as you remove a 10 from the box. Ask how many tens are in the box. [7] How many ones are in the box? [5] What number is in the box? [75]

Drop five more bundles of 10 into the box. Ask how many tens are in the box. [12] How many ones are in the box? [5] Point out that 12 tens is too many to write. Have the children watch while you take 10 tens out of the box and place a rubber band around them to make a big bundle. Tell the children that the big bundle contains one hundred sticks. One hundred equals 10 tens. Place the big bundle into the box and ask what is in the box. [1 hundred, 2 tens, and 5 ones] Show the class how to write this number.

Do another similar example. Place 98 in the box, then add six more bundles of 10. Make a big bundle and name the new number. Emphasize that when you have too many tens to write the number, make a big bundle.

✕ ✦ ᴄ ACTIVITY 5.17   Trading Ten

Follow the procedures of Activities 5.15 and 5.16, except use base-10 blocks to represent the numbers. When you have too many to write, trade 10 ones for a 10 or trade 10 tens for a 100.

✕ ✦ ᴄ ACTIVITY 5.18   See, Say, and Show

Form the class into groups of four students. Give each group a set of base-10 blocks.

Use the blocks to show the number 381. Ask how many hundreds, tens, and ones there are. Demonstrate how to say the number. [Three hundred eighty-one] Use the blocks to show the number 526. Demonstrate how to say the number. [Five hundred twenty-six] Use the blocks to show the number 642. Ask a child to say the number.

Place the number 354 in a box. Have a child come forward, look in the box and say the number. Then each group should use their blocks to show that number. When everyone is finished, take the three hundreds out of the box and show them to the class. Did all the groups have the right number of hundreds? Do the same with the tens and then with the ones. Have everyone say the number together. Repeat this procedure with 269, 524 and 915.

ACTIVITY 5.19 Hear, Show, and Write

Form the class into groups of four students. Give each group a set of base-10 blocks. Write 538 on a sheet of paper. Have a child come forward and read the number to the class.

Each group should then use their base-10 blocks to show the number. After showing the number with the blocks, the group should agree on how to write the number correctly and someone in the group should write the number.

When all the groups are finished, hold up your number so each group can see it and check their own number. Repeat this procedure with 219, 526, and 645.

ACTIVITY 5.20 One Amount, Many Names

On the chalkboard, write a base-10 chart like the one pictured.

Use base-10 blocks to represent the number 645. Record the number on the base-10 chart.

Trade a 10 for 10 ones and record the result. Point out that we still have the same amount, but this is another way to name that amount.

Trade a 100 for 10 tens and record the result. This is just another name for the same amount. Make other trades to get other names for the same amount.

Start with another number and make trades to get other names for the same amount.

Hundreds	Tens	Ones
6	4	5
6	3	15
5	13	15

Rounding Numbers

The most effective way to develop the concept of rounding numbers is to help the children to visualize the numbers on the number line. If the tens are highlighted on the number line, it is not difficult for children to decide which 10 the number is closest to. For example, if you want to round 87 to the nearest 10, first draw a number line that has the tens written in a different color.

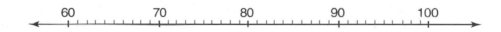

Then, locate the number 87 on the number line.

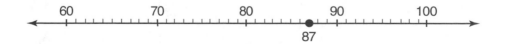

The children will see that 87 is between 80 and 90, but it is closer to 90. So, since 90 is the nearest 10, we say that 87, rounded to the nearest 10, is 90.

Similarly, we would say that 32, rounded to the nearest 10, is 30.

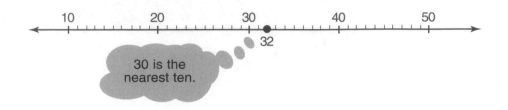

65 is exactly halfway between 60 and 70. Neither of these tens is nearer to 65 than the other.

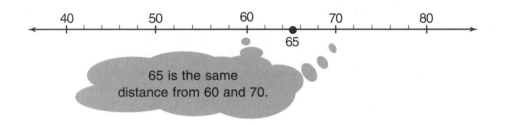

In cases like this, there are a number of conventions that can be adopted, but the most common at the elementary school level is to round numbers like this up to the next higher 10.

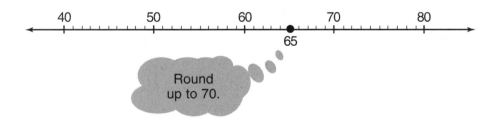

As the children are exposed to a variety of examples, they may be able to generalize the rule: If the ones digit is five or more, round up. If the ones digit is less than five, round down. It is important that the rule not be presented rotely. Rather, arrive at the rule as a generalization of many examples. Ideally, the children should be led to state the rule themselves as a summary of what they have discovered. Then the children will understand the rule. Retention of the rule will be much better, because it is always easier to remember things that we can visualize and connect to other things that we know.

The following activity sequence suggests how a teacher could develop the concept of rounding numbers to the nearest 10.

×+٩ ACTIVITY 5.21   The Closest Girl

Line up 15 chairs at the front of the room. Have three girls come forward and seat one girl in the third chair, one in the eighth chair, one in the thirteenth chair.

Then have a boy come and sit in any of the empty chairs. Ask which girl is the boy closest to. Repeat the activity with several other boys.

Next seat three boys in the chairs, have a girl sit in an empty chair, and decide which boy is closest. Repeat the activity with several other girls.

×+٩ ACTIVITY 5.22   The Closest 10

Line up 15 chairs at the front of the room, with their backs toward the children. Tape the number 20 to the back of the third chair, and tape the number 30 to the back of the thirteenth chair.

Point to the chair with 20 on its back and ask, "If this is chair number twenty, then what number chair would the next one be?" [21] Have the children figure out the numbers for several other chairs.

Next, have a child sit in any chair. Ask, "What is the number of that chair?" Then ask if 20 or 30 is closest. If the child sits in chair number 25, be sure that everyone agrees that chair is the same distance from 20 and from 30.

Repeat the activity with several other children.

Have the children line up 25 chairs in the hallway and label the second chair with a 40, the twelfth chair with a 50, and the twenty-second chair with a 60. Follow the same procedures described above.

×+٩ ACTIVITY 5.23   Find the Nearest 10

Draw a number line on the chalkboard. Label the tens with colored chalk, but do not label the rest of the numbers. Prepare cards with all the missing numbers. Shuffle the number cards and pass them out to the class.

Have children come forward, one at a time, and tape their numbers in the proper place on the number line. After taping the numbers to the number line, have them tell which is the nearest 10.

Repeat the activity with several other children.

Adapting a Lesson

Now we examine a lesson from grade 1. The lesson plan parallels the teaching activities that would typically be suggested in a teacher's guide. We have organized the plan around the components: objective, lesson opener, development, monitoring learning, practice, and closure.

LESSON OBJECTIVE

The student will recognize and write numbers from 13 through 19.

Lesson Opener

Write the numbers 7 through 12 on the chalkboard and place about 20 counters on the table. Point to the 8 and call on a child to tell what that number is. Have another child come forward and give you that many counters. Then have a third child check to see if it is the correct number of counters. Repeat the process with the number 12. Tell the class that today they will learn to recognize and write the numbers 13 through 19.

Development

Show the class 14 popsicle sticks. Tell them that there are 14 sticks. While they watch, count out 10 of the sticks and put a rubber band around those ten sticks. Show them that there are four sticks left over, and tell them that 14 is 10 and 4. Record the number on a place value chart. Explain that this is how we write fourteen, and then write 14 next to the chart.

Repeat this process with the numbers 16 and 19.

Direct the attention of the class to the first page of the lesson in the student book. Lead them through the first example. Point out that one group has 10 dots and the other group has five dots. Point out how the number 15 is written.

Monitor Learning

Have the children complete the rest of the teaching examples on the page. Move around the room, observing the children's work. Identify those who are having difficulty.

Practice

Have the class complete the practice exercises on the second page of the student lesson. Have students who are having difficulty complete the reteaching worksheet instead.

Closure

When you are getting near the end of the math period, get the attention of the class and remind them that today they learned how to recognize and write the numbers 13 through 19.

Adapting the Lesson for a Diverse Group of Students

To adapt this traditional lesson plan into one that is appropriate for all learners, we need to accomplish the following five goals.

Increase the amount of development. We want to develop the concepts more thoroughly and relate the "new" numbers more completely to other numbers with which the children are already familiar.

Provide more visual information. The original lesson did a good job of providing visual information, but we need to expand the use of visuals to be sure that the children acquire strong mental imagery for their number concepts. Every time a new mathematical concept is introduced, the children should "see what it looks like."

Add more kinesthetic activity. We want the children to be up, out of their seats, doing math. Children need to be active participants in demonstrating concepts, in addition to the teacher's showing them. Active physical involvement encourages active intellectual involvement.

Plan for more oral communication about mathematics from and among the children. Encourage the children to question and conjecture. We want them to discuss and explain. Ask questions instead of lecturing.

Plan for continual monitoring of learning. The teacher needs to be aware of how well the children are learning during every part of the lesson. Continual assessment of learning allows the teacher to know who understands and who does not, who can use the skills being taught and who cannot, which students might be grouped together for remedial instruction, what content needs to be retaught, and when content needs to be taught with a different approach.

Remember that these adaptations make the lesson appropriate for almost all students. But, remember also, that some students with severe needs may require further instructional adaptations.

LESSON OBJECTIVE

The student will recognize and write numbers from 13 through 19.

Lesson Opener

Prepare sets of three cards for each of the numbers 5 through 12. One card should have the numeral, one card should have a picture of that many dots without any apparent grouping, and the third card should have a picture of that many dots grouped by fives and tens. See the examples below.

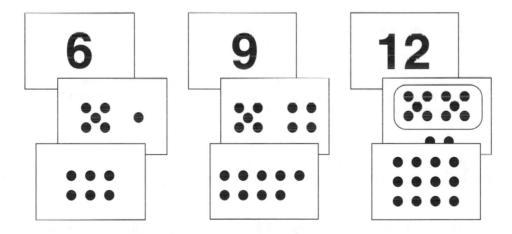

Shuffle the cards and pass them out to the children. Have them to get together with the others who have the same number. When all the children are with their partners, have them explain what is on their cards. [For example, "I have 9." "I have 9 dots." "I have 5 dots and 4 dots. That's the same as 9."]

Monitor Understanding

Observe to be sure that all the children understand how to find their partners. Provide further explanation to children who are having difficulty.

For the numbers 10, 11, and 12, use a place-value chart to show how we write numbers that are 10 or more.

Explain to the class that today they will learn about the numbers 13 through 19.

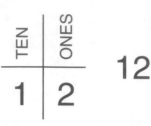

Development

Have the children work with one or two partners. Give each set of partners 13 popsicle sticks. Tell them to separate their sticks into two groups. Ask how many sticks they placed in each of the two groups. Have children come forward and record combinations that they have discovered. Discuss all the different combinations that the children discovered. [For example, "13 is the same as 9 and 4 more." "6 and 7 more is also 13." "11 and 2 is 13."] Be sure the discussion includes 12 and 1 more and 10 and 3 more. Use the place-value chart to show how to write 13.

Monitor Understanding

Listen to the children explain the different combinations that they found. Ask leading questions when they need help to understand. Observe to be sure the children are able to record their results.

Give the partners one additional stick (now they have 14). Tell them to discover and record as many combinations as they can. Discuss what they find. Ask which combinations tell them the most about the number 14. During the discussion, emphasize the importance of 10 + 4 and 13 + 1. Use the place-value chart to show how to write 14.

Monitor Understanding

Move around the room, observing and listening to the children's discussion. Ask leading questions when they need help to understand. Be sure the children understand how to record their results.

Repeat the process with the numbers 16 and 18.

Direct the attention of the class to the first page of the lesson in the student book. Lead them through the first example. Point out that one group has 10 dots and the other group has five dots. Have a child come to the chalkboard and record that number on a place-value chart. Have another child come forward and show how the number 15 is written without using the place-value chart.

Monitor Learning

Have the children complete the rest of the teaching examples on the first page of the lesson. Move around the room, observing the children's work. Identify those who are having difficulty.

Practice

Pair the children with partners. Have them complete the practice exercises on the second page of the student lesson, one at a time. After both partners have completed an example, they should compare results to see if they agree. If they have different results, they should discuss the example and agree on an answer.

Monitor Learning

Move around the room, observing the children's work. Identify those who are having difficulty and provide assistance. Emphasize forming a group of 10 and then counting to see how many are left.

Closure

Near the end of the math period, ask the class what they have learned today. Ask how to write the numbers 13 through 19.

Follow Up

Pass out copies of a sheet of paper with 17 dots on it. Have the children take the paper home and use it to show a parent how to write the number.

Exercises and Activities

1. Read "Standard 6: Number Sense and Numeration" on pages 38–40 of *Curriculum and Evaluation Standards for School Mathematics*, published by the National Council of Teachers of Mathematics. Also read the discussion of the Number and Operations Standard on pages 32–36 of *Principles and Standards for School Mathematics*, also published by the National Council of Teachers of Mathematics. Compare and contrast the recommendations in the standards with the recommendations in this chapter.

2. Study the adapted lesson plan on pages 91–92. Identify activities in the plan that implement the recommendations in Standard 6 of the *Curriculum and Evaluation Standards for School Mathematics* and *Principles and Standards for School Mathematics*.

3. Study the traditional and adapted lesson plans on pages 90–92. Identify the changes in the adapted plan that increase the development of the number concepts.

4. Study the traditional and adapted lesson plans on pages 90–92. Identify the changes in the adapted plan that increase the student communication about the number concepts.

5. Study the traditional and adapted lesson plans on pages 90–92. Identify the changes in the adapted plan that increase the visual information about the number concepts.

6. Study the traditional and adapted lesson plans on pages 90–92. Identify the changes in the adapted plan that provide for more kinesthetic activity.

7. Develop an instructional sequence for rounding numbers to the nearest hundred. The instructional sequence should parallel the one on pages 87–89.

8. Develop an instructional sequence for teaching two-digit numbers and numeration.

9. Choose a lesson on the topic "number and numeration," from a published elementary school mathematics textbook series.
   a. Write a lesson plan that follows the teaching suggestions in the teacher's guide.
   b. Identify the parts of the lesson that develop the concept(s) or skill(s)
   c. Expand the developmental part of the lesson by adding activities that build mental imagery for the concepts or skills being taught or that build connections between the numbers being taught in the lesson and numbers with which the students are already familiar.

10. Choose a lesson on the topic "number and numeration" from a published elementary school mathematics textbook series.
    a. Write a lesson plan that follows the teaching suggestions in the teacher's guide.
    b. Identify the parts of the lesson that provide visual information about the concept(s) or skill(s) being taught.
    c. Expand the lesson by adding activities that use more visual information about the concepts or skills being taught.

11. Choose a lesson on the topic "number and numeration" from a published elementary school mathematics textbook series.
    a. Write a lesson plan that follows the teaching suggestions in the teacher's guide.
    b. Identify kinesthetic activity that is included in the lesson.
    c. Add more kinesthetic activity to the lesson.

12. Choose a lesson on the topic "number and numeration" from a published elementary school mathematics textbook series.
    a. Write a lesson plan that follows the teaching suggestions in the teacher's guide.
    b. Identify parts of the lesson that include student communication about the concept(s) or skill(s) taught in the lesson.

c. Add more opportunities for communication from or among students to the lesson.

13. Choose a lesson on the topic "number and numeration" from a published elementary school mathematics textbook series.

   a. Write a lesson plan that follows the teaching suggestions in the teacher's guide.

   b. Identify the parts of the lesson designed to assess the learning of the students.

   c. Add more continual assessment (monitoring of learning) to the lesson plan.

14. Study the adapted lesson plan on pages 91–92. Make further changes in the lesson plan to make it more appropriate for a child with a history of breaking manipulatives.

15. Study the adapted lesson plan on pages 91–92. Make further changes in the lesson plan to make it more appropriate for a child whose learning disability includes figure-ground confusion.

16. Study the adapted lesson plan on pages 91–92. Make further changes in the lesson plan to make it more appropriate for a child who has limited understanding of English.

References and Related Readings

Ehrenburg, S. D. (1981). Concept learning: How to make it happen in the classroom. *Educational Leadership*, 39(1), 36–43.

Greenes, C., Schulman, L., & Spungin, R. (1993). Developing sense about numbers. *Arithmetic Teacher: Mathematics Education through the Middle Grades*, 40, 279–284.

National Council of Teachers of Mathematics. (1989). *Curriculum and evaluation standards for school mathematics*. Reston, VA: NCTM.

National Council of Teachers of Mathematics. (2000). *Principles and standards for school mathematics*. Reston, VA: NCTM.

Schram, P., Feiman-Nemser, S., & Ball, D. L. (1990). *Thinking about teaching subtraction with regrouping: A comparison of beginning and experienced teachers' responses to textbooks*. East Lansing, MI: Michigan State University (NCRTE Research Report 89-5).

Web Sites

http://www.sasked.gov.sk.ca/docs/elemath/numop.html
(A scope and sequence chart for numbers and operations.)

http://www.edu.org/LTT/CDT/TBI.html
(Teaching Big Ideas.)

CHAPTER 6

ADDING AND SUBTRACTING WHOLE NUMBERS:

Combining and Separating Quantities

THE ASSESSMENT STANDARD

"...making assessment an integral part of classroom practice is associated with improved student learning" (National Council of Teachers of Mathematics, 2000, p. 22).

THE NUMBER AND OPERATIONS STANDARD

"An understanding of addition and subtraction can be generated when young students solve "joining" and take away problems by directly modeling the situation..." (NCTM, 2000, p. 83).

THE PROBLEM SOLVING STANDARD

"Teachers should ask students to reflect on, explain, and justify their answers so that problem solving both leads to and confirms students' understanding of mathematical concepts" (NCTM, 2000, p. 121).

THE COMMUNICATION STANDARD

"Teachers... should expect students to explain their thinking and should give students many opportunities to talk with, and listen to, their peers" (NCTM, 2000, p. 130).

THE REPRESENTATION STANDARD

"Through class discussions of students' ways of thinking and recording, teachers can lay foundations for students' understanding of conventional ways of representing the process of adding numbers" (NCTM, 2000, p. 68).

Teaching Addition of Whole Numbers

An Overview of the Development of Computation

When teaching any operation on whole numbers, there are three distinct instructional tasks that the teacher must complete. They are developing the meaning of the operation, developing the basic facts, and developing the algorithm(s). A closer examination of these instructional tasks yields a clear pattern of development.

The Meaning of the Operation. When teaching the meaning of the operation, teachers need to lead the child to accomplish two things. First, the child must associate the arithmetic operation with some physical operation. This association provides a basis for modeling the operation and establishes mental imagery for the operation. Second, the child must learn to use some already available skill to figure out the answer. When established in this way, the meaning of the operation provides the child with a way to discover answers to specific examples.

The Basic Facts. Some facts are committed to memory while others are "figured out" using a step-by-step procedure. Basic facts are those needed to figure out the others. Basic facts serve as the basis for the rest of the facts. Normally, children are initially taught a body of easy basic facts for an operation, and then later they are taught the harder basic facts for that operation. However, for both the easy basic facts and the hard basic facts, there are three things that the children should be led to do.

First, the children should discover the answers for themselves. The meaning of the operation is applied to find answers to the easy facts. However, as the numbers get larger, the skills used in the application of the meaning are too inefficient. So, more efficient thinking strategies need to be developed for finding answers to the hard basic facts.

Second, the children should recognize relationships that exist among the facts. There are two major benefits of this emphasis on relationships. The emphasis on relationships improves retention, because it is easier to remember things that are related to other things that we already know. Also, recognition of those relationships drastically reduces the amount of memorization needed.

Third, the children should commit the facts to memory. Of course, if the meaning of the operation has been effectively taught, the child can figure out the answers to basic facts. So, why is it important that they be memorized? Remember that the basic facts are used to find computation answers. If the basic facts are not memorized, the computation process becomes so slow and tedious that mathematics learning grinds nearly to a stop. If the basic facts are not memorized, children develop a sense of "can't do."

The Algorithm(s). The algorithms are the step-by-step computation procedures that are followed to complete multi-digit examples. Since the algorithms are procedures, it is tempting to resort to teaching a series of rote rules that describe the procedures. Memorization of rote rules traditionally has been the predominant method for learning algorithms for arithmetic operations. Rules are generalizations, usually important ones. However, effective teachers de-emphasize rote rules. The problem with learning rules rotely is that rote rules are meaningless rules. The word, rote, literally means mechanically and without intelligent attention.

Rote rules are also confusing. Children often learn them slightly wrong. Rote rules are often only slightly different from other rote rules, and children mix them up. They tend to use them in the wrong context. Retention is poor. Although the teacher may get what appears to be quick mastery after intense practice of a rote rule, that so-called mastery often goes away as soon as the practice stops. A weekend away from practice will have a devastating effect on retention. And, if we carefully consider the content of rote rules as they are taught, most of them are not even true. Every rote rule that is commonly taught is only true within some very narrow context. Eventually, as the setting changes, the rule has to be corrected with a new rule. This adds to the confusion. The child's dilemma becomes: When do I use that rule? When do I use this rule? Is either rule the right one?

Instead of teaching rote rules, the teacher should instead emphasize big ideas that explain the process (Thornton, Tucker, Dossey, & Bazik, 1983). Big ideas are ideas that are constantly recurring. Each recurrence of a big idea becomes an extension of something already learned. The algorithms should be taught using effective physical or pictorial models. Modeling a concept or skill lets the children see what the concept or skill looks like and helps the children to develop clear mental imagery. Modeling gives meaning to the algorithms. Note that we are not contending that children should not learn rules in mathematics. Indeed, with meaningful teaching, *the children still learn rules*. However, the *rules arise out of patterns observed by the children* as they use appropriate models that allow them to visualize the mathematical procedures. Rules are simply *statements of helpful ways to do the work*. Meaningful rules *make sense to the children* and are not "what we do because the teacher told us to."

Now we examine this developmental sequence as it is applied to establishing the meaning of addition.

Developmental Sequence for the Addition of Whole Numbers

Developing the Meaning of Addition.   Children need to *associate addition with the combining of quantities*. This association should become so strong that when the children see the symbols 3 + 4, they visualize three things being combined with four things. When seeing a situation where quantities are being combined, the child thinks "That's addition!" After addition has been mastered, the child will see problem settings where things are being combined and will think "I can use addition to solve this problem." But association of addition with the combining of quantities is not enough. After those quantities have been combined, children must understand that they can *count to find the answer*. The following activity illustrates how a teacher might begin development of the meaning of addition.

✗ + ч ACTIVITY 6.01   Altogether

Write the number 4 on the chalkboard. Have a child place that many blocks in your hands. Ask the other children how many blocks you have. Place the four blocks into a box, out of sight. Ask the children how many blocks are in the box. About 10 inches to the right of the number 4, write the number 2 on the chalkboard. Have a child give you two blocks. Ask the other children how many blocks are in your hands.

Place these two blocks into the box with the first four blocks. Point out that you put four blocks into the box and then put two more blocks into the box. Ask if anyone can tell you how many blocks are in the box now. Have someone count them to see how many.

Repeat the activity with other pairs of numbers.

Tell the children that when you put two amounts together you are adding.

This first activity starts out like it is just another activity relating number and numeral. But then the physical operation, combining, is introduced and the mathematical name for it (adding) is introduced. Notice that no effort is made at this time to introduce the plus sign. That comes very soon, but for now, we are modeling addition (combining quantities) and introducing the new term, add. When the children see addition modeled, they should be able to tell what they see using appropriate mathematical language.

Modeled Addition ⟶ Verbal Description

In the next activities, the plus sign and then the equal sign are introduced, and we begin using the written notation for addition.

Modeled Addition ⟶ Written Notation

An Activity to Introduce the Plus Sign.

---

x + y **ACTIVITY 6.02   Give Me a Sign**

Write the numbers 3 and 6 side-by-side and about 8 inches apart on the chalkboard. Have a child place three blocks on the table. Have another child place six blocks on the table. Tell the children to watch what you do. Place the three blocks and then the six blocks into a box, out of sight. Ask the children what we call it when we put two amounts together. [Adding.]

Tell the children that we use a plus sign to show that the two numbers have been added. Write a plus sign between the numbers. Point to it and say, "This is a plus sign." Tell the children that what is written on the board is three plus six. Ask what it means. [3 and 6 are added.]

Repeat the activity with other pairs of numbers.

An Activity to Introduce the Equal Sign.

---

x + y **ACTIVITY 6.03   This Equals That**

Place a group of two blocks and a group of five blocks on the table. Have a child come forward, count the blocks in each group, and announce the numbers to the class. Tell the children to watch what you do. Place the two blocks and then the five blocks into a box, out of sight. Ask the children what we call it when we put two amounts together. [Adding.] Ask a child to come forward and write the addition on the chalkboard, using a plus sign to show the addition.

Next, ask a child to come forward and check to see how many blocks there are altogether. Tell the children that we use an equal sign to tell how many blocks there are altogether. Write 2 + 5 = 7 on the board. Point to each symbol as you read it.

Repeat the activity with other pairs of numbers. Have different children write the symbols and other children read what is written.

Finally, the children should learn to model addition examples that they are given either in writing or verbally.

Written Example ⟶ Modeled Form

Spoken Example ⟶ Modeled Form

Two Activities to Introduce the Process of Finding Answers.

✕ + ◁ ACTIVITY 6.04   Make Sum for Me

Write 4 + 3 on the chalkboard. Ask a child to come forward and use the blocks and the box to show this addition. When the child has placed four blocks and then three blocks together into the box, ask the other children how we can find how many blocks there are altogether. [Count them.]

Have a child come forward and count the blocks. Ask the children how to write the answer. [Write = 7 after 4 + 3.] Use the equal sign to record the answer.

Repeat the activity with other addition examples.

Point out that the children now know how to figure out answers by themselves.

✕ + ◁ ACTIVITY 6.05   Show Me Sum

Place some blocks and a box on the table. Choose a child to come to the table. Tell this child to listen carefully and then use the blocks and the box to show the addition that you are going to say. Slowly say, "Two plus three." If the child has difficulty, allow other children to make suggestions.

After the child has combined the blocks together in the box, ask how to find how many there are altogether. [Count them.]

Have someone count the blocks to see how many there are. Then say the result, "So, two plus three equals five." Have someone come forward and write the facts on the chalkboard.

Repeat the activity with several other examples. Point out again that the children know how to figure out answers by themselves.

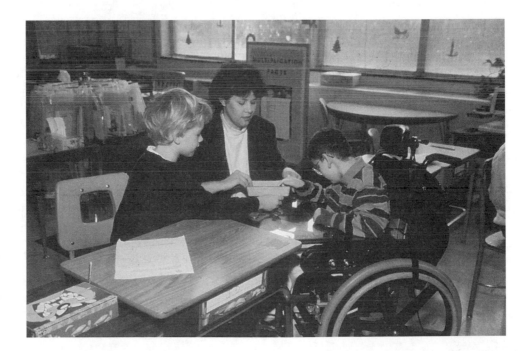

To reinforce the meaning of addition, the children should encounter a wide variety of addition examples using objects that are familiar to them, such as lunch boxes, pencils, ball caps, cookies, or even other children. They should use appropriate terminology to describe verbally the addition and use the plus sign and equal sign to write it. In every example, the children should figure out the answer for themselves, and the teacher should continually emphasize that this is easy. They can find the answers by themselves.

Making the Process of Finding Answers More Efficient. Of course, the meaning of the operation is dependent on counting to find the answer. For example, to find the answer to 6 + 3, the process would look something like this:

First, count out six objects.
Next, count out three objects.
Then combine these two groups.
And finally count all the objects to see how many.

You will note that the process requires a lot of counting. Anything that can speed up the process should be done. In the preceding example, when we counted the nine objects that we have altogether, we recounted objects that had already been counted. We do not need to recount the group of six; we already know that there are six objects in that group. So instead, start with that group and add the objects from the other group to it, one at a time.

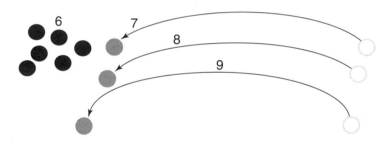

Start with 6 in the larger group. Add one of the objects from the other group; now there are 7. Add the next object from the other group; now there are 8. Add the last object from the other group; now there are 9. There are nine altogether. *Counting on* is the process in which we count on from the largest number to find the sum. Since we do not have to recount the larger group, it is a quicker and more efficient way to find the answer.

Developing the Easy Basic Addition Facts

As the children begin developing the basic addition facts, the first focus is on mastery of the easier ones (Thornton, et al., 1983). This generally includes basic facts with sums of 10 or less. The children should not be given the facts with answers included. Rather, it is important that the children find the answers for themselves. The benefits that result from the children finding basic fact answers for themselves are the following:

- Since they use the meaning of the operation to find the answers, the process of finding those answers reinforces the meaning.
- They realize that they do not need to rely on someone else for an answer. They can do it themselves, and they become more confident.

- They know that the answers are correct, because they figured them out.
- If there is ever a question about the accuracy of an answer, they do not have to rely on someone else to tell them. They can check their own answers.
- As their self-esteem improves, they develop an "I can do it" approach to basic facts. This positive approach spills over into the development of other mathematics concepts and skills.

Activities to Help Children Discover the Facts. The process of finding answers should be as interesting as the teacher can make it. The following series of activities illustrates the variety of methods that could be employed.

---

x + y **ACTIVITY 6.06 Fact Finder**

Assign the children to work in pairs. Give each pair 10 objects, such as 10 pencils, 10 blocks, 10 frog cut-outs, or 10 crayons.

The children take turns going first. One child takes some of the objects. The other child takes some of the remaining objects.

Both children write both numbers with a plus sign between them. Then they combine the objects that were chosen, and each child figures out how many there are altogether. Each child writes an equal sign and the answer. Then they compare results to see if both did the addition correctly.

Repeat the activity to do other additions.

---

x + y **ACTIVITY 6.07 I Can Do Sum**

Form groups of three or four children. Each child should have 10 counters. Each group should have two cubes with numbers printed on the faces. The first cube should have the numbers 4, 5, 6, 4, 5, and 6. The second cube should have the numbers 0, 1, 2, 3, 3, and 4.

Children take turns tossing the two cubes. After each toss, each child uses his or her counters to find the sum of the two numbers showing on the cubes. After finding the answer, the child should record the fact on a sheet of paper.

When everyone is finished, they compare results and correct errors.

---

x + y **ACTIVITY 6.08 Finger Split**

Have children work with partners. Each pair of partners will need a 10-inch piece of colored yarn.

One child holds his hands up with boths hands open and palms outward. The partner hangs the yarn between any two of the first child's fingers. This separates the 10 fingers into two groups. The children identify the addition fact and record it on a sheet of paper.

This fact is 4 + 6 = 10.

Repeat the activity to find other sums of 10.

Discovering Relationships Among the Facts. Once the children have found answers for a body of easy basic addition facts, the teacher should lead them through the process of accumulating them into an organized list. The facts should be organized in many different ways to help the children see patterns. The patterns that the children see help them to discover relationships that exist among the facts.

For example, we might have the children make a list of all the facts where 1 is being added. The children could then see that when we add 1 to a number, we get the next number (next in the counting sequence). When listing all the facts where 0 is being added, the children can easily see that whenever 0 is added we get the same number. If the teacher points out 2 + 3 = 5 and 3 + 2 = 5, 5 + 1 = 6 and 1 + 5 = 6, 5 + 3 = 8 and 3 + 5 = 8, and other similar pairs, the children can see that rearranging the numbers does not change the answer. If the children are led to organize the facts so that facts with the same answer are together, they can discover that there are many different ways to name a number. For example, 6 + 1, 4 + 3, 1 + 6, 2 + 5, 0 + 7, 5 + 2, 3 + 4, and 7 + 0 are all names for the same number, 7.

The emphasis on relationships provides two benefits. First, the interrelationships among the facts make them easier to remember. And, once the facts have been memorized, the interrelationships will improve retention. *It is always easier to remember things that are related to other things that we know.*

Second, the emphasis on relationships substantially reduces the quantity of information to be learned. Suppose we consider the addition facts with sums of 10 or less to be easy basic addition facts. These facts are displayed in the table below. Note that there is a total of 64 easy facts. That's a lot to have to learn.

+	0	1	2	3	4	5	6	7	8	9
0	0	1	2	3	4	5	6	7	8	9
1	1	2	3	4	5	6	7	8	9	10
2	2	3	4	5	6	7	8	9	10	
3	3	4	5	6	7	8	9	10		
4	4	5	6	7	8	9	10			
5	5	6	7	8	9	10				
6	6	7	8	9	10					
7	7	8	9	10						
8	8	9	10							
9	9	10								

Notice that there are 19 facts that involve addition of zero. But when we study relationships among the facts we find that when adding zero we always get the other number. That is only one thing to learn instead of 19 things.

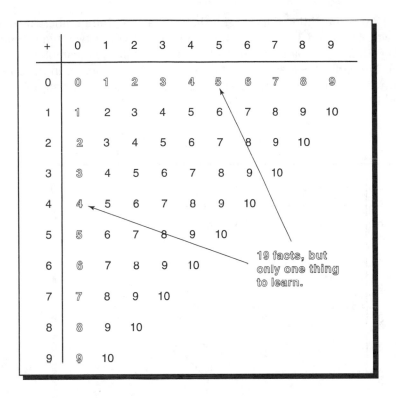

19 facts, but only one thing to learn.

The facts, 1 + 0 and 0 + 1, were included above. There are 17 other facts where 1 is being added. In the exploration of patterns and relationships, the children have already seen that, when we add 1, we get the next number in the counting sequence. So, instead of needing to learn these 17 facts as separate things, the children have only one thing to learn.

+	0	1	2	3	4	5	6	7	8	9
0	0	1	2	3	4	5	6	7	8	9
1	1	2	3	4	5	6	7	8	9	10
2	2	3	4	5	6	7	8	9	10	
3	3	4	5	6	7	8	9	10		
4	4	5	6	7	8	9	10			
5	5	6	7	8	9	10				
6	6	7	8	9	10					
7	7	8	9	10						
8	8	9	10							
9	9	10								

17 facts, but only one thing to learn.

Now if the children have seen that rearranging the numbers does not change the answer, 6 + 3 and 3 + 6 can be learned together, not as two things to learn, but as one thing. This is, of course, what mathematicians call the commutative property of addition. Similarly, 2 + 8 and 8 + 2 become one thing to learn. In the 64 easy basic facts that we are considering, there are 12 of these commutative pairs. That is, 24 facts, but only 12 things to learn.

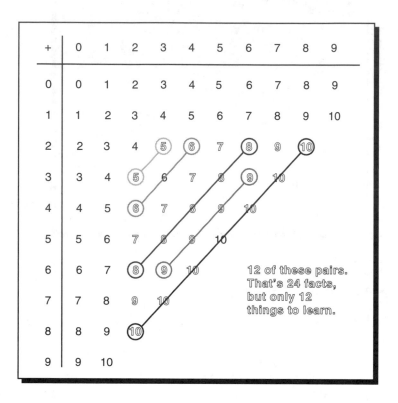

We have now considered all but four of the easy basic addition facts. These are the doubles: 2 + 2, 3 + 3, 4 + 4, and 5 + 5. They must be learned as separate facts, but children generally find them relatively easy to learn. Let's review how these few relationships reduce the amount of memorization that is necessary.

Group of Facts	Number of Facts	Things to Learn
Adding 0	19	1
Adding 1	17	1
Commutative Pairs	24	12
Doubles	4	4
All Easy Facts	**64**	**18**

Activities for Exploring Relationships. The following activities illustrate ways to help children explore patterns and discover relationships among the addition facts.

Adding 1

⟨x + y⟩ ACTIVITY 6.09   Just Another One

You will need a box and 10 blocks.

Show the children that the box is empty. Place the box on a table or desk where all the children can see. Tell them to watch and listen carefully. Drop three blocks into the box, one at a time. Ask how many blocks are in the box. Tell the children that you are going to add one more block. Drop another block into the box. Ask how many blocks are in the box. [4] Write $3 + 1 = 4$ on the chalkboard.

Repeat the activity, starting with different numbers (for example, 6, 4, or 9). In each case record the result. [$6 + 1 = 7$, $4 + 1 = 5$, and so on.]

Place 15 blocks into the box. Tell the children that there are 15 blocks. Have them watch and listen as you add one more block. Ask how many there are now. Write $15 + 1 = 16$.

Write $11 + 1 =$ on the chalkboard. Ask what the answer is. If no one knows, use the blocks and box to find the answer. Continue with other examples until the children have generalized the notion that *when we add 1 we get the next number* in the counting sequence.

Adding 0

⟨x + y⟩ ACTIVITY 6.10   The Empty Box

Form groups of three or four children. Each group will need three boxes and 10 blocks.

Write 6 on the chalkboard. Have someone in each group place that many blocks into one of the boxes. Write 0 on the board about 6 inches to the right of the 6. Point to the 0 and have someone in each group put that many blocks in another box.

Write a plus sign between the two numbers and tell the children that we are going to add the two numbers. Have them empty the blocks from the first box and the blocks from the second box into the third box. Ask how many there are altogether. Does everyone agree?

Repeat the activity with $0 + 8$, $4 + 0$, and $0 + 9$. Then write $7 + 0 =$ on the board and ask if anyone knows the answer. Repeat with $0 + 13$. Ask what is always true.

Rearranged Pairs

⟨x + y⟩ ACTIVITY 6.11   Number Split

Have the children work with partners. Each pair needs 10 counters and a 12-inch length of yarn. Have them place some of the counters on the table between them. (For example, they might place eight of the counters on the table.)

Then have them use the yarn to separate the counters into two groups.

Help them to see that when the two parts are added, the answer is all of the counters. Have them write the two facts that are shown by the counters and yarn. [$3 + 5 = 8$ and $5 + 3 = 8$.]

Have them repeat the process to produce other pairs of facts. Have the children report the pairs of facts that they found.

Record them on the chalkboard. Have the children look at the pairs of facts and explain the pattern. What happens to the answer if you rearrange the numbers? [It does not change.]

On large cards (about 8.5 × 5.5), print two facts. Each pair should demonstrate one of the relationships discussed earlier. One fact should have the answer. The other should not.

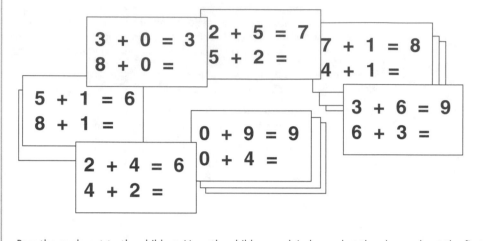

Pass the cards out to the children. Have the children explain how what they know about the first fact can help them figure out the second fact.

Memorization of the Easy Basic Addition Facts

After the easy basic facts have been investigated for helpful relationships, there needs to be a concentrated and sustained effort to help the children commit those facts to memory. As practice activities with the objective of memorization are planned, several principles should be kept in mind:

1. Children should be aware that the objective is to memorize the facts. They should be told to remember. (Surprisingly, children often are not told to remember the facts.)
2. The activities should use an interesting and fun format.
3. They should have a high level of involvement. Minimize time spent waiting. Maximize time spent thinking about the facts.
4. They should focus on a small number of unmemorized facts at any given time.
5. Some already memorized facts should be mixed in with the target unmemorized facts. This will improve retention.
6. If a child does not know an answer, he or she should be required to figure it out. This implies that the child will have time to figure it out.
7. To figure out an answer, the child should think about what he or she already knows that will help find the answer. What other facts already known will help? What relationship already known will help? Counting should be used only as a last resort.
8. Emphasize accuracy, not speed. Accuracy is of great importance. Speed is of little importance. Speed will come after accuracy and confidence.

The following are examples of activities that might be used when working on memorization of the easy basic addition facts.

✕ + ◄ ACTIVITY 6.13   Facts of the Day

Identify two facts of the day. Have the children find the answers. Write the facts on the chalkboard. Tape a sheet of paper over the answer to each fact. Tell the children to remember these facts. Call on a child. Ask for the answer to one of the facts. If the child does not know, have the child figure it out. Then tell the child to remember it.

Throughout the day, ask different children for the answers to these facts. Have them write the facts and put them in their pockets.

✕ + ◄ ACTIVITY 6.14   Easy Ones

Prepare flashcards with the numbers 0 to 9 printed on them. Also prepare flashcards with these facts printed on them.

$0 + 1 =$	$1 + 0 =$	$1 + 1 =$	$2 + 1 =$
$1 + 2 =$	$3 + 1 =$	$1 + 3 =$	$4 + 1 =$
$1 + 4 =$	$5 + 1 =$	$1 + 5 =$	$6 + 1 =$
$1 + 6 =$	$7 + 1 =$	$1 + 7 =$	$8 + 1 =$
$1 + 8 =$	$9 + 1 =$	$1 + 9 =$	

Call on a child. Show one of the numbers. Have the child tell you the number that is one more. When the children can correctly give the number that is one more, switch to the addition-fact flashcards.

✕ + ◄ ACTIVITY 6.15   Today's Pairs

Identify four facts of the day. They should consist of two commutative pairs, for example,

$$4 + 3 = 7, \ 3 + 4 = 7, \ 6 + 2 = 8, \text{and } 2 + 6 = 8$$

Ask the children how these facts are related. Have the children find the answers. Write the facts on the chalkboard. Tape a sheet of paper over the answer to each fact. Tell the children to remember these facts. Call on a child. Ask for the answer to one of the facts in a commutative pair. Then ask for the answer to the other fact in that pair. If the child does not know, have him or her figure it out. Remind the children of the relationship between these facts. Then tell him or her to remember it.

Throughout the day, ask different children for the answers to these facts. Have them write the facts and put them in their pockets.

✕ + ◄ ACTIVITY 6.16   One More

Prepare flashcards for addition facts through sums of eight.

Show a card. Have the child give the answer. If he or she cannot, have him or her figure it out.

Then ask for the answer to a fact that is one more. For example, after the child gives the answer to $4 + 2 =$, ask, "What is $4 + 3$?" After the child has answered $3 + 5 =$, ask, "What is $4 + 5$?" After the child has answered $4 + 3 =$, ask, "What is $4 + 4$?"

Thinking Strategies for Hard Basic Addition Facts

When developing the hard basic addition facts (sums of 11 through 18), answers can still be found by counting. However, with the larger numbers, counting is inefficient and consequently very slow. So, at this point in the development, more efficient strategies are needed to allow the child to find answers quickly and accurately (Thornton, et al., 1983). A wide variety of fact strategies are taught to children. The objective is to committ these facts to memory. Some fact strategies seem to lead to memorization while others do not. The strategies that successfully lead to memorization have two common characteristics.

First, *successful strategies are mental strategies.* They consist of a series of quick, easy, mental procedures. They are not pencil/paper strategies, though they can be recorded using mathematical notation. They are not mechanical strategies. They are not performed by manipulating fingers or other objects, although the fingers or other physical materials could be used to establish mental imagery for the strategies.

Second, *successful strategies require the child to use facts that are already memorized to figure out the facts that are not yet memorized.* The child is constantly thinking about what he or she already knows that can help him or her figure out what he or she does not know. The child has a sense of building on what is already known. New knowledge is closely related to existing knowledge, and it is always easier to remember things that are related to other things that are known.

One More.   The simplest thinking strategy for hard basic addition facts is the one-more strategy. The thinking is simple, so it is an easy strategy for children to use. Every hard fact can be thought of as being one more than another fact. Think of that other fact and then add one more.

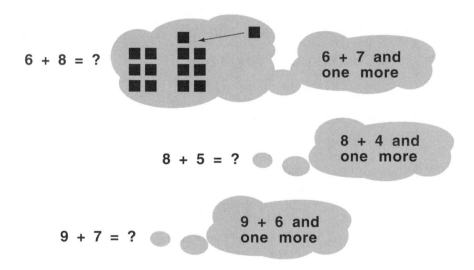

Of course, a child cannot use this strategy to find 6 + 8 unless he or she already knows 6 + 7. He or she cannot find 8 + 5 unless 8 + 4 is already known. The answer to 9 + 7 cannot be found unless 9 + 6 is known.

This strategy works particularly well in a clinical setting where the instructor is working with one child. However, in the classroom children learn the facts at different rates. They do not learn them in the same sequence. One child may know 6 + 8 = 14, but the next child may not know that fact. One child is able to use the one-more strategy to find the answer to 6 + 9, but another cannot. To use this strategy successfully, the teacher must know exactly which facts the child already knows in order to know which one the child will be able to figure out. With one child, this is possible, but with a classroom full of children it is not. So, even though the one-more strategy is easiest for the child to use, and even though the strategy works well with an individual child, it is not manageable with a class.

Doubles.   Researchers (Thornton, et al., 1983) have found that the doubles (6 + 6, 8 + 8, and so on) tend to be easier for children to commit to memory than are other hard basic addition facts. A reasonable approach might be to get the doubles memorized and then build on them to find answers to other facts, In fact, the doubles strategy is one of the more successful ones.

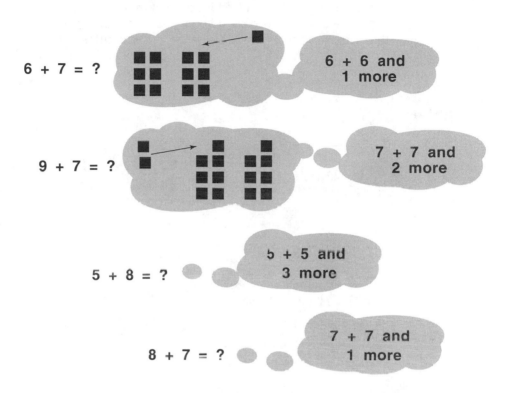

The thinking process requires "counting on" from the double. Counting on is easy if the target fact is only one or two away from the double. However, if the fact is three or more away from the double, the strategy is less effective.

Adding by counting on requires two simultaneous counts. For example, to find the answer to 8 + 6 we would begin with 8 and count on from there: 8, 9, 10, 11, 12, ... But how far do we count? When do we stop counting? At the same time that we are counting on from eight, we must also count from one. Otherwise, we don't know when to stop.

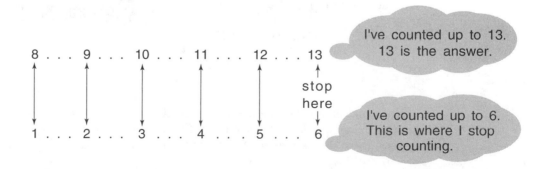

Because the doubles method requires two simultaneous counts starting with different numbers, when the target fact is more than two away from a double, children usually are unable to complete the process mentally. They typically do one count mentally and keep the other count on their fingers. Finger counting slows the process down and becomes more mechanical. The mental link between the problem and its answer is cluttered. Practice using this strategy does not effectively lead to memorization of facts that are more than two away from the double.

Make Ten. Another strategy that has been shown to be effective is the "make ten" strategy. It is based on the understanding that basic addition facts with sums of 10 are typically learned before the basic addition facts with sums greater than 10. In this strategy, the purpose is to mentally rearrange the quantities being combined to form a group of 10 and some leftovers. The strategy is taught easily when some device such as a ten-frame is used to provide mental imagery for the process.

To find 8 + 6, place the larger number in the 10-frame and place the other number outside the 10-frame.

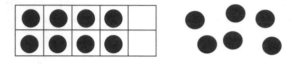

Use some of the smaller number (the 6) to fill the 10-frame.

You can see that the answer is 10 + 4. So, 8 + 6 = 14.

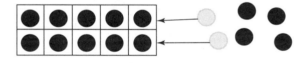

To find 3 + 9, place 9 in the 10-frame and place 3 outside the 10-frame.

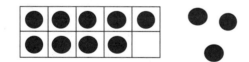

You need to move 1 to fill the 10-frame.

That leaves 2 outside the 10-frame.

So, the answer is 12. 3 + 9 = 12.

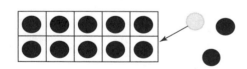

The children should practice using the 10-frame to find answers until mental imagery for the process is established. Then children are able to get answers by just thinking about how they would use the 10-frame. For example, to find the answer to 8 + 7, the series of mental steps becomes:

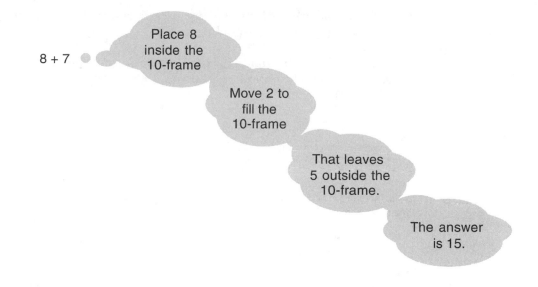

8 + 7

Place 8 inside the 10-frame

Move 2 to fill the 10-frame

That leaves 5 outside the 10-frame.

The answer is 15.

The child can easily learn the process through a series of self-directed questions. To find 7 + 9:

What number goes inside? |9|

How many do I move? |1|

What's left outside? |6|

What's the answer? |16|

The make-10 strategy is a general strategy in that it works for all of the hard basic addition facts. As a result, the children can always use it without having to decide what to do with each fact. It uses a process very much like the regrouping process used in the addition algorithm, so learning the make-10 strategy makes it easier to learn the addition algorithm.

Teachers must decide which fact strategy to teach and whether to use a single strategy or a combination of strategies. Some prefer to use a single strategy to improve the speed in finding answers, which also speeds up memorization. Some prefer allowing the child to choose from a variety of strategies the one that is best for each fact.

Teaching the Hard Basic Addition Facts

After the children have learned to use an efficient strategy to find answers to the hard basic addition facts, rapid progress can be made toward mastery of those facts. As when working on the easy facts, the children need to figure out the answers to the hard facts. The children should recognize and use relationships among the hard facts and commit them to memory.

If children do not know a hard fact, saying "I don't know" is not acceptable. They need to figure out the answer. Since we want them to do that efficiently and quickly, we encourage (almost require) them to use the thinking strategy that they learned. The children have, at this point, been using counting for over a year to find addition fact answers. The children are comfortable with counting—even when it takes a long time. Consequently, they will automatically fall back on counting because they are so comfortable with it. So, the teacher must continually lead the children to use the thinking strategy instead of counting.

If children do not know the answer to a fact, they need to think about what they already know that will help them find that answer. If children continually think about the relationships among the facts, they end up with fewer things to learn, and their retention of what they have learned is better.

Some Activities for Memorization of the Hard Basic Addition Facts. The following sequence of activities illustrates how the teacher might help children to memorize the hard basic addition facts.

✗ + ◆ ACTIVITY 6.17 What Do You Know That Helps?

This activity requires a set of addition-fact flashcards. Select some cards that show facts that have already been mastered. Mix in some cards for facts that are not yet mastered. Shuffle the cards.

Show a flashcard to a child. If the child gives an answer, ask the rest of the class if it is correct. If the child does not know the answer, show related facts and ask if they help.

For example, if the fact on the flashcard is 6 + 8, ask if the child knows 8 + 6. Does the child know 6 + 6? Does the child know 8 + 5? If none of the related facts helps, then lead the child through a thinking strategy to find the answer.

✗ + ◆ ACTIVITY 6.18 Match Me

Prepare large cards showing facts without answers. Include pairs of facts with the same answer. Mix in some facts that have already been mastered with facts that are not yet mastered. Shuffle the cards. Give a card to each child. Have everyone find a partner whose fact has the same answer. If there is an odd number of children, the teacher should participate so everyone has a partner.

Have the children stand in a circle with partners standing together. They should hold their cards so everyone else can see. Have the children check to see if all the partners match.

Collect the cards, reshuffle them, and repeat the activity.

✗ + ◆ ACTIVITY 6.19 Fact War

Prepare a set of cards with one-digit numbers on them. Make five cards for each number.

Form a group of 3 or 4 children. Shuffle the deck and place it face down on the table.

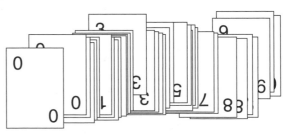

On each play, all players take two cards from the top of the deck. Each child lays his cards face up and says the sum. Whoever has the greatest sum takes the cards used in that play. When all the cards have been played, the one who has taken the most cards is the winner.

If there is a disagreement about a sum or about which is greater, the children should use counters to discover who is right.

ⅹ + ᵕ ACTIVITY 6.20 Make 11

Use cards like those described in Activity 6.19. Form a group of 3 or 4 children. Shuffle the cards and place the deck face down on the table. Turn three starter cards face up on the table.

Players take turns. On each play, the player takes the top card from the deck and places it face up on the table with the starter cards. The player then looks at all the cards that are face up. If two of them have a sum of 11, the player takes those two cards, and the player's turn is over. If the player is unable to find two cards with a sum of 11, the turn is over. The number of starter cards for each player will increase or decrease depending on whether the previous player found two cards with a sum of 11.

When all the cards have been played, the one who has taken the most cards is the winner.

ⅹ + ᵕ ACTIVITY 6.21 Make 12

Use cards like those described in Activity 6.19. Form a group of 3 or 4 children. Shuffle the cards and place the deck face down on the table. Turn three starter cards face up on the table.

Follow the procedures of Activity 6.20, except the players find two cards with a sum of 12.

ⅹ + ᵕ ACTIVITY 6.22 Lucky Number Concentration

From cards like those described in Activity 6.19, take the following 20 cards: three 4s, three 5s, four 6s, four 7s, three 8s, and three 9s.

Form a group of 2 to 4 children. Place the cards face down on the table in four rows of five cards. Have the children play concentration, looking for pairs of numbers that have a sum of 13.

Players take turns. On each turn, the player turns two cards over. If they have a sum of 13, the child takes the cards and the turn is over. If they do not have a sum of 13, they are turned face down again and the turn is over. When all the cards have been taken, the child who has taken the most cards is the winner.

Teaching the Addition Algorithm

After mastery of the basic addition facts, the child is ready to begin work on the addition algorithm. Remember that the addition algorithm is the step-by-step process by which the basic facts are used to find answers to any other whole-number addition example. To say it another way, the addition algorithm is what we use to do multi-digit addition, addition of numbers with more than one digit. Remember, that when teaching the algorithm, we want to do several things:

Let the children see what it looks like. Carefully model the operation with an appropriate physical or pictorial model. Use a model that lets them see what happens to the basic units—ones, tens, hundreds, and so on—when we add.

De-emphasize rote rules. We might end up with rules, but they should be meaningful. They should arise out of the modeling process.

Emphasize big ideas. These are the important generalizations that describe the process. They arise out of the modeling process.

Let the written algorithm simply be a recording of what happens when the algorithm is modeled. Everything we write should match something we do.

Watch our language. The language we use should describe what the children see when the operation is modeled, not language that describes what we write down.

The next three activities introduce the first of the big ideas.

---

x + y ACTIVITY 6.23   Sticks and Stones

Bring nine small sticks and nine small stones to class.

Have a child come forward and place three of the sticks and five of the stones into a box. Record on the chalkboard what was placed in the box.

    3 sticks   5 stones

Have another child come forward and place two more sticks and three more stones into the box. Record on the chalkboard what was placed in the box.

    3 sticks   5 stones
    2 sticks   3 stones

Ask what is in the box. Ask how they know. Repeat the activity with different numbers of sticks and stones.

---

x + y ACTIVITY 6.24   Gloves and Socks

Bring nine gloves and nine socks to class.

Have a child come forward and place six gloves and one sock into a box. Record on the chalkboard what was placed in the box.

    6 gloves   1 sock

Have another child come forward and place three more gloves and two more socks into the box. Record on the chalkboard what was placed in the box.

Ask what is in the box. Ask how they know. Repeat the activity with different numbers of gloves and socks.

    6 gloves   1 sock
    3 gloves   2 socks

---

x + y ACTIVITY 6.25   What's in the Box?

Use popsicle sticks and bundles of 10 popsicle sticks.

Write the number 26 on the chalkboard.

    26

Have a child come forward and show the number using the bundled sticks. Place the bundled sticks that the child selected into a box. Then write the number 53 about 6 inches to the right of the 26. Have a child come forward and show the number using the bundled sticks. Place those bundled sticks into the box also. Point out that you have put those two numbers together. Ask what we call it when you do that. [Adding.] Write a plus sign between the numbers.

    26   53

    26 + 53

Ask what is in the box altogether. Ask how they know.

Repeat the activity with different numbers. Repeat the activity with three-digit numbers.

Always Add Like Units. Out of experiences like those illustrated above, it becomes apparent to the children that to decide what is in the box, they only need to think about what was put into the box. If sticks and stones are in the box, then they need to think about how many sticks and how many stones are in the box. If gloves and socks are put into the box and later some more gloves and socks are put into the box, then to tell what is in the box they need only to think about how many gloves are in the box and how many socks are in the box. And how can they figure this out? Add the number of gloves that were put into the box at first to the number of gloves put into the box later. To decide how many socks are in the box, add the number of socks that were put into the box at first to the number of socks that were put into the box later. This is so obvious to the children that it rarely needs to be pointed out. Why do they not add the number of gloves to the number of socks? Because in this setting that would make no sense.

When adding 26 and 53 by representing these numbers with a model that allows the children to see the basic units and then combining the numbers together, the children know the answer because they can see what it looks like. They can see that they only need to tell how many tens there are and how many ones there are. There is no tendency to add the number of tens to the number of ones. That makes no sense.

If they use the model to add 142 + 35, they will not be inclined to add the 1 and the 3. That does not make sense. However, if the typical rote rules are taught, children frequently combine "always go left to right" and "you must line up the columns" to get:

$$\frac{142}{|\ 35}$$

This obviously is not correct. It makes no sense. When an appropriate model is used to help the children see what multi-digit addition looks like, children will not make this common error. They can see what needs to be added to what (Tucker, 1989).

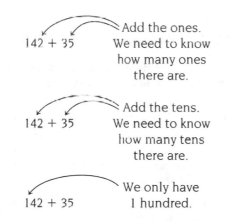

142 + 35   Add the ones. We need to know how many ones there are.

142 + 35   Add the tens. We need to know how many tens there are.

142 + 35   We only have 1 hundred.

We add ones to ones. We add tens to tens. *We always add like units.* This is the first of two big ideas that are used in the addition algorithm. Let's consider this big idea.

First, addition of like units is a constantly recurring idea. How do we add decimals? We add like units.

2.481 + 47.2 = 49.681   To find out how many tenths there are, tenths are added to tenths. *We must add like units.* It is interesting to note, though, that the decimal points do not need to be lined up. That's another rote rule that isn't even true.

Why is it easier to add $\frac{2}{5} + \frac{1}{5}$, than to add $\frac{2}{5} + \frac{1}{3}$? Because in $\frac{2}{5} + \frac{1}{5}$, the fractional units are the same in both fractions. In $\frac{2}{5} + \frac{1}{3}$ the fractional units are not the same. We *add like units*. In this case, we call them like denominators, but it is the same big idea.

When adding polynomials in algebra, we would add as follows.

$$(2x + 5y + 4xy) + (7x + 3xy) = 9x + 5y + 7xy$$

Why do we add the *x*s together? Why do we add the *xy*s together? Why did we not add the 5*y* to anything? Because *we add like units*. In this case, we call them like terms, but it is the same big idea.

Although we don't need to point it out to first-grade children, this big idea (always add like units) is really an application of the distributive property:

$$23 + 42 = (20 + 3) + (40 + 2)$$
$$= 2 \times 10 + 3 \times 1 + 4 \times 10 + 2 \times 1$$
$$= 2 \times 10 + 4 \times 10 + 3 \times 1 + 2 \times 1$$
$$= [2 + 4] \times 10 + [3 + 2] \times 1$$
$$= 6 \times 10 + 5 \times 1$$
$$= 65$$

The second of the two big ideas that are the basis of the addition algorithm also arises out of the modeling process. We first provide experiences to establish that a number can be named in many ways. We then create an addition dilemma and use the children's understanding of renaming numbers to resolve it. The following activities illustrate how this can be done.

$x + y$ ACTIVITY 6.26   Same Amount—New Name

Using bundled popsicle sticks, represent the number 34. Write the number on the chalkboard. Ask how many tens and how many ones there are. Record this on the board.

3 tens & 4 ones

Tell the children to watch carefully. Then remove the rubber band from one of the bundles. Ask the children what you did. Did you add any sticks? [No.] Did you remove any sticks? [No.] Do you still have the same number of sticks? [Yes.] Point out that even though the number of sticks is the same, the sticks are not bundled the same. Ask how many bundles of 10 there are now. Ask how many unbundled sticks there are now. Record this result.

3 tens & 4 ones
2 tens & 14 ones

Remove the rubber band from another bundle. Have the children tell what you have now. Record the result. Point out that for each of these, there are really the same number of sticks, but we can see three different names for the same number.

3 tens & 4 ones
2 tens & 14 ones
1 ten & 24 ones

Repeat the activity with a different number.

Repeat the activity starting with two bundles of 10 and 56 unbundled sticks (2 tens and 56 ones). Find other names for this number by making new bundles of ten from the unbundled sticks (3 tens and 46 ones, four tens and 36 ones, and so on).

✗ + ✓ ACTIVITY 6.27 AKA

Ask the children if they know what AKA means. [It stands for **A**lso **K**nown **A**s. It is another name for someone.] Write 45 on the chalkboard. Tell the children that 45 has a lot of names. Below the 45, write AKA 40 + 5. Tell the children to get out pencil and paper and write another name for 45. Have the children share with the class their AKAs. Record the different names for 45. The AKAs might include 44 + 1, 43 + 2, 42 + 3, 10 + 35, 30 + 15, and so on. If necessary, remind the children of the new names you get if you unbundle a 10.

✗ + ✓ ACTIVITY 6.28   Too Many to Write

Write the addition problem 54 + 28 on the chalkboard in vertical form. Have a child come forward and represent the two numbers using bundled popsicle sticks or base-10 blocks. Have the child place the numbers into a box. Ask the class to tell you what is in the box. How many tens are there? [7] Record this under the tens.

$$\begin{array}{r} 54 \\ + 28 \\ \hline \end{array}$$

Ask how many ones are in the box. [12] Record this under the ones. Restate that we have 7 tens and 12 ones. Point to the answer on the board. Ask if this looks like 7 tens and 12 ones. [No, it looks like 7 hundreds, 1 ten, and 2 ones.]

$$\begin{array}{r} 54 \\ + 28 \\ \hline 7 \end{array}$$

Ask if anyone knows what is wrong. [When you write 12 ones it does not look like 12 ones.] Point out that we only have room, in each position, for a 1-digit number. In this case, *we have too many to write.* Ask what we can do to get rid of this problem. [Trade 10 ones for a ten.]

$$\begin{array}{r} 54 \\ + 28 \\ \hline 712 \end{array}$$

Have children help you make a trade. Ask what we have after the trade. Point out that this is another name for the same number.

Repeat the activity with other numbers.

When There Are Too Many to Write, Make a Trade. The second of the two big ideas that are the basis for the addition algorithm is: *When there are too many to write, make a trade,* meaning too many to write in standard notation. If the example given in Activity 6.28 had been done using a base-10 chart, there would have been no confusion caused by the way the answer was written. But, neither would there have been a need to make the trade.

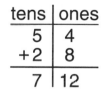

tens	ones
5	4
+2	8
7	12

So, building on the children's experiences with the model, we can show that there are only two things in the addition algorithm to do: Add like units and, when there are too many to write, make a trade. That is all there is to the addition algorithm. When the children learn these two things, they can add any two whole numbers. It does not make any difference whether we are adding three-digit numbers without regrouping, adding two-digit numbers with regrouping from ones to tens, adding five-digit numbers with regrouping from tens to hundreds and also regrouping from hundreds to thousands, or adding any combination of whole numbers. And, looking ahead to addition of decimals, there will not be anything new, because we just add like units and make a trade when there are too many to write.

Summary of the Developmental Sequence for Addition

Establish the meaning of the operation	1. Associate addition with combining quantities. 2. Learn to use counting to find answers.
Develop the easy basic facts	1. Find the answers using the meaning of addition. 2. Discover relationships among the facts. 3. Memorize the facts.
Develop thinking strategies for hard addition facts that:	1. Are mental strategies. 2. Use memorized easy facts to find answers for the hard facts.
Develop the hard basic facts	1. Find the answers using the thinking strategies. 2. Review helpful relationships among the facts. 3. Memorize the facts.
Develop the algorithm	1. Always add like units. 2. If there are too many to write, make a trade.

Teaching Subtraction

The developmental sequence for teaching whole-number subtraction is similar to that for addition. The first step is to establish the meaning of the operation by associating subtraction with a physical operation. Two physical settings are related to subtraction. One setting calls for comparison subtraction, and the other calls for take-away subtraction.

Developing the Meaning of Subtraction

Comparison Subtraction. We first consider comparison subtraction. Beginning with two quantities, we compare them to find the difference.

 **ACTIVITY 6.29   Extras**

Form two groups, one with five children, the other with nine. Have the two groups stand on opposite sides of the room.

Ask if the two groups have the same number. Ask which group has more children. Ask if anyone would like to guess how many more. After some guesses have been made, have the members of the smaller group go hold hands with someone in the other group.

Point out that the extras that are not holding hands are the difference. The difference is four children.

ACTIVITY 6.30   So, What's the Difference?

Show the children a group of four shoes and a group of 10 socks.

Ask if there are the same number of shoes and socks. Ask if there are more socks or more shoes. Have children come forward and match a shoe with a sock until you run out of shoes.

Point out that the extras are the difference. The difference is six socks. Tell the children that this is a kind of subtraction. Write the subtraction sentence on the chalkboard. Explain each of the symbols used.

The process used to find the difference is one-to-one matching. Children can easily learn to use this matching process to find answers to specific subtraction examples. The next two activities illustrate how the teacher can lead children to find answers in comparison subtraction.

ACTIVITY 6.31   Compare for Differences

Write 8 — 3 on the chalkboard. Tell the children that we are going to find the difference between 8 and 3.

Use counters to show the two numbers.

Then match counters from the first number with counters from the second number so the children can see that the difference is 5. Record the answer on the chalkboard.

Repeat the activity with several other examples. Sometimes, have a child write the problem. Sometimes have a child get the counters to show the two numbers. Sometimes have a child do the matching. Sometimes have a child write the answer. Sometimes, have a child do the whole thing.

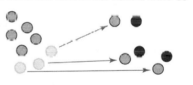

ACTIVITY 6.32   Spin and Compare

Make spinners. Straighten one end of a paper clip to make the pointer. Hold the pointer in place with the point of a pencil. Spin the pointer to get a number.

Have children work with partners. Each partner spins a number and then shows the number with counters. The children then match counters to find the difference. They should write the subtraction sentence for each example (that is, they should record their results).

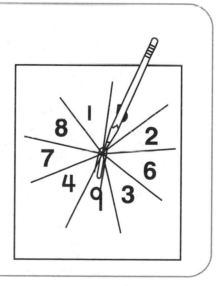

Take-Away Subtraction. Now we consider the second of the physical settings that children should associate with subtraction. In this setting, we start with one number, take some of it away, and find the remainder (Page, 1994). The following activities can be used with children to illustrate take-away subtraction.

×+૫ ACTIVITY 6.33   Give Me Four

Show the children seven toy cars. Write the number 7 on the chalkboard. Tell the children that you are going to pretend to give some of the cars away. Call on another child to come to the front. Have that child say, "Give me four cars." Write 4 on the chalkboard about 8 inches to the right of the 7.

Tell the child to take away four cars. When this is done, tell the children that when you take away part of a number, this is called subtraction. Write a minus sign between the two numbers. Tell them that we read this as seven minus four.

Explain that the answer to the subtraction is the number that remains. Ask how many cars remain after we have taken away four of them. Record the answer on the chalkboard and read the resulting subtraction sentence, seven minus four equals three.

Repeat the activity using different numbers. Start with different numbers of cars. Let the children decide how many to give away.

×+૫ ACTIVITY 6.34   It's in the Bag

Have the children work with partners. Give each pair of partners a paper bag, 10 crayons, and pencil and paper. They take turns going first.

The first child places some of the crayons in the bag. That child writes the number (for example, 8) on the paper to show how many crayons are in the bag.

$$8$$

The second child takes some of the crayons out of the bag, and records how many crayons were taken out of the bag (for example, 3).

$$8 - 3$$

The first child counts to see how many crayons are left in the bag and records the rest of the subtraction sentence.

$$8 - 3 = 5$$

They should continue the activity until they have generated at least 10 subtraction examples.

We see that there are two distinct types of subtraction. Children need to become familiar with both comparison and take-away situations and to relate both to subtraction. They will encounter both kinds of situations in solving problems. They need to recognize that *we can use subtraction here.* However, once the meaning of subtraction has been established, take-away subtraction is used almost exclusively in the development of whole number subtraction.

Developing the Easy Basic Subtraction Facts

The children should find the answers to the easy basic subtraction facts. Their understanding of the meaning of subtraction allows them to do this. Activities like Activity 6.34, It's in the Bag, are effective for this purpose. As they discover the facts, their results should be compiled in some organized form. As the facts are organized, the teacher should lead the children to discover several relationships.

They should notice that any time a number is subtracted from itself, the answer is zero. There are 10 of these facts, but once they see the relationship, there is only one thing to remember. The children should notice that whenever we subtract zero from a number, the answer will be that same number. There are also 10 of these facts, but only one thing to remember. They should notice that when we subtract one from any number, we get the number that comes before it in the counting sequence. There are 10 of these facts, but again only one thing to remember. Recognition of these relationships reduces the amount of memorization that is necessary.

There are other relationships that should also be discovered because they provide connections to other things that the child knows. And, *it is always easier to remember things that are related to other things that we know.* Every subtraction fact is related to an addition fact. For example:

$$8 - 2 = 6 \qquad 5 - 1 = 4 \qquad 10 - 7 = 3 \qquad 9 - 3 = 6$$
$$6 + 2 = 8 \qquad 4 + 1 = 5 \qquad 3 + 7 = 10 \qquad 6 + 3 = 9$$

Every subtraction fact is related to another subtraction fact. For example:

$$5 - 2 = 3 \qquad 8 - 1 = 7 \qquad 10 - 6 - 4 \qquad 7 - 2 = 5$$
$$5 - 3 = 2 \qquad 8 - 7 = 1 \qquad 10 - 4 = 6 \qquad 7 - 5 = 2$$

The children need to see what these relationships look like. So, as the relationships are being discovered, the children should be exposed to physical representations of those relationships. The following activities illustrate how this can be accomplished.

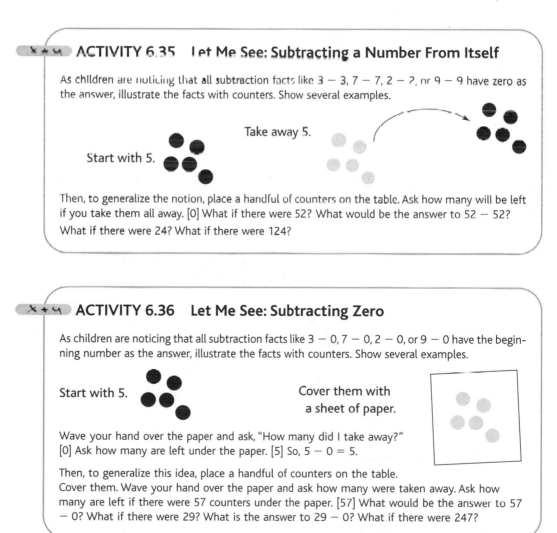

✗ + ↰ ACTIVITY 6.35 Let Me See: Subtracting a Number From Itself

As children are noticing that all subtraction facts like 3 − 3, 7 − 7, 2 − 2, or 9 − 9 have zero as the answer, illustrate the facts with counters. Show several examples.

Start with 5.

Take away 5.

Then, to generalize the notion, place a handful of counters on the table. Ask how many will be left if you take them all away. [0] What if there were 52? What would be the answer to 52 − 52? What if there were 24? What if there were 124?

✗ + ↰ ACTIVITY 6.36 Let Me See: Subtracting Zero

As children are noticing that all subtraction facts like 3 − 0, 7 − 0, 2 − 0, or 9 − 0 have the beginning number as the answer, illustrate the facts with counters. Show several examples.

Start with 5.

Cover them with a sheet of paper.

Wave your hand over the paper and ask, "How many did I take away?" [0] Ask how many are left under the paper. [5] So, 5 − 0 = 5.

Then, to generalize this idea, place a handful of counters on the table. Cover them. Wave your hand over the paper and ask how many were taken away. Ask how many are left if there were 57 counters under the paper. [57] What would be the answer to 57 − 0? What if there were 29? What is the answer to 29 − 0? What if there were 247?

ACTIVITY 6.37   Let Me See: Related Subtraction and Addition Facts

As children are noticing that subtraction facts are related to addition facts, for example, $3 - 1 = 2$ and $2 + 1 = 3$, $7 - 4 = 3$ and $3 + 4 = 7$, or $9 - 5 = 4$ and $4 + 5 = 9$, illustrate the facts with counters. Show several examples.

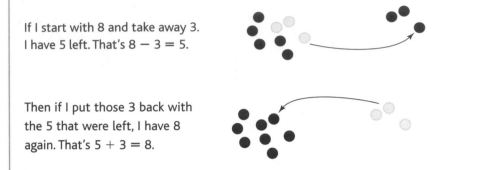

If I start with 8 and take away 3. I have 5 left. That's $8 - 3 = 5$.

Then if I put those 3 back with the 5 that were left, I have 8 again. That's $5 + 3 = 8$.

Then, to generalize, place a handful of counters on the table. Tell the children that you think there are 51 counters. Take away all but 3 of them. Ask how many are left. [3] Replace the counters that were taken away. Ask how many there are now. [51 — as many as we started with.] Write $128 - 54 = 74$ on the chalkboard. Tell the children that this means we started with 128, took 54 away and had 74 left. Ask how many there would be if we put the 54 back with the 74 that were left. [128]

ACTIVITY 6.38   Let Me See: Related Subtraction Facts

As children are noticing that there are pairs of related subtraction facts like $3 - 1 = 2$ and $3 - 2 = 1$, $7 - 4 = 3$ and $7 - 3 = 4$, or $9 - 5 = 4$ and $9 - 4 = 5$, illustrate the relationship with counters. Show several examples.

Show 8 counters. Lay a length of yarn through the counters to separate them into a group of 3 and a group of 5.

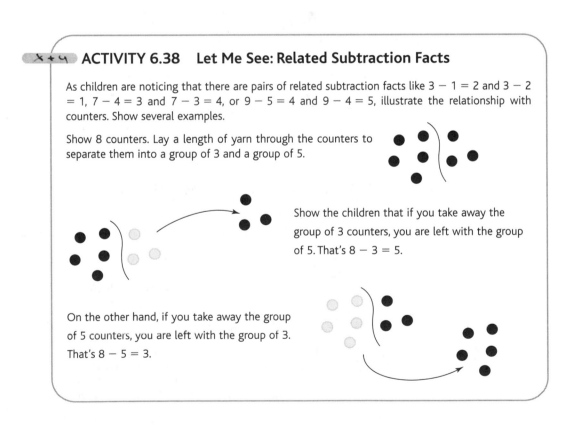

Show the children that if you take away the group of 3 counters, you are left with the group of 5. That's $8 - 3 = 5$.

On the other hand, if you take away the group of 5 counters, you are left with the group of 3. That's $8 - 5 = 3$.

After discovering these helpful relationships, the children are ready to begin memorization of the easy basic subtraction facts. Some of the memorization activities that follow emphasize thinking about the relationships.

<hr />

ACTIVITY 6.39   Related Pairs

Prepare large cards with pairs of related subtraction facts on them. The answer should be included for one of the facts, but not for the other.

8 − 2 = 6		8 − 5 = 3		9 − 3 = 6
8 − 6 =	4 − 1 = 3	8 − 3 =	6 − 2 = 4	9 − 6 =
	4 − 3 =		6 − 4 =	

Show the cards, one at a time. Have children give the missing answer. Ask how the first answer can help them get the missing answer. If they cannot give the missing answer, ask how the first answer can help them figure it out.

Use counters to show the related facts if needed (see Activity 6.38).

✕＋� ACTIVITY 6.40 Put Them Together and Take Them Apart

Prepare flashcards for the following subtraction facts.

$$8 - 3 = \qquad 5 - 2 = \qquad 9 - 6 = \qquad 6 - 3 =$$
$$4 - 2 = \qquad 7 - 5 = \qquad 8 - 4 = \qquad 6 - 4 =$$
$$7 - 4 = \qquad 8 - 6 = \qquad 9 - 4 = \qquad 9 - 2 =$$

Write these addition facts on the chalkboard.

$$2 + 2 = 4 \qquad 3 + 2 = 5 \qquad 3 + 3 = 6 \qquad 1 + 4 = 6$$
$$2 + 5 = 7 \qquad 3 + 4 = 7 \qquad 5 + 3 = 8 \qquad 4 + 4 = 8$$
$$2 + 6 = 8 \qquad 3 + 6 = 9 \qquad 5 + 4 = 9 \qquad 7 + 2 = 9$$

Show a flashcard. Whether or not the child can give the answer, ask which of the addition facts on the board helps to figure out the answer. Use counters to show the related facts if needed (see Activity 6.37).

✕＋� ACTIVITY 6.41 Peek If You Need To

When an individual child is having difficulty remembering a particular fact, for example, $9 - 4$, fold a small piece of paper, write the problem on the outside, write the answer on the inside, and tape it to the child's desk.

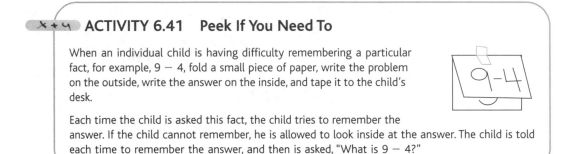

Each time the child is asked this fact, the child tries to remember the answer. If the child cannot remember, he is allowed to look inside at the answer. The child is told each time to remember the answer, and then is asked, "What is $9 - 4$?"

✕＋� ACTIVITY 6.42 Fact Maker

Prepare 20 cards with one-digit numbers on them. There should be two cards for each of the digits 0 through 9. Also prepare seven cards with minus signs and seven with equal signs.

Give the cards to a child and have the child form as many subtraction facts as possible.

✕＋� ACTIVITY 6.43 Complete Your List

Prepare lists of five subtraction facts without answers. Tape answer cards around the room.

Form groups of three children. Give each group a list. Have them find the answers to all the facts on their list and bring them to the teacher. Be sure there are enough copies of the answers that occur more than once.

As the children bring you the answers to their fact lists, have them tell you what answers go with what problems.

Thinking Strategies for Hard Basic Subtraction Facts

Answers to the hard basic subtraction facts (minuends of 11 through 18) can still be found by counting. However, with the larger numbers, counting is inefficient and slow. At this point more efficient strategies need to be developed that allow the child to find answers to the hard basic subtraction facts quickly and accurately.

Our objective is for these facts to be committed to memory, and the strategies that successfully lead to memorization have two common characteristics. They are mental strategies, and they require the child to use facts that are already memorized to figure out the facts that are not yet memorized. The children should be constantly thinking about what they already know that can help them figure out what they do not know. The children should build on what they already know. New knowledge is closely related to old knowledge, and it is always easier to remember things that are related to other things that are already known.

Think of a Related Addition Fact. Among the thinking strategies for hard basic subtraction facts that have been used, two have been particularly successful. The first of these is the one most loved by mathematicians—think of a related addition fact. This strategy is based on the inverse-operation relationship between subtraction and addition, allowing subtraction to be defined in terms of addition: $a - b = c$, where c is the unique number such that $c + b = a$. So, if we want to find the answer to $a - b = ?$, we can think about what number can be added to b to produce a sum of a ($? + b = a$).

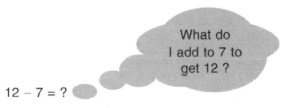

This is a good strategy. It is mathematically strong. It is a universal strategy; that is, it will work for all hard basic substraction facts. However, as a strategy for finding answers to hard subtraction facts, it has one flaw. Using this strategy to find $12 - 7 = 5$ requires that the child already know $5 + 7 = 12$. To find $17 - 9 = 8$, the child must already know $8 + 9 = 17$. This strategy requires that the child already know the hard addition facts. Unfortunately, children who are having difficulty mastering the hard subtraction facts are most frequently the same children who have not yet mastered the hard addition facts. This strategy will not work for these children.

Subtract from Ten. A second strategy that has proven successful for finding answers to the hard basic subtraction facts requires the children to already know the facts having a minuend of 10 ($10 - 5$, $10 - 7$, $10 - 4$, and so on.) It uses the idea that the teen numbers can be thought of as 10 and some more.

This strategy is the reverse of the make-ten strategy that was suggested for finding answers to the hard addition facts. Since subtraction from 10 is easy, we will have the children subtract from ten to find answers to all the hard basic subtraction facts. The 10-frame is an effective tool for developing understanding of and mental imagery for the subtract-from-ten thinking strategy. For example, suppose we want to find the answer to $13 - 7$. We begin by using the 10-frame to represent 13, the number that we start with.

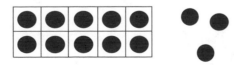

When we take away 7, we will take seven counters from the 10-frame.

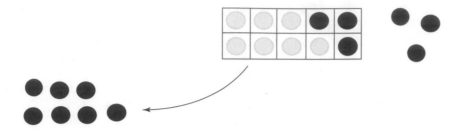

Three counters are left in the 10-frame. Altogether, 3 + 3, or six counters are left. So, 13 − 7 = 6. Or, suppose we want to find 14 − 8.

Start with 14.

Take 8 from the 10.

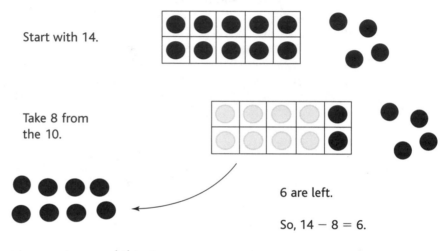

6 are left.

So, 14 − 8 = 6.

This is a nice way to record the steps.

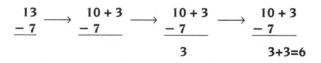

$$\begin{array}{c} 13 \\ -\,7 \\ \hline \end{array} \longrightarrow \begin{array}{c} 10 + 3 \\ -\,7 \\ \hline \end{array} \longrightarrow \begin{array}{c} 10 + 3 \\ -\,7 \\ \hline 3 \end{array} \longrightarrow \begin{array}{c} 10 + 3 \\ -\,7 \\ \hline 3 + 3 = 6 \end{array}$$

After adequate time has been spent with the 10-frame to develop mental imagery for the process, another device to help children to think through the process is to give the child a card with a zero in one corner. Have them cover parts of the minuend to assist their thinking.

Write the problem.   Subtract from 10.   Then, add the 5.

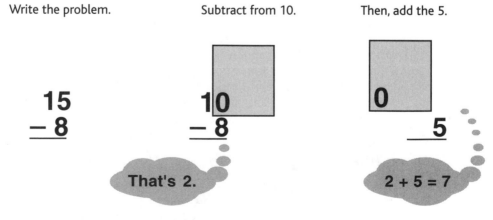

The subtract-from-ten strategy is easy to teach. It is a universal strategy that can be used for all the hard basic subtraction facts. And, it only requires that the children know easy facts.

Teaching the Subtraction Algorithm

After mastery of the basic subtraction facts, the children are ready to begin work on the subtraction algorithm. Remember that the subtraction algorithm is the step-by-step process by which one can use the basic facts to find answers to any other whole-number subtraction example. Remember also, that when teaching the algorithm, we want to do several things:

- *Let them see what it looks like.* Carefully model the operation with an appropriate physical or pictorial model. Use a model that lets the children see what happens to the basic units—ones, tens, hundreds, and so on—when we subtract.
- *De-emphasize rote rules.* We might end up with rules, but they should be meaningful. They should arise out of the modeling process.
- *Emphasize big ideas.* These are the important generalizations that describe the process. They also arise out of the modeling process.
- *Let the written algorithm simply be a recording* of what happens when the algorithm is modeled. Everything we write should match something we do.
- *Watch our language.* The language used should be language that describes what the children see when the operation is modeled, not language that describes what we write down.

In the next activity we introduce the first of the two big ideas that are the basis for the subtraction algorithm.

✕ ◆ ꜒ ACTIVITY 6.44   What's Left in the Box ?

Write 74 on the chalkboard. Have a child come forward and get the base-10 blocks that represent 74. Put them in a box. Write   31 to the right of the 74. Ask what this means. [Take away 31 from 74.]

Have a child come forward and take 31 out of the box. Ask how many tens are left in the box. [4] Ask how they know that. How many ones are left in the box? [3] Ask how they know that. Record the answer on the board.

Repeat the process with other examples, but do not use examples that require regrouping. Use some examples with three-digit numbers. Record some examples horizontally and record some vertically.

Always Subtract Like Units.   The children will never try to take the ones from the tens or take the tens from the hundreds. That makes no sense when they see what it looks like. It is not necessary to tell the children how to subtract two- and three-digit numbers. The children's common sense will tell them. We take the hundreds from the hundreds. We take the ones from the ones. We take the tens from the tens. We *always subtract like units.* This is the first of two big ideas that are used in the subtraction algorithm.

The second big idea comes just as naturally as did the first one. Set up an example in which the children encounter a dilemma and then let the children tell you how to deal with it. Activity 6.45, which is really a continuation of activity 6.44, illustrates how this might be done.

ACTIVITY 6.45   What's the Problem? What'll We Do?

Write 75 on the chalkboard. Have a child come forward and get the base-10 blocks that represent 75. Put them into a box. Write −27 below the 75. Ask what this means. [Take away 27 from 75.]

Have a child come forward to take 27 out of the box. Suggest that the child take the seven ones out of the box first. When the child cannot do it, ask what the problem is. [There are not enough ones.] Ask the other children what to do. How can we get more ones? [Trade a ten for 10 ones.] Have the child make that trade.

Have the children tell what you have after the trade. Now, how many tens are there? How many ones are there? Record the trade.

Ask if there are enough ones now to take away seven ones.

$$\begin{array}{r} {\scriptstyle 6\,15} \\ 7\!\!\!/5 \\ -\ 27 \\ \hline \end{array}$$

Complete the subtraction, recording each step as it is completed.

Repeat the process with other examples. Use some examples with three-digit numbers. Record them vertically. Do some examples where there are not enough ones and some where there are not enough tens. Do some examples where there are not enough ones and also not enough tens. Emphasize that it does not make any difference what you are short of, whenever you do not have enough, you make a trade.

Have children do the modeling and the writing.

When There Are Not Enough, Make a Trade.   The second of the two big ideas that are the basis for the subtraction algorithm is: *When there are not enough, make a trade.* Out of the children's experiences with the model, we can show that there are only two things that we do in the subtraction algorithm. *Subtract like units* and, *when there are not enough, make a trade.* That is all there is to the subtraction algorithm. When the children learn to do these two things, they can complete any whole-number subtraction example. It does not make any difference whether we are subtracting three-digit numbers without regrouping, subtracting two-digit numbers with regrouping from tens to ones, subtracting five-digit numbers with regrouping from hundreds to tens and also regrouping from thousands to hundreds, or any combination of whole numbers. *Always subtract like units. When there are not enough, make a trade.* And looking ahead to subtraction of decimals, there will not be anything new, because we just subtract like units and make a trade when there are not enough.

Summary of the Developmental Sequence for Subtraction

Establish the meaning of the operation

1. Associate subtraction with comparison and with take away.
2. Learn to use counting to find answers.

Develop the easy basic facts

1. Find the answers using the meaning of subtraction.
2. Discover relationships among the facts.
3. Memorize the facts.

Develop thinking strategies for hard subtraction facts

1. Use mental strategies.
2. Use memorized easy facts to find answers for the hard facts.

Develop the hard basic facts	1. Find the answers using the thinking strategies.
	2. Review relationships among the facts.
	3. Memorize the facts.
Develop the algorithm	1. Always subtract like units.
	2. If there are not enough, make a trade.

Adapting a Lesson

Now, we adapt another lesson, this time, an early lesson on subtraction. Again, we begin with a traditional plan, taken directly from suggestions that might be found in a teacher's guide of a published program. You should note that this plan is a good one. However, its focus is to teach the textbook page. This lesson will be adapted to make it more effective in meeting the learning needs in a diverse classroom.

LESSON OBJECTIVE

The student will create subtraction sentences with minuends of 1 to 6.

Lesson Opener

Show four counters and two boxes. Tell the children that you are going to put some of the counters into one box and the rest into the other box. Ask, if you place three counters into one box, how many will be in the other box? If you place two into one box, how many will be in the other box? Tell the children that today they will be creating subtraction sentences.

Development

Place the blue lake transparency on the overhead projector. Place four fish cutouts in the lake. Take one of the fish out of the lake. Ask how many fish are left in the lake. Write the subtraction sentence, $4 - 1 = 3$, on the chalkboard.

Tell the children to watch while you do another example. Place three fish in the lake and then remove two of them. Ask what subtraction sentence tells what you did. Write the subtraction sentence on the board.

Monitor Learning

Have everyone do the *Check Understanding* example. Observe to identify children who do not understand.

Practice

Have children who had difficulties with the *Check Understanding* example complete the reteaching worksheet. Have the rest of the children use their lake work mats and fish counters to complete the examples on the practice page.

Closure

At the end of math time, point out to the children that they have been using their fish counters to create subtraction sentences.

The adapted lesson plan that follows includes an increased amount of developmental instruction. Notice the shift in instructional emphasis from teaching the pages of the student book toward an emphasis on teaching the concept. We have also increased visual input, kinesthetic activity, student communication, and monitoring of learning. Remember that these adaptations will make the lesson appropriate for almost all students. But, remember also, that some students with severe needs may require further instructional adaptations.

LESSON OBJECTIVE

The student will create subtraction sentences with minuends of 1 to 6.

Lesson Opener

Show four counters and a box. Tell the children that you want to put some of the counters into the box. Have a child come forward to help. Ask the class how many to place into the box. Have the child who is helping place that many into the box. Without showing the remaining counters, ask how many are left. Have your helper check to see if they were right. Have two children come forward to help. Show the class five counters. Have one helper put them into the box. Ask how many are in the box. Have the second helper write that number on the chalkboard. Tell the class that you want to take some out of the box. Ask how many they want to take out of the box. Ask what we call it when you start with a number and then take some away. [Subtraction.] Ask how many were subtracted. Have your helper who is writing on the chalkboard record this subtraction. Ask how many are left in the box. Have the first helper look in the box to check the answer. Have the second helper record the answer. **Monitor Understanding** Observe the children carefully throughout this activity. Direct questions to children who may not understand. Provide further explanation or additional examples as needed.

Monitor Understanding

Explain that when we write a subtraction fact (in horizontal form), we call it a subtraction sentence. Tell the class that today they will be creating subtraction sentences.

Development

Direct the attention of the class to the bulletin board. (Before school you should place three bird cutouts on the bulletin board.) Call on a child to come forward and remove two of the birds. Ask how many birds we started with. Ask how many were taken away. Ask how many are left. Have another child come forward and write the subtraction sentence. **Monitor Understanding** Observe the children carefully throughout this activity.

Place six chairs in a line at the front of the room. Have six children come sit in the chairs. Have four children get up and go to the back of the room. Ask how many children we started with. Ask how many moved to the back of the room. Ask how many are left. Have a child come forward and write the subtraction sentence. **Monitor Understanding** Observe the children carefully throughout this activity.

Monitor Understanding

Place the blue lake transparency on the overhead projector. Tell the class that you have six fish. Ask how many of your fish you should place in the lake. Have a child come to the front to help. Tell the class that your helper is fishing in the lake. Ask the class how many of the fish they think your helper will catch. Have your helper remove that many fish from the lake. Ask how many fish are left in the lake. Ask how many fish were in the lake to start with. Ask how many were taken out of the lake. Ask how many are left. Have another child come forward and write the subtraction sentence on the board.

Use the fish to complete another example, except have all the children use pencil and paper to write the subtraction sentence at their seats. **Monitor Understanding** Move around and check the children's work. Provide extra explanations as needed.

Direct the children's attention to the *Check Understanding* example. Have the children use their lake work mats and fish counters to complete the example. **Monitor Understanding** Move around the room to check the children's work. Provide extra explanations as needed.

Practice

Have children work with partners and use their lake work mats and fish counters to complete the first four examples on the practice page.

Closure

At the end of the math time, ask the class what they have been doing today. Ask what they have learned how to do. Do one more example using sunflower seeds. Have the children tell you what the subtraction sentence is.

Follow Up

Give each child a baggie with six sunflower seeds. Tell them that you want them to take the sunflower seeds home and use them to explain to their parents what they learned today.

Teaching Problem Solving Using Addition and Subtraction

Problem solving is a high priority topic in the elementary school mathematics curriculum. As stated in the NCTM *Curriculum and Evaluation Standards for School Mathematics*,

> Problem solving should be the central focus of the mathematics curriculum. As such, it is a primary goal of all mathematical activity. Problem solving is not a distinct topic but a process that should permeate the entire program and provide the context in which concepts and skills can be learned. (p. 23)

An early part of the development of the ability to use addition and subtraction to solve problems is found in the way that the meanings of the operations are developed. When the arithmetic operations are related to physical operations, the child is better able to look at problem situations and determine if addition or subtraction can be used to find the solution.

If the essence of the problem is that some of a quantity is being taken away, the child can look at the situation and tell that subtraction should be used to find the answer. If the essence of the problem situation is that quantities are being combined and we want to find how many altogether, the child can look at the situation and tell that addition should be used to find the answer. If the essence of the problem situation is that two quantities are being compared and you want to find which is more and how much more, the child can look at the situation and tell that subtraction should be used.

Translating Word Problems into Situations. When problems are posed as word problems, the children should not be taught to look for key words like "and" or "of," but rather they should think about the situation being described and think about what is happening to the quantities. They should think about what operation they see happening in the problem. The reason many children are unable to solve word problems is that they have not learned to convert the word problem (a bunch of words) into a situation. It is not that they lack the needed mathematical understanding and ability. Most often, once they are able to "see" the situation, the solution is simple for them.

Sometimes special help must be provided so the children can make the conversion from a bunch of words to a situation. Among techniques that have proven to be successful are dramatization of the problem, modeling the problem, partnering, and group explanations. These techniques are illustrated in the following activities.

ACTIVITY 6.46 Act It Out

Form groups of children. Give each group a word problem. Have each group plan how to act out their problem before the rest of the class. When they are ready, have each group act out their problem and then ask the question that needs to be answered. The other class members must figure out the answer. The teacher should use some children to show the first one.

ACTIVITY 6.47 Show It With Stuff

Form groups of children. Give each group a word problem. Have each group plan how to use materials like counters and boxes to show their problem to the rest of the class. When they are ready, have each group show their problem and then ask the question that needs to be answered. The other class members must figure out the answer. The teacher should do the first one.

ACTIVITY 6.48 Partners Can

Have the children work with partners. Give the partners a word problem. Have them discuss the problem and agree on how to explain what is happening in the problem. When the partners are ready, the teacher should go to them and have them explain the problem. What is happening? What do we want to find out?

ACTIVITY 6.49 Teacher's a Dummy

Have the children look at a word problem. Tell them that you don't understand the problem. You don't know what to do. Ask them to explain the problem to you. Try to get even the weakest students involved. Play dumb. Ask really stupid questions. Loosen up and have fun with it.

Use Things That Children Care About.   Suppose a friend poses a problem that you do not care about. When this happens, the friend has a problem but you really do not have a problem because you just don't care. A "problem" is not a problem to you unless you want to get a solution. You might play along with your friend to help solve the problem, but you will be easily bored by it. And if something comes along that is important to you, you will quickly drop the "problem" and do what is important to you.

Remember that children are like that, too. If they don't really care about getting a solution, finding a solution will have a low priority. Anything else that they do care about will draw their attention away. But, there is something that will help keep the children involved.

Use Things That Are Real to Children. It is important that children experience problems that come from everyday situations. The problems they experience should include numerical situations involving things that they are familiar with, and things encountered in natural settings. If they are farm children, problems about chickens or cows might make sense. If they are city children, similar mathematical situations that involve taxicabs would probably be more meaningful and more interesting.

It is recommended that the teacher find out what objects are common to each child in the class and pose problems involving objects from the world of each child. Whenever others do not know about those objects, that child can then be the "expert" and explain about them. In this way, a thoughtful teacher can arrange circumstances so that every child, at some time, can be looked on by the other children as an expert.

Use Mixed Problem Examples. It is also important that problem solving be mixed. It is not enough for the child to be able to use addition to solve problems included in the unit on addition. The child must be able to decide when to add *and when not to add*. Within the unit on addition the child should encounter examples of addition problems *and nonexamples of addition problems* The child should be required to think about the problem setting and decide when to add, when to subtract, and when not to do either. This will only happen when there is a conscious effort to provide an effective mix of problem settings.

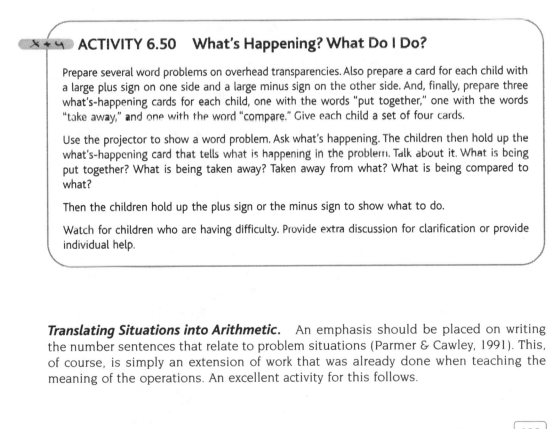

ACTIVITY 6.50   What's Happening? What Do I Do?

Prepare several word problems on overhead transparencies. Also prepare a card for each child with a large plus sign on one side and a large minus sign on the other side. And, finally, prepare three what's-happening cards for each child, one with the words "put together," one with the words "take away," and one with the word "compare." Give each child a set of four cards.

Use the projector to show a word problem. Ask what's happening. The children then hold up the what's-happening card that tells what is happening in the problem. Talk about it. What is being put together? What is being taken away? Taken away from what? What is being compared to what?

Then the children hold up the plus sign or the minus sign to show what to do.

Watch for children who are having difficulty. Provide extra discussion for clarification or provide individual help.

Translating Situations into Arithmetic. An emphasis should be placed on writing the number sentences that relate to problem situations (Parmer & Cawley, 1991). This, of course, is simply an extension of work that was already done when teaching the meaning of the operations. An excellent activity for this follows.

✗ ＋ ✗ ACTIVITY 6.51 Headlines

Show the children a newspaper. Show them two or three articles in the paper. Point out the headline for each article. Explain that the headline tells, in a very small amount of space, what is in the story.

Show this story on the overhead projector. Talk about the story. Since some of Billy's cars are being taken away, we can write it as subtraction. The subtraction sentence that goes with the story is $10 - 4 = 6$.

Billy brought 10 toy cars to school. He gave four of the cars to his friend Ben to play with. He had six cars left.

Since this subtraction sentence tells what is in the story, it would make a good headline for the story. Write $10 - 4 = 6$ above the story.

Repeat the process with an addition story. Write the addition sentence above the story as a headline.

Give the children several number stories. Have them work with partners to write a headline above each story.

Give them some headlines. Have them work with their partners to make up a story that goes with each headline.

Exercises and Activities

1. Compare the two early subtraction lesson plans.
   a. Identify where the adapted plan provides more kinesthetic activity.
   b. Identify where the adapted plan provides more opportunity for communication from the children.
   c. Identify where the adapted plan provides more opportunity for communication among the children.
2. Adapt Activity 6.38 so that it could be used with a child with a severe visual impairment.
3. Choose a lesson on either addition or subtraction of whole numbers from a published elementary school mathematics textbook series.
   a. Write a lesson plan that follows the teaching suggestions in the teacher's guide.
   b. Identify the parts of the lesson that develop the concept(s) or skill(s).
   c. Expand the developmental part of the lesson by adding activities that build mental imagery for the concepts or skills being taught or that build connections between the numbers being taught in the lesson and numbers with which the students are already familiar.
4. Choose a lesson on either addition or subtraction of whole numbers from a published elementary school mathematics textbook series.
   a. Write a lesson plan that follows the teaching suggestions in the teacher's guide.
   b. Identify the parts of the lesson that provide visual information about the concept(s) or skill(s) being taught.
   c. Expand the lesson by adding activities that provide more visual information about the concepts or skills being taught.

5. Choose a lesson on either addition or subtraction of whole numbers from a published elementary school mathematics textbook series.
   a. Write a lesson plan that follows the teaching suggestions in the teacher's guide.
   b. Identify kinesthetic activity that is included in the lesson.
   c. Add more kinesthetic activity to the lesson.

6. Choose a lesson on either addition or subtraction of whole numbers from a published elementary school mathematics textbook series.
   a. Write a lesson plan that follows the teaching suggestions in the teacher's guide.
   b. Identify parts of the lesson that include student communication about the concept(s) or skill(s) taught in the lesson.
   c. Add more opportunities for communication from or among students to the lesson.

7. Choose a lesson on either addition or subtraction of whole numbers from a published elementary school mathematics textbook series.
   a. Write a lesson plan that follows the teaching suggestions in the teacher's guide.
   b. Identify the parts of the lesson designed to assess the learning of the students.
   c. Add more continual assessment (monitoring of learning) to the lesson plan.

8. Study the adapted lesson plan on pages 130–131. Make further changes in the lesson plan to make it more appropriate for a child with a history of breaking manipulatives.

9. Study the adapted lesson plan on pages 130–131. Make further changes in the lesson plan to make it more appropriate for a child whose learning disability includes figure-ground confusion.

10. Study the adapted lesson plan on pages 130–131. Make further changes in the lesson plan to make it more appropriate for a child who has limited understanding of English.

11. An interesting process can be used to change a hard subtraction fact into an easier one. If we think of the answer as the difference between the two numbers, that difference can be illustrated on the number line.

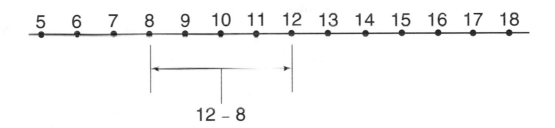

Notice that if 2 is added to both numbers, they shift two spaces to the right on the number line, but they are the same distance apart.

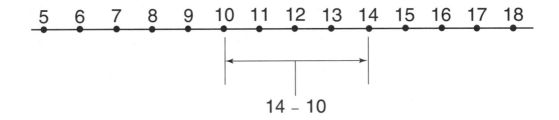

Adding the same number to both numbers does not change the difference. Notice that although the difference (the answer) is the same, this new fact is a lot easier.

  a. Use this equal-additions process to change 15 − 8 into an easier fact.

  b. Develop an activity to teach children to use this strategy to find answers to the hard basic subtraction facts.

12. A variation of the process described on page 125–126 for teaching the subtract-from-10 thinking strategy, is to use an **L**-shaped card as pictured below. After subtracting from ten, record the difference in the ones place as shown before completing the process.

Explain how this process might help a child with short-term memory problems.

13. Read "Summary of Changes in Content and Emphasis in K–4 Mathematics," on pages 20 and 21 of the *Curriculum and Evaluation Standards for School Mathematics*, published by the National Council of Teachers of Mathematics. How do the teaching suggestions provided in this chapter relate to the recommended changes?

14. Read the sections related to the Number and Operations Standard, on pages 32–36 and pages 78–88 of *Principles and Standards for School Mathematics*, published by the National Council of Teachers of Mathematics. How do the teaching suggestions provided in this chapter relate to this standard?

15. Read "Teaching and Learning Creatively: Using Children's Narratives" by LoCicero, LaCruz, and Fuson, in the May, 1999 issue of *Teaching Children Mathematics*. Explain how the article relates to the section of this chapter on teaching children to use addition and subtraction to solve problems (pp. 131–134).

16. The following addition results illustrate an error pattern like those that were related by Robert Ashlock, in his book, *Error Patterns in Computation: A Semi-programmed Approach*.

$$
\begin{array}{r} 8\ 4 \\ +\ 5\ 6 \\ \hline 1310 \end{array}
\qquad
\begin{array}{r} 35 \\ +\ 72 \\ \hline 107 \end{array}
\qquad
\begin{array}{r} 69 \\ +\ 28 \\ \hline 817 \end{array}
\qquad
\begin{array}{r} 1\ 8 \\ +\ 9\ 7 \\ \hline 1015 \end{array}
$$

  a. What is this student's error pattern? What is the student doing to produce the incorrect answers?

  b. Plan a mini-lesson to correct this student's error pattern.

References and Related Readings

Ashlock, R. B. (1998). *Error patterns in computation: A semi-programmed approach* (7th ed.). Upper Saddle River, NJ: Merrill/Prentice Hall.

LoCicero, A. M., LaCruz, Y., & Fuson, K. C. (1999). Teaching and learning creatively: Using children's narratives. *Teaching Children Mathematics, 5*, 544–547.

National Council of Teachers of Mathematics. (1989). *Curriculum and evaluation standards for school mathematics.* Reston, VA: NCTM.

National Council of Teachers of Mathematics. (2000). *Principles and standards for school mathematics.* Reston, VA: NCTM.

Page, A. (1994). Helping children understand subtraction. *Teaching Children Mathematics, 1*, 140–143.

Parmar, R. S., & Cawley, J. F. (1991). Challenging the routines and passivity that characterize arithmetic instruction for children with mild handicaps. *Remedial and Special Education, 12*(5), 25.

Thornton, C. A., Tucker, B. F., Dossey, J. A., Bazik, E. F. (1983). *Teaching mathematics to children with special needs.* Menlo Park CA: Addison-Wesley.

Tucker, B. F. (1981). Give and take: Getting ready to regroup. *The Arithmetic Teacher, 28*(8), 24–26.

Tucker, B. F. (1989). Seeing addition: A diagnosis/remediation case study. *The Arithmetic Teacher, 36*(5), 10–11.

Web Sites

http://www.proteacher.com/100009.shtml
(Lesson plans on addition and subtraction by teachers.)

http://www.forum.swarthmore.edu/
(Math forum links to math discussions and ideas.)

http://www.sasked.gov.sk.ca/docs/elemath/numop.html
(A scope and sequence chart for numbers and operations.)

CHAPTER 7

MULTIPLYING AND DIVIDING WHOLE NUMBERS:

Combining Equal-Sized Groups and Separating Quantities into Equal-Sized Groups

THE NUMBER AND OPERATIONS STANDARD

"Modeling multiplication problems with pictures, diagrams, or concrete materials helps students learn what the factors and their products represent in various contexts" (National Council of Teachers of Mathematics, 2000, p. 151).

THE ALGEBRA STANDARD

"In grades 3–5, students can investigate properties such as commutativity, associativity, and distributivity of multiplication over addition" (NCTM, 2000, p. 160).

THE PROBLEM SOLVING STANDARD

"Listening to discussions, the teacher is able to assess students' understanding" (NCTM, 2000, p. 187).

THE REPRESENTATION STANDARD

"Representations can help students organize their thinking. Students' use of representations can help make mathematical ideas more concrete and available for reflection." (p. 68).

Teaching Multiplication of Whole Numbers

Developmental Sequence for Teaching Multiplication

Now we examine the developmental sequence as it is applied to teaching whole-number multiplication. As when teaching addition and subtraction, the first major instructional task is to establish the meaning of multiplication.

Developing the Meaning of Multiplication

Children need to *associate multiplication with the combining of equal-sized quantities*. The association must be so strong that when children see the symbols 3 × 4, they visualize three groups of four things being combined. When the child sees a situation where equal quantities are being combined, the child will think "That's multiplication!" After multiplication has been mastered, the child will see problem settings where equal quantities are being combined and think "I can use multiplication to solve this problem."

The children must also realize that, after those equal quantities have been combined, they can *count to find how many there are altogether*.

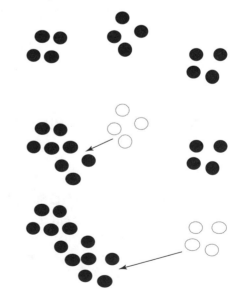

If I combine three groups of 4,

I can count them to see that there are 12 altogether. So, 3 × 4 = 12.

Since counting this many objects becomes tedious and is time consuming, we want to lead the children to understand that we can also use addition to find the answer.

Start with 3 groups of 4.

Combine two of the groups.
That's 4 + 4.

Then, I can add the other group
of 4. That's 4 + 4 + 4.

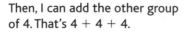

We can figure out the answer to multiplication examples in two ways. We can count to get the answer, or we can add to get the answer. If the children already have developed a level of proficiency with simple addition, it is easier and quicker to get multiplication answers by adding. These are two ways that work, but the children should be encouraged to use the most efficient method.

Introduce the operation of multiplication using physical materials. During this introduction, use concepts and language that are already available to the children. In this natural setting we then introduce the new mathematical terms and the notation that is used to write them.

In the next activities, multiplication is introduced as a physical operation on equal-sized groups. Then the language of multiplication is introduced along with the times sign. Finally we begin using the written notation for multiplication.

×+ч ACTIVITY 7.01   Putting Bunches Together

Bring about 25 small sticks that are about the same size to class.

Using rubber bands, have children make three bunches of five sticks. Have them put the three bunches into a box. Write on the chalkboard what is in the box. [3 bunches of 5.] Ask how we can figure out how many sticks are in the box. [We count them.]

Point out that the bunches are being combined. Ask what we call it when we put numbers of things together. [Addition.] Show how addition can be used to find how many sticks. [First put 2 bunches together into the box. That's 5 + . Then add the other bunch. That's 5 + 5 + 5.] Have the children find how many sticks are in the box using both methods. Write the answer. [3 bunches of 5 is 15.]

Repeat the activity using other numbers.

×+ч ACTIVITY 7.02   Money in My Pocket

Bring to class about 30 pennies. Have four children come forward. Give each of them six pennies. Have them put the pennies in their pockets. Have the class figure out how to find how many pennies there are in all four pockets. [By taking them out, combining them and counting. By adding.] Have the children find the answer both ways.

Repeat the activity with different numbers.

×+ч ACTIVITY 7.03   The Way to Say It

Have six children come to the front of the room and get four blocks each. Then have the other children watch carefully as your four helpers, one at a time, place their blocks in a paper bag.

Ask the class to describe what was done. [4 was placed in the bag 6 times.] Have the children figure out how many blocks are in the bag. Write four, 6 times = 24 on the chalkboard.

Do another example (for example, seven, 3 times) and write it on the chalkboard. Then explain to the children that instead of four, six times, we usually say 6 times 4. Point to the other example and ask how we usually say it. [3 times 7.]

Finally, introduce the multiplication sign [×] and show how to use it to write the examples. [6 × 4 = 24, 3 × 7 = 21.] Tell the children how to read each example. [6 times 4 equals 24, 3 times 7 equals 21.]

Do other examples with the blocks and paper bag. Have the children use multiplication language and notation to say, write, and read the examples.

✖ ✦ ᐟ ACTIVITY 7.04 Fact Finders

Prepare two spinners, one with the numbers 2 to 9, to determine the size of the groups, and the other with the numbers 2 to 4 to determine the number of groups.

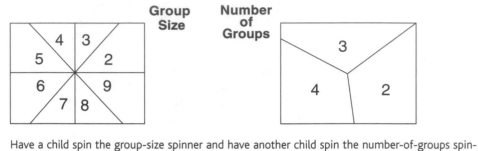

Group Size   **Number of Groups**

Have a child spin the group-size spinner and have another child spin the number-of-groups spinner. Have children form and combine the groups and then figure out the total number. Have them use appropriate multiplication language to describe what they are doing. Have them use appropriate multiplication notation to write their results. Have them read what is written.

As they figure out answers, encourage them to use the most efficient method.

To reinforce the meaning of multiplication, the children should encounter a wide variety of multiplication examples using objects that are familiar to them. They should use appropriate terminology to describe verbally the multiplication and use the times sign and equal sign to write it. In every example, the children should figure out the answer for themselves, and the teacher should continually emphasize how easy it is. They can find the answers by themselves. Three examples of instructional activities follow that illustrate how this can be accomplished.

✖ ✦ ᐟ ACTIVITY 7.05 How Much Paper Do I Need?

Tell the children that you are thinking about doing an art activity where each person needs five sheets of paper. Ask the class to figure out how many sheets of paper are needed for a group of four children.

Get out some paper, and use it to check the answer.

✖ ✦ ᐟ ACTIVITY 7.06 What Do We Need to Play the Game?

Show this game to the children. Have cards, each having one letter on them. Shuffle the cards and give seven cards to each of three children. They are to use their cards to spell the longest word that they can. But, before spelling their words, they may trade three cards if someone else is willing to trade with them. After the trades, whoever spells the word with the most letters wins.

Have the children figure out how many cards were used in the game. How many cards would be needed if there were four players? five players?

ACTIVITY 7.07   Is That Enough Milk?

Have the children count to find out how many students are in the class. Then explain that we would like to get enough cartons of milk so that they can all have one to drink. How many cartons are needed?

Tell them that one person can carry four cartons without dropping them. Have four children come to the front. Ask the class whether there would be enough milk if each of these children brought back four cartons. Would there be enough if five students went for milk? Six students?

Note that this requires a lot of adding. We want to speed up the process as much as possible. One way to accomplish this is to have the children think about what multiplication they have already done that might help with this one. Often several related multiplications are done together or in succession, For example, if you have just found the answer to 3 × 6 by adding 6 + 6 + 6, then 4 × 6 is easy.

$$4 \times 6 = 6 + 6 + 6 + 6$$

I already know that this is 18,
so the answer to 4×6 is

$$4 \times 6 = 18 + 6$$
$$= 24$$

The teacher should continually emphasize that with every problem that they face, the children should first think about what they already know that will help.

Teaching the Easy Basic Multiplication Facts

After the meaning of multiplication has been established, and children can confidently find answers on their own, we focus on the easier basic multiplication facts, with our goal being commiting those facts to memory. Which multiplication facts are included in the easy ones will vary from program to program, but whichever ones are included, there is a sense that these are easier than the others. For purposes of our discussion here, we will consider multiplication facts with multipliers of 0 to 3 to be the easy ones. There are 64 of these easy basic multiplication facts.

While focusing on the easy facts, in addition to figuring out the answers for themselves, we want the children to discover helpful relationships that exist among the multiplication facts. In particular, the teacher needs to assure that the children discover four relationships.

First, the children should recognize that the facts where one of the numbers being multiplied is a zero all have something in common. The answer for these facts is always zero.

X	0	1	2	3	4	5	6	7	8	9
0	0	0	0	0	0	0	0	0	0	0
1	0	1	2	3	4	5	6	7	8	9
2	0	2	4	6	8	10	12	14	16	18
3	0	3	6	9	12	15	18	21	24	27
4	0	4	8	12						
5	0	5	10	15						
6	0	6	12	18						
7	0	7	14	21						
8	0	8	16	24						
9	0	9	18	27						

$$0 \times 4 = 0 \qquad 0 \times 7 = 0 \qquad 6 \times 0 = 0$$

$$9 \times 0 = 0 \qquad 0 \times 3 = 0 \qquad 4 \times 0 = 0$$

$$0 \times 8 = 0 \qquad 1 \times 0 = 0$$

There are 19 facts with the multiplier or the multiplicand equal to zero. That's 19 of the 64 easy basic multiplication facts, but because of this relationship it is only one thing for the children to learn.

A second important relationship is evident in the next group of facts.

$$1 \times 4 = 4 \qquad 1 \times 7 = 7 \qquad 6 \times 1 = 6$$

$$9 \times 1 = 9 \qquad 1 \times 3 = 3 \qquad 4 \times 1 = 4$$

$$1 \times 8 = 8 \qquad 1 \times 1 = 1$$

There are 19 basic multiplication facts in which one of the numbers being multiplied is 1. In each of these cases, the answer will be the other number. Two of those are $0 \times 1 = 0$ and $1 \times 0 = 0$, and they have been dealt with earlier. So, we have 17 new facts in this group. But, because of this relationship it is only one thing to learn.

The next relationship that we want the children to recognize is that certain pairs of facts are related.

$$3 \times 4 = 12 \quad \text{and} \quad 4 \times 3 = 12$$

$$9 \times 2 = 18 \quad \text{and} \quad 2 \times 9 = 18$$

$$4 \times 5 = 20 \quad \text{and} \quad 5 \times 4 = 20$$

$$4 \times 8 = 32 \quad \text{and} \quad 8 \times 4 = 32$$

Children should recognize from these pairs of facts that changing the order of the numbers being multiplied does not change the answer. This rearrangement principle tells us that the answer to 5×6 is also the answer to 6×5. The answer to 3×9 is also the answer to 9×3. And, 8×74 has the same answer as 74×8.

An important relationship between other pairs of facts should also be recognized by the children. This time the relationship is between certain multiplication facts and certain addition facts.

$$2 \times 4 = 8 \quad \text{and} \quad 4 + 4 = 8$$

$$2 \times 9 = 18 \quad \text{and} \quad 9 + 9 = 18$$

$$2 \times 5 = 10 \quad \text{and} \quad 5 + 5 = 10$$

$$2 \times 8 = 16 \quad \text{and} \quad 8 + 8 = 16$$

Multiplying 2 times a number is exactly the same as adding that number to itself. This is a direct result of the meaning of multiplication. Children who recognize this relationship realize that these are just the doubles that were already memorized as addition facts, so there is nothing new to learn here. Also since the numbers being multiplied may be rearranged without affecting the answer, $4 \times 2 = 2 \times 4$. Therefore, 4×2 is also a double. There are 13 of these doubles that have not been previously dealt with as multiplication by zero or by one. If the children are aware of how multiplication is related to addition, they will already know these 13 facts. That's 13 facts, but nothing new to learn.

There are just six remaining rearranged pairs that were not included in multiplication by zero, by one, or by two. That's 12 multiplication facts, but if the child has learned that rearranging the numbers does not change the product, it is only six things to learn. So, of the 64 easy basic multiplication facts, the only one not yet discussed is $3 \times 3 = 9$. That's one fact to learn. Let's summarize the impact of such an emphasis on relationships.

Group of Facts	Number of Facts	Things to Learn
$\times 0$	19	1
$\times 1$	17	1
$\times 2$	15	0
Commutative Pairs	12	6
3×3	1	1
All Easy Facts	64	9

The emphasis on relationships provides a tremendous advantage to the child. The 64 easy basic multiplication facts can be mastered by only learning nine new things. This certainly increases the number of children who actually have the facts committed to memory and increases the speed with which memorization takes place. But, even more important, it significantly increases retention of those facts once they have been memorized. Remember, *it is always easier to remember things that are related to other things that are already known.*

After the children understand the relationships among the facts, they should commit the easy basic multiplication facts to memory. The instructional activities that are selected to lead the children to memorizing the easy basic multiplication facts should have certain characteristics. These are the same characteristics presented in Chapter 6 for addition facts.

1. Children should be aware that the objective is to memorize the facts. Tell them to remember the facts.
2. The activities should use an interesting and fun format.
3. Activities should have a high level of involvement. Minimize waiting time. Maximize thinking time.
4. Activities should focus on a small number of unmemorized facts at any given time.
5. Some already memorized facts should be mixed in with the target unmemorized facts. This will improve retention.
6. If a child does not know an answer, then he or she should figure it out. Allow enough time to figure it out. Discourage guessing by asking, "How did you figure that out?"

7. To figure out an answer, the child should think about what he or she already knows that will help find the answer. What other facts that I already know will help? What relationship that I know will help? Counting or adding should be used only as a last resort.

8. Accuracy should be emphasized, not speed. Accuracy is of great importance. Speed is of little importance. Speed will come after accuracy and confidence.

The following examples of memorization activities demonstrate these characteristics.

✕ + ⊣ ACTIVITY 7.08 They're Still Doubles

Have a student come to the front and demonstrate 2 ✕ 6 using counters. As the child shows six objects two times and then combines them, say, "But, that looks, like 6 + 6." Repeat the process with a child showing 2 ✕ 4. As the child shows four objects, two times and then combines them, say, "But that looks like 4 + 4." Repeat with several other doubles to assure that the children see that multiplication by 2 is the same as a double in addition.

Then have them think about the doubles in addition as they figure out answers when multiplying by 2. Emphasize that they already know these answers.

✕ + ⊣ ACTIVITY 7.09 Doubles and One More

Have a student come to the front and demonstrate 3 ✕ 6 using counters. After the child has shown three groups of 6, suggest that the child start by combining two of the groups. Point to the two groups of 6 that have been combined. Point out that is 6 + 6. Point out that it is also 2 ✕ 6. Then point out that there is still one more 6. Three 6s are the same as two 6s and one more 6. Write it on the chalkboard.

$$3 \times 6 = 2 \times 6 + 6$$

Emphasize that they already know the double, so they just need to add one more 6.

Repeat this process with other multiplications by 3: 3 ✕ 7, 3 ✕ 5, 3 ✕ 9, 3 ✕ 4, 3 ✕ 8, 3 ✕ 3.

✕ + ⊣ ACTIVITY 7.10 Facts of the Day

Identify two facts that a student needs to work on. Have the child figure out the answers and write each fact on a piece of paper. Tell the child to remember both of the facts. Immediately ask the child for both answers. Tell the child again to remember them. Frequently during the day, ask the child to give you one or the other of these answers. Each time, tell the child to remember. At the end of the day send the two pieces of paper with the facts written on them home with the child along with a note explaining what you are doing. Ask the parents to ask the child to give them the answers to both facts.

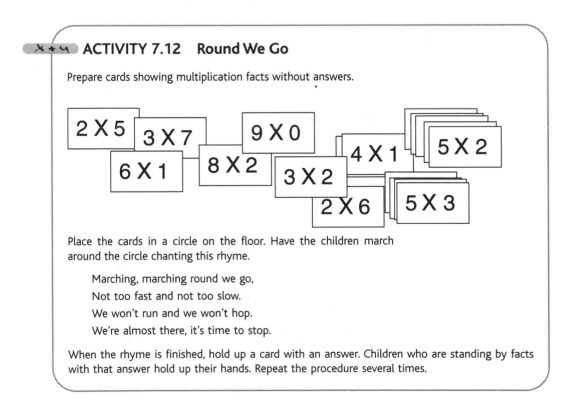

✖ ÷ ⊕ ACTIVITY 7.11   Match Me

Prepare cards, some with multiplication facts without answers, and some with the answers.

Hand a card to each child. Have them find their partners so that they make a complete fact. If there is an odd number of children, you should take a card and participate so everyone has a partner.

Have the partners stand together so everyone can see their fact. Have the children check everyone's work. Are the partners correct?

You might wish to have several copies of the same facts that you are emphasizing, but mix in a few facts that the children already know for review. Mix up the cards, hand them out, and have the children find their new partners.

✖ ÷ ⊕ ACTIVITY 7.12   Round We Go

Prepare cards showing multiplication facts without answers.

Place the cards in a circle on the floor. Have the children march around the circle chanting this rhyme.

> Marching, marching round we go,
> Not too fast and not too slow.
> We won't run and we won't hop.
> We're almost there, it's time to stop.

When the rhyme is finished, hold up a card with an answer. Children who are standing by facts with that answer hold up their hands. Repeat the procedure several times.

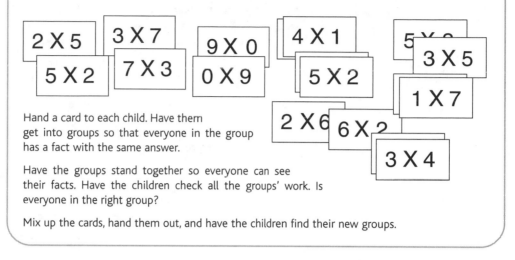

✕ ✦ ◁ ACTIVITY 7.13   Match My Group

Prepare cards showing multiplication facts without answers. Be sure there are facts with the same answers.

Hand a card to each child. Have them get into groups so that everyone in the group has a fact with the same answer.

Have the groups stand together so everyone can see their facts. Have the children check all the groups' work. Is everyone in the right group?

Mix up the cards, hand them out, and have the children find their new groups.

Thinking Strategies for Hard Basic Multiplication Facts

When developing the hard basic multiplication facts (for example, those with multipliers greater than 3), answers can still be found by counting or by adding. However, with the larger numbers, both counting and adding are inefficient and consequently very slow. At this point in the development, more efficient strategies are needed that allow the child to find answers quickly and accurately.

Our objective is for these facts to be committed to memory. Remember from our discussion of strategies for the hard basic addition facts that some strategies seem to lead to memorization while others do not. Recall also, that the strategies that are successful have two common characteristics.

Successful strategies are mental strategies. They consist of a series of quick, easy, mental procedures. They are not pencil-and-paper strategies, nor or they performed by manipulating fingers or other objects. Also, *successful strategies require the child to use facts that are already memorized to figure out the facts that are not yet memorized.* The child is constantly thinking about what he or she already knows that can help figure out what he or she does not know. The child has a sense of building on what is already known. New knowledge is closely related to existing knowledge, and it is always easier to remember things that are related to other things that we know.

One More.   The simplest thinking strategy for hard basic multiplication facts is the one-more strategy. The thinking is very simple, so it is easy for children to use. Every hard basic multiplication fact can be found using this strategy. If we want to find 6 × 8, we think of six 8s as being five 8s and one more 8. We visualize 6 × 8 as six rows of 8 objects.

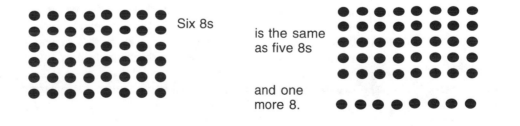

If we know what five 8s is equal to, then we simply need to add one more 8. That will give the answer to six 8s.

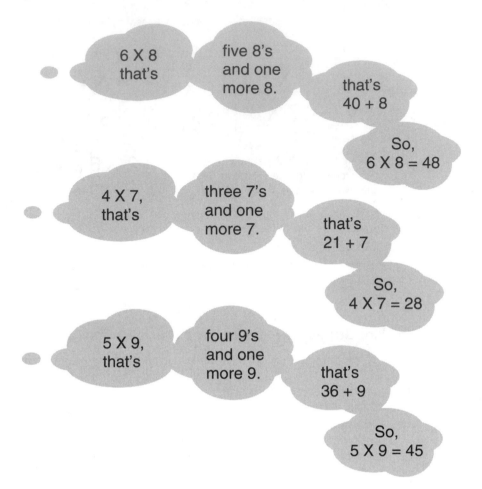

To use the one-more strategy to find answers to a hard basic multiplication fact, in each case we must know another fact first. For example, to find 6 × 8, we must already know 5 × 8. To find 7 × 9, we must already know 6 × 9. To find 5 × 7, we must already know 4 × 7. To find 6 × 6, we must already know 5 × 6.

Textbooks frequently use the one-more strategy to develop the hard facts in a carefully controlled sequence. The authors know which facts have previously been developed and all new facts build on them. However, in practice, the children do not memorize the facts in the same sequence they are developed in the textbook. They typically remember some and not others. As a result, at any given time, the children in any class will have mastered varied combinations of facts, and, of course, they will not have mastered other combinations.

When it is time for the children to figure out the answer to 6 × 8, we cannot be sure that they already know 5 × 8. When we are ready for the children to figure out the answer to 7 × 9, we cannot depend on their already knowing 6 × 9. Some children already know the necessary facts. Some do not. Although the one-more strategy works well in the textbook, and though it may work well when you are working with a single child (where you can keep track of which facts are already memorized), it is difficult to use in a large group setting (where it is hard to keep track of which facts each child has already memorized). But, there is another thinking strategy that seems to work more effectively in a whole-class setting.

The other thinking strategy for hard basic multiplication facts that has proven to be more successful in a whole-class environment is the partial-products strategy. In fact, the one-more strategy is really a special case of the partial-products strategy. The simplest description of this strategy is that we take the "big" fact that we do not know and break it into easier facts that we do know. For example, suppose we do not know the answer to 6 × 7. We visualize this as 6 rows of 7 objects. We break it into two easy parts and then combine those two parts.

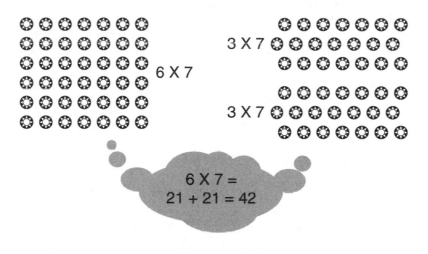

Other examples of this strategy are given below.

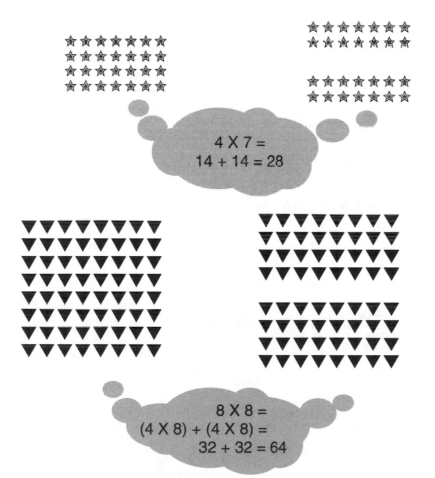

Success with this strategy depends on getting the children to think about what easier facts they already know that can help them find the answer. This kind of thinking is good problem-solving behavior, and we would want them to think like this even if it did not help them with their multiplication facts.

Teachers who use the partial-products strategy find that a fair amount of time and effort are required to get the children to use this thinking pattern. But, after the children get comfortable with it, they are able to find answers much more quickly, and they make rapid progress toward mastery of the multiplication facts. In addition to providing quicker mastery of the hard basic multiplication facts, this strategy introduces the concept of partial products which will later be used in multi-digit multiplication. In other words, the instructional goal is achieved more quickly if time is spent on learning the thinking strategies.

After the children have learned to use an efficient strategy to find answers to the hard basic multiplication facts, rapid progress can be made toward mastery of these facts. As when working on the easy facts, the children should be able to figure out the answers to the hard facts. The children need to recognize and use relationships among the hard facts. And, we want the children to commit the hard facts to memory.

If children do not know a hard multiplication fact, they cannot just say "I don't know." They must figure out the answer. And since we want them to figure out the answer efficiently and quickly, we encourage (almost require) them to use the thinking strategy that has been learned. The children have, at this point, been using repeated addition for over a year to find multiplication fact answers. They are comfortable using repeated addition—even when it takes a long time. Consequently, they will automatically fall back on repeated addition because they are comfortable with this process. So, the teacher must continually lead the children to use the thinking strategy instead.

If children do not know the answer to a hard basic multiplication fact, they need to think about what they already know that will help them with the fact that they do not know. If children continually think about the relationships among the facts, they end up with fewer things to learn, and their retention of what they have learned is better.

Activities for Memorization of the Hard Basic Multiplication Facts. The following group of activities demonstrates how a teacher can help students to think about what they already know that will help them with what they are trying to figure out.

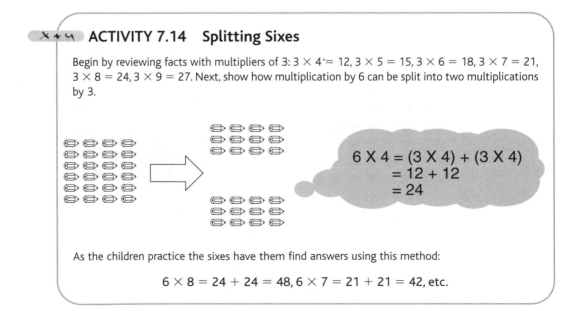

× + ◁ ACTIVITY 7.14   Splitting Sixes

Begin by reviewing facts with multipliers of 3: $3 \times 4 = 12$, $3 \times 5 = 15$, $3 \times 6 = 18$, $3 \times 7 = 21$, $3 \times 8 = 24$, $3 \times 9 = 27$. Next, show how multiplication by 6 can be split into two multiplications by 3.

$$6 \times 4 = (3 \times 4) + (3 \times 4)$$
$$= 12 + 12$$
$$= 24$$

As the children practice the sixes have them find answers using this method:

$$6 \times 8 = 24 + 24 = 48, 6 \times 7 = 21 + 21 = 42, \text{ etc.}$$

✕ ÷ ⊲ ACTIVITY 7.15 Thirty-Six vs. Twenty-Four

Prepare a set of 50 cards with one-digit numbers on them. Each of the numbers 0 through 9 should appear on five cards. This is a game for two players.

Shuffle the deck and place it face down on the table between the players. Turn one card face up. The players take turns. One player tries to find pairs of numbers with a product of 36. The other player tries to find pairs of numbers with a product of 24. On each turn, the player turns over an additional card and looks at all the numbers that are showing. If the player sees two numbers with his product, he or she takes those two cards.

After all the cards in the deck have been turned, the game is over, and the player who has taken the most cards is the winner. Most of the cards will not be used and will remain on the table.

✕ ÷ ⊲ ACTIVITY 7.16 Finding My Answers

Prepare a set of 50 cards like those described for Activity 7.15. This is a game for three players.

Shuffle the deck and place it face down on the table. Turn one card face up. The players take turns. One player tries to find pairs of numbers with a product of 63, 48, or 49. The second player tries to find pairs of numbers with a product of 72, 64, or 42. The third player tries to find pairs of numbers with a product of 81, 56, or 32. On each turn, the player turns over an additional card and looks at all the numbers that are showing. If the player sees two numbers with one of his or her products, he or she takes those two cards.

After all the cards in the deck have been turned, the game is over, and the player who has taken the most cards is the winner. Most of the cards will not be used and will remain on the table.

✕ ÷ ⊲ ACTIVITY 7.17 Some Easy and Some Hard

Prepare a set of 50 cards like those described for Activity 7.15.

Follow the procedures of Activity 7.16, except have the players find the following sets of products: 12, 16, or 56; 8, 36, or 48; and 6, 25, or 42.

✕ ÷ ⊲ ACTIVITY 7.18 Line Up

Prepare large flashcards showing multiplication facts without answers. Include the facts that are currently being emphasized. Include enough so that every child will have one. Shuffle them and give one card to each child.

Separate the class into two groups. Have one group go to one side of the room and have the other group go to the opposite side of the room. Tell the two groups to line up so that the answers to their multiplication facts are in order. Allow them to talk and help each other. When they are lined up, have them hold their cards so the other group can see them. Each group should then check the other group.

Collect the cards, reshuffle them, and repeat the activity.

ACTIVITY 7.19   Scavenger Hunt

Prepare five lists of answers to multiplication facts. Each list should have seven answers. Also prepare cards showing the multiplication facts that have the answers on the lists, but do not include the answers on these cards. Be sure that there is a fact card for each answer on each list, but include some extra fact cards that do not go with any of the answers.

Tape the fact cards on the walls all around the classroom. Form five teams and give each team one of the lists of answers. Tell the teams that they must find facts to go with all the answers on their lists.

The first team to collect facts for all their answers wins.

Teaching the Multiplication Algorithm

When the basic multiplication facts have been mastered, the child is ready to begin work on the multiplication algorithm. The multiplication algorithm is the step-by-step process by which we use the basic facts to find answers to any other whole-number multiplication example. We use the multiplication algorithm to do multi-digit multiplication. Several principles related to teaching algorithms have been mentioned earlier. Let's review those principles.

- *Let them see what it looks like.* Carefully model the operation with an appropriate physical or pictorial model. We should use a model that lets the children see what happens to the basic units—ones, tens, hundreds, and so on—when we multiply.
- *De-emphasize rote rules.* We may end up with rules, but they should be meaningful. They should arise out of the modeling process.
- *Emphasize big ideas.* These are the important generalizations that describe the procedures. They also come from the modeling process.
- *Let the written algorithm simply be a recording* of what happens when the algorithm is modeled. Everything we write should match something we do.
- *Watch our language.* The children should use language that describes what they see when the operation is modeled, not language that describes what we write down.

The first of the big ideas that form the basis of the multiplication algorithm is *multiplication by ten*. It is important that the child discover that multiplication by ten is really easy. It is not unusual to see a child multiply by ten something like this:

$$
\begin{array}{r}
236 \\
\times\ 10 \\
\hline
000 \\
236 \\
\hline
2360
\end{array}
$$

When we see this, we know that the algorithm has been taught rotely, and the child has not been taught the first big idea for the multiplication algorithm. Most adults know (and who knows how they learned it) that when multiplying by ten, we simply "add a zero." Multiplication by ten is easy. But we do not want to just give them this "rule" without teaching it meaningfully. To do this, we need a model for numbers that lets the child see ones, tens, and hundreds. For our discussion here we begin by using bundled sticks.

We begin by using the bundled sticks to represent 21.

Then we use the bundled sticks to represent 21 ten times, and we write 10×21 on the board.

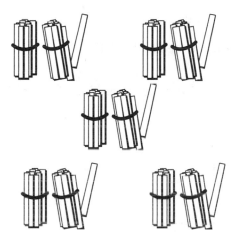 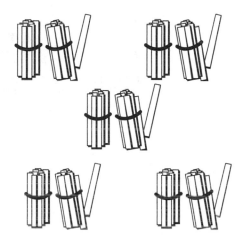

Next, we put all the tens together and put all the ones together.

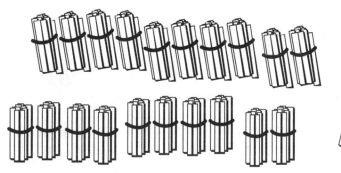

And finally, we group the tens together to make hundreds and group the ones together to make a ten.

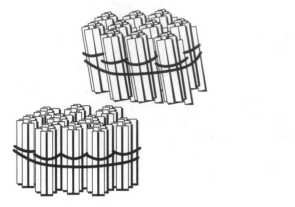

And we record the result on the board. $10 \times 21 = 210$

We repeat this process with a variety of examples and record all the results together on the chalkboard. For example, we might use:

$$10 \times 21 = 210$$
$$12 \times 10 = 120 \ \ (10, \text{ twelve times})$$
$$10 \times 36 = 360$$
$$42 \times 10 = 420$$
$$10 \times \ \ 8 = 80$$

When these examples have been completed by using the model to get the answers, we ask the students if they see a pattern. Do they see how we might get the answer without using the model? When it has been suggested that you can just "add" a zero to get the answer, write another example (for example, 10×18) on the board, and ask what the answer is. Record the answer that the children give, but then do this example with the model to verify that the children's answer is correct.

Out of experiences like those illustrated above, it becomes apparent to the children that multiplication by ten is easy, that you "just add a zero." The next step is to extend the notion of multiplication by ten as follows.

$$30 \times 7 = 10 \times 3 \times 7$$

This is 30.

We have a basic fact (3×7) and a multiplication by 10.

The answer is $10 \times 21 = 210$.

Similarly, $50 \times 9 = 10 \times 5 \times 9 = 10 \times 45 = 450$. Again, we have a basic fact and a multiplication by 10. $4 \times 60 = 4 \times 6 \times 10 = 240$, which again is a basic fact and a multiplication by 10. Answers to all of the examples, 70×8, 30×6, 7×20, 40×3, 5×80, and so on, are easily found by multiplying the answer to a basic fact by 10.

The answer to an example like 30×70 can be found by extending the notion of multiplication by ten still further.

$$30 \times 70 = \overset{30}{\overbrace{10 \times 3}} \times \overset{70}{\overbrace{10 \times 7}} = 10 \times 10 \times 3 \times 7 = 2100$$

In this case we end up with a basic fact and two multiplications by ten. Each multiplication by 10 "adds a zero." Similar examples also result in a basic fact and two multiplications by ten.

$$40 \times 30 = 4 \times 3 \times 10 \times 10 = 1200$$
$$20 \times 90 = 2 \times 9 \times 10 \times 10 = 1800$$
$$50 \times 70 = 5 \times 7 \times 10 \times 10 = 3500$$
$$80 \times 50 = 8 \times 5 \times 10 \times 10 = 4000$$

> This one has 3 zeros. Why?

One final extension of multiplication by ten is needed. Since $100 = 10 \times 10$ and $1000 = 10 \times 10 \times 10$, $600 = 6 \times 10 \times 10$ and $4000 = 4 \times 10 \times 10 \times 10$, it follows then, that

$$7 \times 600 = 7 \times 6 \times 10 \times 10 = 4200 \quad \text{(A basic fact and two multiplications by 10)}$$

$$70 \times 600 = 7 \times 6 \times 10 \times 10 \times 10 = 42000 \quad \text{(A basic fact and three multiplications by 10)}$$

$$4000 \times 30 = 4 \times 3 \times 10 \times 10 \times 10 \times 10 = 120{,}000 \quad \text{(A basic fact and four multiplications by 10)}$$

> This one has 4 zeros. Why?

$$60 \times 500 = 6 \times 5 \times 10 \times 10 \times 10 = 30{,}000 \quad \text{(A basic fact and three multiplications by 10)}$$

After each step in the development of the concept of multiplication by ten and the extensions of that concept, the children need to have a variety of experiences where they practice and apply their current level of understanding. The following activities illustrate ways to practice this concept.

$x + 4$ **ACTIVITY 7.20 Easy Tens**

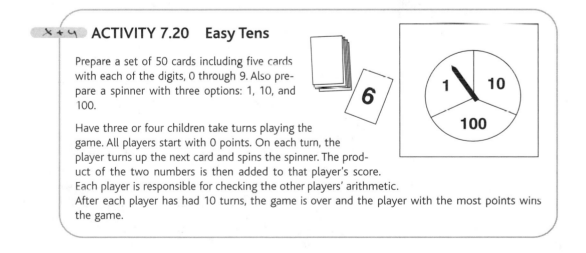

Prepare a set of 50 cards including five cards with each of the digits, 0 through 9. Also prepare a spinner with three options: 1, 10, and 100.

Have three or four children take turns playing the game. All players start with 0 points. On each turn, the player turns up the next card and spins the spinner. The product of the two numbers is then added to that player's score. Each player is responsible for checking the other players' arithmetic. After each player has had 10 turns, the game is over and the player with the most points wins the game.

ACTIVITY 7.21   Tossing for Points

Draw a series of shapes on the bottom of the inside of a box and write a number like 5, 30, 4, 200, 70, 8 in each shape. Also prepare a cube with 4, 5, 6, 7, 8, and 9 written on the six faces. Place the box against one wall, and use masking tape to place a line on the floor about 6 feet from the wall.

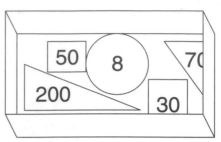

Have a small group of children play. Players take turns standing behind the line and tossing the cube into the box. If the cube lands on one of the shapes, the player's score for that toss is the product of the number in the shape and the number on the cube. If the cube is not touching a shape, the player's score for that toss is the number on the cube. If the cube is touching two shapes, the player's score is the product of the number on the cube times the greater of the numbers in the two shapes. After each player has had five tosses, the one with the greatest total score wins.

ACTIVITY 7.22   That One!!!

Prepare a set of about 30 cards with multiplication examples like 6 × 80, 200 × 4, 30 × 60, 800 × 70, 300 × 200, 90 × 80, and 600 × 6.

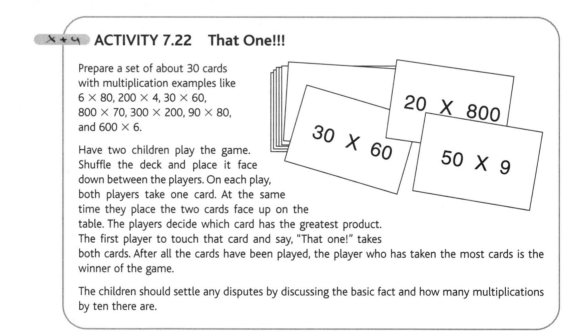

Have two children play the game. Shuffle the deck and place it face down between the players. On each play, both players take one card. At the same time they place the two cards face up on the table. The players decide which card has the greatest product. The first player to touch that card and say, "That one!" takes both cards. After all the cards have been played, the player who has taken the most cards is the winner of the game.

The children should settle any disputes by discussing the basic fact and how many multiplications by ten there are.

The second of the two big ideas that are the basis of the multiplication algorithm also develops from the modeling process. This big idea was used earlier when we worked on the hard basic multiplication facts. It is the notion of *partial products*. Recall that when we were faced with a hard multiplication fact that we did not know the answer to, we could use partial products to break it into easier facts. For example, 8 × 7 can be broken into 4 × 7 + 4 × 7.

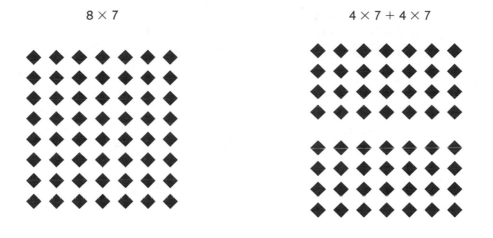

$$8 \times 7 \qquad\qquad 4 \times 7 + 4 \times 7$$

Similarly, if we want to multiply a one-digit number by a two-digit number, we can break this hard-to-find product into two easy parts, called partial products. To multiply 12×7,

$$12 \times 7 \qquad\qquad 10 \times 7 + 2 \times 7$$

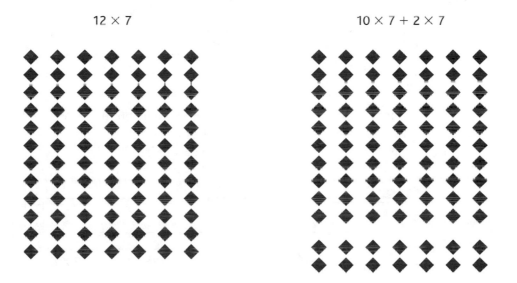

And, since $10 \times 7 = 70$, and $2 \times 7 = 14$, $12 \times 7 = 70 + 14 = 84$. In the same way, $36 \times 4 = 30 \times 4 + 6 \times 4$.

$$30 \times 4 \qquad\qquad\qquad\qquad\qquad 6 \times 4$$

30×4 is a basic fact and a multiplication by ten, and 6×4 is a basic fact. So, we have broken 36×4 into two easy partial products.

$$36 \times 4 = 30 \times 4 + 6 \times 4 = 120 + 24 = 144$$

When the notion of area of rectangles has been developed, the array model for multiplication evolves into the area model. If the sides of a rectangle are 8 and 3, the area of that rectangle is 8 × 3 = 24.

In the same way, 36 × 4 can be represented by a rectangle with sides of 36 and 4. The area of this rectangle is equal to 36 × 4.

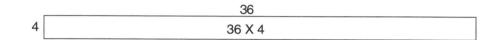

If we cut the rectangle into two parts we see a representation of the two partial products.

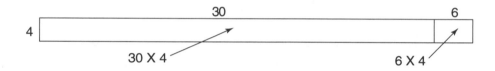

In this example we also end up with nothing but basic facts and multiplication by ten. If we follow the same procedure with 53 × 8, we have 53 × 8 = 50 × 8 + 3 × 8. Once again, there is nothing but basic facts and multiplication by ten.

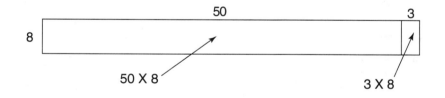

Partial products can also be used to break an example like 29 × 70 into easy partial products.

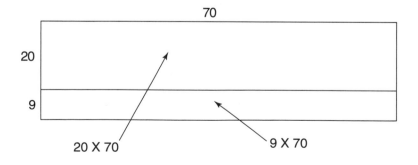

Notice that 20 × 70 is a basic fact and two multiplications by ten, while 9 × 70 is a basic fact and one multiplication by ten.

When multiplying two multi-digit numbers, partial products still allow us to find the answer using only basic multiplication facts and multiplication by ten. For example consider 35 × 46 and 179 × 38.

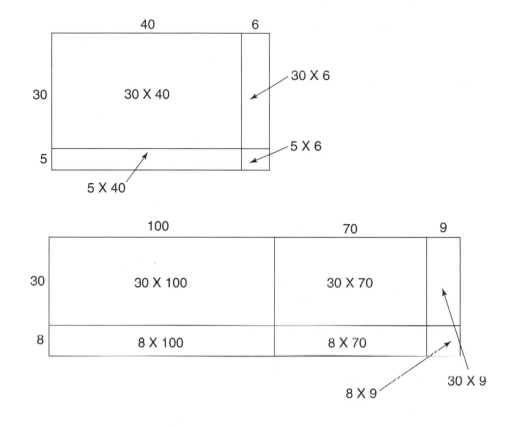

In every whole-number multiplication example, regardless how large or small the numbers, partial products allow us to find the answer using only basic facts and multiplication by ten. Once the partial products have been found, they are added to get the total product. We find then that the algorithm for multi-digit multiplication consists of a series of easy steps.

When multiplying a three-digit number by another three-digit number, we have nine partial products. When multiplying two four-digit numbers we have 16 partial products. Keeping track of such a large number of partial products is a problem. So, to condense the recording of the algorithm, regrouping is done as it is in addition. First, consider 54 × 7.

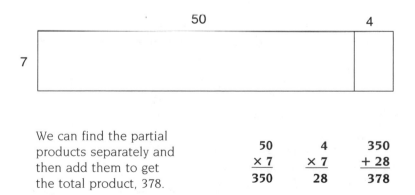

We can find the partial products separately and then add them to get the total product, 378.

50	4	350
× 7	× 7	+ 28
350	28	378

Or we can do the two multiplications, and use regrouping to find the answer. First multiply 7 times 4. That's 28— or 2 tens and 8 ones. Record the 8 ones in the ones place and keep track of the 2 tens.

$$\begin{array}{r} \overset{2}{5}4 \\ \times\ 7 \\ \hline 8 \end{array}$$

Next, we multiply 7 times 50. That's 7 times 5 tens or 35 tens. But we already had 2 tens, so, altogether, we have 37 tens. That's the same as 3 hundreds and 7 tens.

$$\begin{array}{r} \overset{2}{5}4 \\ \times\ 7 \\ \hline 378 \end{array}$$

We use regrouping in a similar fashion to multiply 3 × 486.

First, multiply 3 times 6. That's 18, or 1 ten and 8 ones. Record the 8 ones in the ones place and keep track of the ten.

$$\begin{array}{r} \overset{1}{4}86 \\ \times\ 3 \\ \hline 8 \end{array}$$

Next, multiply 3 times the 8 tens. That's 24 tens. With the ten that we already had, we have 25 tens or 2 hundreds and 5 tens. Record the 5 tens in the tens place and keep track of the 2 hundreds.

$$\begin{array}{r} \overset{2\,1}{4}86 \\ \times\ 3 \\ \hline 58 \end{array}$$

Finally, multiply 3 times the 4 hundreds. That's 12 hundreds. But we already had 2 hundreds, so that's 14 hundreds, or 1 thousand and 4 hundreds. Record this.

$$\begin{array}{r} \overset{2\,1}{4}86 \\ \times\ \ 3 \\ \hline 1458 \end{array}$$

If the student can use regrouping to find 54 × 7 = 378, then 54 × 70 is the same except there is also a multiplication by ten. If the student can use regrouping to find 483 × 6 = 2898, then 483 × 600 is the same except there are also two multiplications by ten. To multiply 342 × 90,

I know I will multiply by 9 and also by ten. Since I can multiply in either order, I'll multiply by ten first. I know to "add a zero" to the answer, so I'll go ahead and write the zero.

$$\begin{array}{r} 342 \\ \times\ 90 \\ \hline 0 \end{array}$$

Now, I'll multiply 9 times 2. That's 1 ten and 8 ones. Record the 8 ones and keep track of the ten.

$$\begin{array}{r} \overset{1}{3}42 \\ \times\ 90 \\ \hline 80 \end{array}$$

Now, I'll multiply 9 times 4 tens. That's 36 tens. But we already had 1 ten, so that makes 37 tens. That's the same as 3 hundreds and 7 tens.

$$\begin{array}{r} \overset{3\,1}{3}42 \\ \times\ 90 \\ \hline 780 \end{array}$$

Now, I'll multiply 9 times 3 hundreds. That's 27 hundreds. But we already had 3, so that makes 30 hundreds. That's the same as 3 thousands and no hundreds.

$$\begin{array}{r} \overset{3\,1}{3}42 \\ \times\ 90 \\ \hline 30780 \end{array}$$

Similarly, the student can multiply 264 × 400.

There are two multiplications by ten. I'll do that first. I'll need to add two zeros.

$$\begin{array}{r} 264 \\ \times\ 400 \\ \hline 00 \end{array}$$

Then, I'll multiply 264 by 4.

$$
\begin{array}{r}
\overset{2\,1}{264} \\
\times\ \ 400 \\
\hline
105600
\end{array}
$$

We can now do any whole-number multiplication example using an efficient, written algorithm. For example, consider 316 × 274.

First multiply by 4.

$$
\begin{array}{r}
316 \\
\times\ 274 \\
\hline
1264
\end{array}
$$

Next multiply by 70.

$$
\begin{array}{r}
316 \\
\times\ 274 \\
\hline
1264 \\
22120
\end{array}
$$

Then multiply by 200.

$$
\begin{array}{r}
316 \\
\times\ 274 \\
\hline
1264 \\
22120 \\
63200
\end{array}
$$

Finally, add the partial products.

$$
\begin{array}{r}
316 \\
\times\ 274 \\
\hline
1264 \\
22120 \\
\underline{63200} \\
86584
\end{array}
$$

The following activities illustrate how a teacher might introduce and have the students use partial products.

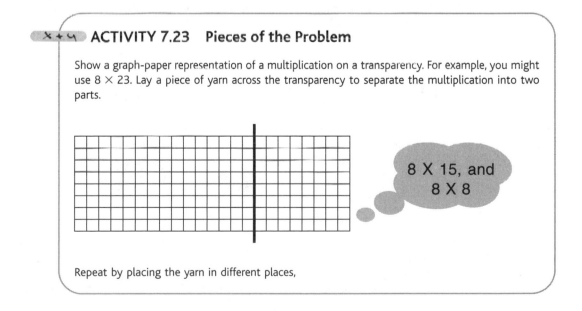

x ÷ ◁ ACTIVITY 7.23   Pieces of the Problem

Show a graph-paper representation of a multiplication on a transparency. For example, you might use 8 × 23. Lay a piece of yarn across the transparency to separate the multiplication into two parts.

8 X 15, and
8 X 8

Repeat by placing the yarn in different places,

This is a continuation of Activity 7.23. Show a graph-paper representation of another multiplication example on a transparency. For example, you might use 7 × 27. Lay a piece of yarn across the transparency to separate the multiplication into two parts. Have the children name the two parts.

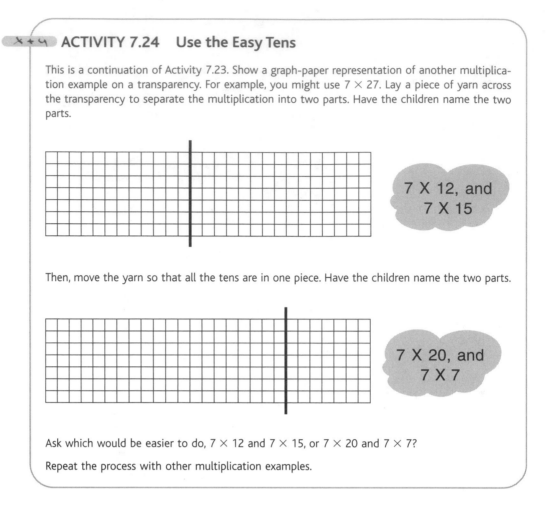

7 X 12, and
7 X 15

Then, move the yarn so that all the tens are in one piece. Have the children name the two parts.

7 X 20, and
7 X 7

Ask which would be easier to do, 7 × 12 and 7 × 15, or 7 × 20 and 7 × 7?

Repeat the process with other multiplication examples.

× + ÷ **ACTIVITY 7.25   Putting the Pieces Together**

Prepare sets of three cards. In each set, one card will show a multiplication example where a two-digit number is being multiplied by a one-digit number. The other two cards in the set will show the two partial products.

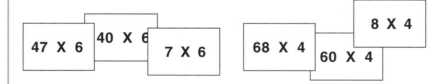

47 X 6   40 X 6   7 X 6   68 X 4   60 X 4   8 X 4

Pass out the cards and have the children find their two partners. When the three partners are together, they then find answers to the two partial products and add them to get the total product.

So, we find that the two big ideas on which the multiplication algorithm is based are *multiplication by ten* and *partial products*. Multiplication by ten is easy, and using partial products reduces the algorithm into a series of steps that involve nothing but basic multiplication facts, multiplications by ten, and addition with regrouping.

Curriculum and Evaluation Standards for School Mathematics identifies complex paper-and-pencil computations as an area that should have decreased emphasis. In the *Standards* the following remarks are made about the availability and use of calculators and the resulting effect on how students should be taught whole-number computation.

> The thoughtful use of calculators can increase the quality of the curriculum as well as the quality of children's learning. Calculators do not replace the need to learn basic facts, to compute mentally, or to do reasonable paper-and-pencil computation. Classroom experience indicates that young children take a common sense view about calculators and recognize the importance of not relying on them when it is more appropriate to compute in other ways. The availability of calculators means, however, that educators must develop a broader view of the various ways computation can be carried out and must place less emphasis on complex paper-and-pencil computation (p. 19).

The authors of this text are in full agreement with the *Standards* on this point. Therefore, when teaching the two big ideas, *multiplication by ten* and *partial products*, as the basis of the multiplication algorithm, our goal is not to develop a high level of skill with the algorithm. The goal is, rather, to develop a high level of understanding of the algorithm and of how it simplifies multiplication with large numbers. In practice, for example, we would want the student to know how to use the algorithm to find 2794 × 2836, but we would not make a homework assignment that includes more than one exercise like this. Rather, we would have the student think about the partial products to mentally estimate such products and then have the student use a calculator to check the accuracy of the estimates.

The following activities describe two estimation games where the students think about the partial products. To encourage this kind of thinking, the teacher should have the student who wins explain to the other players how to make good estimates in a hurry.

x ÷ ÷ ACTIVITY 7.26   Shuffle

Prepare a set of 30 cards showing multiplication examples. The examples should include some with one-digit multipliers, and some with two-digit, three-digit and four-digit multipliers.

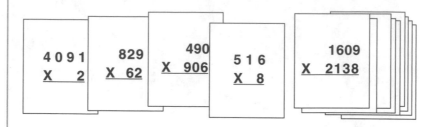

Form a group of 2 to 4 children. Shuffle the deck. Players take turns being the dealer. On each play, the dealer gives each player five cards, face down. When the dealer says go, the players race to arrange their cards in order from least answer to greatest answer. The first player to finish says done, and play stops. If everyone agrees that the answers are in order, that player gets a point.

If there is a disagreement about the order of the answers, the children should each explain their reasons. If they cannot agree, then they should use a calculator to resolve the disagreement.

The game continues until a player has five points. That player wins.

x ÷ ÷ ACTIVITY 7.27   Guestimation

Prepare a set of cards like those described in Activity 7.26. Form a group of 2 to 4 children. Shuffle the deck and place it face down on the table.

One card is turned over and all the players write their best estimate of the answer. They are not to do any written computation. The estimate must be done mentally. When everyone is finished, they use a calculator to find the exact answer. The player with the best estimate gets one point.

If there is a disagreement about which estimate is closest to the answer, the children should each explain their reasons. If they cannot agree, then they should use the calculator to resolve the disagreement by finding the difference between the estimates and the answer.

The game continues until a player has 10 points. That player wins.

Summary of Developmental Sequence for Multiplication

Establish the meaning of the operation

1. Associate multiplication with combining groups of the same size.
2. Learn to use addition to find answers.

Develop the easy basic facts

1. Find the answers using the meaning of multiplication.
2. Discover relationships among the facts.
3. Memorize the facts.

Develop thinking strategies for hard multiplication facts that:

1. Are mental strategies.
2. Use memorized facts to find answers for the hard facts.

Develop the hard basic facts	1. Find the answers using the thinking strategies.
	2. Review relationships among the facts.
	3. Memorize the facts.
Develop the algorithm	1. Multiply by ten.
	2. Use partial products.

Adapting a Multiplication Lesson

Now we adapt a fourth-grade lesson on multiplication. As we have done before, we begin with a traditional plan, taken directly from suggestions like those that might appear in a teacher's guide of a published textbook program. You should note that this plan is a good one. However, its focus is to teach the textbook page. Notice also that the developmental part of the lesson consists of a detailed explanation of a single example, and that the lesson consists mainly of practice. (It was pointed out earlier that the most important thing a teacher can do to make a lesson appropriate for all students is to thoroughly develop the concepts and skills.)

LESSON OBJECTIVE

The student will multiply a two-digit number and a one-digit number.

Lesson Opener

Have students find each of the following products:

$$10 \times 5 \quad 31 \times 3 \quad 7 \times 34$$
$$2 \times 18 \quad 42 \times 3 \quad 26 \times 2$$

Ask students if they have estimated how many people are in a room by using multiplication. For example, they may have estimated by multiplying a row of 10 by 5 (the number of rows). Explain that this will help them to understand the multiplication of a two-digit number and a one-digit number.

Development

Direct the attention of the class to the example on the first page of the lesson, 4×34. Point out that 34 is between 30 and 40, so 4×34 will be between 4×30 and 4×40. Ask what 4×30 equals. [120] What does 4×40 equal? [160] So, the answer to 4×34 must be between 120 and 160.

Point out the picture of the base-ten blocks used to illustrate the example. Multiply the ones. Record it as 1 ten and 6 ones. Point out the second picture that shows the renaming. Multiply the tens. Add the extra ten. Write the tens.

Ask if this answer is reasonable. Is it between 120 and 160?

Monitor Learning

Have the students do the *Check Understanding* examples. Watch for students who add the extra ten to the tens digit before multiplying.

Practice

Have students complete the practice exercises on the second page of the lesson. Students who had difficulty with the *Check Understanding* examples may be assigned the reteaching worksheet instead of the practice exercises.

This lesson will be adapted to make it more effective in meeting the needs in a diverse classroom. The adapted lesson plan that follows includes an increased amount of developmental instruction. Notice the shift in instructional emphasis from teaching the pages of the student book toward an emphasis on teaching the concept. We have also increased visual input, kinesthetic activity, student communication, and monitoring of learning.

LESSON OBJECTIVE

The student will multiply a two-digit number and a one-digit number.

Lesson Opener

Prepare pairs of cards. One card of each pair will show a multiplication example like 30 × 7. The other card of the pair will show the answer to the multiplication.

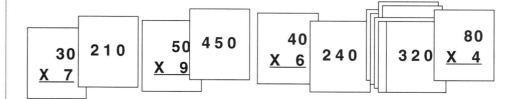

Shuffle the cards and give a card to each student. If there is an odd number of students, the teacher should keep a card and participate. Have the students find their partners. After everyone has found a partner, call on several students to tell how they were able to figure out the correct answers. **Monitor Understanding.** Observe the children carefully throughout this activity. Direct leading questions to children who are unable to find their partners. (For example, ask "How many tens are you starting with? How many times do you have those tens?")

Write 4 × 90 on the chalkboard. Point out that this is an easy multiplication to do. Then write 4 × 93 on the board, and tell the class that today they will learn that multiplying these numbers is also easy.

Development

Show 6 × 8 as an array of squares. Draw a line through the array to show that 6 × 8 can be broken into two easy parts.

6 × 8, is the same as, 3 × 8 + 3 × 8.

Monitor Understanding. Observe the children carefully throughout this activity. If a child seems not to understand, explain the two partial products by showing them in the pictorial model.

Next, use the same model to show that 6 × 14 is the same as 6 × 10 plus 6 × 4.

Next, show that 4 × 28 is the same as 4 × 20 + 4 × 8.

Monitor Understanding. Continue to observe the students to see if they understand. Provide extra explanations as needed.

Next, use base-ten blocks to model similar examples. Show 4 × 36. Show the students that the 6 ones are there four times, and that the 3 tens are there four times.

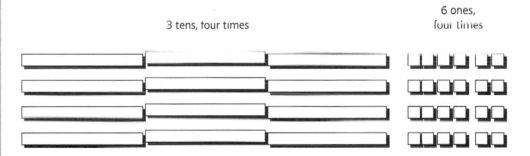

3 tens, four times

6 ones,
four times

Help the students to see that these two parts show the two multiplications that must be completed to get the answer to the original problem: 4 × 30 and 4 × 6. Have the students find these two partial products and add them to get the final product. **Monitor Understanding.** Watch the students to be sure that they understand.

Also use the base-ten blocks to show the multiplication of 6 × 43.

6 × 40   6 × 3

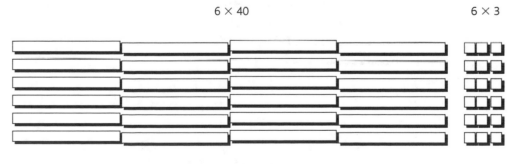

Once again, have the students find the two partial products and add them to get the final product.

Point out to the children that although it is necessary to do both multiplications, it is not really necessary to write the two partial products separately. Redo the two previous examples using base-ten blocks to illustrate how to use regrouping. Be sure to record each step so that the students can see the relationship between the written steps and the steps using the model. Show 4 × 36 and write it on the chalkboard in vertical form.

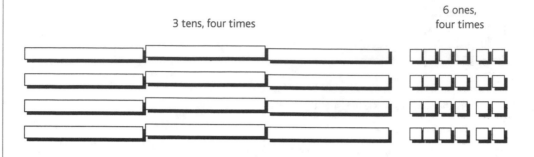

3 tens, four times

6 ones, four times

Point out that we have some tens and we have some ones. We think first about how many ones there are. We have 6 ones, four times. That's 24 ones. But, as we learned in relationship to addition, that is too many to write, so we must make a trade. We trade 20 of the ones for 2 extra tens. **Monitor Understanding.** If students do not understand, a short review of regrouping in addition may be needed.

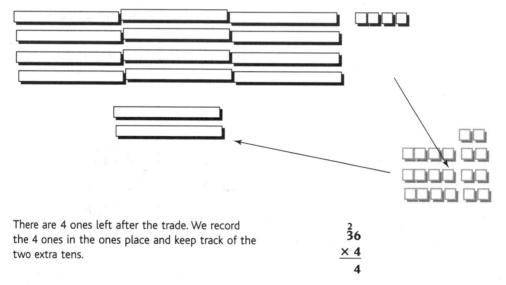

There are 4 ones left after the trade. We record the 4 ones in the ones place and keep track of the two extra tens.

$$\begin{array}{r} \overset{2}{36} \\ \times\ 4 \\ \hline 4 \end{array}$$

Next, we think about how many tens we have. There are 3 tens, four times. That's 12 tens. But we must also count the two extra tens that we traded for, so altogether we have 14 tens. But that's too many to write, so we trade 10 tens for a hundred.

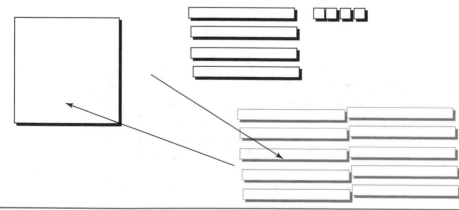

That leaves us with 4 tens. We record the 4 tens and the 1 hundred that we traded for.

$$\overset{2}{36} \\ \underline{\times\ 4} \\ 144$$

Use the base-ten blocks to show the multiplication of 6 × 43.

6 × 40   6 × 3

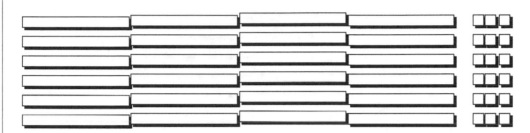

There are 18 ones. That's too many to write, so we make a trade.

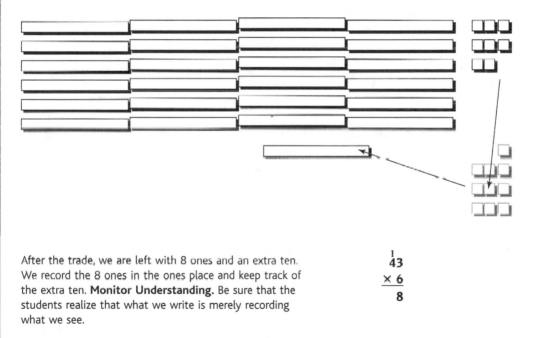

After the trade, we are left with 8 ones and an extra ten. We record the 8 ones in the ones place and keep track of the extra ten. **Monitor Understanding.** Be sure that the students realize that what we write is merely recording what we see.

$$\overset{1}{43} \\ \underline{\times\ 6} \\ 8$$

There are 6 × 4, or 24 tens, plus the extra ten that we traded for, so altogether we have 25 tens. That's too many to write, so we must make a trade.

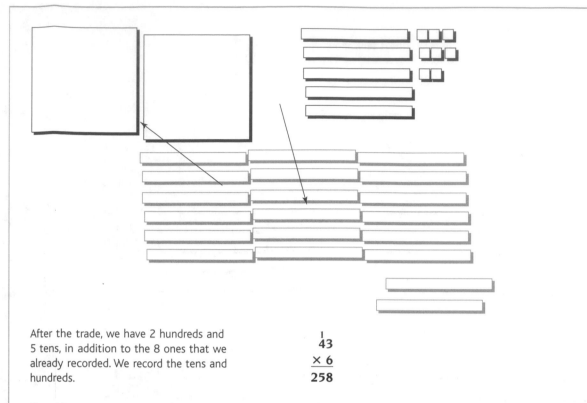

After the trade, we have 2 hundreds and 5 tens, in addition to the 8 ones that we already recorded. We record the tens and hundreds.

$$\begin{array}{r} 1 \\ 43 \\ \times\ 6 \\ \hline 258 \end{array}$$

Practice

Have children work with partners to complete practice examples 10, 13, and 17.

Closure

Ask the class what they learned today. Hand out papers with one multiplication example. Have the children take this example home and show a parent how to do it.

Teaching Division of Whole Numbers

Developmental Sequence for Teaching Division

The same developmental sequence used for addition, subtraction, and multiplication is used to teach whole-number division. As with the other operations, the first major instructional task is to establish the meaning of division.

Developing the Meaning of Division. There are several different ways that division can be approached. However, when division is introduced at the elementary school level, it is nearly always considered to be the separation of a quantity into equal-sized parts. Therefore, we want children to *associate division with separating a quantity into equal-sized parts.* The association should be so strong that when children see the symbols 12 ÷ 4, they visualize a group of twelve things being separated into equal groups. When the child sees a situation where a quantity is being separated into equal parts, the child will think "That's division!" After division has been mastered, the child will see problem settings where quantities are being separated into equal parts and will think "I can use division to solve this problem."

Measurement Division   There are two distinct kinds of division where a quantity is being separated into equal parts: measurement division and partition division. The easiest way to understand the difference between them is to consider an example of each. Suppose in a game where players use chips, there are 20 chips and all 20 must be used. If we know that each player must use four chips, how many players must there be in the game? To answer this question, we set aside four chips (that's enough for one player), then set aside four more chips (that's enough for another player), and continue this process until all the chips have been set aside. We then count the groups of four chips to see how many players there would be. Since there are five groups of four chips, there would be five players.

In this example, we know how many chips we are starting with and we know the size of the groups. We want to find out how many groups there are. The division we described is 20 ÷ 4 = 5.

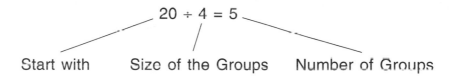

$$20 \div 4 = 5$$

Start with   Size of the Groups   Number of Groups

This is called measurement division. *In measurement division, we know the beginning number, we know the size of the groups, and we want to find the number of groups.*

Partition Division   Now let's consider the other type of division. Suppose this time, there is another game where the players use chips. In this game there are also 20 chips and every chip must be used. However, there are four players and every player must have the same number of chips. This time we know that there are four groups of chips (one group of chips for each player), but we don't know how many chips are in each group. To find out how many chips each player gets, we designate four players and give each of them a chip. Then we give each of them another chip, and continue this process until all the chips have been passed out. Finally, we count to see how many chips each of the four players has after all the chips have been passed out.

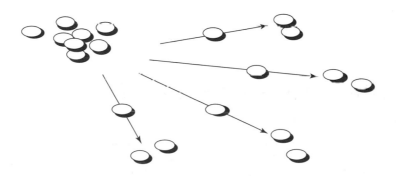

In this example, we know how many chips we are starting with and we know the number of groups. We want to find out how many chips are in each group. The division that we described is 20 ÷ 4 = 5.

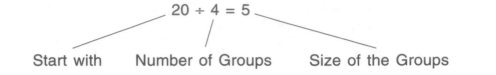

$$20 \div 4 = 5$$

Start with　　Number of Groups　　Size of the Groups

This kind of division is called partition division. *In partition division, we know how many we are starting with, we know the number of groups, and we want to find out how many are in each group* (Tucker, 1973; Moyer, 2000).

These two kinds of division seem to be the same, but actually they are different because we know different information: In measurement division we know the size of the groups; in partition division we know the number of groups. They are different because we want to find different things. In measurement division we want to find the number of groups, while in partition division we want to find the size of the groups. We use different procedures to get the answer. In measurement division we repeatedly remove (subtract) the same amount, while in partition division we distribute (pass out) the objects equally.

Since the students encounter both kinds of division situations, it is important that they be exposed to both as they are learning the meaning of the operation. The following activities illustrate how a teacher might lead students to understand the meaning of division. The activities provided here illustrate only partition division. Development of similar activities for measurement division is left as an exercise for the reader.

×÷٩ ACTIVITY 7.28　Equal Sharing

Place a transparency on the overhead projector. Put 24 raisins in one corner. Use a marker to draw four 3-inch circles on the transparency.

Explain that you have four children to whom you want to give the raisins, and that you want them all to have the same number. Tell the students that you want to put each child's raisins in one of the four circles.

Ask the students how to do it. Follow their directions exactly until there are the same number of raisins in each circle. If the students' directions do not lead to equal groups, let them figure out what to do. When the groups are all the same size, write the word "divide" on the chalkboard. Explain that when you separate a number of things into equal-sized groups, it is called division.

Repeat the activity, but this time, start with 36 raisins.

×÷٩ ACTIVITY 7.29　Equal Sharing—Write It

Follow the procedures of Activity 7.28, but for the first two examples, write the division sentence.

Write 24 ÷ 4 = 6, and explain that 24 is the number that you start with (24 raisins), 4 is the number of equal groups (there are 4 children), and 6 is the number in each group (each child gets 6 raisins). Also explain the division sign and demonstrate how to read the division sentence.

On the third example, have a student read the division sentence. For the rest of the examples, ask a student to tell you what the division sentence is, and have another student write the division sentence.

ACTIVITY 7.30   Acting Out Division

Write $12 \div 3 = 4$ on the chalkboard. Ask the children to help you figure out what the division sentence means. Point to the 12. Ask what that number tells us. [It's the number of objects that we start with.] Point to the division sign. Ask what it tells us. [It tells us to separate the 12 into equal groups.] Point to the 3. Ask what it tells us. [We have 3 equal groups.] Point to the = 4, and ask what it tells us. [It tells us the number in each group.] Identify 12 objects and do what the number sentence says.

Next, write $27 \div 3 =$. Explain that this time we don't have the entire division sentence. Ask what we know. [We know that we are to start with 27 objects and separate them into 3 equal groups.] Identify 27 objects and carry out the division to find how many are in each group. When finished, write the answer part of the division sentence.

Repeat this procedure with other examples: $15 \div 5$, $24 \div 6$, $35 \div 7$.

ACTIVITY 7.31   Fact Finders—Division

Prepare lists of four division facts without the answers. The lists should be different, but be sure that each fact that you include appears on two lists. Form groups of two or three students. Give each group a list and a set of objects. It is best if you are able to provide each group with objects that are different from the ones used by other groups. For example, one group may be given small stones, another group blocks, and another group pencils.

Have each group use their objects to figure out the answers to all their facts. When everyone is finished, talk about the answers. When each answer is given, ask if anyone else had that same problem. Did they get the same answer?

Teaching the Easy Basic Facts.   To reinforce the meaning of division, the children should encounter a wide variety of division examples using familiar objects. They should use appropriate terminology to describe verbally the division and use the division sign and equal sign to write the division sentence. In each example, they should figure out the answer for themselves, and the teacher should continually say how easy it is. Emphasize that they can find the answers by themselves.

Discovering Relationships Among the Easy Basic Division Facts   After the meaning of division has been established, and children can confidently find answers on their own, we focus on the easier basic division facts. For purposes of our discussion here, we consider division facts with divisors of 1 to 5 to be the easy ones. There are 50 of these easy basic division facts.

As these facts are discovered, organized, and reorganized, the students are led to discover as many relationships among them as possible. Many of these relationships, in effect, reduce the amount of memorization that is necessary. All of them contribute to improved retention of the facts that are memorized. It is always easier to remember things that are related to other things that are already known. Among the relationships that the teacher should be sure to emphasize are the following ones:

1. When 0 is divided by any number, the answer will always be 0. (There are 5 of these facts among the 50 facts that we are considering easy basic division facts. That's *five facts* but *only one thing to remember.*)

2. When any number is divided by 1, the answer will be the starting number. (In addition to $0 \div 1$, there are nine of these facts among the 50 easy basic division facts. That's *nine facts* but *only one thing to learn.*)

3. When any number is divided by itself, the answer will always be 1. (In addition to $1 \div 1$, there are four of these facts among the 50 easy basic division facts. That's *four facts* but *only one thing to learn.*)

4. There are several pairs of facts that are related:

$$6 \div 2 = 3 \text{ and } 6 \div 3 = 2 \qquad 8 \div 2 = 4 \text{ and } 8 \div 4 = 2$$

$$10 \div 2 = 5 \text{ and } 10 \div 5 = 2 \qquad 12 \div 4 = 3 \text{ and } 12 \div 3 = 4$$

$$15 \div 3 = 5 \text{ and } 15 \div 5 = 3 \qquad 20 \div 4 = 5 \text{ and } 20 \div 5 = 4$$

Each of these pairs has the same dividend, and the numbers that are the divisor and quotient in one fact of the pair are the quotient and divisor in the other fact of the pair. The two facts in a pair should be learned together. Then each pair of facts becomes one thing to learn. (That's *twelve facts* but *only six things to learn.*)

5. Every division fact is related to a multiplication fact. For example, consider these pairs of facts:

$$12 \div 2 = 6 \text{ and } 6 \times 2 = 12 \qquad 18 \div 3 = 6 \text{ and } 6 \times 3 = 18$$

$$21 \div 3 = 7 \text{ and } 7 \times 3 = 21 \qquad 24 \div 4 = 6 \text{ and } 6 \times 4 = 24$$

$$30 \div 5 = 6 \text{ and } 6 \times 5 = 30 \qquad 36 \div 4 = 9 \text{ and } 9 \times 4 = 36$$

Once this relationship is discovered, students can use it to find answers to division facts without counting objects. However, they are only able to do this if they already know the related multiplication facts.

Memorizing the Easy Basic Division Facts   When the students have become familiar with the helpful relationships among the easy basic division facts, we can expect them to make fairly rapid progress toward memorizing these facts. The instructional activities that are selected to lead the children to memorizing the easy basic division facts should have certain characteristics. These are the same characteristics presented earlier in this chapter for multiplication facts.

1. Children should be aware that they are to memorize the facts.
2. The activities should use an interesting and fun format.
3. Activities should have a high level of involvement.
4. Activities should focus on a small number of unmemorized facts at any given time.
5. Some already memorized facts should be mixed in with the target unmemorized facts. This will improve retention.
6. Children should be allowed enough time to figure out facts that they do not know.
7. To figure out answers, children should think about what they already know that helps them find this answer. What other facts or relationships do they already know that help?
8. Accuracy should be emphasized, not speed.

The following examples of memorization activities have these characteristics.

$\times \div \div$ ACTIVITY 7.32　One Is Important!

Write the following problems on the chalkboard.

$$4 \div 1 = \qquad 8 \div 1 = \qquad 3 \div 1 =$$

Have the children figure out the answers. Ask them what the pattern is. Once they are sure of the pattern, have them use it to find the answers to these examples.

$$7 \div 1 = \qquad 5 \div 1 = \qquad 6 \div 1 =$$

Erase the chalkboard and write these examples:

$$3 \div 3 = \qquad 9 \div 9 = \qquad 7 \div 7 =$$

Have the children figure out the answers. Ask them what the pattern is. Once they are sure of the pattern, have them use it to find the answers of these examples.

$$2 \div 2 = \qquad 8 \div 8 = \qquad 5 \div 5 =$$

Finally use flashcards showing a mixture of the two types of division illustrated above. Show a flashcard. Call on a child to answer. Ask the other students if the answer is correct. Ask how they know. What pattern are they using?

$\times \div \div$ ACTIVITY 7.33　Related Pairs

Write the following pairs of problems on the chalkboard.

$$15 \div 3 = \qquad 20 \div 5 = \qquad 6 \div 3 =$$
$$15 \div 5 = \qquad 20 \div 4 = \qquad 6 \div 2 =$$

Have the children figure out the answers. Ask them what the pattern is. Once they are sure of the pattern, write these facts on the board.

$$8 \div 2 = 4 \qquad 10 \div 5 = 2 \qquad 12 \div 3 = 4$$
$$15 \div 5 = 3 \qquad 6 \div 2 = 3 \qquad 20 \div 4 = 5$$

Use flashcards showing the facts $6 \div 3 =$, $8 \div 4=$, $10 \div 2 =$, $12 \div 4 =$, $15 \div 3 =$, and $20 \div 5 =$. Show a card. Call on a student. Ask which of the facts on the board can help us with this one.

$\times \div \div$ ACTIVITY 7.34　Line Up

Prepare large cards showing easy basic division facts without the answers. Distribute one card to each student. Separate the class into two groups. Have one group move to one side of the room, and have the other group move to the opposite side of the room.

Tell the students to line up with the others in their group so that the answers to their problems are in order from least to greatest. Allow them to talk to help one another. If they have difficulty, have them think about the helpful relationships.

When they are lined up, have them hold their cards so that the other group can check to see if they are in the correct order. If they think someone in the other group is not lined up correctly, they should tell that student what other fact(s) to think about to get the correct answer.

ACTIVITY 7.35   Problems and Answers

Prepare about 25 pairs of cards. In each pair, one card should show an easy basic division fact without the answer. The other card in the pair should show the answer to the fact.

Form a group of 2 or 3 students. Shuffle the cards and place the deck, face down, on the table. To start play, each player draws three cards. Players take turns playing. On each play, the player draws one card from the deck and then lays down any matching problem cards and answer cards that he has. Other players check each fact to be sure it is correct. If a fact is incorrect, the player must pick up the incorrectly matched cards.

Play continues until all the cards have been drawn from the deck. The player who has completed the most facts is the winner.

Developing Efficient Thinking Strategies for the Hard Basic Division Facts.   Before beginning work on the harder basic division facts, it is important that the students have learned to use an efficient thinking strategy to figure out answers. The most effective fact strategies have two characteristics: they are mental strategies, and they require the student to use facts that are already memorized to figure out the ones that are not memorized. We consider two of those strategies.

Partial Quotients   The partial quotients stragegy for hard basic division facts is similar to the partial products strategy that was used for hard basic multiplication facts. In this strategy, the student thinks about what easier division facts with the same divisor can help. For example, suppose the student needs to find 48 ÷ 6.

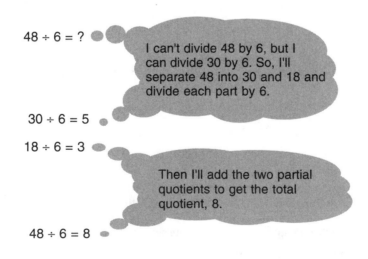

$48 \div 6 = ?$

I can't divide 48 by 6, but I can divide 30 by 6. So, I'll separate 48 into 30 and 18 and divide each part by 6.

$30 \div 6 = 5$

$18 \div 6 = 3$

Then I'll add the two partial quotients to get the total quotient, 8.

$48 \div 6 = 8$

If the student does not know the answer to 56 ÷ 8, he or she can break 56 into two easy parts and use partial quotients to find the answer.

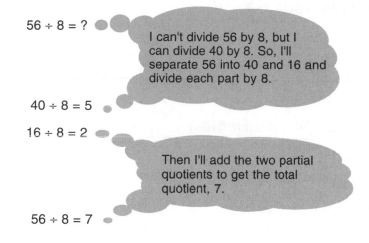

$56 \div 8 = ?$

I can't divide 56 by 8, but I can divide 40 by 8. So, I'll separate 56 into 40 and 16 and divide each part by 8.

$40 \div 8 = 5$

$16 \div 8 = 2$

Then I'll add the two partial quotients to get the total quotient, 7.

$56 \div 8 = 7$

In the same way, we can find the answer to $28 \div 7$. Separate 28 into $14 + 14$. Divide each part by 7 and add the partial quotients to get the total quotient, 4. Using this strategy lays the groundwork for the algorithm that is taught later. However, partial quotients are seldom used in textbooks for basic division facts.

Think of a Related Multiplication Fact   The strategy that is most commonly taught in elementary school mathematics textbooks comes from one of the relationships that exists among the basic facts. Most commonly, the thinking strategy taught for hard basic division facts is *think of a related multiplication fact*. For example, if we need to find the answer to $36 \div 9$, think "what number times 9 will equal 36."

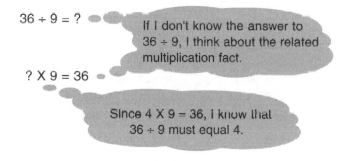

$36 \div 9 = ?$

If I don't know the answer to $36 \div 9$, I think about the related multiplication fact.

$? \times 9 = 36$

Since $4 \times 9 = 36$, I know that $36 \div 9$ must equal 4.

Similarly, if we do not know the answer to $72 \div 8$, we can think about the related multiplication fact: "What number times 8 equals 72?" Since $9 \times 8 = 72$, we know that $72 \div 8 = 9$. This strategy works well if the students are thoroughly familiar with the relationship between division facts and multiplication facts and if they have mastered the required multiplication facts before they try to use them to find answers to division facts.

A Remediation Note   Students who have difficulty using related multiplication facts to find answers to the hard basic division facts often have that difficulty because they have not yet mastered the hard basic multiplication facts. *We cannot use facts that we do not know.*

Teaching the Hard Basic Facts.   Once students have developed an efficient thinking strategy to quickly and accurately find answers to the hard basic division facts, it is relatively easy for them to achieve mastery of those facts. The teacher should *revisit the relationships* that were discovered when dealing with the easy division facts to assure that the students realize that they also apply to the hard division facts. And, the students should *work toward memorization* of those facts.

Developing the Division Algorithm.   After the basic division facts have been mastered, it is possible to develop the division algorithm very quickly. Rapid success depends however, on the application of the same principles that were presented for each of the other operations.

> *Let them see what it looks like.* Carefully model the operation with an appropriate physical or pictorial model. We should use a model that lets the students see what happens to the basic units—ones, tens, hundreds, and so on—when we divide.
> *De-emphasize rote rules.* We may end up with rules, but they should be meaningful. They should arise out of the modeling process.
> *Emphasize big ideas.* These are the important generalizations that describe the procedures. They also come from the modeling process.
> *Let the written algorithm simply be a recording* of what happens when the algorithm is modeled. Everything we write should match something we do.
> *Watch our language.* The language that we use should describe what we see when the operation is modeled, not language that describes what we write down.

Although the division algorithm can be developed using measurement division, there are many points at which difficulties arise (Tucker, 1973). Consequently, in recent years, textbook writers have used, almost without exception, partition division to develop the algorithm. We also use partition division in our development. We proceed by describing how a physical model can be used to clarify and give meaning to the algorithm. We then see how the entire algorithm is based on the application of two big ideas.

Consider the example, 48 ÷ 4. We want to divide 48 into 4 equal parts. To do this, we begin by using bundled sticks to represent 48.

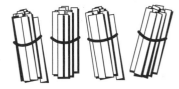

Next, we write the division problem on the chalkboard.

$$4\overline{)48}$$

We want to separate 48 into four equal parts, so we designate four places to put those four equal parts. We begin by distributing the tens.

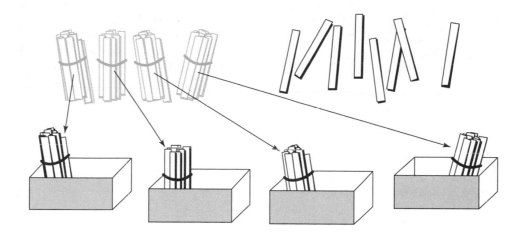

We record that one ten is placed in each of the equal parts.

$$\begin{array}{r} 1 \\ 4\overline{)48} \end{array}$$

And, we record that 4 tens are taken away from the original number. After the subtraction, we see that we still have 8 ones to distribute.

$$\begin{array}{r} 1 \\ 4\overline{)48} \\ -4 \\ \hline 8 \end{array}$$

Next, we distribute the ones. We are able to place 2 ones in each of the equal parts.

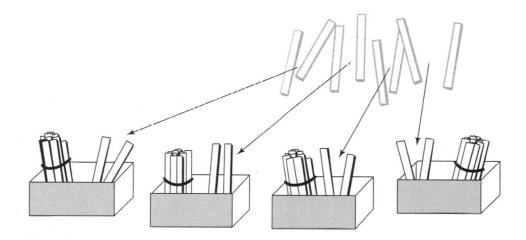

Finally we record the 2 ones that we placed in each of the equal groups, record that we took 8 ones away from what was left of the beginning number, and record that nothing is left of the original number to be distributed. We were able to place one ten and two ones (12) in each of the four equal parts.

$$\begin{array}{r} 12 \\ 4\overline{)48} \\ -4 \\ \hline 8 \\ -8 \\ \hline 0 \end{array}$$

One key to successfully teaching the division algorithm or any of the algorithms is to get the students to understand that the written algorithm is nothing more than an orderly recording of what is being done with the model. To accomplish this, the process must be modeled one step at a time, and each step should be recorded immediately after it is completed. We look at one more example, 639 ÷ 3. This time we use base-ten blocks to model the process. We begin by writing the problem and representing the beginning number with the model.

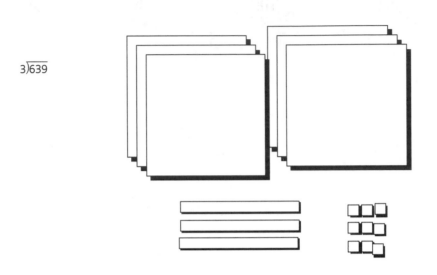

Then we designate three locations where we place the three equal parts.

We distribute the hundreds first. We have 6 hundreds, so we can place 2 hundreds in each of the three equal parts.

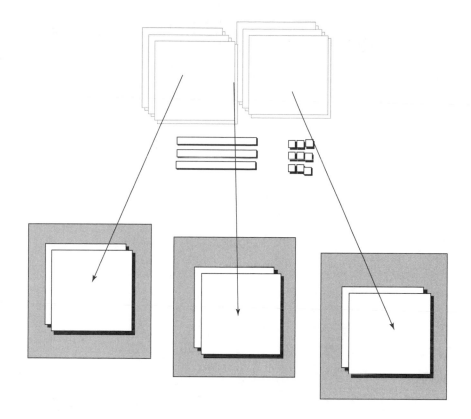

We took 6 hundreds away from our beginning number. We record that and see that after the subtraction, we still have 3 tens and 9 ones to distribute.

$$\begin{array}{r} 2 \\ 3\overline{)639} \\ -\ 600 \\ \hline 39 \end{array}$$

Next, we distribute the tens. We have 3 tens to distribute, so we are able to place 1 ten in each of the three equal parts.

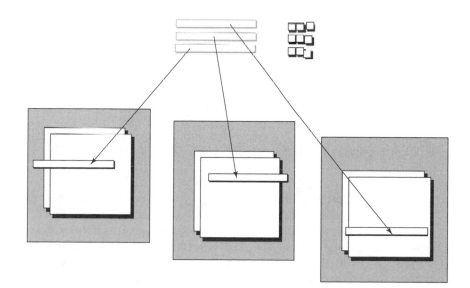

We took 3 tens away from what was left of the beginning number. We record that and find that there are still 9 ones to be distributed.

$$\begin{array}{r} 21 \\ 3\overline{)639} \\ -6 \\ \hline 39 \\ -3 \\ \hline 9 \end{array}$$

Finally, we distribute the 9 ones. We are able to place 3 ones in each of the three equal parts.

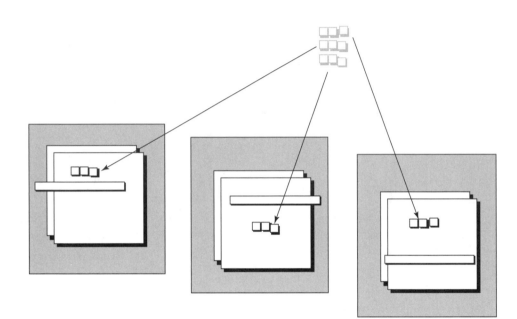

We record the 3 ones that we placed in each of the equal parts. In this step, we distributed 9 ones. These were taken away from what was left of the beginning number, so we record this subtraction. We have nothing left to distribute.

$$\begin{array}{r} 213 \\ 3\overline{)639} \\ -6 \\ \hline 39 \\ -3 \\ \hline 9 \\ -9 \\ \hline 0 \end{array}$$

We are able to place 2 hundreds, 1 ten, and 3 ones in each of the three equal parts. The answer to the division problem is 213.

Divide One Unit at a Time   In these two examples, we see the first of the two big ideas that are the basis of the division algorithm, *divide one unit at a time*. What we are really doing is using *partial quotients* in the same way that they were suggested for simplifying hard basic division facts. The second big idea for the division algorithm also arises out of the modeling of division examples. This time, we begin with $92 \div 4$. First, we write the division problem and represent 92 (the number that we start with) using base-ten blocks.

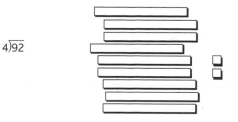

$4\overline{)92}$

We designate four locations where we place the four equal parts.

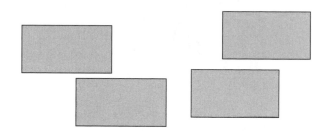

We begin the division process by distributing the tens. Since there are 9 tens, we have enough to place 2 tens in each of the four equal parts. Notice that there is one ten left over.

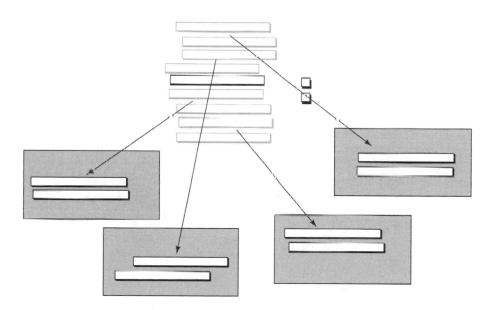

We place 2 tens in each of the 4 equal parts. We took 8 tens away from the starting number. We are left with 1 ten and 2 ones.

$$
\begin{array}{r}
2 \\
4\overline{)92} \\
-8 \\
\hline
12 \\
\end{array}
$$

Now we are faced with a problem that we have not seen before. What do we do with the ten that we were unable to distribute? Whenever we have "leftovers," we trade them for smaller units. So, in this case, we trade the leftover ten for 10 ones.

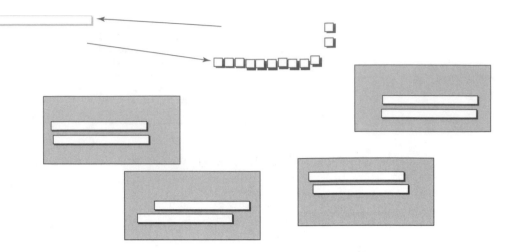

Before the trade, we had 1 ten and 2 ones. After the trade we have 12 ones.

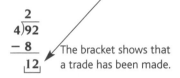

$$\begin{array}{r} 2 \\ 4\overline{)92} \\ -8 \\ \underline{\lfloor 12 \rfloor} \end{array}$$

The bracket shows that a trade has been made.

These 12 ones need to be distributed to the four equal parts. We can place 3 ones in each of the 4 equal parts.

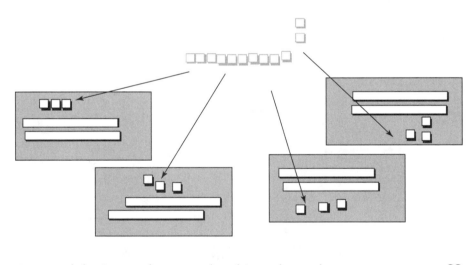

We record the 3 ones that were placed in each equal part. In this step, we took 12 ones from what was left of the beginning number. We record this subtraction and see that there is nothing left to be distributed.

$$\begin{array}{r} 23 \\ 4\overline{)92} \\ -8 \\ \underline{\lfloor 12 \rfloor} \\ -12 \\ \hline 0 \end{array}$$

The answer to the division problem is 23.

Trade Remainders for Smaller Units We examine another example, one where it is necessary to *trade remainders for smaller units*. To find the answer to 625 ÷ 5, we write the problem and represent the beginning number, 625, with base-ten blocks. We begin by distributing 1 hundred to each of 5 equal parts.

$5\overline{)625}$

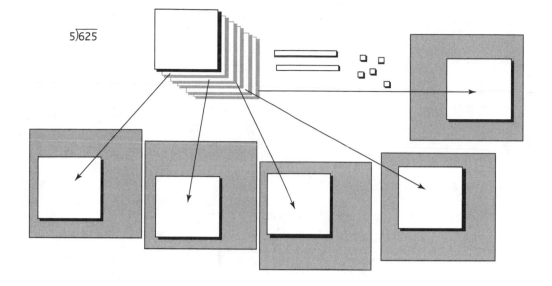

In this step we took 5 hundreds away from our beginning number. After we record this subtraction, we have 1 hundred, 2 tens, and 5 ones that still need to be distributed.

$$\begin{array}{r} 1 \\ 5\overline{)625} \\ -\ 5 \\ \hline 125 \end{array}$$

The remaining hundred can be traded for 10 tens. We now have 12 tens.

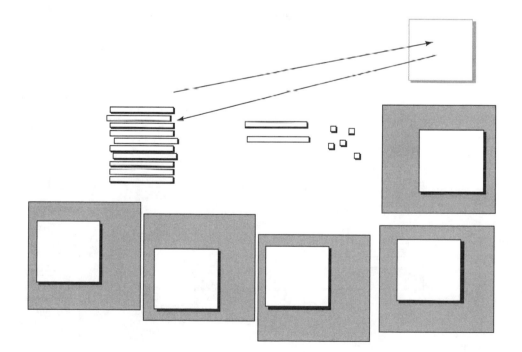

Now, we can place 2 tens in each of the 5 equal parts.

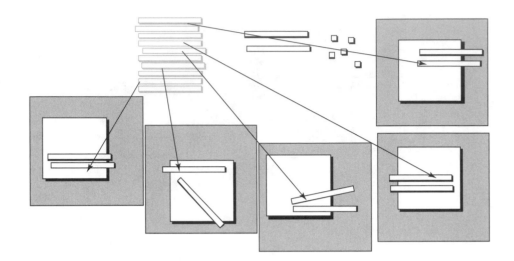

We record the 2 tens that we placed in each of the equal parts. To do this, we take 10 tens away from what is left of our starting number. We record this subtraction and we have 2 tens and 5 ones left to distribute.

$$
\begin{array}{r}
12 \\
5\overline{)625} \\
-\ 5 \\
\hline
12\!\!\downarrow5 \\
-\ 10 \\
\hline
25
\end{array}
$$

We then trade the remaining 2 tens for 20 ones. Now we have 25 ones to distribute.

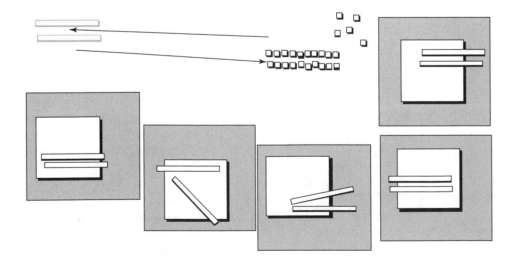

We place 5 ones in each of the 5 equal parts.

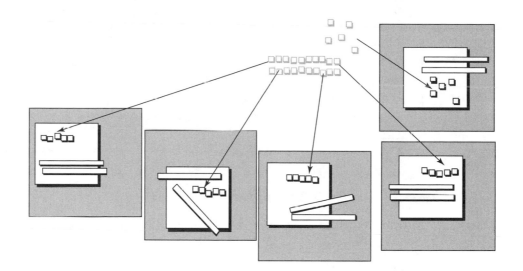

Finally, we complete the recording of the process. We record 5 in the ones place, and since we took 25 ones away from what was left of the beginning number, we record this subtraction. We see that there is nothing left to distribute. 625 ÷ 5 = 125.

$$
\begin{array}{r}
125 \\
5\overline{)625} \\
-\ 5 \\
\hline
125 \\
-\ 10 \\
\hline
25 \\
-\ 25 \\
\hline
0
\end{array}
$$

Both big ideas for the division algorithm arise out of experiences as we model division examples: *divide one unit at a time*, and *trade remainders for smaller units*. Regardless of what the numbers are, that's all there is to the division algorithm.

Notice that all the examples examined above had one-digit divisors. If we want students to be able to use pencil-and-paper computation to divide by large divisors, a great deal of time must be spent teaching them to estimate partial quotients. However, we should seriously question the practice of using pencil-and-paper computation for these examples. With the availability of calculators, we do not need to teach today's students to do complex, pencil-and-paper division computation. The time can be better spent on literally hundreds of other things—things that will be far more useful to the students.

In the spirit of the NCTM *Standards*, it is more important for students to understand how the algorithm works than for them to become proficient with long division involving multi-digit divisors. It is more important that they can use the principles that are the basis of the algorithm to make quick and accurate estimates. It is also more important that they become able to intelligently decide whether it is appropriate to estimate the answer, use a calculator to get the exact answer, or use pencil-and-paper computation.

The following activities illustrate how a teacher might introduce the first big idea, divide one unit at a time. Notice that the early examples involve common objects.

✕ ÷ ⊣ ACTIVITY 7.36   Rocks and Blocks

Bring about 20 small rocks to class. Place 18 rocks into a box with 12 wooden blocks. Write "18 rocks and 12 blocks" on the chalkboard. Have six students come to the front of the room. Tell the class that you want to share the rocks and blocks equally among these six people, but that you want the class to tell how to do the sharing so it will be equal.

Call on other students to give directions. Do exactly as you are told, but keep asking, "Is that right?" "Now What do I need to do?" "Are we done yet?"

When the sharing is complete, repeat the process by sharing 20 rocks and 15 blocks among five students.

✕ ÷ ⊣ ACTIVITY 7.37   Buttons and Bows

Follow the procedures of Activity 7.36, except use buttons and bows instead of rocks and blocks.

✕ ÷ ⊣ ACTIVITY 7.38   Nuts, Bolts, and Screws

Follow the procedures of Activity 7.36, except use groups of three different kinds of objects: nuts, bolts, and screws.

✕ ÷ ⊣ ACTIVITY 7.39   Pennies and Dimes

Share nine dimes and six pennies among three people.

Record the results as a division example. Point out how you can share the tens (the dimes) first and then share the ones (the pennies).

The following activities illustrate how a teacher might introduce the second big idea, *trade remainders for smaller units*. Once again the early examples involve common objects.

✕ ÷ ⊣ ACTIVITY 7.40   Eggs and More Eggs

Bring several egg cartons to class. Fill the egg cartons by placing a block in each space. Place seven full cartons and six blocks on a table. Explain that the blocks represent eggs. Write 7 cartons and 6 eggs on the chalkboard. Tell the students that you want to divide the eggs into 3 equal groups.

Start with the cartons. Ask how many eggs are in each carton. [12] Ask how many cartons should be placed in each of the 3 groups. [2] Do that. Then, ask what to do with the extra carton of eggs. [Take them out of the carton.] Ask how many eggs still need to be divided. [12 + 6 = 18] Ask how many eggs go into each of the 3 groups. [6 eggs.]

Write the final result on the board. Each group has two cartons and six eggs.

ACTIVITY 7.41 Sharing Beads

Prepare about 12 strings of beads. Place seven beads on each string.

Place the 12 strings of beads on the table with one extra bead. Point out to the students that each string has seven beads on it. Explain that you want to divide the beads into five groups with the same number of beads in each group.

Divide the strings of beads first. Cut the two strings that were left over and take the beads off the strings. Divide the resulting 15 beads.

ACTIVITY 7.42 More Pennies and Dimes

Share nine dimes and six pennies among four people.

Record the results as a division example. Point out how you can share the dimes first, trade the leftover dime for 10 pennies, and then share the 16 pennies.

The following activities illustrate how a teacher can encourage students to use the principles of the division algorithm to estimate division answers.

ACTIVITY 7.43 Best Guess

Write 12)384 on the chalkboard. Tell the class that you want everyone to guess what the answer is and to write it on sheet of paper.

When everyone has written a guess, start to work through the example.

Ask how many hundreds are in each part. [There are 12 parts but only 3 hundreds. We cannot put any hundreds in each part.] Ask what to do with the 3 hundreds. [Trade them for 30 tens. We now have 38 tens.]

Ask how many tens can be placed in each part. [3 tens can be placed in each part.] Ask if anyone's guess had 3 tens.

Continue until the example is finished. Decide whose guess was closest to the answer. Repeat the process with other examples.

ACTIVITY 7.44 Guesstimation

Prepare cards with division examples on them. Some should have one-digit divisors and some should have two-digit divisors. Form a group of 2 or 3 students. Shuffle the cards and place the deck face down on the table.

On each play, one card is turned over and the students estimate the answer and write down the estimate. Then they should use a calculator to find the answer. The student with the best estimate gets a point. If there is a tie, all who tied get a point. After each play, the one(s) with the best estimate must explain how the estimate was figured out.

When all the cards have been played, the one with the most points wins.

Adapting a Division Lesson

Now we adapt a fourth-grade lesson on division. As we have done before, we begin with a traditional plan that follows the kind of suggestions that would be found in a teacher's guide of a published textbook program. Note that this plan is a good one. As with previous textbook lessons that we examined, the focus is to teach the textbook page, the developmental part of the lesson consists of a detailed explanation of a single example, and the lesson consists mainly of practice.

LESSON OBJECTIVE

The student will record the steps in division computation.

Lesson Opener

Have students find each of the following quotients:

$$30 \div 3 \qquad 60 \div 3 \qquad 80 \div 4 \qquad 40 \div 2$$

Have students separate 26 pennies into 3 equal parts. How much is in each part? How much is left over?

Development

Direct the attention of the class to the example on the first page of the lesson. 42 cents (4 dimes and 2 pennies) is being separated into 3 equal parts. Refer to the pictures on the page. The dimes are separated first. One dime is placed in each part and one dime remains. Point out the written steps that are shown on the page.

The next picture shows 10 pennies in place of the dime. Altogether, there are 12 pennies to be divided. 4 pennies are placed in each part. Point out the written steps that are shown on the page.

Ask if the students understand that the written division is just the recording of the steps.

Monitor Learning

Have the students do the *Check Understanding* examples.

Practice

Have students complete the practice exercises on the second page of the lesson. Students who had difficulty with the *Check Understanding* examples can be assigned the reteaching worksheet instead of the practice exercises.

Closure

Ask students what they learned about recording division.

Next we adapt this lesson to make it more effective in meeting the learning needs in a diverse classroom. We increase the amount of developmental instruction, visual input, kinesthetic activity, and student communication, and we make monitoring of learning a more integral part of the lesson. These adaptations make the lesson appropriate for almost all students. But, remember that some students with severe needs might require further instructional adaptations.

LESSON OBJECTIVE

The student will record the steps in division computation.

Lesson Opener

Make enough copies of the following division examples so that there will be enough for all the students.

30 ÷ 3	40 ÷ 2	40 ÷ 4	50 ÷ 5
60 ÷ 2	60 ÷ 3	60 ÷ 6	80 ÷ 2
80 ÷ 4	80 ÷ 8	90 ÷ 3	90 ÷ 9

Place the numbers 10, 20, 30, and 40 at different locations on the wall. Tell the students that the numbers on the wall are the answers. Have the students go stand by the answers to their problems. **Monitor Understanding.** Watch the students during this activity to be sure that they understand. Provide help as it is needed.
Explain that today the class will divide two-digit numbers and will learn how to record the steps.

Development

Show the students seven strings of beads with six beads on each string and nine beads not on strings. Ask the students to tell you how to separate the beads into three equal groups. Record the steps using a chart like this one. Begin by placing two strings of beads in each part. Record the two strings that were placed in each part and subtract the six strings that were distributed.

STRINGS	BEADS	
2		In each group
7	9	Starting amount
6		
1	9	

Ask what to do with the leftover string of beads. [Take them off the string.] Record this result. **Monitor Understanding.** On each step, watch for students who do not understand. Provide extra explanation as needed.

STRINGS	BEADS	
2		In each group
7	9	Starting amount
-6		
X̶	Ø̶	
	15	

Distribute the 15 beads. Record the number placed in each group, and subtract the number that was used.

STRINGS	BEADS	
2	5	In each group
7	9	Starting amount
-6		
X̶	Ø̶	
	15	
	-15	
	0	

Using blocks to represent eggs, show the students five cartons of eggs and eight eggs not in cartons. Tell them that you want to separate the eggs into four equal groups. Follow the steps outlined for the previous example and record the steps on a chart like this one.

CARTONS	EGGS
5	8

In each group
Starting amount

Monitor Understanding. On each step, watch for students who do not understand. Provide extra explanation as needed. For example, you might need to remind some students that there are 12 eggs in each carton.

Show the students 75 cents (seven dimes and five pennies). Tell them that you want to separate the money into five equal parts. Follow the same procedures that were used in the previous two examples.

DIMES	PENNIES	
		In each group
7	5	Starting amount

Record the steps on a chart like this one.

Monitor Understanding. Continue watching for students who do not understand. Provide help as needed.

Tell the students that you are now going to do this example again, but that you will record the steps a little bit differently. Point out that since each dime is equal to 10 pennies, we can think of the dimes and pennies as tens and ones. Write the division and record the steps using standard division notation.

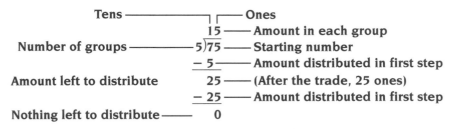

Monitor Understanding. Be sure that students understand that everything we write is a recording of something that we do.

Direct the attention of the class to the example on the first page of the lesson. 42 cents (four dimes and two pennies) is being separated into three equal parts. Refer to the pictures on the page. The dimes are separated first. One dime is placed in each part and one dime remains. Point out the written steps that are shown on the page.

The next picture shows 10 pennies in place of the dime. Now, there are 12 pennies to be divided. Four pennies are placed in each part. Point out the written steps that are shown. **Monitor Understanding.** Ask if the students understand that the written division is just the recording of the steps.

Form groups of four students. Give each group eight dimes and 16 pennies. Write the example 7)84 on the chalkboard and have each group use the dimes and pennies to find the answer to the division example. Have them record each step the way you have been doing it. **Monitor Understanding.** Move around to observe the work in the groups. If a group is having difficulty, ask leading questions to help them. Emphasize the recording of the steps.

Practice

When all the groups have finished, have the students do the *Check Understanding* examples for practice. **Monitor Understanding.** Move around the room, checking the students' work. Catch the errors and misconceptions and get them corrected. If some students need reteaching, form a group and reteach the concepts and skills.

Closure

Pick one more example and ask for volunteers to come to the front to find the answer. Have a student separate the dimes and pennies. Have the other student record the steps.

Follow Up

Assign one example for homework. Tell the students that they are to explain to a parent how to do the division and record the steps.

Using Multiplication and Division to Solve Problems

The beginning of the ability to solve problems involving multiplication and division is found in the way that the meanings of those operations are developed. If the essence of the problem is that several equal-sized quantities are being combined, the student can look at the situation and tell that multiplication can be used to find the answer. If the essence of the problem situation is that a quantity is being separated into equal parts, the student can look at the situation and tell that division can be used to find the answer. Students should be led to analyze the problem situation, decide what "physical action" is taking place, and relate that physical action to the appropriate arithmetic problem.

All of the remarks in Chapter 6 about teaching students to solve problems using addition and subtraction also apply when teaching students how to use multiplication and division to solve problems. The students should experience *problems that they care about* and that involve *familiar objects*. The students should experience *mixed examples and nonexamples* where they must decide when they can and cannot use each of the operations. And, finally, when solving word problems, the students should be led to focus, not on key words, but on what is happening in the problem situation.

Exercises and Activities

1. Compare the two multiplication lesson plans on pages 167–172 of this chapter.
   a. Identify where the adapted plan provides more developmental work.
   b. Identify where the adapted plan provides more kinesthetic activity.
   c. Identify where the adapted plan provides more opportunity for communication from the children.
   d. Identify where the adapted plan provides more opportunity for communication among the children.

2. Suppose you were about to teach the lesson presented on pages 168–172 of this chapter, but you have a child with a severe visual impairment in the class. What additional adaptations would you make so that the lesson would be appropriate for that child?

3. Adapt Activities 7.28–7.31 so that measurement division is being developed and used.

4. Develop an instructional activity that uses a physical model to help children understand relationship 4 on pages 174–175.

5. Develop an instructional activity that uses a physical model to help children understand relationship 5 on page 176.

6. Following the steps described on pages 184–186, develop an instructional activity that has children use $1, $10, and $100 bills to divide 852 by 3.

7. Revise Activity 7.28 to make it more kinesthetic.

8. Develop a kinesthetic practice activity for multiplication of two-digit numbers by one-digit numbers.

9. Develop a kinesthetic practice activity for division of two-digit numbers by one-digit numbers.

10. All of the generalizations that are referred to in this text as big ideas are direct results of the properties of operations in the set of real numbers. What properties give us the big idea of partial products?

11. Describe activities similar to Activities 7.28, 7.29, and 7.30 to develop the concept of measurement division.

12. Develop an activity similar to Activity 7.33 which will encourage students to think about related multiplication facts to find answers to division facts.

13. All of the generalizations that are referred to in this text as big ideas are direct results of the properties of operations in the set of real numbers. Division distributes over addition from the right. Explain how the big idea "divide one unit at a time" results from this property.

14. Read Tucker's 1973 article, "The Division Algorithm," in The *Arithmetic Teacher*, *Volume* 20, Issue 8. Can you identify the two types of division (partition division and measurement division) in the article?

15. Choose a lesson on either multiplication or division of whole numbers from a published elementary school mathematics textbook series.
    a. Write a lesson plan that follows the teaching suggestions in the teacher's guide.
    b. Identify the parts of the lesson that provide visual information about the concept(s) or skill(s) being taught.
    c. Expand the lesson by adding activities that provide more visual information about the concepts or skills being taught.

16. Choose a lesson on either multiplication or division of whole numbers from a published elementary school mathematics textbook series.
    a. Write a lesson plan that follows the teaching suggestions in the teacher's guide.
    b. Identify all kinesthetic activity that is included in the lesson.
    c. Add more kinesthetic activity to the lesson.

17. Choose a lesson on either multiplication or division of whole numbers from a published elementary school mathematics textbook series.
    a. Write a lesson plan that follows the teaching suggestions in the teacher's guide.
    b. Identify parts of the lesson that include student communication about the concept(s) or skill(s) taught in the lesson.
    c. Add more opportunities for communication from or among students to the lesson.

18. Choose a lesson on either multiplication or division of whole numbers from a published elementary school mathematics textbook series.
    a. Write a lesson plan that follows the teaching suggestions in the teacher's guide.
    b. Identify the parts of the lesson designed to assess students' learning.
    c. Add more continual assessment (monitoring of learning) to the lesson plan.

19. Study the adapted lesson plan on pages 168–172. Explain how this lesson accommodates the needs of a child who has difficulty remembering how to complete multi-step tasks.

20. Study the adapted lesson plan on pages 193–194. Make further changes in the lesson plan to make it more appropriate for a child with limited upper-arm mobility.

21. Study the adapted lesson plan on pages 168–172. Make further changes in the lesson plan to make it more appropriate for a child who has a limited visual field.

22. Read the article, "Using Modeling, Manipulatives, and Mnemonics with Eighth-Grade Students," by David H. Allsopp, which is in the November/December, 1999 issue of *Teaching Exceptional Children*.
    a. How do the teaching suggestions made in the article agree or disagree with those included in this text?
    b. Where the teaching suggestions made in the article disagree with those included in this text, which approach do you prefer? Explain why.

23. Read the discussion related to "Standard 7: Concepts of Whole Number Operations," which is found on pages 41–43 of *Curriculum and Evaluation Standards*

for *School Mathematics*, published by the National Council of Teachers of Mathematics. Relate the teaching suggestions in this chapter to Standard 7.

24. The following multiplication results illustrate an error pattern like those that were related by Robert Ashlock, in his book, *Error Patterns in Computation: A Semi-programmed Approach.*

$$
\begin{array}{cccc}
\overset{1}{14} & \overset{3}{34} & \overset{5}{47} & \overset{4}{68} \\
\times\,4 & \times\,9 & \times\,8 & \times\,5 \\
\hline
86 & 546 & 726 & 500
\end{array}
$$

   a. What is this student's error pattern? What is the student doing to produce the incorrect answers?

   b. Plan a mini-lesson to correct this student's error pattern.

25. The following division results illustrate an error pattern like those that were related by Robert Ashlock, in his book, *Error Patterns in Computation: A Semi-programmed Approach.*

$$
\begin{array}{cccc}
33 & 24 & 69 & 37 \\
2\overline{)66} & 4\overline{)168} & 3\overline{)288} & 5\overline{)365} \\
60 & 160 & 270 & 350 \\
\hline
6 & 8 & 18 & 15 \\
\underline{6} & \underline{8} & \underline{18} & \underline{15}
\end{array}
$$

   a. What is this student's error pattern? What is the student doing to produce the incorrect answers?

   b. Plan a mini-lesson to correct this student's error pattern.

References and Related Readings

Allsopp, D. H. (1999). Using modeling, manipulatives, and mnemonics with eighth-grade children. *Teaching Exceptional Children, 32,* 74–81.

Ashlock, R. B. (1998). *Error patterns in computation: A semi-programmed approach* (7th ed.) Upper Saddle River, NJ: Merrill/Prentice Hall.

Moyer, P. (2000). A remainder of one: Exploring partitive division. *Teaching Children Mathematics, 6,* 517–521.

National Council of Teachers of Mathematics. (1989). *Curriculum and evaluation standards for school mathematics.* Reston, VA: NCTM.

National Council of Teachers of Mathematics. (2000). *Principles and standards for school mathematics.* Reston, VA: NCTM.

Tucker, B. F. (1973). The division algorithm. *The Arithmetic Teacher, 20,* 639–646.

Web Sites

http://www.proteacher.com/100009.shtml
(Lesson plans on multiplication and division by teachers.)

http://www.forum.swarthmore.edu/
(Math Forum Links to Math Discussions and ideas.)

http://www.sasked.gov.sk.ca/docs/elemath/numop.html
(A scope and sequence chart for numbers and operations.)

CHAPTER 8

FRACTIONS:

Working with Units Smaller Than One

THE TEACHING PRINCIPLE

"Because students learn by connecting new ideas to prior knowledge, teachers must understand what their students already know" (p. 18).

THE NUMBER AND OPERATIONS STANDARD

"Through the study of various meanings and models of fractions—how fractions are related to each other and to the unit whole and how they are represented—students can gain facility in comparing fractions" (p. 149).

THE REASONING AND PROOF STANDARD

"In grades 3–5, students can investigate properties such as commutativity, associativity, and distributivity of multiplication over addition" (p. 192).

THE PROBLEM-SOLVING STANDARD

"Teachers should look for opportunities for students to revise, expand, and update generalizations they have made..." (p. 187).

THE COMMUNICATION STANDARD

"Well-posed questions can simultaneously elicit, extend, and challenge students' thinking and at the same time give the teacher an opportunity to assess the students' understanding" (p. 197).

The National Council of Teachers of Mathematics. (2000). *Principles and Standards for School Mathematics* (pp. 18, 149, 187, 192, 197). Reston, VA: NCTM.

Defining Fractions

There are three ways that a fraction can be interpreted. In other words, there are three distinct meanings for each fraction. For example, $\frac{2}{3}$ can be interpreted as two divided by three.

Suppose we start with 2.

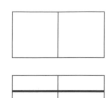

Now, we divide 2 by 3. That is, we divide 2 into 3 equal parts.

One of these 3 equal parts (the shaded part) is $\frac{2}{3}$. It is 2 divided by 3.

The fraction $\frac{2}{3}$ can be interpreted as a ratio, which is a kind of comparison. Suppose we want to compare 2 and 3. The ratio is 2 to 3, which can be written as $\frac{2}{3}$. We can say that 2 is $\frac{2}{3}$ as big as 3.

The fraction $\frac{2}{3}$ can also be interpreted as 2 of 3 equal parts. If we have a quantity that is equal to 1 and divide that quantity into 3 equal parts, then 2 of those 3 equal parts would be written as $\frac{2}{3}$.

The shaded part is equal to $\frac{2}{3}$.

This last interpretation is typically used when children are first learning about fractions.

Three Sides of Fractions

Children should be able to achieve three goals with numbers (Thornton, et al., 1983). First, they should be able to identify the quantity that is named by the number. They should be able to show how much it is. Second, they should be able to name the number and be able to say it. Third, they should be able to write the number clearly using standard notation that communicates the number unambiguously. Indeed, these goals imply that there are six tasks that the child should be able to complete. This is just as true when the numbers are fractions as when they are whole numbers.

1. If the child is shown some fractional quantity, he or she should be able to say the number (the fraction) that names that quantity.
2. If the child is shown some fractional quantity, he or she should be able to write the number (the fraction) that names that quantity.
3. If the child is shown a numeral (a fraction), he or she should be able to show that fractional quantity.
4. If the child is shown a numeral (a fraction), he or she should be able to say the number (the fraction).
5. If the child hears a number (a fraction) spoken, he or she should be able to show that fractional quantity.
6. If the child hears a number (a fraction) spoken, he or she should be able to write the number (the fraction).

Since we want children to be able to perform these tasks with fractions, our instruction must be designed so that these abilities are explicitly taught.

Fractional Units

Fractions are introduced to children very early (kindergarten or first grade). Although this early encounter with fractions is normally limited, it lays important groundwork for a later, more formal treatment of the topic. Usually, at this beginning level, children are only introduced to $\frac{1}{2}$ and $\frac{1}{3}$. The three big emphases at this level are that one of something is separated into *equal parts*, the number on the bottom (*the denominator*) *tells how many parts*, and the number on top (*the numerator*) indicates that we are considering *one of those equal parts*.

The equal parts are the *fractional units*. If the fraction is $\frac{1}{3}$, then the fractional unit is thirds. Since the numerator is 1, we are considering one of those fractional units (one third). Fractions with a numerator of 1 are called unit fractions because they name one fractional unit. $\frac{1}{2}$ is also a unit fraction, but the fractional unit is halves. When learning $\frac{1}{2}$, the children need to see many examples where objects are separated into two equal parts. The objects must be cut exactly in half. The children should see many nonexamples where objects are cut into more than two equal parts and other nonexamples where objects are cut into unequal parts. When learning $\frac{1}{3}$, the children need to see many examples where objects are cut into three equal parts. The objects must be cut into exact thirds. The children should see many nonexamples where objects are cut into more than or less than three equal parts and other nonexamples where objects are cut into unequal parts.

The children should learn to identify the fractions, to say the fraction names, and write the fractions. The following activities illustrate the way that the fraction $\frac{1}{2}$ can be taught. It is left as an exercise for the reader to develop similar activities for teaching other fractions.

ACTIVITY 8.01   Fair Sharing

Bring two apples and a knife to class. You also need three sheets of paper, three 1-foot lengths of yarn, and a pair of scissors.

Hold up one of the apples, and tell the class that you want to cut the apple into two parts. Cut the apple into two parts that are unequal. Have two children come to the front of the class. Give each child one of the two parts of the apple. Have them hold their pieces so the class can see. Ask if they both got a fair share. [No.] Ask why not. [One got more. One didn't get as much. The two parts were not equal. They weren't the same size.] Hold up the second apple. Ask what to do so that both children will get a fair share. [Cut into two equal parts.]

Cut the second apple into two equal parts and give each child one part. Ask if they both got a fair share. [Yes.] Write the fraction $\frac{1}{2}$ on the chalkboard. Tell the class that this is a fraction. It is one half. Point out the top number and the bottom number. Tell the class that the 2 tells us that there are two equal parts. Show the two equal apple parts. Hold up one of these parts and tell the class that this is one half of the apple. Hold up the other part and tell the class that this is also one half of the apple.

Show the class the two unequal apple parts. Ask if they are the same size. [No.] Hold up one of the unequal parts and tell the class that since the parts are not equal, this is not one half of the apple.

Repeat the activity using the three lengths of yarn. Cut one length of yarn into two equal parts to illustrate one half. Cut the second length of yarn into two unequal parts to illustrate a non-example of one half. Cut the third length of yarn into three equal parts to illustrate another nonexample of one half. For each nonexample, ask why it is not one half.

Repeat the activity again using the three sheets of paper.

✕ ✦ ⊣ ACTIVITY 8.02   Putting Halves Together

Prepare a number of shapes. Cut each shape into two equal parts. Be sure that you make enough shapes so that there will be enough for all the children.

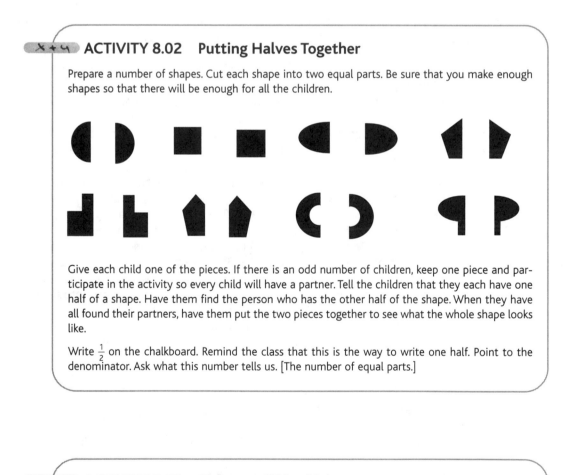

Give each child one of the pieces. If there is an odd number of children, keep one piece and participate in the activity so every child will have a partner. Tell the children that they each have one half of a shape. Have them find the person who has the other half of the shape. When they have all found their partners, have them put the two pieces together to see what the whole shape looks like.

Write $\frac{1}{2}$ on the chalkboard. Remind the class that this is the way to write one half. Point to the denominator. Ask what this number tells us. [The number of equal parts.]

✕ ✦ ⊣ ACTIVITY 8.03   Halves and Not Halves

Prepare a number of shapes like those used for Activity 8.02. Cut some of them into two equal parts. Cut some into two unequal parts. Cut the rest into three parts. Use a piece of yarn to divide the bulletin board into two sections. Place a card showing the fraction $\frac{1}{2}$ in the middle of one section of the bulletin board.

Show the children the parts of each shape. Let the children decide whether the shape was cut into halves. If it was cut into halves, place the two halves on the section of the bulletin board with the fraction one half. If the children decide that the shape was not cut into halves, place the parts of the shape in the other section of the bulletin board.

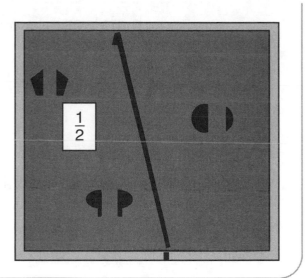

x + 4 **ACTIVITY 8.04   Writing Fractions**

Prepare a number of shapes like those used for activity 8.02. Cut some of them into two equal parts. Cut some into two unequal parts. Cut the rest into three parts. Tape the parts of each shape side by side on the chalkboard.

Show the children the parts of each shape. Let the children decide which shapes are cut into halves. If the children decide that a shape is cut into halves, have a child come forward and write $\frac{1}{2}$ below the parts of that shape. Draw an arrow from the fraction to one of the two equal parts.

Beyond Unit Fractions

After children have had early experiences with unit fractions (usually $\frac{1}{2}$, $\frac{1}{3}$, and $\frac{1}{4}$), the fraction concepts are generalized to include fractions with numerators other than 1. This is usually accomplished by the end of the second grade. The notion that the parts must be equal is revisited, and then the child learns to write a numerator to indicate how many of the equal parts are being considered and a denominator to indicate the total number of equal parts.

For example, when a shape is divided into four equal parts and three of the parts are shaded, then the fraction $\frac{3}{4}$ names the shaded part of the shape.

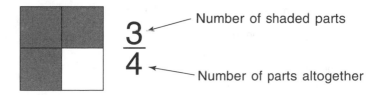

Number of shaded parts

$$\frac{3}{4}$$

Number of parts altogether

Once again, we want the children to be able to show the fractional quantity, name the fractional quantity using appropriate fraction terminology, and write the fraction name using appropriate fraction notation.

✗ ⊹ ⊌ ACTIVITY 8.05   Naming Fractions

Prepare cards showing pictures of fractional quantities.

Show the pictures to the children. Call on individuals to give the fraction name for the shaded part in the pictures. Ask how they can tell what the fraction name is.

✗ ⊹ ⊌ ACTIVITY 8.06   Find the Fraction

Show the children a set of fraction circles.

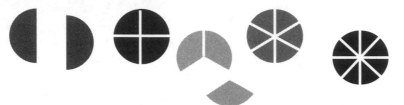

Write $\frac{2}{3}$ on the chalkboard. Point out the circle that is divided into thirds. Pick up two of those three parts and tell the class that this is $\frac{2}{3}$ of the circle.

Write other fractions on the board and call on children to come to the front and use the fraction circles to show the fractions.

✗ ⊹ ⊌ ACTIVITY 8.07   Fraction Match

Prepare pairs of cards. One card of each pair should show a picture of a fraction. The second card should show the fraction.

Shuffle the cards and give each child a card. If there is an odd number of children, the teacher should keep a card and participate in the activity so everyone has a partner.

Have the children find their partners so that one partner has the fraction and the other partner has the picture of that fraction.

When everyone has a partner, they should hold their cards so that the other children can check to see if they are correct.

✗ ⊹ ⊌ ACTIVITY 8.08   Around We Go

Place cards, some showing pictures of fractions and some showing fractions, in a circle on the floor. Have the children march around the circle chanting this rhyme:

> Marching, marching, round we go,
> Not too fast and not too slow.
> I won't run and I won't hop.
> I'm almost there. It's time to stop.

When they say stop, each child should stand by one of the cards. The teacher then names a fraction. Children who are standing by the fraction or by a picture of the fraction that the teacher has named should raise their hands.

Fractions of a Set

Another way that fractions are used is to name a part of a set of objects. For example, consider the set of circles pictured below.

Since four out of six circles are blue, we can name the part of the set consisting of blue circles using the fraction $\frac{4}{6}$. We can find another fraction name by forming groups of two circles.

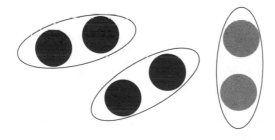

We can see that two out of three groups are blue, so $\frac{2}{3}$ is another fraction name for the part of the set made up of blue circles.

Now consider this set of shapes. Three of the five shapes are squares, so we can say that $\frac{3}{5}$ of the shapes are squares.

But, all the shapes are not the same size. This illustrates the primary difference between the way we use a fraction to name a part of a region and the way we use a fraction to name a part of a set. When naming a *fraction of a region*, all the *parts must be the same size*. But, when naming a *fraction of a set*, all the *parts must have the same number of objects*.

In this set of people, even though the men are not the same size as the women, half of the set is men. There are the *same number* of men as women.

Equivalent Fractions

When two different fractions name the same quantity, the fractions are equal. We say that they are equivalent fractions. Consider this square which has been divided by a vertical line into two equal parts. The shaded part is $\frac{1}{2}$ of the square.

$$\frac{1}{2}$$

Suppose we cut the square with horizontal lines into three equal parts. Notice that each of the two original parts has been cut into three equal parts, leaving us with six equal parts. Three of those six parts are shaded, so another name for the shaded part of the square is $\frac{3}{6}$. The fractions $\frac{1}{2}$ and $\frac{3}{6}$ are equal. They are equivalent fractions. A similar procedure is illustrated below to show other pairs of equivalent fractions: $\frac{2}{3} = \frac{6}{9}$, $\frac{3}{4} = \frac{6}{8}$, and $\frac{2}{5} = \frac{4}{10}$.

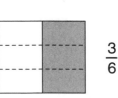

$$\frac{3}{6}$$

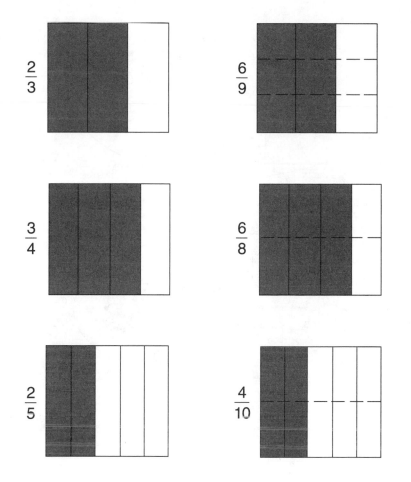

Fractions of sets can also be used to develop the idea of equivalent fractions. For example, in this set of objects, 12 out of 18 are pentagons. One fraction name for the part of the set that is made up of pentagons is $\frac{12}{18}$.

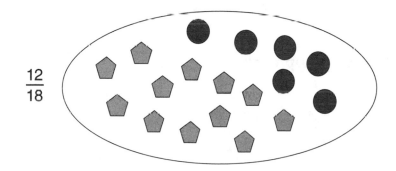

By grouping the objects we can see other fraction names for the same part of the set.

$\frac{2}{3}$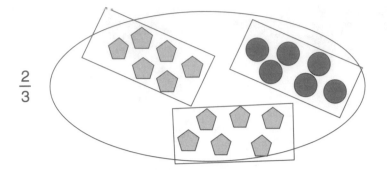

$\frac{4}{6}$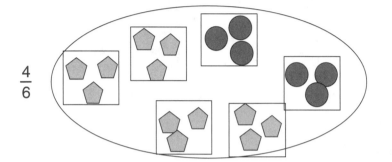

$\frac{6}{9}$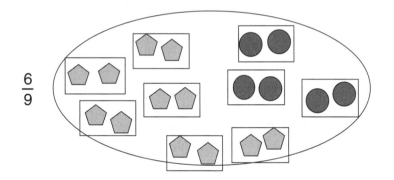

Using the Laboratory Approach

One effective way to teach equivalent fractions is to use the laboratory approach that was described in Chapter 3. Recall that in the laboratory approach, the students are led through a series of steps.

1. *Explore (or experiment)*. In this step a physical or pictorial model is used to find a variety of results (answers). Since the student can see where the answer came from, common sense tells the student whether the answer is correct.
2. *Keep an organized record of results*. The results are recorded in a way that facilitates recognition of the patterns that the teacher wants the student to notice.
3. *Identify patterns*. The children identify patterns that suggest ways to get the result (answer) without using the model.

4. *Hypothesize (or generalize) how to get results without the model.* In their own words, the children state the process that will produce the correct result.

5. *Test the hypothesis (the generalization).* Use the hypothesized procedure to get result(s). Then, do the same example(s) using the model to verify that the process does produce correct result(s).

Next we examine how the laboratory process can be used to develop the concept of equivalent fractions.

1. *Explore.* Use fraction squares to find a new name for the same fractional quantity.
2. *Record each result.*

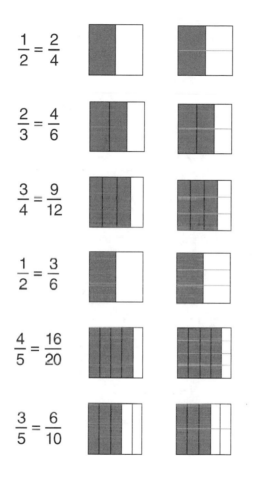

3. *Identify the pattern* that is the relationship between the two equal fractions. Students notice that, "In the second fraction, both numbers are bigger." The teacher points to $\frac{3}{5} = \frac{6}{10}$ and asks, "How much bigger are they?" We want the students to see that both numbers are twice as big. The numerator was multiplied by 2 and the denominator was multiplied by 2.

In another example, we find that $\frac{3}{4} = \frac{9}{12}$. In this case, the numbers in the second fraction are three times as big. The numerator and denominator were both multiplied by 3 to produce an equivalent fraction.

In still another example, $\frac{4}{5} = \frac{16}{20}$, the numerator and denominator were both multiplied by 4. Point out that the horizontal lines separate every part into four smaller parts. So, we have four times as many parts altogether. The horizontal lines also separate every shaded part into four smaller parts, so we have four times as many shaded parts.

$$\frac{4}{5} \times 4 = \frac{}{20}$$

$$\frac{4 \times 4}{5 \times 4} = \frac{16}{20}$$

4. *Generalize the pattern.* Help the students to see the same kind of pattern in all the other examples.

$$\frac{1 \times 2}{2 \times 2} = \frac{2}{4} \qquad \frac{2 \times 2}{3 \times 2} = \frac{4}{6}$$

$$\frac{3 \times 3}{4 \times 3} = \frac{9}{12} \qquad \frac{1 \times 3}{2 \times 3} = \frac{3}{6}$$

$$\frac{3 \times 2}{5 \times 2} = \frac{6}{10}$$

Ask the students if they think this always works. Can we always get an equivalent fraction if we multiply the numerator and denominator by the same number?

5. *Verify the generalization.* Write a fraction, for example $\frac{3}{4}$. Ask how to get an equivalent fraction. [Multiply numerator and denominator by the same number.] Do this to get an equivalent fraction. Then use the model to verify the result. For example, if numerator and denominator were multiplied by 4 to find an equivalent fraction, the result would be:

$$\frac{3 \times 4}{4 \times 4} = \frac{12}{16}$$

To verify this result, start with a picture of $\frac{3}{4}$. To change from four equal parts to 16, each of the original parts must be cut into four pieces. When this is done, we can see that the shaded part of the square is 12 out of 16 equal parts.

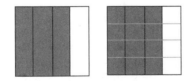

So we see that we obtain the correct result by multiplying numerator and denominator by 4.

A natural extension of this idea is to find an equivalent fraction with a particular denominator. For example, we wish to find a fraction equivalent to $\frac{2}{3}$ that has a denominator of 15. It is left as an exercise for the reader to develop an instructional activity to teach this.

Comparison of Fractions

There are four distinct steps in the development of the ability to compare fractions. In the first step, when fractions with the same numerator are being compared, extra attention must be given to the development of strong mental imagery for the fractional units. And, along with this mental imagery, must come an awareness that if the denominator is greater, there are more parts. And, if an object is divided into more parts, the parts are smaller. A natural sequence is first to compare unit fractions, such as $\frac{1}{2}$, $\frac{1}{3}$, $\frac{1}{4}$, $\frac{1}{5}$, $\frac{1}{7}$, or $\frac{1}{15}$. After the students are able to correctly compare unit fractions, the second step is to teach them to compare nonunit fractions that have the same numerators. For example, they might compare $\frac{2}{7}$ and $\frac{2}{4}$. The third step is to teach students to compare fractions with the same denominators, comparing $\frac{5}{8}$ and $\frac{7}{8}$, for example. Finally, the fourth step is to teach the students to compare fractions that have unlike numerators and unlike denominators. In this final step the students encounter, and must learn to use, the one big idea of comparison: *compare like units*.

The following set of activities illustrates how a teacher can develop students' abilities to compare fractions.

ACTIVITY 8.09   Big and Little Pieces

Ask the class if they like candy. Ask if they would rather share a candy bar with two other people or with three other people. Ask why. What would be the difference? Show them two two-by-six rectangles of paper. Tell them to imagine that they are two candy bars. Have the class tell you how to cut the first "candy bar" so it could be shared with two other people. [It needs to be cut into 3 equal pieces.] Have the class tell you how to cut the second candy bar so it could be shared with three other people. [It needs to be cut into 4 equal pieces.] Hold up a piece from each candy bar for the class to compare. Point out that the larger piece is $\frac{1}{3}$, and the smaller piece is $\frac{1}{4}$.

Point to the denominators and remind the students that when the denominator is bigger, the candy bar was cut into more pieces. So, the pieces are smaller.

Write $\frac{1}{3}$ and $\frac{1}{4}$ on the chalkboard, and ask which is more.

ACTIVITY 8.10   More Big and Little Pieces

Show the class a set of fraction circles.

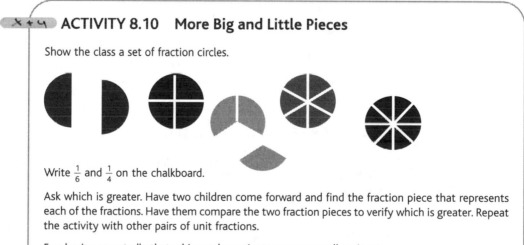

Write $\frac{1}{6}$ and $\frac{1}{4}$ on the chalkboard.

Ask which is greater. Have two children come forward and find the fraction piece that represents each of the fractions. Have them compare the two fraction pieces to verify which is greater. Repeat the activity with other pairs of unit fractions.

Emphasize repeatedly that a bigger denominator means smaller pieces.

✕ ÷ ◢ ACTIVITY 8.11   When 3 Pieces is More than 3 Pieces

Tell the class to imagine that two people each have a candy bar. One cuts her candy bar into four equal parts. The other cuts hers into six equal parts. If both are willing to give you three pieces, who would be giving you more? Why?

Which is more, $\frac{3}{4}$ or $\frac{3}{6}$?

Show the class a set of fraction circles.

Write $\frac{3}{4}$ and $\frac{3}{6}$ on the chalkboard.

Ask which is greater. Have two children come forward and find the fraction pieces that represent each of the fractions. Have them compare the fraction pieces to verify which fraction is greater. Repeat the activity with other pairs of fractions. For example, you could use $\frac{2}{3}$ and $\frac{2}{6}$, $\frac{4}{6}$ and $\frac{4}{5}$, or $\frac{5}{8}$ and $\frac{5}{9}$.

Emphasize repeatedly that a bigger denominator means smaller pieces.

✕ ÷ ◢ ACTIVITY 8.12   Fractions with Like Units

Show the class a set of fraction circles.

Write $\frac{5}{6}$ and $\frac{3}{6}$ on the chalkboard.

Ask which is greater. Have a child come forward and use the fraction circles to show the two fractions. Repeat the activity with other pairs of fractions with the same denominators. For example, you could use $\frac{3}{4}$ and $\frac{1}{4}$, $\frac{3}{8}$ and $\frac{5}{8}$, or $\frac{7}{9}$ and $\frac{8}{9}$.

Emphasize repeatedly that since the denominators are equal the fractional units are the same. The numerator tells how many of those units you have. $\frac{8}{9}$ is greater than $\frac{7}{9}$ because eight of those units is more than seven of those units.

✕ ÷ ◢ ACTIVITY 8.13   Getting Like Units

Write "7 feet" and "97 inches" on the chalkboard. Below them, write "23 yards" and "31 yards." Point to the top two lengths and ask which is longer. Then point to the bottom two lengths and ask which is longer.

Ask why the second pair of lengths is easier to compare. [The units are the same.]

Write "84 eggs" and "76 eggs" on the chalkboard. Below them, write "71 eggs" and "6 dozen eggs." Point to the top two amounts and ask which is more. Then point to the bottom two amounts and ask which is more.

Ask why the first pair of eggs is easier to compare. [The units are the same.] Explain that when comparing quantities, it is always easier when we compare like units.

Write $\frac{5}{8}$ and $\frac{3}{8}$ on the chalkboard. Below them, write $\frac{3}{4}$ and $\frac{7}{9}$. Point to the top two fractions and ask which is greater. Then point to the bottom two fractions and ask which is greater.

Ask why the first pair of fractions is easier to compare. [The units are the same.] It is always easier to compare quantities when the units are the same.

Write "13 inches" and "1 foot" on the chalkboard. Ask how many inches are equal to 1 foot. Mark out 1 foot and write 12 inches above it. Point out how easy it is to compare the two lengths when we rewrite them using the same units.

Write $\frac{2}{3}$ and $\frac{3}{4}$ on the chalkboard. Explain that you are going to show the class how to rewrite these fractions so that they have the same units. Show representations of these two fractions on an overhead transparency.

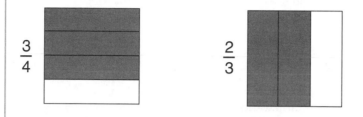

Tell the class that you want to cut the pieces so that you will have the same size pieces in both fractions. You can do that by cutting the first fraction vertically into three equal parts and cutting the second fraction horizontally into four equal parts. Do this on the transparency.

After doing this, write the new names for the fractions.

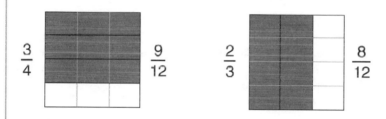

Ask the class to look at the new fraction names and decide which fraction is greater.

[$\frac{3}{4}$ is greater than $\frac{2}{3}$.]

Show the class that you can get the new names for the two fractions by multiplying numerator and denominator by the same number.

$$\frac{3 \times 3}{4 \times 3} = \frac{9}{12} \qquad \frac{2 \times 4}{3 \times 4} = \frac{8}{12}$$

Cross multiplying is a process for comparing fractions that is often taught to elementary children. It is quick and easy to use. Unfortunately, though, it is most often taught as a rote process, and consequently, it is generally not retained. Cross multiplying works as follows.

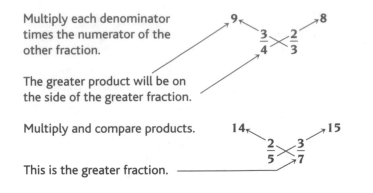

Multiply each denominator times the numerator of the other fraction.

The greater product will be on the side of the greater fraction.

Multiply and compare products.

This is the greater fraction.

Let's consider how cross multiplication can be taught with meaning. We know that to compare $\frac{2}{5}$ and $\frac{3}{7}$, we need to rename the fractions using the same unit (the same denominator).

$$\frac{2 \times 7}{5 \times 7} = \frac{14}{35} \qquad \frac{3 \times 5}{7 \times 5} = \frac{15}{35}$$

The cross multiplication process gives us the numerators of the renamed fractions that have the same fractional unit.

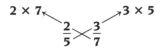

Since the units of these renamed fractions are the same, what we actually compare are the numerators (which tell us how many of those units we have). Although we need to know that the denominators are the same, we do not need to actually compute those denominators. When we use cross multiplication we are merely finding the numerators of the renamed fractions.

Adding Fractions

Recall that for whole numbers two big ideas were identified for addition. The first of those big ideas was *always add like units*. The same big idea holds for addition of fractions. Addition of fractions with the same units (like denominators) is easy. The most effective way to show students how easy it is to add like fractions is to use a physical model such as fraction circles. For example, suppose we want to add $\frac{3}{8}$ and $\frac{2}{8}$. We represent both fractions with the fraction pieces and then combine them. We have three of "these things" and two more of "these things." Altogether, there are five of "these things." "These things" are eighths, so $\frac{3}{8} + \frac{2}{8} = \frac{5}{8}$.

If we are adding like units (like fractions), we have only to think about how many of those units we have altogether. For $\frac{4}{7} + \frac{2}{7}$, we have four sevenths and two more sevenths. Altogether, we have six sevenths.

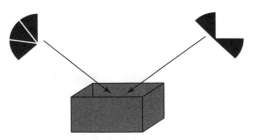

Addition of like fractions is easy if we use a physical model so the students can visualize combining the fractional units. If the fractions do not have the same fractional units (like denominators), then the students must be led to understand that the fractions can be renamed so that the fractional units are the same. That is, we change to equivalent fractions that have a common denominator. The students' previous work with equivalent fractions should have provided the needed understanding and skills, but rather than assuming that they remember, it is wise to redevelop the key ideas. It is not easy to add the fractions $\frac{3}{4}$ and $\frac{2}{3}$ because the fractional units are not the same. If we rename the two fractions so that both have the same denominator, 12, the addition becomes easy, because we can *add like units*.

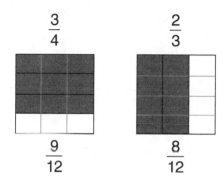

If we follow the same process for renaming fractions, it is easy to quickly rename the original fractions using a common denominator. After seeing several examples completed using the fraction-squares model, and after examining the results, the students notice that in every case, the product of the two given fractions can serve as a common denominator for the addition.

We can use 5 × 8 as the common denominator.

$$\frac{2}{5} + \frac{3}{8}$$

In the first fraction, we multiplied the denominator by 8, so we must also multiply the numerator by 8.

$$\frac{2 \times 8}{5 \times 8} + \frac{}{5 \times 8}$$

In the second fraction, we multiplied 5 times the denominator, so we must also multiply 5 times the numerator.

$$\frac{2 \times 8}{5 \times 8} + \frac{5 \times 3}{5 \times 8}$$

This process for obtaining common denominators is simple and easily justified using the pictorial fraction-squares model. Using the model, children can quickly master addition of unlike fractions. Some teachers are not comfortable with it, however, because although the product of the two denominators is always a common denominator, it is not always the least common denominator.

When most teachers learned to add unlike fractions as elementary children, they were taught that the least common denominator must first be found. They have been convinced by their own training that the least common denominator must be used when adding unlike fractions. This, of course, is not really true. Indeed, addition of fractions is typically defined in algebra as:

$$\frac{a}{b} + \frac{c}{d} = \frac{ad + bc}{bd}$$

So then, does teaching children to find least common denominators not have any value? Of course least common denominators have value, and we should continue to teach children how to find them. However, it is actually much more difficult for children to find least common denominators than it is for them to add unlike fractions. It is recommended here to first master addition of fractions and then, at a later time, revisit the topic with a focus on least common denominators.

Subtracting Fractions

Developing understanding of subtraction of fractions exactly parallels the development of addition of fractions. Subtraction of fractions with like denominators is taught immediately after addition of like fractions. As with addition, subtraction of like fractions is most effectively taught using a physical model. Select fraction pieces to represent the minuend, take away the pieces that represent the subtrahend, and recognize that the remaining fraction pieces represent the answer. It is good to point out how the process of subtracting fractions is like the process of subtracting whole numbers—we start with a number, take away a number, and see what number is left.

Immediately after addition of unlike fractions is taught, the children are taught subtraction of unlike fractions. The first of the big ideas for subtraction, *always subtract like units*, also applies to subtraction of fractions. So, subtraction of unlike fractions requires that we rename the two fractions using the same fractional unit (a common denominator). Just as with addition, fraction squares are an excellent model for justifying the product of the two denominators as a common denominator. Once the two fractions have been renamed with a common denominator, the children can easily apply their ability to subtract like fractions.

$$\frac{a}{b} - \frac{c}{d} = \frac{ab}{bd} - \frac{bc}{bd} = \frac{ad - bc}{bd}$$

Least Common Denominators

Now, we examine least common denominators. Mathematically, the least common denominator of two fractions is the *least common multiple* of the two denominators. The process for finding the least common multiple includes two distinct steps. First, we find the prime factorization of each denominator. Then, we form the least number that contains all the factors of the first denominator and also contains all the factors of the second denominator. This is a complex process to teach and students seldom retain it.

However, by being less mathematical, we can actually simplify the process. First, we help the students to realize that, although the product of the denominators is always a common denominator, sometimes there is another common denominator that is a smaller number.

$$\frac{1}{2} + \frac{1}{4} = \frac{4}{8} + \frac{2}{8} = \frac{6}{8} \quad \text{could be done like this} \quad \frac{1}{2} + \frac{1}{4} = \frac{2}{4} + \frac{1}{4} = \frac{3}{4}$$

$$\frac{5}{6} + \frac{3}{4} = \frac{20}{24} + \frac{18}{24} = \frac{38}{24} \quad \text{could be done like this} \quad \frac{5}{6} + \frac{3}{4} = \frac{10}{12} + \frac{9}{12} = \frac{19}{12}$$

Next we need to help them to understand that, since whole-number computation is generally easier with smaller numbers, fraction computation is also easier if we use smaller denominators. We can accomplish this by comparing several examples where the product of the denominators is a large number.

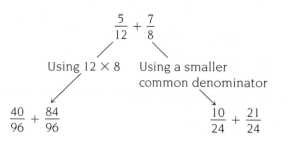

$$\frac{5}{12} + \frac{7}{8}$$

Using 12 × 8   Using a smaller
common denominator

$$\frac{40}{96} + \frac{84}{96} \qquad\qquad \frac{10}{24} + \frac{21}{24}$$

The next step is to discover a method for finding the least common denominator. For each of the two fractions, the students need to think about the denominators for all possible equivalent fractions. We get an equivalent fraction by multiplying numerator and denominator by the same number. We multiply by 2, 3, 4, 5, … to find the various possibilities. We do this for both fractions. Consider, for example, $\frac{2}{3}$ and $\frac{3}{5}$.

$$\frac{2}{3} = \frac{2 \times 2}{3 \times 2} = \frac{4}{6} \qquad \frac{2}{3} = \frac{2 \times 3}{3 \times 3} = \frac{6}{9} \qquad \frac{2}{3} = \frac{2 \times 4}{3 \times 4} = \frac{8}{12} \qquad \frac{2}{3} = \frac{2 \times 5}{3 \times 5} = \frac{10}{15}$$

$$\frac{3}{5} = \frac{3 \times 2}{5 \times 2} = \frac{6}{10} \qquad \frac{3}{5} = \frac{3 \times 3}{5 \times 3} = \frac{9}{15} \qquad \frac{3}{5} = \frac{3 \times 4}{5 \times 4} = \frac{12}{20} \qquad \frac{3}{5} = \frac{3 \times 5}{5 \times 5} = \frac{15}{25}$$

We can then create a list of denominators for fractions equivalent to each of the two fractions. We circle the possible denominators that appear in both lists. These are the possible common denominators.

$\frac{2}{3}$ 3   6   9   12   ⑮   18   21   24   27   ㉚   33   36   39   42   ㊺ …

$\frac{3}{5}$ 5   10   ⑮   20   25   ㉚   35   40   ㊺   50   55   60   65   70   75 …

The smallest of the numbers that appears in both lists is the least common denominator. The least common denominator of $\frac{2}{3}$ and $\frac{3}{5}$ is 15.

Suppose we want to find the least common denominator of $\frac{5}{6}$ and $\frac{3}{8}$.

$\frac{5}{6}$ 6   12   18   ㉔   30   36   42   ㊽   54   60   66   ㉞   78   84   90 …

$\frac{3}{8}$ 8   16   ㉔   32   40   ㊽   56   64   ㉞   80   88   96   104   112   120 …

The least common divisor of $\frac{5}{6}$ and $\frac{3}{8}$ is 24.

The following sequence of activities illustrates how addition and subtraction of fractions can be taught.

✕ ✦ ↳ ACTIVITY 8.14   Name the Rods

This activity uses colored number rods like the Cuisenaire Rods or the Color Factor Rods. Choose any of the rods in the set and let its length be equal to 1.

1

Then find fraction names for all the other rods.

1

Each of these is $\frac{1}{6}$.

1

Each of these is $\frac{1}{3}$.

See if the students can find more than one name for some of the rods.

$\frac{1}{3}$

$\frac{2}{6}$

×+⊣ **ACTIVITY 8.15   Give and Take**

Prepare a large cube with $\frac{1}{8}$ on two faces, $\frac{2}{8}$ on two faces, and $\frac{3}{8}$ on two faces. Also prepare three circles divided into eighths.

Form a group of three children and seat them around a table. Give each child one of the circles cut into eighths, and show the group the cube with fractions on it.

The children take turns playing. On each play, the player tosses the cube and takes the fraction showing on top from the player on his left. Every player must write the fraction that he or she has after each play.

Players must check what everyone else has written. If any player has written an incorrect fraction, the other players must explain why it is not correct. If a player runs out of fraction pieces, he or she is out of the game but must continue to check the other players. After everyone has had three turns, the player with the largest fraction is the winner.

×+⊣ **ACTIVITY 8.16   What Fraction Is in the Box—Addition**

This is a partner activity. The participants must have a set of fraction circles.

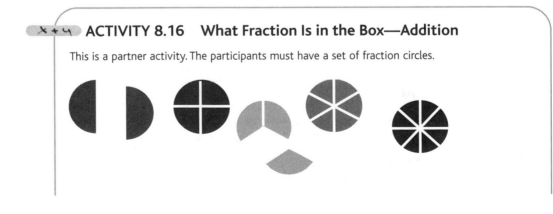

They should also be given a set of cards showing examples of addition of like fractions and a box.

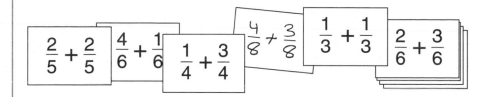

After choosing a card, one child should place the fraction pieces for the first fraction into the box. The other child should place the pieces for the second number into the box. Then they both write what they think the correct answer is. Finally, they look in the box to check their answers.

x ÷ 4   ACTIVITY 8.17   What Fraction Is in the Box—Subtraction

This is a partner activity. The participants must have a set of fraction circles.

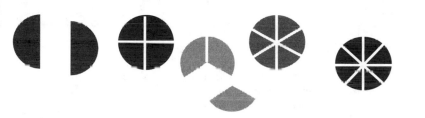

They should also be given a box and a set of cards showing examples of subtraction of like fractions.

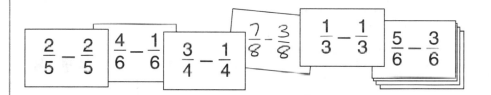

After choosing a card, one child should place the fraction pieces for the first fraction into the box. The other child should take the pieces for the second number out of the box. Then they both write what they think the correct answer is. Finally, they look in the box to check their answers.

x ÷ 4   ACTIVITY 8.18   Predictions

This is a partner activity. The participants must have a set of fraction circles.

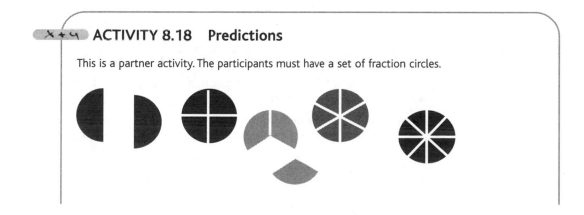

They should also be given a box and a mixture of cards like those used in Activities 8.16 and 8.17.

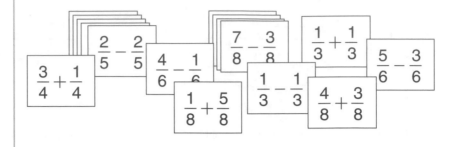

After choosing a card, both children should write what they think the correct answer is. Then they use the fraction pieces to check their answers.

ACTIVITY 8.19 Same Size Units

Prepare several pairs of overhead transparencies showing fraction-square representations of two unlike fractions. One fraction square should be divided vertically and the other horizontally.

For example, one transparency could show $\frac{1}{3}$ and $\frac{1}{4}$.
Write $\frac{1}{3} + \frac{1}{4}$ on the chalkboard and show the transparency.

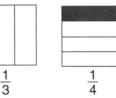

Explain that you want to have the same size pieces (like units) so that you can add the two fractions. Ask how you can cut up the pieces so that they will all be the same size. [Cut the first fraction horizontally into fourths and cut the second fraction vertically into thirds.]

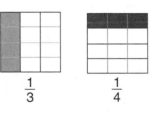

Write the addition using the new fraction names. Emphasize that you are still adding the same amounts.

$$\frac{1}{3} + \frac{1}{4} = \frac{4}{12} + \frac{3}{12}$$

Repeat the process with several other examples. After each example has been completed, write the new result under the previous one.

Ask the class if they can see what they might do in every example to get the new denominator (the common denominator). [The new denominator is the product of the two original denominators.]

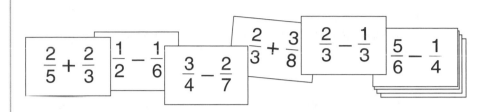

✕ + ⊔ ACTIVITY 8.20   Answer Hunt

Prepare enough cards showing addition or subtraction of unlike fractions so there are enough for all the children.

Also prepare cards with answers for all the addition and subtraction examples. Tape the answer cards to the wall around the room.

Hand out the addition and subtraction cards to the students and have them find the answers to their problems.

Improper Fractions and Mixed Numbers

Fractions with numerators greater than their denominators are called improper fractions. Improper fractions are greater than one. There is not really anything improper about such fractions. In fact mathematicians generally prefer using improper fractions to mixed numbers, because an improper fraction is considered to be a simpler form of the number than the equivalent mixed number. However, there are situations where a mixed number is preferable to an improper fraction. For example, if you went into a fabric store and told the clerk that you would like to buy $\frac{17}{4}$ yards of cloth, the clerk would probably look at you like you were crazy. If a price tag indicated the price of some piece of merchandise as $\frac{874}{100}$ dollars, the customer would probably say, "just forget it."

In their first encounter with improper fractions and mixed numbers, children learn that these are merely two ways to name the same amount. The work focuses on finding mixed numbers equal to given improper fractions and finding improper fractions equal to given mixed numbers. Either physical models or pictorial models can be used effectively to develop the concepts and skills. Using the fraction circles, we can show that $1 + \frac{2}{6} = \frac{8}{6}$:

   One and two sixths is the same amount as eight sixths.

And, using pictorial fraction squares, we can show that $1 + \frac{3}{4} = \frac{7}{4}$.

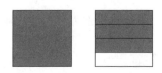   One and three fourths is the same amount as seven fourths.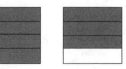

If we record the step where 1 is renamed as a fraction, we can see the steps that would be followed when a model is not being used.

$$1 + \frac{3}{4} = \frac{4}{4} + \frac{3}{4} = \frac{7}{4}$$

This is another name for 1.

We can then follow this same process for conversion of any mixed number to an improper fraction.

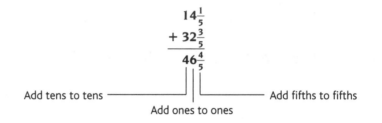

$$1\frac{5}{8} = \frac{8}{8} + \frac{5}{8} = \frac{13}{8} \qquad 3\frac{2}{3} = \frac{3}{3} + \frac{3}{3} + \frac{3}{3} + \frac{2}{3} = \frac{11}{3}$$

And we can follow a similar procedure to change an improper fraction to a mixed number.

$$\frac{14}{9} = \frac{9}{9} + \frac{5}{9} = 1\frac{5}{9} \qquad \frac{18}{7} = \frac{7}{7} + \frac{7}{7} + \frac{4}{7} = 2\frac{4}{7}$$

Addition and subtraction of mixed numbers is almost identical to addition and subtraction of whole numbers. For each operation, the procedures are based on the same two big ideas. When adding, *always add like units.*

$$
\begin{array}{r}
14\frac{1}{5} \\
+\ 32\frac{3}{5} \\
\hline
46\frac{4}{5}
\end{array}
$$

Add tens to tens ——————┘ └—————— Add fifths to fifths

Add ones to ones

We also apply the second big idea of addition, *when there are too many to write in standard* form or as a proper fraction, *make a trade.*

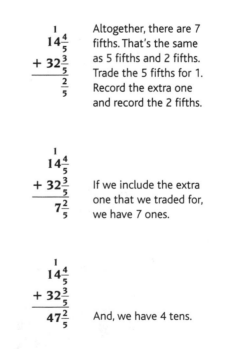

$$
\begin{array}{r}
\overset{1}{14\frac{4}{5}} \\
+\ 32\frac{3}{5} \\
\hline
\frac{2}{5}
\end{array}
$$

Altogether, there are 7 fifths. That's the same as 5 fifths and 2 fifths. Trade the 5 fifths for 1. Record the extra one and record the 2 fifths.

$$
\begin{array}{r}
\overset{1}{14\frac{4}{5}} \\
+\ 32\frac{3}{5} \\
\hline
7\frac{2}{5}
\end{array}
$$

If we include the extra one that we traded for, we have 7 ones.

$$
\begin{array}{r}
\overset{1}{14\frac{4}{5}} \\
+\ 32\frac{3}{5} \\
\hline
47\frac{2}{5}
\end{array}
$$

And, we have 4 tens.

When subtracting, we *always subtract like units.*

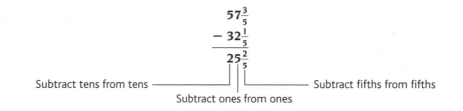

$$57\tfrac{3}{5}$$
$$-\ 32\tfrac{1}{5}$$
$$25\tfrac{2}{5}$$

Subtract tens from tens ──────────┘│└────── Subtract fifths from fifths

Subtract ones from ones

We also apply the second big idea of subtraction—*when there are not enough, make a trade.*

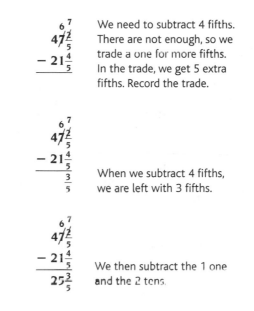

We need to subtract 4 fifths. There are not enough, so we trade a one for more fifths. In the trade, we get 5 extra fifths. Record the trade.

When we subtract 4 fifths, we are left with 3 fifths.

We then subtract the 1 one and the 2 tens.

A Remediation Note. The following incorrect computation illustrates what may be the most common error pattern among children who are subtracting mixed numbers.

In this error pattern, the student is carrying over the rote borrowing procedure from whole number subtraction. The student must be led to understand and the denominator tells how many pieces you get in the trade. Let them see it with a model.

Multiplying Fractions

Three different approaches to modeling multiplication of fractions have appeared in the professional literature. Two of these approaches have been demonstrated to be effective. They are reasonably easy to use and they are meaningful to the students. The third approach is easy to use but it is not meaningful to the student. The rationale for the answer does not make sense. We examine all three approaches and discuss what the students must already understand before they can be used effectively.

In the first approach, the students find a fraction of a fraction.

$$\frac{1}{2} \times \frac{2}{3}$$

This means $\frac{1}{2}$ of $\frac{2}{3}$

The teacher cannot assume that the students understand this. To help the students associate the word "of" with multiplication, begin with some whole-number examples. For example, show a group of three objects. Then show five *of* these groups. Write 5 × 3. Show a seven-inch strip of paper. Then show four *of* these strips end to end. Ask how long they are altogether. Write "4 *of* the strips." Write 4 × 7. Show three cartons of "eggs." Write 3 × 12. Then write "3 *of* the cartons."

Only after the students are comfortable with the relationship between multiplication and the word "of" should this method be attempted. To find $\frac{1}{2}$ of $\frac{2}{3}$, we must begin with $\frac{2}{3}$.

We use a fraction square to represent the beginning fraction. The green part of the square represents $\frac{2}{3}$.

Now we want to find $\frac{1}{2}$ of that fraction. We can find half of the green part of the square by cutting it into two equal parts with a horizontal line. We then shade $\frac{1}{2}$ of the beginning fraction.

The square is now divided into six equal parts. The shaded part is two out of six equal parts, or $\frac{2}{6}$.

$$\frac{1}{2} \text{ of } \frac{2}{3} \text{ is } \frac{2}{6}$$

$$\frac{1}{2} \times \frac{2}{3} = \frac{2}{6}$$

This is exactly what we would have expected if we had used a physical model. If we used the fraction circles to represent $\frac{2}{3}$, we would have two of those pieces. Of course, half of those two pieces is one of those pieces, $\frac{1}{3}$, and $\frac{1}{3} = \frac{2}{6}$.

For another example, we model $\frac{2}{5} \times \frac{3}{4}$. Before we can find $\frac{2}{5}$ of $\frac{3}{4}$, we must first have $\frac{3}{4}$. We use a fraction square to represent $\frac{3}{4}$. We divide the square into fourths with horizontal lines. $\frac{3}{4}$ of the square is red.

Now we divide the square into fifths using vertical lines. We shade $\frac{2}{5}$ of the fraction $\frac{3}{4}$.

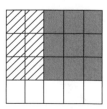

$$\frac{2}{5} \text{ of } \frac{3}{4} \text{ is } \frac{6}{20}$$

$$\frac{2}{5} \times \frac{3}{4} = \frac{6}{20}$$

The second method for modeling fraction multiplication uses the area model that we have already seen when dealing with whole-number multiplication. Recall that the area of a rectangle is equal to the product of the length and the width.

In this model, the length of one side times the length of the other side equals the area.

$3 \times 4 = 12$

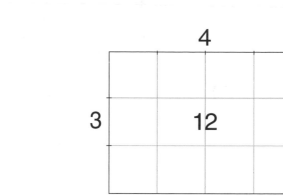

Now, suppose we want to find the answer to $\frac{1}{2} \times \frac{2}{3}$. If we have a rectangle with a length of $\frac{1}{2}$ and a width of $\frac{2}{3}$, then the area of that rectangle would be $\frac{1}{2} \times \frac{2}{3}$. We start with a unit square (a square that is 1 unit on each side). The area of the unit square is also 1. We divide one side into three equal parts and highlight $\frac{2}{3}$ of that side.

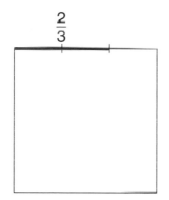

Next, we divide an adjacent side into two equal parts. We highlight $\frac{1}{2}$ of that side. We subdivide the square and shade the rectangle that has a length of $\frac{2}{3}$ and a width of $\frac{1}{2}$. The area of the shaded rectangle is $\frac{1}{2} \times \frac{2}{3}$. The area of the shaded rectangle is also two out of six equal parts of the unit square, so $\frac{1}{2} \times \frac{2}{3}$ and $\frac{2}{6}$ are two names for the same area, and they must be equal. Therefore, $\frac{1}{2} \times \frac{2}{3} = \frac{2}{6}$.

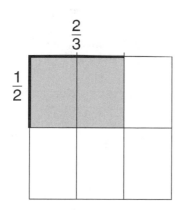

Now, let's consider a second example using the area model. To find the answer to $\frac{4}{5}$ and $\frac{2}{3}$, we begin with a unit square and show $\frac{4}{5}$ on one side and $\frac{2}{3}$ on the other side.

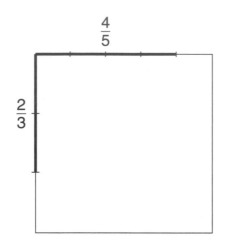

We subdivide the square and shade the rectangle that is $\frac{4}{5}$ on one side and $\frac{2}{3}$ on the other side.

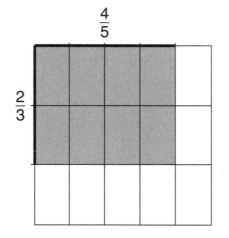

The area of this rectangle is $\frac{4}{5} \times \frac{2}{3}$. The area is also $\frac{8}{15}$. So, $\frac{4}{5} \times \frac{2}{3} = \frac{8}{15}$.

This method of modeling fraction multiplication requires the students to use the area concept. Before expecting them to understand this method, the teacher must assure that they know that the product of the length and the width of a rectangle equals the area of that rectangle.

The third method for modeling fraction multiplication is occasionally recommended, but it is included here only to alert you to a problem that is inherent in its use. *This method is not recommended.* It is quick and easy to use, but it is not a meaningful way to multiply fractions. Suppose we want the answer to $\frac{3}{4} \times \frac{2}{3}$.

In this approach we begin by using diagonal shading in a fraction square to show one of the fractions.

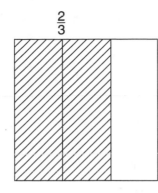

$\frac{2}{3}$

Then we divide the square horizontally to show the other fraction. The shading for this fraction is diagonal in the opposite direction. The part of the square that is shaded both directions is the answer to the multiplication. So, $\frac{3}{4} \times \frac{2}{3} = \frac{6}{12}$.

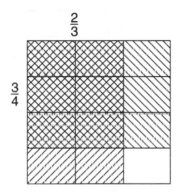

$\frac{2}{3}$

$\frac{3}{4}$

This process produces the correct answer. It is quick and relatively easy to use, but it is not a meaningful method, because the students cannot understand why the part that is shaded both directions is the answer. The rationale for the answer—because it is shaded both directions—is meaningless. It would be just as meaningful (to the student) to say that the answer is the part that is shaded one direction. That is also the correct answer for this example.

To the children, the real reason the part shaded both directions is the answer is that the teacher said it is. So, with this method, we have merely created a rote rule that involves drawing a picture. Even though this method still appears in some teacher materials, *research has shown it to be ineffective.*

Either of the first two methods works well. Both of them are meaningful to the students and provide effective modeling of fraction multiplication. They supply answers that students believe to be correct, because the process used to get those answers makes sense.

Dividing Fractions

Division of fractions is a topic that is often developed poorly. Sometimes the development is based on a set of examples drawn from a couple of special cases and then the procedural rules are generalized from those special cases, for example, $\frac{8}{9} \div 4$, $2 \div \frac{1}{3}$ and $\frac{3}{4} \div \frac{1}{8}$.

For $\frac{8}{9} \div 4$, start with $\frac{8}{9}$ and divide it into 4 equal parts.

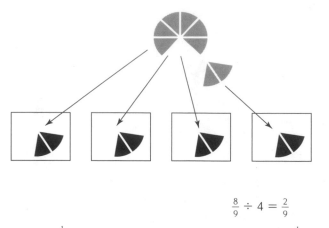

$$\frac{8}{9} \div 4 = \frac{2}{9}$$

For $2 \div \frac{1}{3}$, start with 2 and see how many times $\frac{1}{3}$ is contained in 2. $\frac{1}{3}$ is contained in 2 six times. So, $2 \div \frac{1}{3} = 6$.

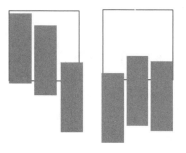

For $\frac{3}{4} \div \frac{1}{8}$, start with $\frac{3}{4}$ and see how many times $\frac{1}{8}$ is contained in $\frac{3}{4}$. The fraction $\frac{1}{8}$ is contained in $\frac{3}{4}$ 6 times. So, $\frac{3}{4} \div \frac{1}{8} = 6$.

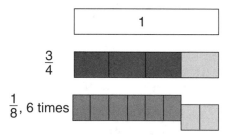

It would appear that we have a good mix of examples, but actually, these are all examples of special cases. In every example, we divided a whole number by a fraction and had a *whole-number* answer, or we divided a fraction by a fraction and had a *whole-number* answer, or divided a fraction by a *whole number* and it came out "even." The most common case is avoided. In these examples we did not divide a fraction by a fraction to get a fraction answer. Because many mathematics educators consider this last type to be difficult to model, there is seldom any attempt to include this most common type of fraction division in the development. Instead, the computational rule for division of fractions is generalized from those easier special cases. As pointed out in Chapter 3, *generalization from special cases is bad mathematics and should be avoided.*

We now examine a developmental sequence that includes examples where a fraction is divided by a fraction to get a fraction answer. We begin with simpler examples to establish the modeling procedures and then proceed to include all types before generalizing the computational rule.

The first thing we do is review measurement division, the kind of division that we will be using. If we want to find the answer to 8 ÷ 2, we need to find out how many 2s are contained in 8.

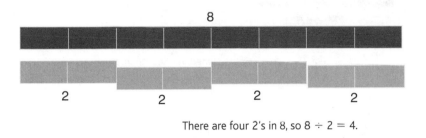

There are four 2's in 8, so 8 ÷ 2 = 4.

We continue by using the same type of division and by following the same modeling procedures to find answers to fraction division examples (Nowlin, 1996). We progress from very easy examples to those that are more difficult to model.

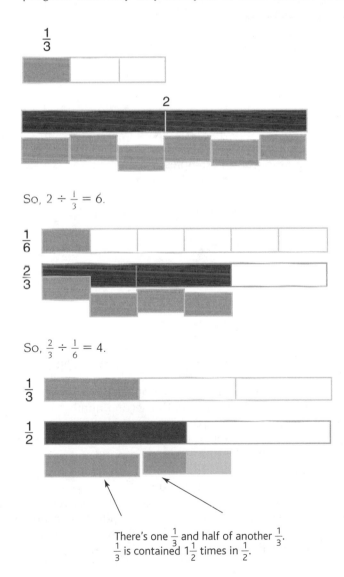

So, $2 \div \frac{1}{3} = 6$.

So, $\frac{2}{3} \div \frac{1}{6} = 4$.

There's one $\frac{1}{3}$ and half of another $\frac{1}{3}$.
$\frac{1}{3}$ is contained $1\frac{1}{2}$ times in $\frac{1}{2}$.

So, $\frac{1}{2} \div \frac{1}{3} = 1\frac{1}{2}$

How many times is $\frac{3}{4}$ contained in $\frac{1}{2}$?

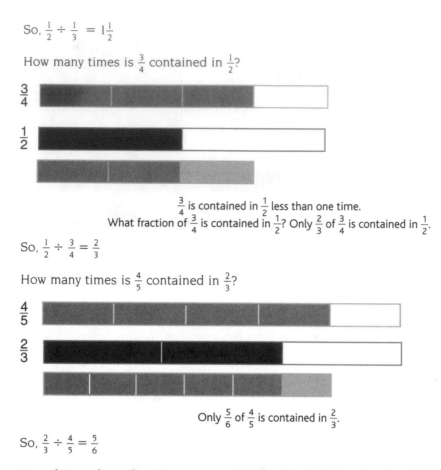

$\frac{3}{4}$ is contained in $\frac{1}{2}$ less than one time.
What fraction of $\frac{3}{4}$ is contained in $\frac{1}{2}$? Only $\frac{2}{3}$ of $\frac{3}{4}$ is contained in $\frac{1}{2}$.

So, $\frac{1}{2} \div \frac{3}{4} = \frac{2}{3}$

How many times is $\frac{4}{5}$ contained in $\frac{2}{3}$?

Only $\frac{5}{6}$ of $\frac{4}{5}$ is contained in $\frac{2}{3}$.

So, $\frac{2}{3} \div \frac{4}{5} = \frac{5}{6}$

Now that we know how to use a model to get answers to fraction-division examples, we can use those results to discover the computation rule. By placing division examples beside related multiplication examples, we can help the student to recognize the pattern. For example, we can use the following pairs. In each pair we use the modeling procedure just discussed to find the division answers, and allow students to use their previously learned ability to multiply fractions to get the multiplication answers.

$$\frac{2}{3} \div \frac{4}{5} = \frac{5}{6} \qquad \frac{2}{3} \times \frac{5}{4} = \frac{5}{6}$$

$$\frac{2}{5} \div \frac{1}{3} = \frac{6}{5} \qquad \frac{2}{5} \times \frac{3}{1} = \frac{6}{5}$$

$$\frac{3}{8} \div \frac{1}{5} = \frac{15}{8} \qquad \frac{3}{8} \times \frac{5}{1} = \frac{15}{8}$$

$$\frac{5}{6} \div \frac{5}{8} = \frac{4}{3} \qquad \frac{5}{6} \times \frac{8}{5} = \frac{40}{30} = \frac{4}{3}$$

The students should notice that the answers are the same for both examples of each pair and that the first fraction is the same for both examples in each pair. They also see that in each pair one example is division and the other is multiplication. They notice that in the multiplication example, the second number is the reciprocal of the second number in the division example.

After they observe these patterns, the students can easily be led to the generalization that the answer to the division example is found by changing the divisor to its reciprocal and changing the division to multiplication. (This, of course, is the rule that all of us learned: invert the divisor and multiply.)

As a point of interest we now discuss a procedure for dividing fractions that is mathematically sound and easy to use. This is a standard procedure in algebra which is seldom included in the elementary school mathematics curriculum. Understanding this procedure depends on students' understanding comparison division.

One way to compare a group of 12 children to a group of four children is to divide. Since $12 \div 4 = 3$, we know that the larger group is three times bigger than the smaller group. If we reverse the groups and compare the group of four children to the group of 12, we have $4 \div 12 = \frac{1}{3}$. This tells us that the smaller group is $\frac{1}{3}$ as big as the larger group.

Suppose we want to compare eggs. In one group we have eight eggs and in the other group, we have two dozen eggs. We cannot just divide the two numbers, $8 \div 2 = 4$, and then say that one group is four times bigger than the other. We must remember the big idea of comparison: *always compare like units*. If we rename the two quantities so that the same unit is used for both, we can divide to make the comparison. We need to rename the two dozen eggs as 24 eggs. Now we can easily compare 8 eggs to 24 eggs. Since $8 \div 24 = \frac{1}{3}$, we can say that eight eggs is $\frac{1}{3}$ as much as 24 eggs.

Now, we think of fraction division as comparison. To find the answer to $\frac{2}{3} \div \frac{4}{5}$, we compare the two fractions. But we have a problem: The fractional units are not the same. Before we can make the comparison we must rename the fractions using the same unit (a common denominator).

$$\frac{2}{3} \div \frac{4}{5} = \frac{10}{15} \div \frac{12}{15}$$

Now that the units are the same, we compare the two fractions, $\frac{10}{15}$ and $\frac{12}{15}$. We compare 10 of those units with 12 of the same units. The comparison is 10 to 12, or $\frac{10}{12}$. So, $\frac{2}{3} \div \frac{4}{5} = \frac{10}{12} = \frac{5}{6}$.

To state the process simply, we rewrite the fractions with a common denominator and compare the two numerators. This process appears in algebra as simplification of complex fractions. In the algebra texts, it would look more like this.

$$\frac{\frac{2}{3}}{\frac{4}{5}} = \frac{\frac{2 \times 5}{3 \times 5}}{\frac{4 \times 3}{5 \times 3}} = \frac{\frac{10}{15}}{\frac{12}{15}} = \frac{\frac{10}{\cancel{15}} \times \cancel{15}}{\frac{12}{\cancel{15}} \times \cancel{15}} = \frac{\frac{10}{1}}{\frac{12}{1}} = \frac{10}{12}$$

The following set of activities illustrates ways that a teacher might develop multiplication and division of fractions.

ACTIVITY 8.21   What Fraction Is in the Box?

Write a fraction on the chalkboard, and using fraction pies (fraction circles), have a student select the fraction pieces that represent that fraction and place the fraction pieces in a box. Have another student come forward and use the fraction pieces to represent the same fraction and then place those fraction pieces in the box with the first representation. Then have a third student do the same thing.

Ask the class how many times the fraction was placed in the box. Point out that since the fraction was placed in the box 3 times, the number in the box is 3 times the original fraction. Ask what number is the box.

Repeat the actvity with other examples.

ACTIVITY 8.22   Length Times Width Is Area

Show the students a rectangle separated into squares. Ask what the length and width of the rectangle are. Ask what the area is. Point out that the length is the same as the number of squares in one row, and the width is the same as the number of rows. The area is the number of rows times the number in each row, 3×6.

Show several rectangles with length and width given. Write each of the areas as a product (5×2, $5 \times n$, $a \times 7$, or $\frac{4}{5} \times \frac{1}{2}$).

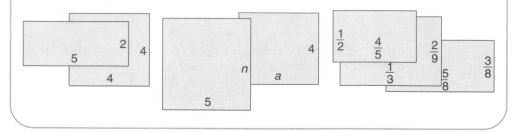

⨉ + ⨅ ACTIVITY 8.23 Two Names for the Area

Show a unit square with its sides subdivided as shown.
Ask how many parts each side is divided into.

Highlight fractional lengths on each side as shown.
Ask what fraction of each side is highlighted.
Label the fractional lengths.

Subdivide the square and then shade the rectangle
with the sides highlighted as shown.

Remind the class that you multiply the length and
width of a rectangle to get the area. Write $\frac{2}{3} \times \frac{1}{2}$.
Point out that this is the area of the shaded rectangle.

Ask how many parts the square was divided into.
Ask how many parts are shaded. What is the
fraction name for the shaded part of the square?

We now have two names for the shaded rectangle, $\frac{2}{3} \times \frac{1}{2}$
and $\frac{2}{6}$, so they must be equal. $\frac{2}{3} \times \frac{1}{2} = \frac{2}{6}$.

Repeat the process with several other examples. Keep a record of
all the results.

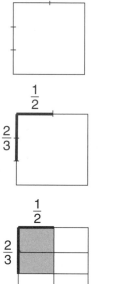

⨉ + ⨅ ACTIVITY 8.24 Match Me

Prepare pairs of cards with one card of each pair showing a fraction multiplication example and
the other card in the pair showing the answer to the example.

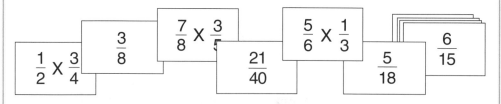

Pass out cards to the students. If there is an odd number of students, the teacher should keep a
card and participate so every student will have a partner. Have them find their partners. Partners
should have problems and matching answers.

When everyone has found a partner, have the partners hold their cards so that everyone can see
and check the answers.

Collect the cards, shuffle them, and repeat the activity.

✕ ÷ ◁ ACTIVITY 8.25 Measuring with Fractions

Prepare strips of colored paper that are the indicated lengths and label them with the indicated labels. Make five of each green strip.

Red Paper	Label	Green Paper	Label
6 inches	6 inches	2 inches	2 inches
8 inches	8 inches		
4 inches	4 inches	8 inches	8 inches
30 cm	1	10 cm	$\frac{1}{3}$
15 cm	$\frac{1}{2}$	6 cm	$\frac{1}{5}$
10 cm	$\frac{1}{3}$	20 cm	$\frac{2}{3}$

Show the class how to measure the 6-inch red strip using the 2-inch green strip as the unit. Show that three of the green strips equal the length of the red strip. Have students measure the 8-inch red strip using the 2-inch green strips. Have them measure the 4-inch red strip with the 8-inch green strip. Fold the green strip so they can see what fraction of the green strip it takes.

Also measure a red strip with the label 1, using the green $\frac{1}{3}$. Measure the red $\frac{1}{2}$ with the green $\frac{1}{5}$ and measure the red $\frac{1}{3}$ with the green $\frac{2}{3}$.

ACTIVITY 8.26 Dividing by Measuring

Create a set of fraction strips and label each strip. Make several copies of each fraction strip. Measure the strips carefully, using the lengths that follow:

$\frac{1}{2}$	15 cm	$\frac{1}{3}$	10 cm	$\frac{2}{3}$	20 cm
$\frac{1}{4}$	7.5 cm	$\frac{3}{4}$	22.5 cm	$\frac{1}{5}$	6 cm
$\frac{2}{5}$	12 cm	$\frac{3}{5}$	18 cm	$\frac{4}{5}$	24 cm
$\frac{1}{6}$	5 cm	$\frac{5}{6}$	25 cm		

Also, prepare a 12-inch strip of paper and three 4-inch strips. Begin with a whole-number division example. Write $12 \div 4$ on the chalkboard. Demonstrate how to find the answer to a division example by measuring. Show that since three 4s are contained in 12, we know that $12 \div 4 = 3$.

Use the fraction strips to demonstrate that since there are four $\frac{1}{6}$-strips in $\frac{2}{3}$, we know that $\frac{2}{3} \div \frac{1}{6} = 4$.

Show that $\frac{1}{2} \div \frac{1}{5} = 2\frac{1}{2}$. Show that $\frac{1}{2} \div \frac{3}{4} = \frac{2}{3}$.

Have students come forward and find the answers to several examples.

ACTIVITY 8.27 Related Multiplication and Division

Following the procedures of Activity 8.26, find the answers to several fraction-division examples. Record the examples in a column with their answers. Then have the students find the answers to multiplication examples that are related to the completed division examples as follows.

$$\frac{1}{2} \div \frac{3}{4} = \frac{2}{3} \qquad \frac{1}{2} \times \frac{4}{3} = \frac{2}{3}$$

$$\frac{1}{3} \div \frac{1}{5} = \frac{5}{3} \qquad \frac{1}{3} \times \frac{5}{1} = \frac{5}{3}$$

Point out that the answers are the same for the division example and the related multiplication example. Ask how you could get the answer to the division without dividing. [You could do the related multiplication.]

Have the students find some answers to division examples by doing the related multiplication. Divide using the fraction strips to check the answers.

ACTIVITY 8.28 Find Three

Prepare sets of three cards. One card shows a division example, the second shows the related multiplication example, and the third shows the answer. There should be enough sets of cards so there will be a set for every two children plus one extra set to use as an example. Shuffle these cards and tape them to the walls around the room.

Point out the cards to the class. Select one of the division cards. Take it off the wall and hold it up so everyone can see. Tell them that there is a card with a related multiplication example. Have the students help you find it. Then tell them that the answer is also somewhere on the walls. Have them help you find it.

Pair all the students with partners. Have each pair of partners find a division card and take it off the wall. When they have done this, tell them to find the multiplication card and the answer card that goes with their division card.

When everyone is finished, have the partners show their cards to the rest of the class. Is everyone correct? Have the class decide.

✕÷✓ ACTIVITY 8.29   Division the Easy Way

Review what the class has learned about fraction division and the related multiplication examples. Have students help you verbalize a rule for changing division to multiplication. (The rule might be something like "invert the divisor and multiply," but try to use the students' words as much as possible.)

Use the rule to do a division example.

Choose a student to come to the front and demonstrate using the rule to do another example. Keep emphasizing how easy it is.

Group the students with partners. Write division examples on the board. Have each student use the rule to find the answer. Then have them check answers with their partners. If they do not agree on the answer, they should figure out who is correct.

Keep emphasizing how easy it is to divide fractions.

Adapting a Lesson on Fractions

We consider now another lesson plan, beginning with a traditional lesson based on suggestions in the teacher's guide. This lesson, which teaches equivalent fractions, was chosen from a fourth-grade textbook.

LESSON OBJECTIVE

The student will write equal fractions using fraction models.

Lesson Opener

Have students name the fraction that is shaded:

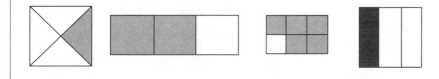

Show students that there are many ways to name the same number. 10 is the same number as $15 - 5$ or $8 + 2$. Have them write the number 10 using as many different names as possible.

Development

Direct the attention of the class to the example on the first page of the lesson. Point out that the child in the picture is placing two fraction pieces for sixths on top of one fraction piece for thirds. Draw their attention to the fact that the two sixths fit exactly on top of the third, so two sixths is the same amount as one third. Write $\frac{2}{6} = \frac{1}{3}$.

Have the students look at the second picture on the page. Point out that six eighths fit exactly on top of three fourths. Ask what number should be placed in the box to make the fraction equation true.

Monitor Learning

Have the students do the three examples in the *Checking Learning* section at the bottom of the page. Identify students who do not understand.

Practice

Assign the practice exercises on the second page of the lesson. Remind the students that they should look at the picture of the fraction strips if they have difficulty. Assign the *Reteaching Worksheet* to students who had difficulty with the examples in the *Checking Learning* section.

Closure

At the end of math time, remind the class that today they learned how to use the fraction model to find equal fractions. Tell the class that their homework is to complete the rest of the assigned exercises.

Following is a revised plan that expands the developmental portion of the lesson. The lesson provides more visual input, is more kinesthetic, and has more opportunities for communication from and among students. Learning will be monitored regularly throughout the lesson. These adaptations make the lesson appropriate for most students. But, remember that some students with severe needs may require further instructional adaptations.

LESSON OBJECTIVE

The student will write equal fractions using fraction models.

Lesson Opener
Have students name the fraction that is shaded:

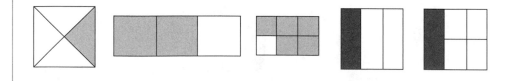

Direct the attention of the students to the last two examples. Ask if they can see how the two pictures are related. [The same amount is shaded.] If no one notices that the same amount is shaded, ask them what they would see if the shaded part of one picture were placed directly on top of the shaded part of the other picture. [They would fit exactly.]

After the students recognize that the same amount is shaded in both pictures, point out that the two fractions name the same amount. These two fractions are just two names for the same amount. Whenever two numbers name the same amount, they are equal. **Monitor Understanding.** Observe the students closely. If any appear not to understand, show an example using prepared overhead transparencies for $\frac{1}{2}$ and $\frac{2}{4}$. Place one transparency on top of the other to help the students see that exactly the same amount is shaded in both fractions.

Explain that in today's lesson, they will learn how to use this idea to find equal fractions.

Development

Tape these pictorial models of fractions on the chalkboard. Leave about 10 inches of boardspace below them.

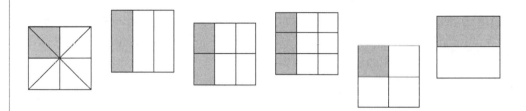

Point to the first fraction. Ask someone to name the fraction. Then have that student write the fraction on the chalkboard below its picture. Ask if anyone can find another fraction that has the same amount shaded. Have them name that fraction and write it below the picture. Ask, "Since these two fractions name the same amount, what can we say about them?" [They are equal.] Write $\frac{2}{8} = \frac{1}{4}$.

Direct the attention of the class to the example on the first page of the lesson. Point out that the child in the picture is placing two fraction pieces for sixths on top of one fraction piece for thirds. Draw their attention to the fact that the two sixths fit exactly on top of one third, so two sixths is the same amount as one sixth. Write $\frac{2}{6} = \frac{1}{3}$.

Continue this process until all the equal fractions have been paired and identified as equal. **Monitor Understanding.** Continue observing to see that everyone understands. Give particular attention to students with a history of poor comprehension. Actively involve these students in the discussion of results.

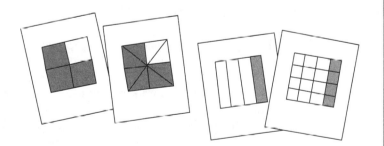

Hand out cards showing pictorial models of fractions. Every fractional quantity used should be on two cards, illustrating two fraction names for the same quantity. Have the students get with the other person that has the same amount pictured. **Monitor Understanding.** Notice if students are having trouble finding others with the same amount shaded. Provide individual help as needed.

When the students are paired correctly, call on them, one pair at a time, to write the equation on the board that says that their fractions are equal. **Monitor Understanding.** Provide help to students who are likely to have trouble, so that they can complete this part of the activity correctly and avoid embarrassment.

Have the students look at the picture on the first page of the lesson in the textbook. Point out that the pictures show children using fraction pieces to do what we have been doing. Tell them to notice that, in the second picture, six eighths fit exactly on top of three fourths. Ask what number should be placed in the box to make the fraction equation true.

$$\frac{3}{4} = \frac{\square}{8}$$

Pair the students with partners. Have the students complete the three examples in the *Checking Learning* section at the bottom of the page. When they are finished, they should compare answers with their partners. If their answers disagree, they are to discuss them and figure out together what the correct answers are.

Monitor Understanding

Move around the room and observe student work. Identify students who do not understand. Provide assistance as needed.

Practice

Have the students continue to work with their partners to complete practice exercises 2, 3, 7, and 9 on the second page of the lesson. Remind the students that the pictures can help them if they have difficulty with any exercise.

Closure

When enough time has been allowed to complete the exercises, ask the class what they learned today about equal fractions. If necessary, ask these questions: How can they tell that two fractions name the same amount? If two fractions name the same amount, what can we say about those two fractions?

Follow Up

Hand out copies of the *Extra Practice Worksheet*. Have the students take the sheet home and show a parent how to do Exercise 6.

Solving Problems Using Fractions

There is little difference between problem solving using fractions and problem solving using whole numbers. It is still necessary to visualize what is happening to quantities, whether they are quantities named by whole numbers or quantities named by fractions. A single quantity can be measured or it can be separated. If there is more than one quantity, those quantities can be combined, or they can be compared.

Suppose we start with a single quantity that is being separated. Subtraction can probably be used to solve the problem. If the quantity is being separated into equal-sized groups, then division can probably be used.

Or we might start with more than one quantity. If those quantities are being combined, addition can probably be used to solve the problem. If the quantities being combined are of equal size, multiplication can probably be used. If quantities are being compared to find a difference, subtraction can probably be used. If quantities are being compared to find how many times bigger one quantity is than another quantity, division can probably be used.

Problem-Solving Strategies

Of course many problems are complex, and they might require a series of steps to arrive at a solution. These successive steps may even require different operations. Because of this complexity, the past 15–20 years have seen a shift in problem-solving emphasis from a focus that was almost exclusively on the solution of word problems toward a strong focus on problem-solving strategies. These strategies are, in effect, coping strategies for complex problem solving. They are ways of attacking problems. They are problem-solving patterns. In a very real sense, they are the big ideas of problem solving.

One problem-solving strategy that is included in almost all elementary school mathematics programs is: *solve part of the problem* or *separate the problem into easier parts*. Another strategy that appears in many programs is: *work backward*.

We examine an example of a problem that makes use of both of these strategies. We separate the problem into easier parts and complete those parts one step at a time, but we work backward beginning with the last step.

> Beth brought some almonds to school one day and decided to share them with three friends. She asked her first friend how many almonds she would like. Her friend asked for three almonds, so Beth gave her three. Her second friend asked if she could have one-third of the almonds that were left, so that's how many Beth gave her. Beth's third friend asked for one half of the remaining almonds, so Beth gave her that many. Beth ate the five almonds that were left. How many almonds did Beth bring to school?

We begin with the last step.

> Beth's third friend asked for one half of the remaining almonds, so Beth gave her that many. Beth ate the 5 almonds that were left.

Beth gave away half and had five left. This means that she was left with as many as she gave away. She must have given away five. So, before that she must have had 10 almonds. Now, we will back up to the previous step.

> Her second friend asked if she could have one third of the almonds that were left, so that's how many Beth gave her.

In this step, Beth gave her friend one third, so she must have been left with two thirds. Since one third is half as much as two thirds, she gave away half as many as she kept. Remember that, at the end of this step, Beth had 10 almonds. She must have given five to her second friend. That means that before doing this she had 15 almonds. Now, we back up to the step where she shared with her first friend.

> She asked her first friend how many almonds she would like. Her friend asked for three almonds, so Beth gave her three

She gave this friend three almonds and had 15 left. Before giving these three almonds away she must have had 18 almonds. This is the number that she brought to school.

Another strategy that appears in most elementary school mathematics programs is: *use a picture or diagram*. In the following problem example, we illustrate the use of this strategy combined with one of the strategies discussed earlier: *separate the problem into easier parts*.

> Ms. Spiffey, a middle school art teacher, arranged for her students to paint one wall of her classroom. They first divided the wall into three equal sections. Then they divided the first of those sections into three equal parts and painted one part red, one part white, and one part blue. They divided the second section into two equal parts and painted one part green

and one part yellow. Finally, they divided the third section into four equal parts and painted one part blue, one part red, one part green, and one part yellow. When they had finished, what fraction of the wall was painted each color?

To simplify the problem we consider one section of the wall at a time. To help us visualize the problem, we draw a picture for each section of the wall. The first section looks like this.

red	
white	
blue	

We can easily see that, so far, $\frac{1}{9}$ of the wall is red, $\frac{1}{9}$ of the wall is white, and $\frac{1}{9}$ of the wall is blue. Now we look at the second section.

| | green | |
| | yellow | |

We can see by examining the picture of this section, that $\frac{1}{6}$ of the wall is painted green and $\frac{1}{6}$ of the wall is painted yellow. Next, we consider the third section of the wall.

		blue
		red
		green
		yellow

In this section, as we can see from the picture, $\frac{1}{12}$ of the wall is blue, $\frac{1}{12}$ of the wall is red, $\frac{1}{12}$ of the wall is green, and $\frac{1}{12}$ of the wall is yellow.

The last thing that we need to do to solve the problem is to add together all the red parts, the white parts, the blue parts, the green parts, and the yellow parts. To be sure that we have not overlooked any parts, we will use another commonly taught strategy: *use a table*.

| Colors | Section | | |
	1	2	3
Red	$\frac{1}{9}$		$\frac{1}{12}$
White	$\frac{1}{9}$		
Blue	$\frac{1}{9}$		$\frac{1}{12}$
Green		$\frac{1}{6}$	$\frac{1}{12}$
Yellow		$\frac{1}{6}$	$\frac{1}{12}$

What part of the wall is red? $\frac{1}{9} + \frac{1}{12} = \frac{4}{36} + \frac{3}{36} = \frac{7}{36}$

What part of the wall is white? $\frac{1}{9}$

What part of the wall is blue? $\frac{1}{9} + \frac{1}{12} = \frac{4}{36} + \frac{3}{36} = \frac{7}{36}$

What part of the wall is green? $\frac{1}{6} + \frac{1}{12} = \frac{2}{12} + \frac{1}{12} = \frac{3}{12} = \frac{1}{4}$

What part of the wall is yellow? $\frac{1}{6} + \frac{1}{12} = \frac{2}{12} + \frac{1}{12} = \frac{3}{12} = \frac{1}{4}$

Exercises and Activities

1. Adapt Activities 8.01–8.03 to develop the concept of three fourths.
2. Develop a learning activity that has children find other fractions equivalent to given fractions using the procedure illustrated on pages 206–207.
3. Develop a learning activity that has children find other fractions equivalent to given fractions using the procedure illustrated on pages 207–208.
4. Develop an instructional activity to teach children how to find a fraction with a particular denominator that is equivalent to a given fraction. The activity should use the fraction-squares pictorial model.
5. Choose a lesson on fractions or mixed numbers from a published elementary school mathematics textbook series.
   a. Write a lesson plan that follows the teaching suggestions in the teacher's guide.
   b. Identify the parts of the lesson that provide visual information about the concept(s) or skill(s) being taught.
   c. Expand the lesson by adding activities that provide more visual information about the concepts or skills being taught.
6. Choose a lesson on fractions or mixed numbers from a published elementary school mathematics textbook series.
   a. Write a lesson plan that follows the teaching suggestions in the teacher's guide.
   b. Identify kinesthetic activity, if any is included in the lesson.
   c. Add more kinesthetic activity to the lesson.
7. Choose a lesson on fractions or mixed numbers from a published elementary school mathematics textbook series.
   a. Write a lesson plan that follows the teaching suggestions in the teacher's guide.
   b. Identify parts of the lesson that include student communication about the concept(s) or skill(s) taught in the lesson.
   c. Add more opportunities for communication from or among students to the lesson.
8. Choose a lesson on fractions or mixed numbers from a published elementary school mathematics textbook series.
   a. Write a lesson plan that follows the teaching suggestions in the teacher's guide.
   b. Identify the parts of the lesson designed to assess the learning of the students.
   c. Add more continual assessment (monitoring of learning) to the lesson plan.
9. Study the adapted lesson plan on pages 236–238. Make further changes in the lesson plan to make it more appropriate for children who are tactile learners.

10. Study the adapted lesson plan on pages 236–238. Make further changes in the lesson plan to make it more appropriate for a child whose learning disability includes figure-ground confusion.

11. Study the adapted lesson plan on pages 236–238. Make further changes in the lesson plan to make it more appropriate for a child who has attention deficit disorder.

12. On page 215 a process for adding unlike fractions is presented. Develop a lesson using the laboratory approach to teach this process for adding unlike fractions.

13. Develop a lesson using the laboratory approach to develop multiplication of fractions. Use the "fraction of a fraction" approach that is discussed on page 224 to model fraction multiplication.

14. Develop a lesson using the laboratory approach to teach multiplication of fractions. Use the area model that is discussed on pages 225–226 to model fraction multiplication.

15. Consider the problem given below. Use the work backward strategy to break the problem into easy parts (see page 239). Then, explain to a friend how to solve the problem.

    Beth brought some almonds to school and shared them with five friends. The first friend was given one fourth of the almonds. Then the second friend was given eight. The third friend was given one half of the remaining almonds, and then the fourth friend was given three. Beth gave the fifth friend one half of what she had left, and had four almonds left over for herself. How many almonds did Beth bring to school?

16. Reread the problem presented on page 239. Adapt the problem for a child who is color blind. After the changes that you make in the problem, it should still require the child to use the same problem-solving steps.

17. Read the discussion of Standard 12, Fractions and Decimals, on pages 57–59 of *Curriculum and Evaluation Standards for School Mathematics*, published by the National Council of Teachers of Mathematics.

18. The following fraction division results illustrate an error pattern like those that were related by Robert Ashlock, in his book, *Error Patterns in Computation: A Semi-programmed Approach.*

    $$\frac{6}{8} \div \frac{3}{8} = \frac{2}{1} \qquad \frac{4}{9} \div \frac{2}{3} = \frac{2}{3} \qquad \frac{9}{17} \div \frac{3}{4} = \frac{3}{4} \qquad \frac{7}{2} \div \frac{2}{5} = \frac{3}{2}$$

    a. What is this student's error pattern? What is the student doing to produce the incorrect answers?

    b. Plan a mini-lesson to correct this student's error pattern.

19. The error pattern illustrated in Exercise 18 was almost a correct procedure. The procedure described in the equation below always produces a correct answer. Use fraction multiplication to demonstrate that this procedure is correct.

    $$\frac{a}{b} \div \frac{c}{d} = \frac{a \div c}{b \div d}$$

References and Related Readings

Ashlock, R. B. (1998). *Error patterns in computation: A semi-programmed approach* (7th ed.). Upper Saddle River, NJ: Merrill/Prentice Hall.

National Council of Teachers of Mathematics. (1989). *Curriculum and evaluation standards for school mathematics.* Reston, VA: NCTM.

National Council of Teachers of Mathematics. (2000). *Principles and standards for school mathematics.* Reston, VA: NCTM.

Nowlin, D. (1996). Division with fractions. *Mathematics Teaching in the Middle School, 2,* 116–119.

Thornton, C. A., Tucker, B. F., Dossey, J. A., & Bazik, E. F. (1983). *Teaching mathematics to children with special needs*. Menlo Park, CA: Addison-Wesley.

Tucker, B. F. (1989). Three methods for modeling multiplication of fractions. *Virginia Mathematics Teacher*, 15(2), 7–9. (Reprinted from *The Illinois Mathematics Teacher*, 37(4), 7–12.)

Web Sites

http://www.eduplace.com/math/mathsteps/3/b/index.html
(Developing the concept of fraction addition.)

http://www.forum.swarthmore.edu/
(Math Forum Links to Math Discussions and Ideas.)

http://ecep1.usl.edu/ecep/math/g/g.htm
(Real-world problems with fractions.)

http://www.ed.gov/databases/ERIC_Digests/ed433184.html
(Resources for teaching fractions.)

http://www.mcn.net/~jimloy/fractn.html
(Fractions and ratios.)

http://teachers.net/lessons/posts/262.html
(Fractions of a set.)

http://www.teachers.net/lessons/posts/17.html
(Fractions of a region.)

http://www.pro-teacher.com/100014.shtml
(Lesson plans by teachers.)

http://forum.swarthmore.edu/paths/fractions/
(Links to fraction sites and lessons.)

http://www.studyweb.com/links/4593.html
(Links to fraction sites. Tips and lessons.)

http://www.newton.mec.edu/Angier/DimSum/Equiv.%20Fraction%20Lesson.html
(A good lesson plan for discussion and adaptation.)

CHAPTER 9

DECIMALS AND PERCENTS:

Working with Base-Ten Units Smaller Than One and Using Hundredths as a Common Denominator

THE NUMBER AND OPERATIONS STANDARD

"... focus should be on developing students' conceptual understanding of fractions and decimals—what they are, how they are represented, and how they are related to whole numbers ..." (National Council of Teachers of Mathematics, 2000, p. 152).

"Teachers can help students extend their understanding of addition and subtraction of whole numbers to decimals by building on a solid understanding of place value ..." (NCTM, 2000, p. 218).

THE PROBLEM-SOLVING STANDARD

"... learning about problem solving helps students become familiar with a number of problem-solving heuristics, such as looking for patterns, solving a simpler of problem, making a table, and working backward" (NCTM, 2000, p. 260).

THE COMMUNICATION STANDARD

"The middle-grades mathematics teacher should strive to establish a communication-rich classroom in which students are encouraged to share their ideas and to seek clarification until they understand" (NCTM, 2000, p. 271).

"Students reveal the ways they are connecting ideas when they answer questions such as, What made you think of that? Why does that make sense? Where have we seen a problem like this before? How are these ideas related? Did anyone think about this in a different way? How does today's work relate to what we have done in earlier units of study?" (NCTM, 2000, p. 274).

Defining Decimals

Decimals can be thought of as fractions, and sometimes as mixed numbers. They are fractions or mixed numbers with denominators that are always equal to the base-ten whole number units. The whole-number base-ten units are ones, tens, hundreds, thousands, ten-thousands, and so on. The decimal fraction units are tenths, hundredths, thousandths, ten-thousandths, and so on. The number one can be thought of as the denominator for the decimal units that are greater than or equal to one. The properties that control what we can do with decimals are the same ones that govern our use of whole numbers and decimals.

As with other numbers that we have considered earlier, we want our students to recognize and name decimal quantities using appropriate terminology, to use appropriate models to show decimal quantities, and to write decimals using appropriate notation. These learning objectives require that we have effective models for decimals. The minimum requirement for a decimal model is the ability to represent the basic units. This means that the chosen model should allow for the representation of ones, tens, hundreds, and so on, as well as tenths, hundredths, thousandths, and so on, or at least the units from this list that are being used in the current lesson.

The base-ten blocks is a model that fits this description. The large cube would represent 1, the flats (each 1 tenth of the large cube) would represent tenths. The longs or the rods (each 1 tenth of a flat and 1 hundredth of a large cube) would represent hundredths. The small cubes (each equal to 1 tenth of a long, 1 hundredth of a flat; and 1 thousandth of a large cube) would represent thousandths. This illustration represents the decimal 1.324 using base-ten blocks.

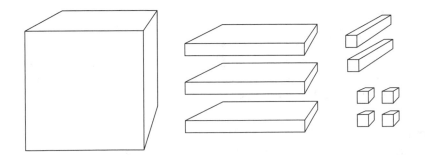

Another option is the decimal square model. This is a two-dimensional model that lends itself to the printed page and it is frequently used in textbooks. A square represents 1. If the square is cut into ten equal-sized strips, the strips represent tenths. If a strip is cut into ten equal squares, these smaller squares represent hundredths. Sometimes the large square is divided into 100 smaller squares and part of the subdivided square is shaded to represent a decimal.

The number 2.47 is represented using both models.

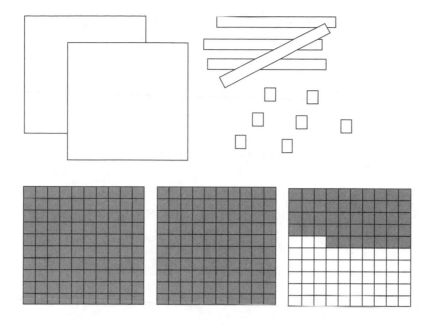

Another model that is sometimes used is the metric-length model. A meter represents 1, a decimeter represents 1 tenth, a centimeter represents 1 hundredth, and a millimeter represents 1 thousandth. This model is not often useful in instructional settings. In instructional settings, one of the other models is invariably more effective.

The money model is another model frequently used to represent decimals. Along with $1-, $10-, and $100-dollar bills to represent ones, tens, and hundreds, this model also uses dimes to represent tenths and pennies to represent hundredths. Since the various pieces of money are capable of being combined, separated, and compared, this model is useful to teach a wide variety of decimal topics.

The final model that we mention is the pocket chart, which is useful when stressing place value. This model is relatively abstract and probably should not be used in the early introduction of decimals. Decimals are represented by markers placed in various positions, and the units associated with those positions must be identified in some way.

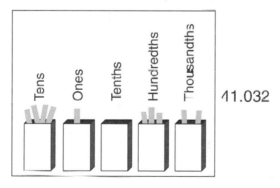 11.032

Place Value for Decimals

When using decimal notation to write decimal fractions, the denominators are not written. Rather, they are indicated by the position of the number. One important task for the teacher, then, is to help students to be able to determine the decimal units from their position. *It is important to first communicate that decimal notation is really an extension of whole-number notation.* Moving from one position to another from right to left, the value of numbers in each position is 10 times the value of numbers in the previous position.

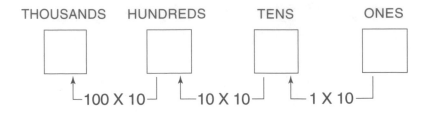

Similarly, moving from one position to another from left to right, the value of numbers in each position is the value of numbers in the previous position divided by 10.

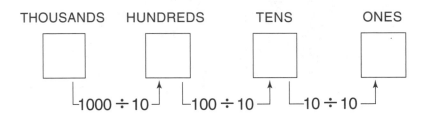

This pattern holds when adding the decimal units that are less than one.

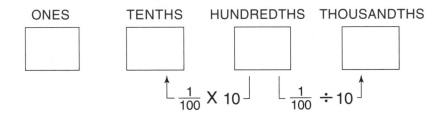

Students also need to understand is that there is symmetry in the decimal numeration system (Thornton, et al., 1983). A common misconception is that the system is symmetric around the decimal point. Actually, *the system is symmetric around the ones*.

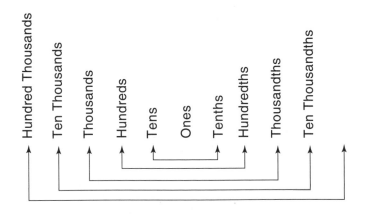

Once we are familiar with the nature of the symmetry, we have the ability to find the value of each place starting from any known position. For example, if we know that the 7 is in the tens place of this number, we can figure out the value of the other places.

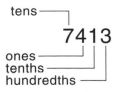

If we know that the 2 in this number is in the tenths place, we can figure out the value of all the other places.

tenths ───────────┐
$$52906$$
ones ──────────────┘
hundredths ──────────┘
thousandths ─────────┘
ten-thousandths ─────┘

If we know that the 8 in this number is in the ones place, we can figure out the value of every other place.

ones ─────────────┐
$$3815$$
tens ───────────────┘
tenths ─────────────┘
hundredths ─────────┘

A device called the decimal point helps us to identify the place values. The decimal point is always placed to the right of the ones place. Once we know which position is the ones place, we use our knowledge of the symmetry of the system to identify the value of all the other positions.

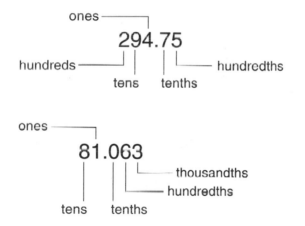

Children should be taught in a meaningful way to read decimals. If the instructional focus is on rote reading procedures, we might appear to gain fast results. However, because so much subsequent reteaching is necessary, we should question the value of such fast results. Remember, it is always harder to remember things that are meaningless. There are, however, several connections that can be developed that improve retention of the rules for reading decimals in a standard way.

Let's begin by looking at two simple related examples from our work with fractions and mixed numbers.

$4 + \frac{2}{3}$ is usually written as $4\frac{2}{3}$ and read as "4 and $\frac{2}{3}$."

$6 + \frac{1}{2} + \frac{1}{4}$ would usually be simplified by adding the two

fractions together to get $6 + \frac{3}{4}$. This would be read as "6 and $\frac{3}{4}$."

The decimal 5.27 literally means $5 + \frac{2}{10} + \frac{7}{100}$. This can be read as 5 and $\frac{2}{10}$ and $\frac{7}{100}$. We can simplify the reading by adding the two fractions. Then we can just read it as a mixed number. To add the two fractions together, we need to rewrite them using a common denominator.

$$5 + \frac{2}{10} + \frac{7}{100} = 5 + \frac{20}{100} + \frac{7}{100} = 5 + \frac{27}{100}$$

Then we can read it as "5 and 27 hundredths." If we look at 5.27 using the decimal square model, we can arrive at the same result.

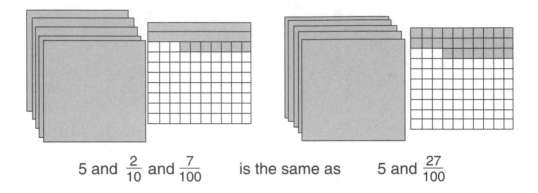

5 and $\frac{2}{10}$ and $\frac{7}{100}$ is the same as   5 and $\frac{27}{100}$

In the same way, we can show that 24.96, which is 24 and $\frac{9}{10}$ and $\frac{6}{100}$, is the same as "24 and $\frac{96}{100}$."

From examples like these, students can be led to understand why a decimal like 207.435 is read as "207 and 435 thousandths." They understand that they are simply reading a mixed number.

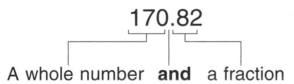

170.82

A whole number **and** a fraction

170 **and** 82 hundredths

When teaching decimals, there are six tasks the student should be able to complete correctly.

1. When shown a decimal quantity (using a decimal model), the student should be able to name the decimal.
2. When shown a decimal quantity (using a decimal model), the student should be able to write the decimal.
3. When the student hears a decimal named, he or she should be able to show the decimal quantity (using a decimal model).
4. When the student hears a decimal named, he or she should be able to write the decimal.
5. When the student sees a written decimal, he or she should be able to name the decimal.
6. When the student sees a written decimal, he or she should be able to show the decimal quantity (using a decimal model).

Instruction should include activities that help the student learn to do these tasks. The following activities illustrate how this can be done.

✗ ➕ ➗ ACTIVITY 9.01   Show and Write

From a roll of adding machine tape, cut nine strips that are 1 meter long, nine strips that are 10 centimeters long, and nine pieces that are 1 centimeter long. Explain that the 1 m strips each represent 1. The 10 cm strips each represent 1 tenth, and the 1 cm pieces each represent 1 hundredth.

Show the class some combination of strips of each size. Have each student write the decimal that is represented. Then ask someone to tell you how many of each unit are included. Write the correct decimal. Ask how many got it right.

Repeat several times with different quantities.

✗ ➕ ➗ ACTIVITY 9.02   Show, Write, and Tell

Use decimal squares to show a decimal quantity. For example, you might show this quantity.

Have every student write the decimal that is represented. Then ask someone to read the decimal. If necessary, discuss why the written decimal shows 4 tenths and 6 hundredths, but we read it as 46 hundredths.

Repeat several times with different quantities.

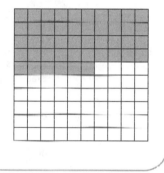

✗ ➕ ➗ ACTIVITY 9.03   I'll Tell, You Show

Hand out copies of the decimal square worksheet shown at the right.

Read aloud a decimal (ones, tenths, and hundredths), and have the students color a representation of that decimal.

Repeat several times with different decimals.

✕ + ⁴ ACTIVITY 9.04   I'll Tell, You Write and Show

Hand out copies of the decimal square worksheet shown at the right.

Read aloud a decimal (ones, tenths, and hundredths), and have the students color a representation of that decimal.

Then have the students write the decimal.

Repeat several times with different decimals.

✕ + ⁴ ACTIVITY 9.05   I'll Tell. You Write and Show Me the Money

Make 8 to 10 packages of play money. Include in each package, four $10 bills, six $1 bills, five dimes, and nine pennies.

Form groups of three students, and give each group a package of money.

Explain that, when you read a decimal, one person in the group will get the money to show that quantity, one person will write the decimal, and the third person will check them to see if they are right. Tell them that they are to take turns doing each job.

Read aloud a decimal (tens, ones, tenths, and hundredths). Be sure that there are no more than 4 tens, 6 ones, 5 tenths or 9 hundredths.

Repeat several times with different decimals. Be sure to monitor the students' work to catch and correct misconceptions.

Comparison of Decimals

Comparison of decimals is not difficult. Virtually every error pattern related to comparing fractions results directly from lack of appropriate mental imagery for the numbers being compared. The student who thinks .98 must surely be greater than 1.2 because 9 and 8 are both more than 1 or 2 is not visualizing the numbers. The student who thinks 6.21 must be greater than 7.3 because three-digit numbers are bigger than two-digit numbers, is not visualizing the numbers.

Almost invariably, error patterns like these can be eliminated by providing mental imagery for the numbers. It seems reasonable, then, that development of appropriate mental imagery should be an integral part of the initial teaching of this topic. Experiences with models that allow the student to literally see when one decimal is greater than another can be used to develop meaningful rules and procedures for comparing decimals.

To compare .2 and .09, we begin by representing both decimals.

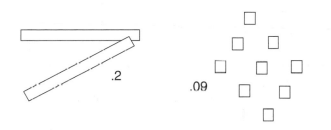

The student can easily see that 2 tenths is greater than 9 hundredths. If unsure, the student can place the hundredths pieces on top of one of the tenths pieces to determine that 9 hundredths is even less than 1 tenth. Then we could ask the students to figure out how many hundredths it would take to equal 2 tenths. This helps to reinforce the comparison.

We use the model to make a lot of comparisons. For example, we might compare 3 and .3, 7.2 and .72, 1.2 and .98.

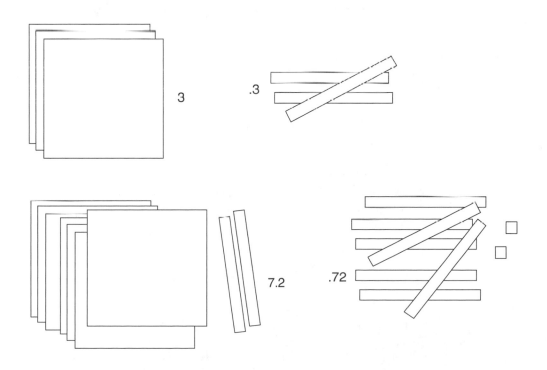

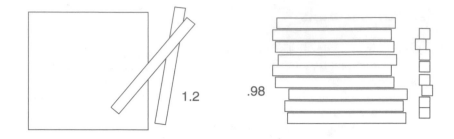

1.2   .98

After recording these and other similar results, the teacher can lead the students to discover a number of helpful patterns.

The value of the number varies according to the position of the digits relative to the decimal point.	$3 > .3$ $7.2 > .72$ $.06 < .60$
The size of the digits is less important than the position of the digits relative to the decimal point.	$.2 > .09$ $.086 < .34$ $1.2 > .98$
Compare numbers by comparing the values of the first nonzero digit	$.206 > .094$ (2 tenths is greater than 9 hundredths.) $.061 > .059$ (6 hundredths is greater than 5 hundredths.) $6.93 < 20.1$ (6 ones is less than 2 tens.)
If the values of the first nonzero digits are equal, then compare the values of the next digits.	$.519 < .523$ (1 hundredth is less than 2 hundredths.) $6.43 > 6.29$ (4 tenths is greater than 2 tenths.) $32.4 < 38.1$ (2 ones is less than 8 ones.)

These patterns can then be fashioned into meaningful rules and procedures for comparing decimals. The rules will be meaningful to the students because they are generalizations from their own discoveries rather than being just "what the teacher said to do."

The following sequence of activities demonstrates how a teacher can develop decimal comparison concepts and skills.

x + y   **ACTIVITY 9.06   Comparing Decimals**

Write two decimals on the chalkboard. Have two students come forward. Have each student represent one of the numbers using squares, strips, and small squares like those illustrated at the right.

After the numbers have been represented with the model, have two other children come forward and check to make sure the numbers were represented correctly.

2.47

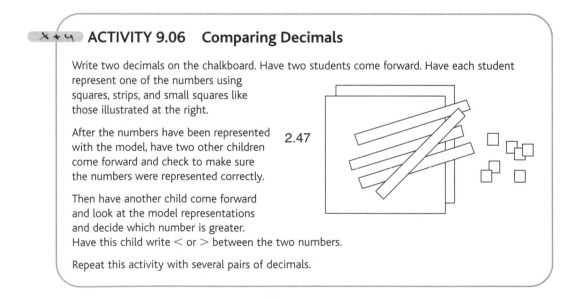

Then have another child come forward and look at the model representations and decide which number is greater.
Have this child write $<$ or $>$ between the two numbers.

Repeat this activity with several pairs of decimals.

✗+4 ACTIVITY 9.07   Partner Comparison

Pair students with partners. Give each pair a set of decimal pieces consisting of 5 ones, 9 tenths, and 9 hundredths.

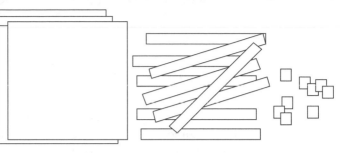

Write two decimals on the chalkboard. Have the partners each use the model to represent one of the numbers. After the numbers have been represented, have the partners decide which number is greater. Then choose a student to come forward and write < or > between the two numbers.

Repeat this activity with several pairs of decimals.

✗+4 ACTIVITY 9.08   Comparison Prediction

Write two decimals on the chalkboard. Tell the students that they will be figuring out which number is greater. Have the students predict which number is greater. If the students agree, call on someone to explain why they think that number is greater. If the students disagree, have students who disagree explain their thinking.

Next, have two students come forward and represent the numbers and check to see if their prediction is correct. Have another child come forward and write < or > between the two numbers.

If a student suggests a clear and correct way to decide which number is greater, write the method on the board and have the class use that method on the next example.

Repeat this activity with several pairs of decimals. Have them sometimes decide which number is less.

✗+4 ACTIVITY 9.09   Comparison Prediction

Prepare a set of about 50 cards showing decimals.

Form a group of 2 to 4 students. Give the group a set of decimal pieces. Shuffle the deck and place it face down on the table.

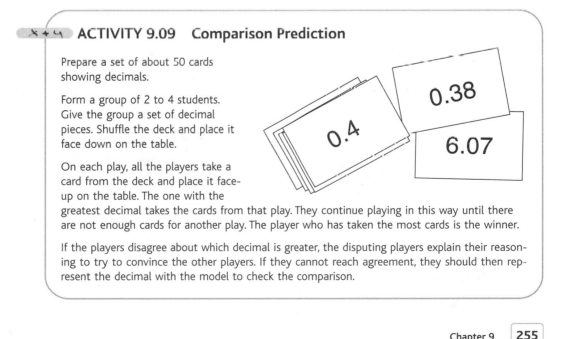

On each play, all the players take a card from the deck and place it face-up on the table. The one with the greatest decimal takes the cards from that play. They continue playing in this way until there are not enough cards for another play. The player who has taken the most cards is the winner.

If the players disagree about which decimal is greater, the disputing players explain their reasoning to try to convince the other players. If they cannot reach agreement, they should then represent the decimal with the model to check the comparison.

Addition and Subtraction of Decimals

The teaching of addition and subtraction of decimals is almost identical to the teaching of addition and subtraction of whole numbers. The same big ideas that govern addition and subtraction of whole numbers are used for adding and subtracting decimals.

For addition: Always add like units.
                      When there are too many to write (in standard form), make a trade.

For subtraction: Always subtract like units.
                      When there are not enough, make a trade.

The only real difference between addition and subtraction of decimals and that of whole numbers is that with decimals, there are more units. We start the instruction by reestablishing the big ideas using a physical model. Using squares, strips, and small squares as a decimal model is an excellent way to illustrate addition and subtraction.

When adding, we model the two numbers, combine them, and record what is there after combining. When subtracting, we model the subtrahend, take away the minuend, and record the remainder.

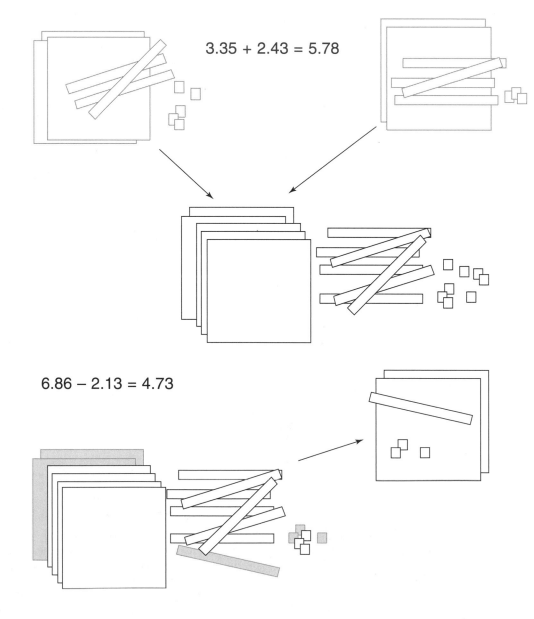

3.35 + 2.43 = 5.78

6.86 − 2.13 = 4.73

Another easy-to-use model for addition and subtraction of decimals is play money. Using $10 bills to represent tens, $1 bills to represent ones, dimes to represent tenths, and pennies to represent hundredths, this representation of decimals can be combined and separated, and when necessary, equal trades can be made.

A Remediation Note. The most common error pattern in addition and subtraction of decimals comes from a rote rule learned when working with whole numbers: The columns must be lined-up. The problem with rote rules is that they are seldom even true beyond certain narrow conditions. And students (even those who have memorized the rules correctly) tend to apply them in inappropriate circumstances. In particular, this rule, when correctly applied in whole-number addition would not produce errors.

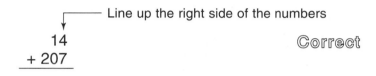

However, when the rule to applied to addition of decimals, the computation is not correct.

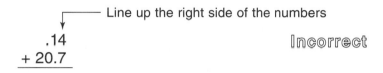

When the teacher identifies this error pattern, it is important that the student not merely be given a new rule (line up the decimal points) to replace the old rule. The reader should not misinterpret this statement. We are not saying that students should not learn to line up the decimal points when adding or subtracting decimals. Lining up the decimal points actually makes the addition or subtraction easier.

What we are suggesting is that when the teacher uses the model to show that if like units are lined up (remember that we *always add like units*), the result is that the decimal points will also be lined up. And, when we line up the decimal points, it turns out that like units are lined up. This is helpful because lining up like units makes it easier to *add like units*. The students still learn the same rule, but the rule is now meaningful. It not only makes sense to the students, but the students also understand why they should follow the rule.

The activity sequence that follows can be used to develop the concepts related to addition and subtraction of decimals.

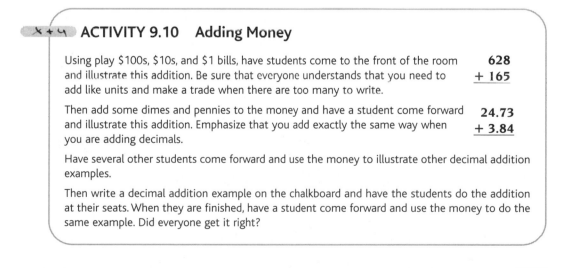

ACTIVITY 9.10   Adding Money

Using play $100s, $10s, and $1 bills, have students come to the front of the room and illustrate this addition. Be sure that everyone understands that you need to add like units and make a trade when there are too many to write.

$$628 + 165$$

Then add some dimes and pennies to the money and have a student come forward and illustrate this addition. Emphasize that you add exactly the same way when you are adding decimals.

$$24.73 + 3.84$$

Have several other students come forward and use the money to illustrate other decimal addition examples.

Then write a decimal addition example on the chalkboard and have the students do the addition at their seats. When they are finished, have a student come forward and use the money to do the same example. Did everyone get it right?

✗ ✦ ↻ ACTIVITY 9.11. Subtracting Money

Follow the procedures described for Activity 9.10, except use subtraction examples.

✗ ✦ ↻ ACTIVITY 9.12 Careful What you Add

Write 42.03 + 615.6 on the chalkboard in horizontal form as shown here. Tell the students that you want to do this addition. Ask what decimal units you will have in the answer. [Hundreds, tens, ones, tenths, and hundredths.] Ask how many ones there will be in the answer. Write 7 on the board with a decimal point after it. Ask how many tens will be in the answer. Record the 5 tens. Ask how many tenths. Record the 3 tenths. Ask how many hundreds. Record the 6 hundreds. Point out that to get the answer you must *add like units*. Model the same addition using play $100 bills, $10 bills, $1 bills, dimes, and pennies to verify that the answer is correct.

As a second example, add 123.4 + 4.567 + 21.02. After completing the addition, explain that even though decimal addition is easy, sometimes you really have to be careful to add only like units (ones to ones, hundredths to hundredths, and so on). Explain that it will be easier to add like units if the like units are written in columns. Rewrite the last example by lining up the like units. Add to demonstrate how much easier it is to add the like units when they are lined up.

As a third example, do 107.64 + 5.193, but this time line up the like units. When you have completed this example, point out that when you place the like units in columns, the decimal points are also lined up. Do another example by lining up the decimal points.

✗ ✦ ↻ ACTIVITY 9.13 If There Aren't Any, Write Zero

Write 42.03 + 615.6 on the chalkboard in horizontal form as shown here. Ask what the smallest unit is in either number. [Hundredths.] Ask how many hundredths there are in the second number. [There are none.] Ask how we could write the number to show that there are no hundredths. [Write a zero in the hundredths place.] Rewrite the addition example as 42.03 + 615.60 and add.

As a second example, write 123.4 + 4.567 + 21.02. Ask what fractional decimal units there are. [Tenths, hundredths, and thousandths.] Rewrite the addition example using zero to indicate when a number has none of some unit. Then add. Emphasize that decimal addition is just like whole-number addition. *Always add like units* and *when there are too many to write, make a trade.*

As a third example, write 107.64 + 5.193. Have the students rewrite the numbers using zeros as they were used in the previous examples. Have them add to get the answer.

✗ ✦ ↻ ACTIVITY 9.14 If There Aren't Any, Write Zero—Subtraction

Write 38.2 − 5.78 on the chalkboard. Ask what units we have to take away. [Ones, tenths, and hundredths.] Point to the subtrahend. Ask how many hundredths we are starting with. [There are none.] Ask how we can rewrite the number to show that there are no hundredths. [Use a zero.]

Rewrite the subtraction example as 38.20 − 5.78. Rewrite it again in vertical form and complete the example. Emphasize that decimal subtraction is just like whole-number subtraction. *Always subtract like units* and *when there are not enough to subtract, make a trade.*

Multiplying Decimals

Multiplication of decimals is also much like multiplication of whole numbers. It is still necessary to use partial products to find answers, but the other big idea of multiplication, multiplication by 10, must be expanded to include multiplication by .1. Once this has been accomplished, there really is little that is new.

The best overall model for multiplication of decimals is the area model. We have already used the area model when learning to multiply whole numbers and fractions. So, it is a small step to use this model to help our students learn to multiply decimals. The essence of the area model is that the length of a rectangle times its width equals the area.

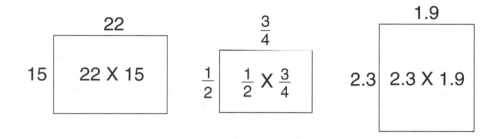

We use the area model to discover answers to some decimal multiplication examples.

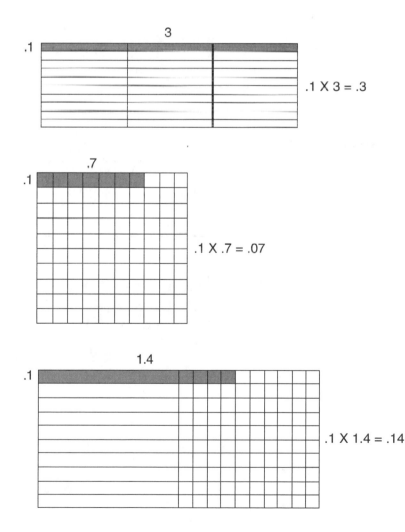

$.1 \times 3 = .3$

$.1 \times .7 = .07$

$.1 \times 1.4 = .14$

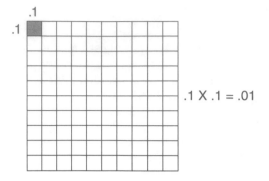

.1 X .1 = .01

The pattern that we want the students to discover is that when multiplying by .1, the effect on the other number is that the decimal point is moved one place to the left. Once this pattern is discovered, we can use the generalization to find other answers. For example, .1 × 3.9,

.1X3.9 =.39

Move the decimal point one place to the left.

3.9

After the students give an answer using the generalization, the next step is to go back to the model to verify that the answer is correct. This confirms that the generalization really works.

.1 X3.9 =.39

It works! You can just move the decimal point one place to the left.

We also need to establish the relationship between multiplication by .1 and multiplication by .01. From the previous generalization about multiplication by .1, we can see that

$$.1 \times .1 = .01$$

In other words, multiplication by .01 is equivalent to two multiplications by .1. This translates into moving the decimal point one place to the left twice, which is, of course, moving the decimal point two places to the left. Similarly,

$$.1 \times .1 \times .1 = .001$$

Multiplication by .001 is equivalent to multiplication by .1, three times, that is, move the decimal point three places to the left.

Now let's see how this information can be used to help us multiply other decimals. Consider the example $.7 \times .34$.

$.7 \times .34 = (.1 \times 7) \times (.01 \times 34)$ We do not need the parentheses here.

$ = .1 \times .01 \times 7 \times 34$ We can rearrange the numbers when multiplying.

We are left with a whole-number multiplication and three multiplications by .1. We know how to multiply the whole numbers.

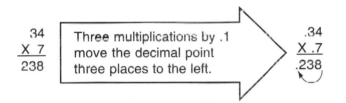

From examples like this, the students should generalize that we multiply as if the numbers were whole numbers and then count the multiplications by .1 to place the decimal point.

After development of the rule, the students should test it by doing some examples and then using the area model for multiplication to verify that the rule does produce the correct results. For example, suppose we want to multiply 3.5×2.7. Using the rule, we get:

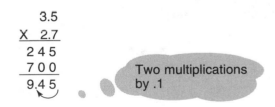

Using the area model, we get:

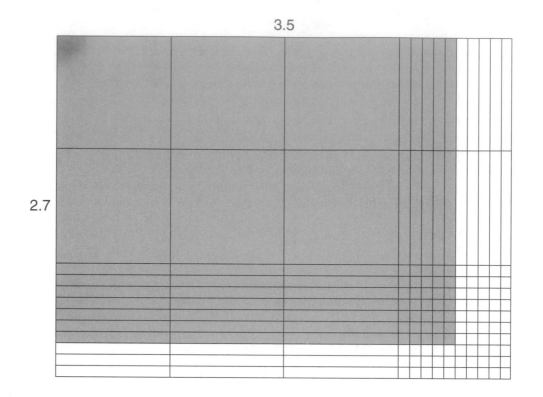

In this piece, we have 6 ones.

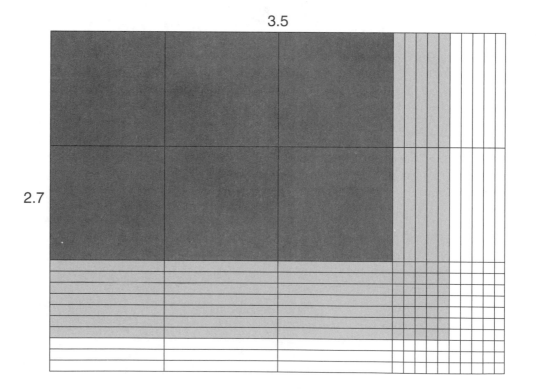

In this piece we have 10 tenths. That's the same as 1.

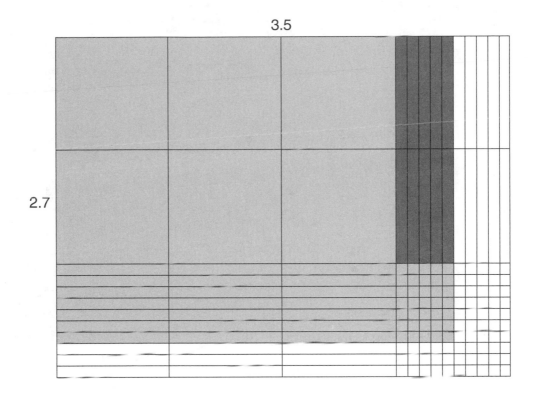

In this piece, we have 21 tenths. That's the same as 2.1.

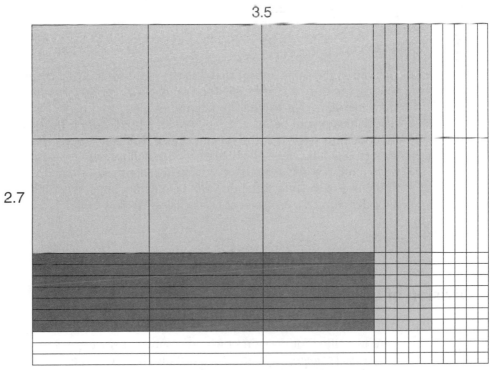

In this piece, we have 35 hundredths.

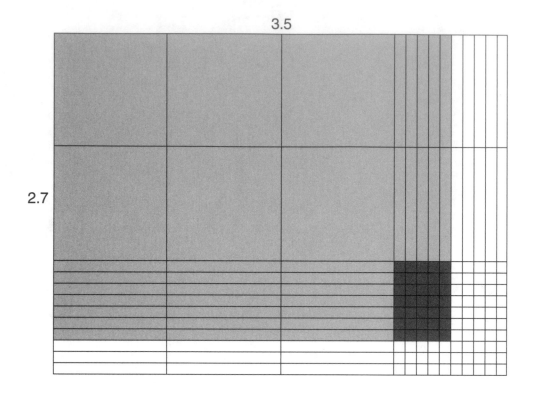

If we add these partial products together, we get:

6.
1.
2.1
.35
9.45

This is the same answer that was produced by applying the rule. It verifies that the rule did produce a correct answer. Two or three verifications like this thoroughly convince students that the rule is a quick, efficient, and correct way to get answers. The rule is meaningful because it was developed out of their own experiences. They used the model to verify that the rule is correct; they can literally see that their answers are correct. It will be viewed as an easy way to multiply decimals, so it will be perceived to be helpful, not just something that the teacher makes them do. They will be confident in the use of the rule. Retention will be outstanding. Remember that *it is always easier to remember things that are connected to other things that you know.*

 Division of Decimals

Division of decimals depends almost entirely on using the same two big ideas that were identified for division of whole numbers: *divide one unit at a time*, and *trade remainders for smaller units.* Compare these two divisions, one a division of a whole number by a whole number and the other a decimal by a whole number.

```
      ┌── hundreds                                    ┌── ones
      │ ┌── tens                                      │ ┌── tenths
      │ │ ┌── ones                                    │ │ ┌── hundredths
      │ │ │                                           │ │ │
     213 R 2                                         2.135
   4)854                                           4)8.54
     -8              Divide one unit                 -8
      54             at a time.                       54
     -4                                              -4
      14             Subtract units                   14
    -12              already divided.               -12
      2                                               20
                     Trade remainders.              -20
                                                      0
```

The procedures are precisely the same. The only difference is that there are some additional units. In the first example, we had a remainder of 2. There were 2 ones left over that could not be traded for smaller units because there were no smaller units. In the second example, the 2 hundredths that were left over could be traded for thousandths and then divided up.

Division of a decimal by a whole number is easy to teach. Using a physical model, we can demonstrate that the process is the same as for whole-number division. Division by a decimal, however, is different. Division of a decimal by a whole number, for example 4, can easily be modeled by separating the decimal units into four equal parts. Division by .4 cannot be modeled so easily. It does not make sense to separate decimal units into four tenths of an equal part. So we need to develop a way to cope with decimal divisors.

Elementary students should discover an interesting pattern that arises out of examples like these.

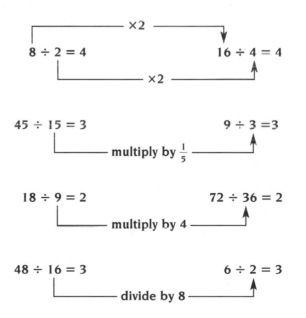

```
        ┌──────── ×2 ─────────┐
        │                     ▼
8 ÷ 2 = 4                16 ÷ 4 = 4
        └──────── ×2 ─────────┘


45 ÷ 15 = 3              9 ÷ 3 = 3
        └──── multiply by 1/5 ────┘


18 ÷ 9 = 2               72 ÷ 36 = 2
        └──── multiply by 4 ────┘


48 ÷ 16 = 3              6 ÷ 2 = 3
        └──── divide by 8 ────┘
```

When we multiply or divide both the divisor and the dividend by the same number, the quotient is unchanged. Sometimes division can be made much easier if we multiply or divide both the divisor and dividend by the same number. For example, consider $450 \div 25$. If we multiply the divisor and the dividend by 4, we have $1800 \div 100$.

Division by 100 is easy. Instead of dividing 414 ÷ 18, we can divide 414 and 18 by 2 and be left with 207 ÷ 9. Division by a one-digit number is usually easier than division by a two-digit number.

This technique can be used to turn any decimal division example into a whole-number division example. The example, 8.21 ÷ .7, can be changed to 821 ÷ 70 when we multiply both the divisor and the dividend by 100. The example, 439 ÷ 3.6, can be changed to 4390 ÷ 36 when we multiply both the divisor and the dividend by 10.

$2.7\overline{)4.98}$	can be changed to	$27.\overline{)49.8}$	when we multiply by 10.
$.36\overline{)21.8}$	can be changed to	$36.\overline{)2180.}$	when we multiply by 100.

We can change any division example with a decimal divisor into an example with a whole-number divisor.

$.23\overline{)6.9}$ **To make the divisor in this example a whole number, we must multiply by 100. So, we will multiply both divisor and dividend by 100.**

$.23\overline{)6.90}$ **Multiplying by 100 moves the decimal point two places to the right.**

$58.9\overline{)4.932}$ **To make the divisor in this example a whole number, we must multiply by 10. So, we multiply both the divisor and the dividend by 10.**

$58.9\overline{)4.9\,32}$ **We move the decimal point in both the divisor and the dividend one place to the right.**

The following sequence of activities illustrates how a teacher can develop the decimal multiplication and division concepts.

×÷ ACTIVITY 9.15   What's in the Box?

Write 4 × 23 on the chalkboard. Ask the students what it means. [23, four times.] Have four students each come forward and use bundled sticks to represent the number 23. Then have each of them put the number into a box. Ask the class how many 23s are in the box. [4] Next, ask who knows what is in the box altogether. How many ones are in the box? [12] Point out that is too many to write in the ones place. Ask what to do. [Make a trade.] Make the required trade and then ask how many ones are left in the box. [2] Ask how many tens are in the box after the trade. [9] Record the answer to the multiplication.

Write 3 × 1.62 on the chalkboard. Follow the same procedures to have the students find the answer. Use dollars, dimes, and pennies to model the decimal.

Repeat with 6 × 21.9, 2 × 3.76, and 7 × 5.8. Emphasize that multiplication of decimals is almost exactly like multiplication of whole numbers.

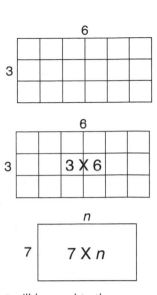

ACTIVITY 9.16   The Product Is the Area

Draw a rectangle on the chalkboard and label the sides 3 and 6. Sketch in the squares to show the area.

Remind the students that you can multiply the length times the width of the rectangle to get the area. Write the product, 3 × 6, on the rectangle.

Draw another rectangle and label the sides 7 and *n*. Tell the students that *n* is the length of the side but you don't know what number *n* is equal to. Ask how we could find the area if we know what *n* is equal to. Label the interior of the rectangle with the product, 7 × *n*.

Show other rectangles and have the students tell what product will be equal to the area. Have them label the interiors of the rectangles with the products.

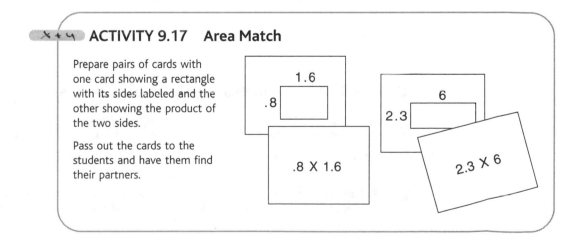

ACTIVITY 9.17   Area Match

Prepare pairs of cards with one card showing a rectangle with its sides labeled and the other showing the product of the two sides.

Pass out the cards to the students and have them find their partners.

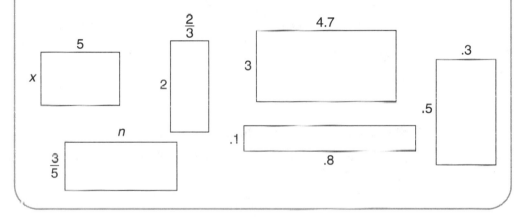

✕ + ◄ ACTIVITY 9.18   Easy Tenths

Use the area model
as shown at the right
to demonstrate that
.1 × 2 = .2.

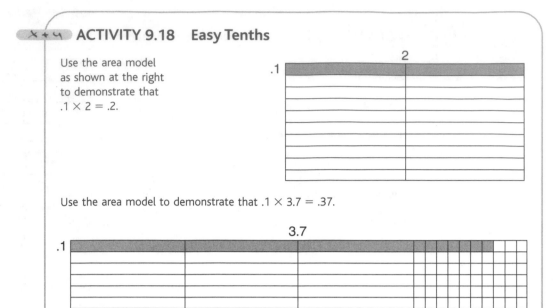

Use the area model to demonstrate that .1 × 3.7 = .37.

Repeat with .1 × 1.4 and .1 × 3.76. Ask what always happens when you multiply by .1. [The decimal point "moves" one place to the left.] Have them tell what they think the answer to .1 × 4.5 will be. [.45] Use the area model to verify the answer.

✕ + ◄ ACTIVITY 9.19   More Easy Tenths

Write 46 × .1 on the chalkboard and then write 46 tenths below it. Ask if these say the same thing. [Yes.] Next, write 40 tenths + 6 tenths. Ask if this is the same thing. [Yes.]

Ask what 10 tenths is equal to. [1] Ask what 40 tenths is equal to. [4] so, 46 tenths must be equal to 4 and 6 tenths. Write 46 × .1 = 4.6.

Write 92 × .1 and ask what is it equal to. If necessary, point out that 90 tenths is 9, so 90 tenths and 2 more tenths is 9 and 2 tenths. Write 92 × .1 = 9.2.

Ask for the answers to 74 × .1, 21 × .1, and 123 × .1.

Ask what always happens when you multiply by .1. [The decimal point moves one place to the left.]

✕ + ◄ ACTIVITY 9.20   Hundredths and Thousandths Are Easy, Too

Ask what always happens when you multiply by .1. [The decimal point moves one place to the left.] Write .1 × .1 on the chalkboard. Ask what the answer is. [.01] Write .1 × .1 = .01.

Point out that since .01 is the same as .1 × .1, multiplying by .01 is the same as multiplying by .1 twice. Write 86 × .01 = 86 × .1 × .1.

Ask again what always happens when you multiply by .1. [The decimal point moves one place to the left.] Ask what would happen if you multiplied by .1 twice. [The decimal point would move two places to the left.]

Write 86 × .01 and ask for the answer. [.86] Ask for the answers to 235 × .01, 45.3 × .01, and 7.98 × .01.

Write .1 × .1 × .1 and ask for the answer. [.001] Write 86.3 × .001 = 86.3 × .1 × .1 × .1. Point out that multiplying by .001 is the same as multiplying by .1 three times. So, you would move the decimal point three places to the left.

Write 86.3 × .001 and ask for the answer. [.0863] Ask for the answers to 235 × .001, 4.53 × .001, and 79.8 × .001.

✕ ÷ ◁ ACTIVITY 9.21   Two-Step Multiplication

Write 23 × 4.5 on the chalkboard. Then rewrite the multiplication as 23 × 45 × .1.

Ask if this is the same thing. Why? [Yes, because 45 × .1 equals 4.5.] Have the students multiply 23 × 45 and then multiply the answer by .1. Remind them that when you multiply by .1, the decimal point moves one place to the left.

Write 35 × 2.14 and then rewrite it as 35 × 214 × .01. Ask if they are equal. Why? Have the students multiply 35 × 214 and then multiply the answer by .01. Remind them that when you multiply by .01, that's the same as multiplying by .1 twice, so the decimal point moves two places to the left.

Write 37 × 3.9 and have the students find the answer. Remind them that they can multiply as though the numbers are whole numbers and then move the decimal point. *Multiply and then place the decimal point.*

Then have them do 21 × .64, 1.36 × 45, and 24 × .061.

✕ ÷ ◁ ACTIVITY 9.22   More Two-Step Multiplication

Write 2.3 × 4.5 on the chalkboard. Then rewrite the multiplication as 23 × .1 × 45 × .1. Ask if this is the same thing. Why? Ask how to rearrange the numbers so that you end up with a whole-number multiplication and multiplications by .1. [23 × 45 × .1 × .1.] Have the students multiply 23 × 45 and then multiply the answer twice by .1. Remind them that when you multiply by .1, the decimal point moves one place to the left. Since there are two multiplications by .1, the decimal point moves two places to the left.

Write 3.5 × 2.14 and ask what two whole numbers are multiplied. [35 and 214.] Ask how many multiplications by .1 there are. [3] Remind them that each multiplication by .1 moves the decimal point one place to the left.

Write 3.7 × 3.9 and have the students find and answer. Remind them that they can multiply as though the numbers are whole numbers and then move the decimal point. *Multiply and then place the decimal point.*

Also have them do .21 × .64, 1.36 × 4.5, and 2.4 × .061.

x ÷ ⊲ ACTIVITY 9.23   Get the Point?

Have the students work with partners. Each pair of partners should have a calculator. Give them a list of decimal multiplication examples. The partners should take turns using the calculator.

On each example, one partner uses the calculator to multiply the related whole numbers. (For example, if the example is 2.76 × 5.4, the student multiplies 276 × 54.) Then the other partner writes the product on a sheet of paper and places the decimal point in the correct position. Finally, the first partner uses the calculator to multiply the original decimals to check the answer.

The partners should then switch roles and continue until all the examples have been completed.

x ÷ ⊲ ACTIVITY 9.24   Dividing Is Dividing

Tell the students that you want to review division. Write $4\overline{)856}$ on the chalkboard. Have a student come forward and use base-10 blocks to represent the number 856. Ask how many equal parts we are to divide this number into. [4] Work through the example, separating the number into four equal parts. Record the steps as you go. Emphasize that you *divide one unit at a time*, and *trade remainders for smaller units*.

Then, beside the first division example, write $4\overline{)8.56}$. Have someone come forward and use dollars, dimes, and pennies to represent the number 8.56. Work through this example, separating the number into four equal parts. Record each step. Emphasize that you *divide one unit at a time*, and *trade remainders for smaller units*.

Point out how decimal division is like whole-number division.

Next, do the two examples, $5\overline{)657}$ and $5\overline{)65.7}$. The first has a remainder of 2 ones. In the second example you also have a remainder, this time 2 tenths. Point out that when working with decimals there are always smaller units to trade for. In the first example, 2 ones can be traded for 20 tenths, which can be separated into five equal parts. In the second example, the 2 tenths (dimes) can be traded for 20 hundredths (pennies), which can be separated into five equal parts.

x ÷ ⊲ ACTIVITY 9.25   Same Answer

Write 18 ÷ 3 on the chalkboard and ask for the answer. Record that answer.

Then ask what you get if you multiply 18 by 3. What if you multiply 3 by 3? Record these new numbers below the 18 and the 3.

Have the students devide 54 by 9. Be sure that they notice that the answer is the same as the answer to the original example.

$$18 \div 3 = 6$$
$$\times 3 \quad \times 3$$
$$54 \div 9$$

$$54 \div 9 = 6$$

Do other examples in the same way. Start with 14 ÷ 2. Multiply by 5 to get 70 ÷ 10. Find both answers. The answers are the same.

Start with 280 ÷ 35. Multiply by 2 to get 560 ÷ 70. Have the students compute the answer to 280 ÷ 35. [8] Ask them to give the answer to 560 ÷ 70 without computing.

ACTIVITY 9.26   Making Division Easier

Write 135 ÷ 5 on the chalkboard. Then tell the class that you are going to multiply both numbers by 2. Write 270 ÷ 10 directly below the original example. Ask what the students know about the answers to these two divisions. [They are the same.] Ask which division they would rather do.

Write 144 ÷ 18 on the chalkboard. Then tell the class that you want to multiply both numbers by $\frac{1}{2}$. Ask what the new numbers would be. [72 and 9.] Write the new division, 72 ÷ 9. Ask what the students know about the answers to these two divisions. [They are the same.] Ask which division they would rather do.

Tell the students that you can sometimes make division easier if you multiply both the divisor and the dividend by the same number.

Write 112 ÷ 16 on the chalkboard. Have the students suggest what we could multiply by to get an easier problem. Try out each suggestion to see if it gives an easier division. [Some good numbers to multiply by are 5 and $\frac{1}{2}$.

×+ч **ACTIVITY 9.27   Always Divide by a Whole Number**

Write $2\overline{)68.96}$ on the chalkboard. Remind the class that this means that we are to divide 68.96 into two equal parts. Write $6\overline{)7.38}$ and remind them that means we are to divide 7.38 into six equal parts. Write $.2\overline{)3.406}$ and ask what this means. Point out that we cannot divide 3.406 into two tenths of an equal part. That doesn't make sense.

Remind the class that we can sometimes change a hard division into an easier one by multiplying both the divisor and the dividend by the same number. Ask what number we could multiply by to change the divisor into a whole number. [Possible answers are 5, 10,….] Choose 10, because multiplication by ten is easy. Multiply the divisor and dividend by 10 to change the division to $2\overline{)34.06}$.

Also do $.9\overline{)34}$. Multiply by 10 to change the division to $9\overline{)340}$. Do $.12\overline{)6.092}$. Multiply by 100 to change the division to $12\overline{)609.2}$. Do $4.32\overline{).7592}$. Multiply by 100 to change the division to $432\overline{)75.92}$. Do $.024\overline{)1.92}$. Multiply by 1000 to change the division to $24\overline{)1920}$.

Fraction Comparison Revisited

Recall that one big idea, *always compare like units*, was identified for comparison. To compare unlike fractions (fractions with different denominators), we normally rename the fractions using a common denominator. Then the comparison is easy. If there are several fractions to compare, finding a common denominator is more complicated. But we must still rename the fractions using the same unit. It is possible to decide ahead of time what fractional unit (denominator) you will use and then "force" the fractional quantities into those units. For example, suppose we decide to compare three fractions using the fractional unit, thirds. Suppose, further, that the fractions are the following.

$$\frac{1}{2} \qquad \frac{3}{4} \qquad \frac{2}{3}$$

The last of these fractions is already in thirds. We need to rename the other two fractions in thirds. We begin by multiplying numerator and denominator of each of these fractions by 3.

$$\frac{1 \times 3}{2 \times 3} = \frac{3}{6} \qquad \frac{3 \times 3}{4 \times 3} = \frac{9}{12}$$

Then we divide numerator and denominator of each fraction by the original denominator.

$$\frac{3 \div 2}{6 \div 2} = \frac{1.5}{3} \qquad \frac{9 \div 4}{12 \div 4} = \frac{2.25}{3}$$

We now have three fractions, all named in thirds, and any comparison that we want to make is easy.

$$\frac{1.5}{3} \qquad \frac{2.25}{3} \qquad \frac{2}{3}$$

Let's look at another example. This time, we will rename all the fractions in fifths.

$$\frac{1}{2} \qquad \frac{1}{4} \qquad \frac{3}{8}$$

We multiply numerator and denominator by 5.

$$\frac{1 \times 5}{2 \times 5} = \frac{5}{10} \qquad \frac{1 \times 5}{4 \times 5} = \frac{5}{20} \qquad \frac{3 \times 5}{8 \times 5} = \frac{15}{40}$$

Then we divide numerator and denominator by the original denominator.

$$\frac{5 \div 2}{10 \div 2} = \frac{2.5}{5} \qquad \frac{5 \div 4}{20 \div 4} = \frac{1.25}{5} \qquad \frac{15 \div 8}{40 \div 8} = \frac{1.875}{5}$$

The resulting fractions are all in fifths.

Or, we can rename all the fractions using the fractional unit, hundredths. We multiply both numerator and denominator by 100 and then we divide numerator and denominator by the original denominator.

$$\frac{5 \times 100}{8 \times 100} = \frac{500 \div 8}{800 \div 8} = \frac{62.5}{100}$$

$$\frac{3 \times 100}{5 \times 100} = \frac{300 \div 5}{500 \div 5} = \frac{60}{100}$$

$$\frac{2 \times 100}{3 \times 100} = \frac{200 \div 3}{300 \div 3} = \frac{66.666...}{100}$$

Defining Percent

The numerators of fractions with a denominator of 100 are called *percents*. 17 percent of a quantity is precisely the same as 17 hundredths of that quantity. The symbol for percent is %.

$$24\% = .24 = \frac{24}{100}$$

$$273\% = 2.73 = \frac{273}{100} = 2\frac{73}{100}$$

Adapting a Lesson on Decimals

Next we examine a lesson plan that follows suggestions that might be found in the teacher's guide of an elementary school mathematics program. Note that it is a good plan. However, it does have some weaknesses that are typical of traditional lesson plans for teaching elementary school mathematics. Notice that:

1. The focus is on teaching the textbook pages.
2. The developmental part of the lesson is minimal.
3. A large amount of practice is recommended using the rule for placement of the decimal point.

Note that when there is a minimum of development, a maximum of practice is always required.

LESSON OBJECTIVE

The student will multiply a decimal by a whole number.

Lesson Opener

Have students find each of these products:

$$8 \times 7 \qquad 6 \times 13 \qquad 16 \times 14 \qquad 28 \times 34$$

Ask: If your grandmother gave you $2.10 every week for three weeks, how much money would she have given you. Use dollar bills and dimes to show $2.10 three times. Count the money to see how much she would have given.

Development

Direct the class's attention to the first page of the lesson. Have them read problem 1. Tell them to look at the money in the picture. This is what Mrs. Sanchez paid Lucita on Monday. Ask how many days Lucita worked for Mrs. Sanchez. [3] Ask how much money Lucita was paid on Tuesday and how much she was paid on Friday. Point out that since she was paid the same amount all three days, multiplication can be used to find how much she was paid altogether. Write the multiplication. Complete the multiplication steps.

$$
\begin{array}{r}
\$\,6.24 \\
\times \quad 3 \\
\hline
\$18.72
\end{array}
\quad
\begin{array}{l}
\text{2 decimal places} \\
\text{0 decimal places} \\
\text{2 decimal places}
\end{array}
$$

Point out that the number of decimal places in the answer is the same as the number of decimal places in the multiplicand. Lead the class through a similar discussion of problem 2. Point out that, in both problems, the number of decimal places in the answer is the same as the number of decimal places in the multiplicand.

Monitor Learning

Have everyone do the four *Check Understanding* examples. Have students who are having difficulty imagine money for the decimal.

Practice

Have the students complete the 48 examples on the practice page. Remind them to place the decimal point. Have them think about correct placement of the decimal point.

Closure

At the end of math time, remind the children that they have learned how to multiply a decimal by a whole number.

We adapt this lesson to increase the amount and depth of the developmental part of the lesson, make the lesson more visual and more kinesthetic, make assessment a continual process that provides feedback about the effectiveness of instruction while that instruction is going on, and increase communication about what is being learned from the students and among the students. These adaptations make the lesson appropriate for almost all students. But, remember that some students with severe needs may require further instructional adaptations.

LESSON OBJECTIVE

The student will multiply a decimal by a whole number.

Lesson Opener

Group students with partners and have each group of partners find the first of these products:

$$6 \times 13 \qquad 28 \times 34$$

When they have finished, have them exchange their work with another group of partners who check their work for accuracy. If the two groups of partners disagree about whether the work of either group is correct, they should discuss the steps in the computation to resolve their differences. Then have the partners do the second example. **Monitor Understanding.** As the groups are working, carefully observe to identify individuals who do not seem to understand how to do the multiplication. Have the groups that include those individuals use a base-10 model such as base-10 blocks or bundled sticks, so that they can see what is happening in the multiplication.

Ask, "If your grandmother gave you $2.10 every week for three weeks, how much money would she have given you?" Using dollar bills and dimes, have three students come forward and show $2.10. Have these three students combine the money to show how much she would have given in three weeks. Have the class tell you, step-by-step, how to figure out how much money there is. Have a student count the money to check the answer. **Monitor Understanding.** Carefully observe those students who had difficulty on the two preceding multiplication examples. Be sure they understand the process.

Development

Ask the class, "If you put some rocks, some crayons, and some paper clips into an empty box, who can tell me what would be in the box. [Some rocks, some crayons, and some paper clips.] Emphasize that the only things that could be in the box would be those things that were put into it. Place ten rocks, a box of crayons, and a box of paper clips on the desk. Write "two rocks, five crayons, and three paper clips" on the chalkboard. Have a student come to the front and place those objects into an empty box. Ask what is in the box. Empty the box.

2 rocks, 5 crayons, and 3 paper clips
× 3
_____

Write ×3 under the list of objects on the chalkboard. Have each of three students come forward and place two rocks, five crayons, and three paper clips in the box. Then ask the class what is in the box. [6 rocks, 15 crayons, and 9 paper clips.] Emphasize that two rocks were placed in the box three times, five crayons were placed in the box three times, and three paper clips were placed in the box three times.

3.82
× 2

Write this multiplication example on the chalkboard. Remind the class that we can use money to represent decimals. Ask how you could use the money to show the decimal 3.82. [3 dollars, 8 dimes, and 2 pennies.] Have a student come forward and represent the number 3.82 two times. Have the student place the two representations of the number together in a box. Ask what is in the box altogether. Emphasize that, since 3.82 was placed in the box two times, each part of that number was placed in the box two times. Two hundredths were placed in the box two times. Eight tenths were placed in the box two times, and three ones were placed in the box two times. Have someone come count the money in the box to check the answer. They will need to trade the 10 extra tenths for a one. **Monitor Understanding.** Continue to observe individuals who do not understand. Be sure to involve them in the procedures.

Following the same steps, lead the class through 6 × 2.37. For this example, emphasize that since we put ones, tenths, and hundredths into the box, that's what we will find in the box. We just have to decide how many of each there are altogether. Point out further that, when there are too many to write, we trade for larger units. **Monitor Understanding.** Continue to observe to identify individuals who are having difficulty understanding. Provide extra help as it is needed.

Direct the class's attention to the first page of the lesson. Have them read problem 1. Tell them to look at the money in the picture. This is what Mrs. Sanchez paid Lucita on Monday. Ask how many days Lucita worked for Mrs. Sanchez. [3] Ask how much money Lucita was paid on Tuesday and how much she was paid on Friday. Point out that since she was paid the same amount all three days, multiplication can be used to find how much she was paid altogether. Write the multiplication. Complete the multiplication steps. Point out the relationship between fractional parts of the multiplicand and the product.

$ 6.24	**tenths and hundredths**
× 3	
$18.72	**tenths and hundredths**

Point out that because both the multiplicand and the product include tenths and hundredths, both numbers have two decimal places.

Lead the class through a similar discussion of problem 2. Point out again that the number of decimal places in the answer is the same as the number of decimal places in the multiplicand. **Monitor Understanding.** Continue to observe as these two problems are completed to identify individuals who are having difficulty understanding. Provide extra help as it is needed.

Monitor Learning

Pair students with partners. Have one of the partners do the first *Check Understanding* example. That student should explain to the partner what is being done and why on each step. For each new example the partners should switch roles, taking turns working out the solution. While the partners are working, move around the room to monitor their work. Have students who are having difficulty use money to help them visualize multiplication of the decimal. Remind them that the answer will have the same fractional units as the multiplicand (hence the same number of decimal places).

Practice

From the 48 examples on the practice page, choose four representative examples and assign them for practice. Be sure that at least one example requires no regrouping (trading), at least one requires regrouping (trading) once, and at least one requires regrouping (trading) twice.

Remind the students that you want every example to be correct. Tell them that you have the answers on a sheet of paper on your desk. Have them come to your desk when they are finished and check their answers. If they have errors, have them show their work to another student and have that person help them find and correct the error.

Monitor Learning

While the students are working to correct their problems, move around the room to monitor the discussions and provide help as needed.

Closure

Near the end of math time, ask the students what kind of multiplication they learned to do today. [They have learned how to multiply a decimal by a whole number.]

Follow Up

Identify an example from the practice page that requires regrouping (trading) one time. For homework, have the students explain to their parents (or some other older person) how to do the example. Tell them to have that person sign the paper and indicate whether or not the explanation was clear.

Using Decimals to Solve Problems

When teaching problem solving using decimals, the same basic principles are applied as when teaching problem solving using other kinds of numbers. The teacher should emphasize that the choice of operation depends on what is happening to the quantities in the problem. If quantities are being combined, then addition can probably be used. If the number names of the quantities are decimals, then those decimals should be added. If the quantities in the problem are being separated into equal parts, then division can probably be used. If the number names of the quantities are decimals, then those decimals should be divided.

As previously noted in Chapter 8, a current instructional emphasis for problem solving in mathematics is the development of and providing experience using a wide variety of problem-solving strategies. We have already seen examples using the following strategies:

Solve part of the problem.
Separate the problem into easier parts.
Work backward.
Use a picture or diagram.
Use a table.

We now examine a problem appropriate for children at about the fourth-grade level. The solution employs one of the strategies demonstrated in Chapter 8 (use a table), and it also uses three additional strategies, *solve a simpler problem*, *try and check* (sometimes called trial and error) and *list the possibilities*.

Juan works at a small store in the mall called "Nuts to You." The store normally sells nuts by the scoop. The price is listed for one scoop of each kind of nuts. For the Christmas season, the store decided to sell prepackaged nuts at $3.00 per package. Juan was asked to figure out how many different mixtures there would be that would sell for $3.00 each if the mixtures were made by combining full scoops of different kinds of nuts.

Price per Scoop	
Peanuts	$ .25
Walnuts	.50
Almonds	.75
Cashews	1.00
Pecans	1.25

We begin by solving several simpler problems. First, suppose the package only contained peanuts. How many scoops would it take?

Since each scoop of peanuts costs 25 cents, the package would have to include 12 scoops of peanuts.

A second simpler problem is: If Juan made a mixture of cashews and peanuts but only included one scoop of cashews, how many scoops of peanuts would be needed?

Since one scoop of cashews costs $1.00, Juan needs to include enough peanuts to make up the other $2.00. The package would have to include eight scoops of peanuts.

A third simpler problem might be: Suppose Juan included two scoops of cashews. In how many different ways could he complete the package?

Since two scoops of cashews costs $2.00, Juan needs to include enough nuts to make up the other $1.00. This can be done in several ways. Juan could use four scoops of peanuts. Juan could use two scoops of walnuts. Juan could use one scoop of almonds and one scoop of peanuts. Juan could use one scoop of walnuts and two scoops of peanuts.

As we discover the different ways to make a $3.00 package of mixed nuts, we need to have an organized way to keep track of the information. To do this, we use a table something like the one on the following page. By *try*ing out different combinations *and check*ing how much each would cost, we can finally arrive at the solution to the problem. There are 46 possibilities.

Pecans $1.25	Cashews $1.00	Almonds $.75	Walnuts $.50	Peanuts $.25
2	0	0	1	0
2	0	0	0	2
1	1	1	0	0
1	1	0	1	1
1	1	0	0	3
1	0	2	0	1
1	0	1	2	0
1	0	1	1	2
1	0	0	3	1

Exercises and Activities

1. Placement of the decimal point when multiplying decimals can be taught using the following fractions approach.

$$3.5 \times 2.7 = \frac{35}{10} \times \frac{27}{10} = \frac{35 \times 27}{10 \times 10}$$

   This approach depends on students' understanding that division by 10 moves the decimal point one place to the left. Develop an instructional sequence to teach students that division by 10 moves the decimal point one place to the left.

2. Develop an instructional sequence to show the meaning of percents as described on page 272. Include visuals and kinesthetic activity.

3. Develop an instructional sequence to teach students how to find percents equivalent to given fractions or decimals.

4. Develop an instructional sequence to teach children how to change percents like $\frac{1}{2}$%, $\frac{3}{4}$%, or $\frac{5}{8}$% to decimals.

5. Complete the table on the top of this page to verify the number of $3.00 mixtures of nuts.

6. Choose a lesson on decimals or percents from a published elementary school mathematics textbook series.
   a. Write a lesson plan that follows the teaching suggestions in the teacher's guide.
   b. Identify parts of the lesson that include student communication about the concept(s) or skill(s) taught in the lesson.
   c. Add more opportunities for communication from or among students to the lesson.

7. Choose a lesson on decimals or percents from a published elementary school mathematics textbook series.
   a. Write a lesson plan that follows the teaching suggestions in the teacher's guide.
   b. Identify the parts of the lesson designed to assess the learning of the students.
   c. Add more continual assessment (monitoring of learning) to the lesson plan.

8. Study the adapted lesson plan on pages 274–276. Make further changes in the lesson plan to make it more appropriate for a child who is paralyzed.

9. Do a web search on *central auditory processing disorder* (CAPD). Find out the symptoms of CAPD and the recommendations for children with CAPD. Then study the adapted lesson plan on pages 274—276. Make further changes in the lesson plan to make it more appropriate for a child whose learning disability includes CAPD.

10. Study the adapted lesson plan on pages 274–276. Make further changes in the lesson plan to make it more appropriate for a child who has limited cognitive abilities.

11. Choose a lesson on decimals or percents from a published elementary school mathematics textbook series.

    a. Write a lesson plan that follows the teaching suggestions in the teacher's guide.

    b. Adapt the lesson plan by adding concept and/or skill development and by adding more kinesthetic activity.

    c. Adapt the lesson plan further to make it appropriate for a child with visual perception problems.

12. Read "Standard 1: Mathematics as problem solving," on pages 23–25 and "Standard 1: Mathematics as problem solving," on pages 75–77 of *Curriculum and Evaluation Standards for School Mathematics*, published by the National Council of Teachers of Mathematics. In what ways are the suggestions presented in this text for teaching problem solving consistent with or inconsistent with those presented in *The Standards*.

References and Related Readings

Bennett, A. B., Nelson, L. T. (1994). A conceptual model for solving percent problems. *Mathematics Teaching in the Middle School, 1*, 20–25.

National Council of Teachers of Mathematics. (1989). *Curriculum and evaluation standards for school mathematics.* Reston, VA: NCTM.

National Council of Teachers of Mathematics. (2000). *Principles and standards for school mathematics.* Reston, VA: NCTM.

Thornton, C. A., Tucker, B. F., Dossey, J. A., Bazik, E. F. (1983). *Teaching mathematics to children with special needs.* Menlo Park, CA: Addison-Wesley.

Web Sites

http://www.forum.swarthmore.edu/
(Math forum links to math discussions and ideas.)

http://forum.swarthmore.edu/library/topics/fractions/
(Links to decimal/fraction sites.)

http://online.edfac.unimelb.edu.au/485129/DecProj/index.htm
(Case studies with video interviews/diagnoses/recommendations. Requires Quicktime which is downloadable from site.)

http://www.ti.com/calc/docs/therole.htm
(All about use of calculators, myths, and concerns.)

CHAPTER 10

MEASUREMENT:

Assigning a Number to a Quantity

THE MEASUREMENT STANDARD

"Measurement is the assignment of a numerical value to an attribute of an object, such as the length of a pencil" (National Council of Teachers of Mathematics, 2000, p. 44).

"Children should begin to develop an understanding of attributes by looking at, touching, or directly comparing objects" (NCTM, 2000, p. 103).

"In grades 3–5, students should … begin to develop and use formulas for the measurement of certain attributes, such as area" (NCTM, 2000, p. 171).

THE COMMUNICATION STANDARD

"Teachers should build a sense of community in middle-grades classrooms so students feel free to express their ideas honestly and openly, without fear of ridicule" (NCTM, 2000, p. 268).

THE CONNECTIONS STANDARD

"The relationship between the diameter and the circumference of a circle can be studied empirically by collecting a variety of circular objects and measuring their circumferences and diameters" (NCTM, 2000, p. 65).

"Many of the formulas students develop and use in the 'Measurement' section draw on their knowledge of algebra, geometry, and measurement" (NCTM, 2000, p. 274).

Measurement and Geometry

This text deals with measurement and geometry separately. However, the elementary school mathematics curriculum typically integrates these two content areas. In fact, elementary school geometry content can hardly be discussed without continual references to measurements of some sort. This chapter shows how measurement concepts are developed. More advanced measurement concepts depend on understanding and use of more advanced geometric concepts.

Defining Measurement

Before discussing the teaching of measurement, we first consider the meaning of measurement. We measure many different kinds of things, including the size of a set of objects, the length of an object, the capacity of a container, the value of an object, or the likelihood of an occurrence. Not only are the things we measure different, but also the processes used to measure them vary from type to type. But, in every case, we are assigning a number to some quantity. In fact, this is precisely what measurement is. *Measurement is the process of assigning a number to a quantity.*

For example, suppose there is a set of children consisting of Ann, Bob, Carl, Denise, Ed, and Fran. A set of children has many attributes that can be measured. We might be interested in how intelligent the group of children is. We might be interested in how long the group is if they were laid end to end. We might be interested in how heavy the group is. We might be interested in how fast the group could run. We might be interested in how nice the children are. All of these things can be measured by assigning a number to the group that represents the attribute being measured. Frequently when a set of objects is being measured, the attribute that we are most interested in is the "numerousness" of the set. How many objects are in the set? In this case, how many children are in the group? If we count the children in the group, we find that there are six children. The number that tells how many is six. We have measured the set.

An important idea in all measurement is the notion of unit. When we measure the set of children, the unit is "child." To find the size of the set, we count to see how many units there are (that is, we count to see how many children there are) in the set. The unit of measurement used to measure the set of children is an example of a *direct unit*. In nonformal language, a direct unit is a piece of the attribute that is being measured. When measuring with direct units, we count how many of those units are contained in the thing being measured.

Measuring Length

Length is measured using direct units. For example, we measure the length of a desk, we decide on a unit of length (a piece of length) and figure out how many of those

The length is 11, 11 crayons.

units equal the length of the desk. If we decide to use a crayon as the unit of length, we could lay crayons end-to-end on top of the desk to see how many crayons equals the length of the desk.

Before beginning to measure length, the children must have a sense of what length is. The meaning of the attribute, length, can be established through a series of gross comparison activities. As the students make these comparisons, they should be sequenced in order to isolate the attribute, length, from the other attributes possessed by the objects being measured.

Which is longer?
The black rectangle is longer.

Which is longer?
This time, the gray rectangle is longer. We are not measuring the color.

Which is longer?
The checkered rectangle is longer. (The direction does not make any difference.)

Which is longer?
The striped rectangle is longer. (The "thickness" is not what we are measuring.)

Which is longer? The black shape is longer. (The shape does not make any difference.)

As the concept of length is developed though these comparisons, the teacher should introduce the vocabulary of length by using it correctly in appropriate contexts. Specifically, the students should become familiar with these terms: long, longer, longest; short, shorter, shortest; and tall, taller, tallest. We encourage the children to use this terminology as they talk about the comparisons being made.

At some point, students should be asked to compare the length of two objects that are nearly the same length, but are arranged so that it is difficult to decide which is longer. For example, two strips of paper could be placed on the bulletin board as pictured here. The students should learn that when the two strips are moved side by side we can easily tell which is longer.

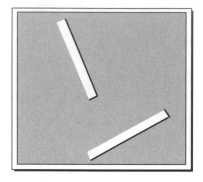

The next step is to present the students with a similar comparison task, but one in which the objects cannot be moved. For example, to compare the length of the chalk tray on a section of chalkboard with the length of a board in the floor, the students should discover that they can stretch a string along the board in the floor to see how long it is and then keep holding that length of string while moving it next to the chalk tray to see which is longer.

With the preceding example, the students used a unit of length, in this case, the length of string. The concept of unit of length can be expanded by making comparisons in settings where a unit of length is inherent in the setting. For example, if two objects are placed on a tile floor, students could make the comparison by counting the tiles. Or, the height of objects in the classroom could be compared by counting spelling books that are stacked next to the objects.

Other arbitrary units that are placed beside the objects can be used to make comparisons. Students can line up paper clips, new pencils, or paper strips that are cut the same length next to the objects being compared. When the students refer to the lengths as some number of paper clips or some number of pencils, they have actually measured those objects.

The following key ideas related to the measurement of length should be emphasized:

- When communicating a length, *the number is meaningless* without the unit. The length of an object might be two pencils long or it might be eight paper clips long. If one object has a length of three and another object has a length of seven, we do not know which is longer unless we know which units were used to measure the two objects.
- *The number of units depends on the size of the unit.* If we use a short unit to measure the length of something it will take more units than if we use a longer unit.

The following sequence of activities can be used to develop the concepts of length, units of length, and measurement of length.

✗ ✦ ↰ ACTIVITY 10.01 Pick the Longest. Pick the Shortest.

Tape strips of paper horizontally to the walls around the room. The strips should be of different colors and very different lengths. Some strips should be wider than others; some should be narrower than others.

Point out two strips and ask which is longer. Talk about the two strips using appropriate length vocabulary. [This strip is longer than that one; That strip is shorter than this one; and so on.] Choose different pairs of strips and have the students decide which is longer and which is shorter. If the strips are too close to decide, have them move the strips side-by-side so they can tell which is longer.

Point out three strips and decide which is longest. Talk about the strips using appropriate vocabulary. [This strip is shorter than both of the other two strips; It is the shortest; That one is the longest; and so on.]

✗ ✦ ⊔ ACTIVITY 10.02   Long, Longer, and Longest

Bring a doll, a baseball bat, a screw driver, and a necktie to class. Lay these objects on the table where the students can see them.

Choose two of the objects and place them side by side with one end of each object at the same edge of the table. Help the students to decide which one is longer and which one is shorter.

Have the children choose different pairs of objects and place the objects with one end right at the edge of the table. Have them use appropriate language to compare the objects.

Choose three objects and decide which is longest. Talk about the objects using appropriate vocabulary. [The baseball bat is longer than both the doll and the screw driver. It is the longest. The screw driver is the shortest.]

Have the children choose three of the objects and compare them. Have them use appropriate vocabulary.

✗ ✦ ⊔ ACTIVITY 10.03   Pick the Longest. Pick the Shortest.

Tape strips of paper to the walls around the room. The strips should be of different colors and the lengths of the strips should be nearly, but not quite, the same length. They should be taped to the wall so that they are not parallel.

Point out two strips, and ask which is longer. Since they are about the same length, it is hard to tell. Ask for suggestions. If someone suggests that the strips be moved together, explain that we could do that, but you want to try a different way.

Ask for two helpers to come help you. Give them some string and show them how to stretch it out along one of the strips and hold their fingers on the string to mark the length. Then have them save that length on the string and take it to the other strip to see which is longer.

Have the children choose two strips. Have everyone guess which is longest. Have two students use the string to let the class decide which is longer. How many guessed right?

Repeat several times with other pairs of strips.

✗ ✦ ⊔ ACTIVITY 10.04   Up-and-Down Length

Stand up several objects (for example, a vase, a statue, a box) around the room.

Point to one of the objects. Explain that when you think about how long something is up-and-down, you are thinking about how tall it is. Use your hands to indicate the vertical length of the object and tell the students that the object is this tall.

Indicate a second object and ask the class which of the two is taller.

Choose other pairs of objects and ask which is taller. If they cannot decide, have them move the objects together to decide. Encourage the students to use appropriate vocabulary (tall, short, taller, shorter, tallest, shortest).

Have the class look at two things (for example, a tree and a building) outside. Which is taller? Which is shorter?

✕ ✦ ✦ ACTIVITY 10.05   Tall, Taller, Tallest

Have the tallest student and the shortest student in the class stand up. Ask who is taller. Ask who is shorter. Then have the shorter student stand on a chair. Ask who is taller now. Be sure that the students understand that the one on the chair is not taller just because his head is higher.

Have two students that are about the same height stand up. Ask who is taller. Ask who is shorter. If they are not sure, ask them how they can make the comparison. [Move them together; use a string.] Allow the class to solve the problem of how to make the comparison.

Repeat the process with other pairs of students.

Have three students stand. Ask who is tallest and who is shortest.

✗ + ↰ ACTIVITY 10.06   Count the Books

Before the students arrive, place some objects on a table or on shelves where the students will be able to see them. Next to each of the objects place a stack of books that are all the same. Depending on your circumstances, the books could be dictionaries, spelling books, reading books, or some other books.

When the students arrive, direct their attention to two of the objects. Ask which is taller. Have the children look at the books next to the objects. Ask how many books it takes to reach the top of each object. Point out that it takes more books to reach the top of the taller object.

Point out another pair of objects. Have the students count the books next to each object. Ask if they can tell which is taller from the number of books. Repeat with other pairs of objects.

✗ + ↰ ACTIVITY 10.07   Comparison by the Book

Place an object in the room and another object outside the room.

Have students stack books next to the object in the room to **see** how many books it takes to reach the top. Then have them take the books to the other object and do the same. Then have them explain how they can tell which object is taller. Repeat the process with two more objects.

✗ + ↰ ACTIVITY 10.08   How Long?

Lay two objects on a checkerboard. Ask if they can use the squares on the board to compare the two objects. Ask how many squares long each object is.

Have them take the checkerboard around the room and use it to see how long other selected objects are.

✗ + ↰ ACTIVITY 10.09   Measuring Length

Form groups of 3 or 4 students. Give each group a box of new crayons.

Lay an object on the table and demonstrate how to lay crayons next to the object to see how many crayons long it is. Explain that you have *measured* the *length* of the object and that the length of the object is that many crayons. Write the length on the chalkboard. For example, you might write 5 crayons.

Have each group choose four things and use their crayons to measure the length of each. Have them make a list of the things they measured and their lengths.

After everyone is finished, have each group report what they found.

✕ ＋ ૫ ACTIVITY 10.10   Units of Length

Show the class an object. Explain that you are going to measure its length. Use several new pencils to measure the length. Write the length on the chalkboard. Then measure the object using paper clips. Write the length on the chalkboard. Then measure the object using crayons and write the length.

Explain that what you use to measure an object is called the unit of measurement. Point out that the number of units will be a big number or a small number, depending on how long the unit is.

Have the students measure several objects and then measure them again using a different unit.

✕ ＋ ૫ ACTIVITY 10.11   Who's Wrong?

You will need two sticks. One should be 11 inches long. The other should be 13 inches long.

Show the class how to measure a length when you only have one copy of the unit. For example, use one pencil to measure the length of a table top by moving it along the table and keeping track of how many times the pencil was used to reach the other end of the table.

Have students measure several things using a pencil, a chalkboard eraser, and a shoe.

Then give a student the 13 inch stick and have that student measure the length of the room. Before the student finishes, have a second student measure the length of the room to check the first student's measurement. But have the second student use the 11-inch stick.

When both students have reported their measurements, ask the class why their answers are different. After they have discussed how one of the students might have made a mistake, hold the two sticks side by side so that the class can see that they are not the same length. Re-emphasize that if the unit is smaller it takes more to make the measurement. If the unit is larger, it does not take as many.

When communicating a measurement to another person, there must be agreement regarding the unit that is used to make the measurement. For example, suppose we are told that a length is 17 pencils. If the measurement is to be unambiguous, we must know how long the pencil is.

Suppose a tailor uses a new pencil to determine that he needs a length of wool cloth that is 26 pencils long. His assistant cuts off a length of cloth that is 26 pencils long. He wants to do it correctly, so he measures very carefully. However, he uses his own pencil which has been sharpened several times. The cloth will be too short because the tailor and his assistant had not agreed on which pencil to use.

Suppose a carpet layer who wears a size 14 shoe uses his foot to measure a piece of carpet for a room, and finds that the carpet needs to be 12 feet wide and 17 feet long. Suppose that he sent his helper, who wears a size 9 shoe to cut the carpet. The piece of carpet cut by the helper would be too short and too narrow because the carpet layer and his helper had not agreed on what foot to use.

The process of agreeing on the length of the units is called standardization of the units. To arrive at a "standard foot," there must first be agreement on what foot to use. And since the person whose foot is to be used cannot be everywhere, everyone using that standard unit must have a copy of the standard foot. Then, length measurements can be communicated unambiguously. Five feet will mean the same thing to everyone, and 42 feet will mean the same to everyone.

Whatever system of standard units of length is to be used can be effectively taught by following these five steps:

- First, justify the need for the system of standard units. That is best accomplished by stressing the need for clear communication of measurements.
- Second, develop mental imagery for each unit. Students should be able to show a reasonable approximation of each unit. This step is essential if they are to have any success in estimating lengths.
- Third, students should be able to estimate lengths using each of the units.
- Fourth, the relationships among the units within the system should be discovered, understood, and learned.
- Fifth, students should become familiar with and proficient in the use of measurement tools that make use of the units in the system (12-inch rulers, yardsticks, meter sticks, tape measures, and so on).

The most common mistake made in teaching length measurement is to begin with the fifth step, without spending sufficient time on the previous four steps. Emphasizing the first through the fourth steps helps students to become proficient in the use of measurement—inside and outside the classroom, in completing measurement exercises and in solving problems that involve measurement, in both common and unusual settings, at times when the need to measure is anticipated and when unexpected needs require measurement.

The following activities illustrate how the concepts of measurement of length can be taught.

First, establish the need for standardized units.

× + ÷ ACTIVITY 10.12   The Captain's Foot

Have students work with partners to trace around their feet. They should cut out the feet. As much as is possible, pair students with partners who are much taller or much shorter than they are.

Choose a pair of partners to measure the length of the room two times, once with each partner's foot. Choose another pair of partners to measure the distance from the classroom door to the next door down the hall. Have other partners measure the length of the chalkboard, the width of the room, the distance from the teacher's desk to the corner of the room, and so on.

In most cases the partners will get two different measurements because their feet are not the same size. Discuss why this could be a problem. Explain the need to agree on what foot to use. Choose a student to be the "captain." Tell the class that the captain has decided that everyone should use his foot. Make copies of the captain's foot for everyone.

Have the partners measure the same things again using the captain's foot. Now their measurements should agree.

ACTIVITY 10.13   The King's Foot

Arrange for another class to cooperate with your class on this activity. Your class will measure using the "captain's" foot. The other class will measure using their teacher's foot. Your class will use a ball of string. The other class will use a roll of adding machine tape. You will need several copies of the order form shown at the right.

Explain that your class will order a strip of paper for your bulletin board from the other class and they will order string for their bulletin board from this class. Decide how much paper to order and complete an order form to send to the other class. The other class will order string from your class in the same way.

> Please send _____ feet of _____ as soon as possible.

After receiving the order from the other class, measure the string or paper, cut it, and send it to the other class. When the string or paper is received, measure it and send a message back to the other class saying, "It was too long," "It was too short," or "It was just right."

For this part of the activity both classes will need several copies of a foot that is exactly 12 inches long. This will be "the king's foot."

Discuss why the measurements might have been wrong. [The other class was not using the "captain's foot."]

Tell the class that you discussed the problem with the teacher of the other class and that the two of you decided that you should use the same foot. Explain that you have decided to use the king's foot. Pass out copies of the king's foot.

Each class should then place another order for paper or string. After receiving the order from the other class, measure the string or paper, cut it, and send it to the other class. When the string or paper is received, measure it using the king's foot and send a message back to the other class saying, "It was too long," "It was too short," or "It was just right."

Hold up a copy of the king's foot. Explain that a long time ago people all over the British Empire decided to use this foot to make measurements. Then, everyone knew how long four feet was. It was the same length all over the Empire.

Second, mental imagery for each unit should be developed.

ACTIVITY 10.14   This Is a Foot

Have the students use a copy of a standard foot (the king's foot) to find objects around the room that are 1-foot long. Have them see if anyone has a length on their body that is exactly 1-foot long (for example, for some students, the distance from the elbow to the knuckles of the closed fist might be 1 foot).

Have the students prepare and attach labels to these objects that say "This is a foot!"

ACTIVITY 10.15 Pick a Foot

Choose several objects that are 1-foot long. Choose an equal number of objects that are not 1-foot long. They should be either shorter than ten inches or longer than fourteen inches in length. Place the objects in pairs around the room. Each pair of objects should have one object that is a foot long and one object that is not a foot long.

Direct the attention of the class to one pair of objects. Ask which one is 1-foot long. Take a vote. Have someone bring a copy of the king's foot to check who was right and who was not.

Continue in this way until all the pairs of objects have been considered. After about five pairs of objects have been looked at and checked, almost everyone should be choosing the foot-long object.

ACTIVITY 10.16 A Foot, or More or Less

Take the class for a walk. Take one copy of the standard foot with you. Along the way, point out objects. Have the students decide if the objects are a foot long, or more than a foot, or less than a foot. For each object, after the students have decided, have someone use the standard foot to see who was right.

Third, students should develop the ability to estimate lengths.

ACTIVITY 10.18 Best Guess

Prepare 10 cardboard strips ranging from 4 inches to 20 inches in length. Also prepare from colored paper two strips that are 10 inches long and 10 strips that are 1 inch long.

Place the cardboard strips under a box so that about 2 inches of each strip can be seen. Place the colored strips in the box.

Form a group of 3 or 4 students. They will each need a sheet of paper and a pencil. They take turns choosing a cardboard strip and pulling it out from under the box. Everyone looks at the strip and guesses how many inches long it is. They each write their guess on their paper.

After everyone has written a guess, the one who chose the strip uses the 10-inch colored strips and the 1-inch colored strips to measure the cardboard strip. The one with the best guess gets a point. If there is a tie for the best guess, everyone who tied gets a point.

Continue until all the cardboard strips have been used. The one with the most points wins.

ACTIVITY 10.19 Place and Guess

Form pairs of partners. Each pair of partners needs two paper clips, 10 ten-centimeter rods, and 10 centimeter cubes.

Both partners close their eyes and place a paper clip on the table between them. Both look at the paper clips, guess how far apart they are, and write the guess on a sheet of paper. Then they use the centimeter cubes and ten-centimeter rods to measure the distance between the paper clips. The one with the best guess gets a point. If they tie, both get a point. The first one to get 10 points wins.

ACTIVITY 10.20   Estimation Walk

Take the class on a walk. Point out things to the class and have them estimate how many feet long they are. After everyone has had a chance to guess, measure the object. Were the guesses close? Who had the best guess? Continue to estimate and check lengths.

There is a great deal of similarity in the three estimation activities. In fact, they are really three versions of the same activity—the same idea packaged in three different ways.

An object is identified.

The measurement is estimated.

The length is measured to check the estimate.

Another object is identified.

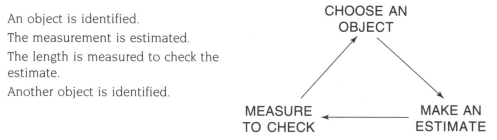

If measurements are made with measuring tools that provide clear imagery of the unit being used, that mental imagery can then be used to make subsequent estimates. The activity provides immediate feedback on the accuracy of each estimate, allowing students to make corrections in their mental imagery before making the next estimate. Accuracy of estimates typically improves dramatically.

We continue with the sample teaching activities.

Fourth, the relationships among the units within the system should be discovered, understood, and learned.

✕ ← ↺ **ACTIVITY 10.21   Equal Trades**

Make several copies of "unit strips." Some should be 1-inch long. Some should be 1-foot long. Some should be 1-yard long.

Form groups of 3 or 4 students. Give each group a set of unit strips. For example, one group might have 1 yard strip, 2 foot strips, and 6 inch strips. Another group might have 2 foot strips and 27 inch strips. A third group might have 1 yard strip and 5 foot strips.

Have each group record what they have. For example, the first group, above would write "1 yard 2 feet 6 inches." The second group above would write "2 feet 27 inches." The third group would write "1 yard 5 feet."

Then have every group compare units and make an even trade with some other group. For example, group 1 might trade 1 yard strip to group 3 for 3 foot strips. After the trades are completed, each group should record what they have after the trade. Have them continue to make trades and record the results.

Point out that the amounts that each group has recorded are all equal.

ACTIVITY 10.22   Scavenger Hunt

Prepare four lists of six measurements as shown below.

8 feet	29 inches	5 feet 3 inches	37 inches
2 yards 14 inches	4 feet 7 inches	1 yard 18 inches	1 yard 25 inches
2 yards 4 feet	3 yards 2 feet	4 feet	2 feet 6 inches
14 inches	7 feet	2 yards 5 feet	4 yards 2 feet
6 feet 8 inches	1 yard 40 inches	20 inches	6 feet
4 yards	8 yards	5 yards	7 yards

Prepare 24 cards, each showing another name for a measurement on one of the lists. Tape these cards to the wall around the room.

Separate the class into four teams. Give one of the lists to each team. (You might want to provide a copy of the list for every member of the team.) Have the teams search for cards that give other names for the measurements on their list.

The first team to finish wins.

ACTIVITY 10.23   Order Three

Prepare sentence strips showing the measurements given below.

8 feet	29 inches	5 feet 3 inches	37 inches
2 yards 14 inches	4 feet 7 inches	1 yard 18 inches	1 yard 25 inches
2 yards 4 feet	3 yards 2 feet	4 feet	2 feet 6 inches
14 inches	7 feet	2 yards 5 feet	4 yards 2 feet
6 feet 8 inches	1 yard 40 inches	20 inches	6 feet
4 yards	8 yards	5 yards	7 yards

Choose three strips and place them in the chalk tray where they can be seen by the class.

Have the class help you arrange them in order from the shortest length to the longest length. Keep asking how they can tell which is longer and which is shorter.

Choose other sets of three measurements to arrange in order. Also arrange sets of four measurements. Arrange sets of five.

ACTIVITY 10.24   Line Up

Prepare sentence strips showing the measurements given below.

8 feet	29 inches	5 feet 3 inches	37 inches
2 yards 14 inches	4 feet 7inches	1 yard 18 inches	1 yard 25 inches
2 yards 4 feet	3 yards 2 feet	4 feet	2 feet 6 inches
14 inches	7 feet	2 yards 5 feet	4 yards 2 feet
6 feet 8 inches	1 yard 40 inches	20 inches	6 feet
4 yards	8 yards	5 yards	7 yards

Shuffle them and pass them out to the class. Separate the class into two groups that are about equal in number. Have one group go to one side of the room and have the other group go to the opposite side. Tell the class that you want each group to line up in order from shortest to longest length. Encourage them to talk to each other when they need help.

Have them hold their measurements so the ones in the other group can see them. Each group should then check the other group to see if they are in the right order. Again, encourage them to talk when they are not sure.

ACTIVITY 10.25   Shuffle

Prepare cards showing measurements like those given below.

8 feet	29 inches	5 feet 3 inches	37 inches
2 yards 14 inches	4 feet 7 inches	1 yard 18 inches	1 yard 25 inches
2 yards 4 feet	3 yards 2 feet	4 feet	2 feet 6 inches
14 inches	7 feet	2 yards 5 feet	4 yards 2 feet
6 feet 8 inches	1 yard 40 inches	20 inches	6 feet
4 yards	8 yards	5 yards	7 yards

Form a group of four students. Shuffle the cards and give the deck to the students. On each play, the dealer should give each player five cards face-down. When the dealer says go, the players turn their cards over and race to get them in order. The winner must explain why each of the cards are in the right position.

The winner then reshuffles the cards and starts a new play. They continue until a player has won five rounds or until the teacher calls time.

Fifth, students should become proficient in the use of measurement tools.

ACTIVITY 10.26   Feet in a Row

The students will need to use their copies of the king's foot (cut-outs of feet that are exactly 12-inches long). Tell the students that you are going to show them a faster way to measure lengths. Have several students bring their copies of the king's foot to the front. Tape the king's feet toe to heel in a row. Number the feet.

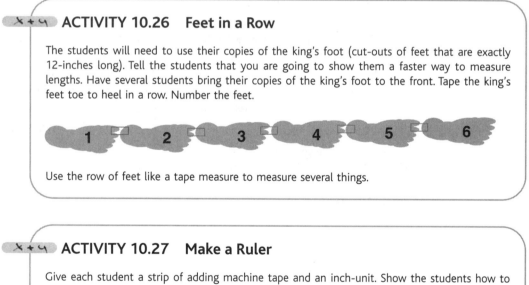

Use the row of feet like a tape measure to measure several things.

ACTIVITY 10.27   Make a Ruler

Give each student a strip of adding machine tape and an inch-unit. Show the students how to mark 1-inch intervals on their strip of adding machine tape to make a ruler. Have them number the inches.

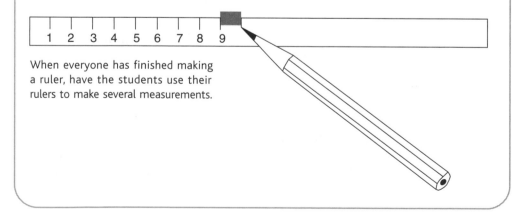

When everyone has finished making a ruler, have the students use their rulers to make several measurements.

ACTIVITY 10.28   To the Nearest Foot

Review rounding of numbers to the nearest 10. Use a number line to help the students visualize the process. Then use a tape measure that shows feet to measure something between 3- and 4-feet long. Show that the length is more than 3 feet but less than 4 feet. Explain that we need to round to the nearest foot. Have the students decide if the length is nearer to 3 feet or 4 feet. Point out the half-way point between 3 feet and 4 feet. Show how to use this half-way point to make the judgment.

> Round to 3 feet.

| | 1 | | 2 | 3 | | 4 | | 5 | |

Measure some other things to the nearest foot.

Teaching Area Measurement

Area is different from length in that we do not, for the most part, actually measure area. In most cases, we measure some combination of lengths and use them in a formula to compute the area. So, the study of area can be separated into two parts. The first part consists of developing the concepts of area and unit of area, and using the units to determine the area. The second part consists of the development of the area formulas. Problem solving, using the level of understanding and skill that has been developed, is found throughout.

The early part of instruction parallels some of the same ideas that were developed for measurement of length.

- The *concept of area* should be developed first by making gross comparisons of the areas of different objects.
- The *concept of a unit of area* as a piece of area should be developed.
- The *concept of measurement of area* as the number of units it takes to cover the area being measured should be developed. Mental imagery for the units should be developed. Students should be able to show a reasonable approximation of the unit.
- Students should develop the *ability to estimate areas* using each of the units.

Although we provide a brief development here, creating teaching and learning activities for developing area concepts is left as exercises for the reader.

Comparisons of area are more complex than comparisons of length. When comparing areas we must take into account length, width, and shape. When the following shapes are compared, children have very little problem deciding which has the bigger area. Shape B is bigger in every way. Students would probably choose shape B even if they did not know what area is.

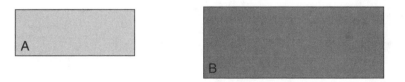

The next two shapes are considerably more difficult because one shape is longer but the other is wider. This forces the child to think beyond one dimension.

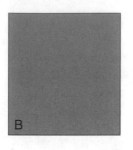

An appropriate way to check the comparison is to cut shape A into parts and rearrange them. Then it can easily be seen that B has a bigger area than A.

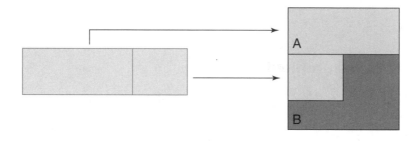

The next pair of figures are even more difficult because, in addition to length and width, the shapes of the figures have an impact on their areas.

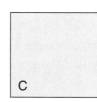

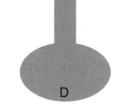

Once again, by cutting and rearranging one of the figures, the comparison can easily be checked. Figure C has the greater area.

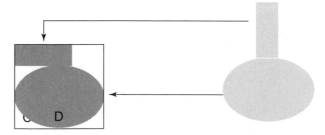

As figures get more complex in shape, look–see comparisons become more difficult, and so we need to introduce the use of units to help with the comparisons. A good way to start is to have students cover the shapes with some common objects, like pennies, in order to help with the comparisons. We want to see how many pennies can be placed inside each shape. We do not want any to go outside the boundary of the shape. Fourteen pennies are required to cover figure A, while 18 pennies are required for figure B. This can help us to decide that figure B has the greater area.

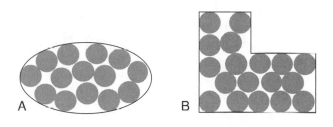

This process breaks down with complex shapes. Consider these two figures. We can place seven pennies on figure C but can only place six pennies on figure D, But does figure C really have the greater area?

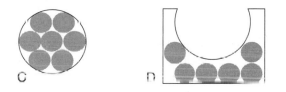

The students will quickly point out that more of the inside of D is left uncovered. The problem is that the pennies do not fit together well. There is space between them that does not get counted. We need to use a unit with a shape that tessellates (a shape that fits together with copies of itself), without any space in between. Among the many shapes that tessellate are a triangle, a parallelogram, a hexagon, and a plus sign.

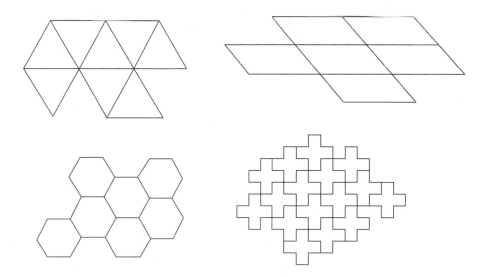

Although there is value in allowing students to explore the measurement of area with the tessellating units just illustrated, the majority of student time should be spent using square units of area. These are the units that are commonly used in area computation formulas. When introducing students to the use of square units, emphasize that the area of a figure is the number of square units it takes to cover the inside of the figure.

The area of this figure is 12 square units.

To cover this area, we use 12 whole squares and three half squares. Altogether, the area is $13\frac{1}{2}$ square units.

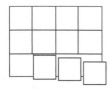

After students are comfortable measuring areas by placing and counting squares, area computation formulas can be taught. The first of these is the area formula for rectangles. This formula can be developed from a series of discoveries made when placing squares on rectangles and determining how many squares there are.

First, because rectangles are the same length from the bottom all the way to the top, every row of squares contains the same number of squares.

In this rectangle, every row has six squares. We can find the total number of squares by multiplying the number in each row times the number of rows.

Area = 6 X 4 = 24 squares

In this rectangle, there are three rows of five squares. The area is $5 \times 3 = 15$ square units.

In this rectangle, there are six squares in the first row, so there must be six squares in every row. There are three rows. The area is 6 × 3 = 18 square units.

So we see that we can compute the area by multiplying the number of squares in each row times the number of rows.

Area of rectangle = Number of squares in each row × Number of rows

Second, if the length and width of the rectangle are given in inches and the area units are square inches, then the number of squares in the first row is the same as the length of the rectangle. The length of this rectangle is 8 inches, so 8 square inches fit in the first row.

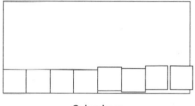

8 inches

Third, if the width is given in inches and the area units are square inches, then the number of rows is the same as the width.

The width of this rectangle is 4 inches, so the area will be four rows of square inches.

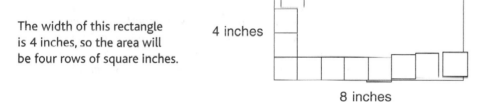

4 inches

8 inches

The area formula can then be written as:

Area = Length of the rectangle × Width of the rectangle

or,   **A = L × W**

The Big Idea for Developing Area Formulas

There is one big idea that constantly recurs as the area computation formulas are developed. This big idea is related to the concept of conservation of area: the amount of area is not changed if the area is rearranged. So, *when we have a figure for which there is no area formula, we rearrange the shape to get a figure for which we have an area formula.* This big idea is used to develop the rest of the area computation formulas.

We now examine how we can rearrange the areas of several common shapes to find the areas. First, consider a parallelogram. We call the base of the parallelogram b and call the height h.

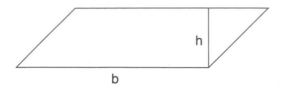

We do not have a formula for area of a parallelogram, but we do have a formula for area of a rectangle. We rearrange the area of the parallelogram into the shape of a rectangle. First, we cut one end of the parallelogram off, leaving square corners.

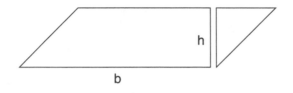

Then we move the piece that we cut off to the other end.

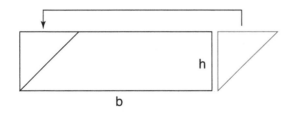

We now have a rectangle with length b and width h. The area of this rectangle is $A = b \times h$, where b is the length of the original parallelogram and h is its height. But this is also the area of the parallelogram because we did not add or take away any area. We just rearranged the area. The area of the parallelogram is:

$$A = b \times h$$

Next, we consider a triangle. The base of this triangle is b and its height is h.

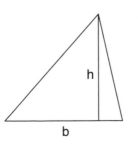

We do not have a formula for area of a triangle, but we do have formulas for areas of rectangles and parallelograms. We need to rearrange the area into the shape of either a rectangle or a parallelogram. To accomplish this, we begin by making a copy of the triangle. When we have done this, we will have twice as much area as we started with.

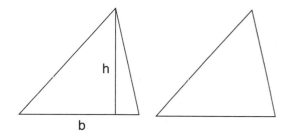

We then rotate the copy and place it on the other side of the original triangle.

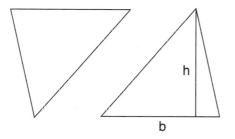

Then we join the two triangles together to form a parallelogram. The area of this parallelogram is $A = b \times h$, where b is the base of the original triangle and h is the height of the original triangle.

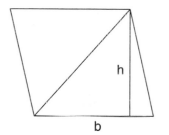

But, remember that, because we included a copy of the original triangle, we have twice the original area. To get the actual area, we multiply by $\frac{1}{2}$. The formula for area of a triangle, then, is

$$A = \frac{1}{2} \times b \times h$$

Now, consider a trapezoid. Trapezoids have two bases, which are parallel sides. The height is the distance between the bases. We label the bases b_1 and b_2 and label the height h.

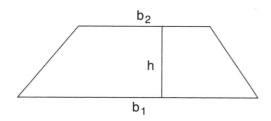

As we did with the triangle, we copy the trapezoid. Remember that this doubles the area.

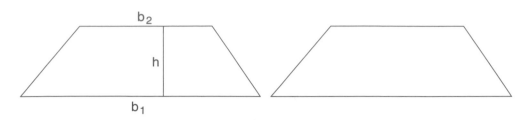

We rotate the copy and join it to the original trapezoid. Together, the two trapezoids form a parallelogram.

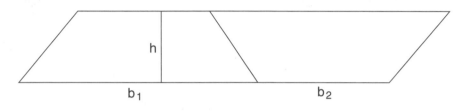

We can find the area of this parallelogram by multiplying the base times the height: $A = (b_1 + b_2) \times h$.

But, remember that we doubled the area, so this area is twice what we want. We need to multiply by $\frac{1}{2}$ to get rid of the extra area. That leaves us with the area formula for trapezoids.

$$A = \frac{1}{2}(b_1 + b_2)h$$

To discover the formula for area of a circle, the students already need to know the relationship between the diameter of a circle (the width of the circle) and the circumference of the same circle (the perimeter or the distance around the circle).

This relationship can be discovered through an exploratory activity where students measure the diameter and circumference of several round things—some big, some small, and some in between. Then, for each circle, the student divides the circumference by the diameter. In every case, the distance around the circle is a little bit more than three times the distance across. Although, because of measurement error, the quotient of the circumference and diameter will vary slightly from circle to circle, the ratio is the number that we call pi (π). The relationship between the circumference and the diameter is given by this formula.

$$C = \pi d$$

Since the diameter is twice the radius, another way to express this relationship is given by these formulas.

$$C = \pi \times 2r \quad \text{or} \quad C = 2\pi r$$

Now, consider this circle. We want to find the area, but do not have a formula for the area of a circle. We try to rearrange the area into a shape for which we have one.

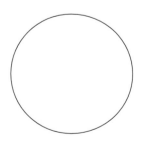

Notice that if we cut the circle into fourths and rearrange them, the area is in a shape with two straight sides, but the shape does not resemble a shape for which we have an area formula.

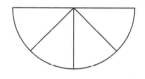

We cut the circle into eighths and separate it into two equal parts.

Then we arrange the pieces as pictured. We can see that the shape is very much like a parallelogram.

If we cut the circle into twelfths and rearrange the pieces in the same way, the shape looks even more like a parallelogram.

The more parts the circle is cut into, the more the rearrangement of the pieces looks like a parallelogram. So, we can imagine 100 parts and a shape that is almost exactly in the shape of a parallelogram. Regardless of the number of pieces, the base of this "parallelogram" is half the circumference (πr), and the height of the "parallelogram" is the radius (r). To find the area of this "parallelogram," we multiply the base times the height.

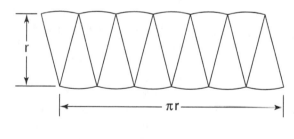

$$A = (\pi r)r$$

This result is the formula for the area of a circle.

$$\mathbf{A = \pi r^2}$$

When students have learned to find areas of unfamiliar shapes in this way—*when the shape is unfamiliar, change it into a familiar shape*—area problems involving composite shapes are typically not difficult. For example, suppose we want to find the area of the following figure.

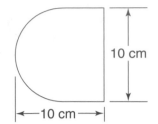

The figure consists of half of a circle with a radius of 5 cm

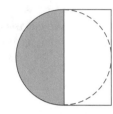

and a rectangle that is 5 cm by 10 cm. The areas of these two parts can be added to find the area of the original figure.

No instructional activities for developing the area formulas are included here, but they are left to the reader as exercises.

Teaching Volume Measurement

Strong parallels exist between area concepts and volume concepts. Units of area are pieces of area. Units of volume are pieces of volume. We measure area by finding how many units it takes to cover the interior of the shape. We measure volume by finding how many units it takes to fill the interior of the shape. We do not normally actually measure area; we measure linear dimensions and compute the area using formulas. We do not normally actually measure volume; we measure linear dimensions and compute the volume using formulas. The one big idea when developing area formulas is: *when we have a shape for which we do not have an area formula, we rearrange the area into a shape for which we do have a formula.* The one big idea when developing volume formulas is similar: *when we have a shape for which we do not have a volume formula, we rearrange the volume into a shape for which we do have a formula.*

We begin the development of volume concepts by establishing meaning for the term volume. We talk about the size of the inside of the shape and make gross comparisons. For example, we can see that box A will hold more than box B, so we say that the volume of box A is greater than the volume of box B.

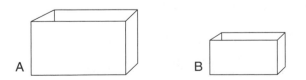

On the other hand, because they are shaped differently, it is harder to tell which of the two boxes C and D would hold more.

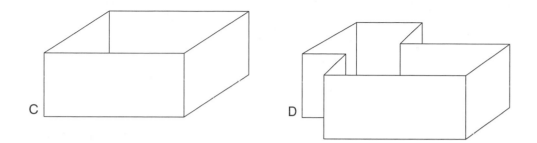

If we fill both shapes with marbles, we can count the marbles to see which shape holds more.

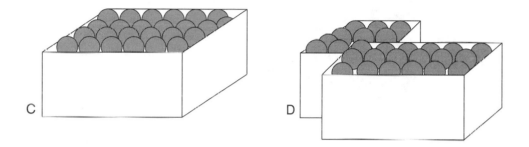

But now we can see a problem similar to the one we saw when we used circular units of area. There is space between the marbles that is not being measured. So, we want to use a unit of volume that completely fills the shape without leaving space between the units. There are actually a lot of shapes that would work, but the volume computation formulas require the use of units in the shape of a cube. We begin experimenting with cubic units to measure the volume of rectangular prisms (or boxes)

As students fill boxes with cubes and count the cubes, they learn that the measure of the volume of the box is the number of cubes it takes to fill the box.

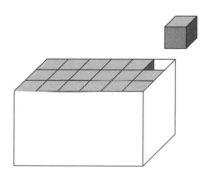

Students can also easily discover that, since the box is the same size and shape from the bottom all the way to the top, every layer of cubes contains the same number.

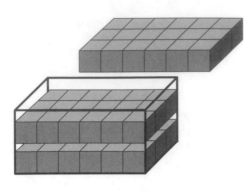

So the volume will be the number in each layer times the number of layers.

Volume = Number of cubes in the first layer × Number of layers

In this transparent box, we see that the first layer contains 18 cubes, and can also see that there are three layers. The volume is 3 × 18, or 54 cubes.

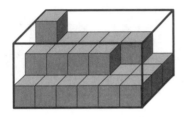

If the area of the base (bottom) of the box is marked off in squares, then in the first layer of cubes, a cube will be on top of every square. So, the number of cubes in the first layer is equal to the area of the base of the box.

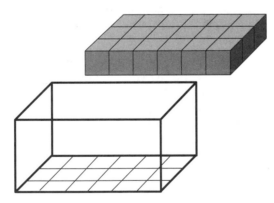

The number of layers is the same as the height of the box. In this example, the height is 3 units and there are three layers.

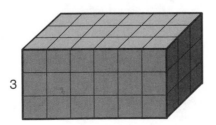

The volume is equal to the number of cubes in the first layer times the number of layers. But since the number of cubes in the first layer is equal to the area of the base and the number of layers is equal to the height, we let B represent the area of the base, let h represent the height, and write the formula for volume of a box (rectangular prism) as:

$$V = Bh$$

The same formula works for any box as long as the box is the same size and shape from the bottom to the top.

A round box (a circular prism, or cylinder).

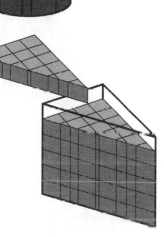

A triangular box (a triangular prism)

Or, even a strangely shaped box (an unusual prism-like figure)

For any box that is the same size and shape from the bottom to the top (called prisms or prism-like figures), the same volume formula will work.

$$V = Bh$$

There is another formula for volume of a cylinder, $V = \pi r^2 h$. However, the area of the base of a cylinder is πr^2 so the cylinder formula is exactly the same as the formula for all the other prism-like figures, $V = Bh$. If students know all the situations where the formula for prism-like figures can be used, they will, in effect, have fewer formulas to remember.

Suppose we have a set of water containers that have prism-like shapes. If one of the shapes is unusual and it is difficult to find the volume, we could fill the unusual container with water and then pour that water into a rectangular, box-shaped container.

We then have rearranged the shape of the water (which is the volume) into a shape for which we have a volume formula.

We can use this technique to discover a volume formula that works for an entire class of three-dimensional shapes.

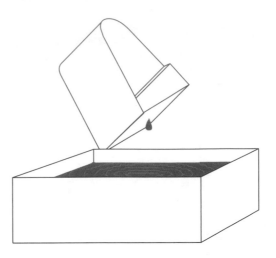

Consider the two figures pictured below. One is a rectangular prism. The other is an inverted pyramid. We do not have a volume formula for pyramids, but we do have one for prisms. These figures have identical bases; that is, the base of the prism is the same size and shape as the base of the pyramid. Also, the height of both figures is the same.

If we fill the pyramid with water and then pour it into the prism, we find that the water fills $\frac{1}{3}$ of the prism.

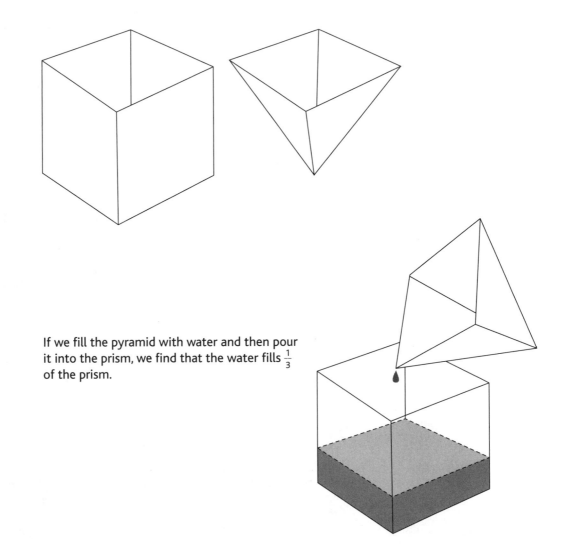

Now, consider these figures. One is a triangular prism. The other is a triangular pyramid. Again both figures have the same base and the same height.

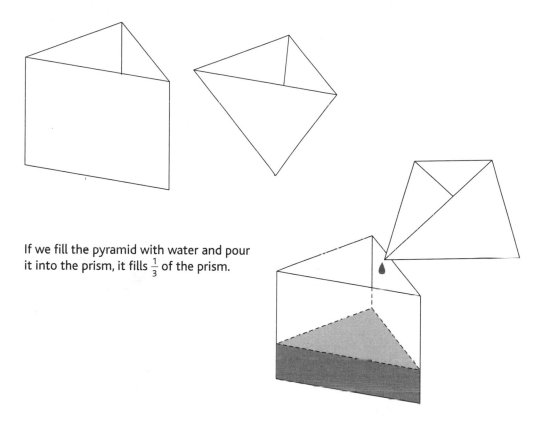

If we fill the pyramid with water and pour it into the prism, it fills $\frac{1}{3}$ of the prism.

The next two figures are a prism-like figure and a pyramid-like figure with the same base and the same height.

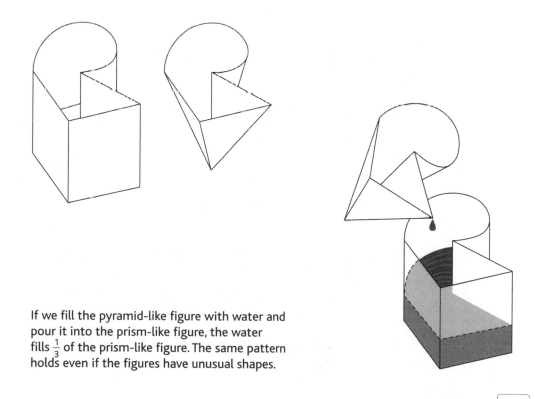

If we fill the pyramid-like figure with water and pour it into the prism-like figure, the water fills $\frac{1}{3}$ of the prism-like figure. The same pattern holds even if the figures have unusual shapes.

As we expect, we see the same relationship between cones and cylinders. This cylinder has the same base and height as the cone.

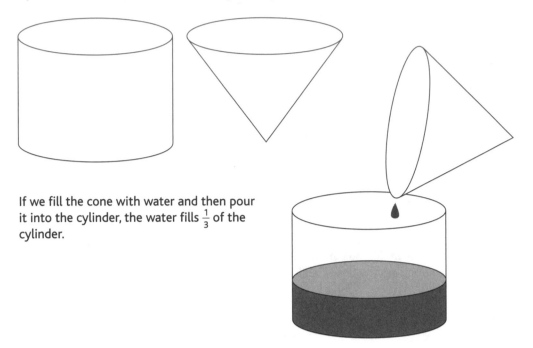

If we fill the cone with water and then pour it into the cylinder, the water fills $\frac{1}{3}$ of the cylinder.

The relationship between the volume of pyramid-like figures (including cones) and prism-like figures with the same base and height gives us the volume formula for all pyramid-like figures. For the same base and height, the volume of the pyramid-like figure is always $\frac{1}{3}$ the volume of the prism-like figure. Since the volume of a prism-like figure is $B \times h$ the volume of a pyramid-like figure is $\frac{1}{3}$ of that.

$$V = \tfrac{1}{3}Bh$$

The following are activities that a teacher might use to develop volume concepts.

×+◁ ACTIVITY 10.29 Pick the Big Box

Assemble a variety of boxes of different sizes and shapes.

Choose two of them and ask the students which will hold the most. Repeat this process with several pairs of boxes. If the students are unable to decide which of a pair of boxes is bigger, set that pair of boxes aside.

×+◁ ACTIVITY 10.30 How to Decide?

Point out one of the pairs of boxes for which the students were unable to identify the biggest.

Conduct a brainstorming session, asking students to think of ways to decide which box is bigger. Remind them that the bigger box is the one that would hold more.

Write every suggestion on the chalkboard, regardless of how good or how practical it is. Then ask the students to decide which methods are most reasonable (make the most sense, are easy to use).

Then try some of the suggested methods to see how they work.

ACTIVITY 10.31   How Can You Fill It Full if There Aren't Enough Cubes?

Construct six small boxes that have the following interior dimensions:

      5 in. by 8 in. by 3 in.   6 in. by 6 in. by 4 in.
      5 in. by 7 in. by 6 in.   4 in. by 9 in. by 7 in.
      7 in. by 6 in. by 5 in.   4 in. by 8 in. by 5 in.

Form six groups. Give each group one of the boxes and about 300 inch-cubes. Have each group fill their box with cubes to see how many cubes are needed.

Take away all but 60 cubes from each group. Then have the groups exchange boxes. Point out that they no longer have enough cubes to fill the boxes. Tell them that you want each group to try to use the cubes that they have to figure how many cubes it would take to fill the box.

Have each group report to the class how they were able to complete the task. Emphasize that every layer of cubes will contain the same number of cubes.

ACTIVITY 10.32   Even Fewer Cubes

Form six groups of students. Give each group one of the boxes prepared for Activity 10.31. (Be sure that no group has a box that they previously worked with.) This time give each group just 22 cubes. Have them see if they can figure out the number of cubes needed to completely fill the box when they only have 22 cubes.

After each group is finished, have the groups report how they figured out the answer. During the discussion ask how they figured out how many cubes would be in the first layer. Also ask how they figured out how many layers there would be.

ACTIVITY 10.33   The Bottom of the Box

Cut a piece of white paper to fit exactly on the bottom of the inside of each of the boxes prepared for Activity 10.31. Draw lines to make 1-inch squares on each piece. Place the papers inside the boxes.

Form six groups and give a box to each group. Also give each group about 50 inch-cubes.

Point out that they can look at the paper on the bottom of the box and see the area of the bottom. Ask each group to figure out the area of the bottom of their box.

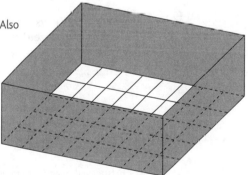

Next, have the students place a cube on top of every square in the area. Ask how the area of the bottom is related to the number of cubes it takes to make one layer.

Collect all but 10 cubes from all the groups and have the groups exchange boxes. Tell the groups to use what they have to find how many cubes will fit in their boxes.

When they are finished, ask how to find how many cubes it takes to fill the box. Emphasize that the number of cubes in the first layer times the number of layers is the number needed to fill the box.

✗ + ◁ ACTIVITY 10.34   Using a Ruler

Form six groups of students. Give each group one of the boxes prepared for Activity 10.31. (Be sure that no group has a box that they previously worked with.) This time give each group a ruler. Tell the students that you want each group to see if they can use the ruler to figure out how many inch-cubes will fit in their box.

After each group is finished, have the groups report how they figured out the answer. Ask how you can tell how many cubes will be in the first layer. Ask how you can tell how many layers there will be.

Write the formula for volume of a box on the chalkboard.

$$V = lwh$$

Place parentheses around the *lw*

$$V = (lw)h$$

Explain that when you multiply these numbers you have the area of the bottom of the box. Remind the students that this area is the same as the number of cubes in the first layer. Also remind them that the height tells how many layers of cubes you have.

✗ + ◁ ACTIVITY 10.35   Odd Boxes

Construct several boxes with unusual shapes like these. Draw squares showing the area of the bottom of each box.

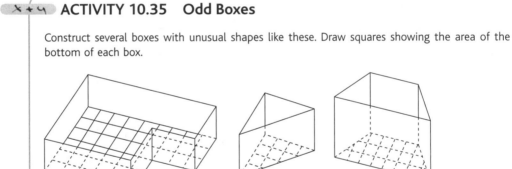

Have students figure out the volume of each box. Let them use a ruler to measure the height of the boxes. Emphasize that the area of the base tells how many cubes are in the first layer and the height tells how many layers there are.

✗ + ◁ ACTIVITY 10.36   Build a Box and Pyramid

Construct a box and a pyramid out of stiff cardboard. The base of the box and the base of the pyramid will be identical. The height of the box will also be the same as the height of the pyramid.

Have a student fill the pyramid with beans and then pour the beans into the box. The student will find that the beans will fill the box one-third full.

Ask how the volume of the pyramid is related to the volume of the box.

> ## ✕ ✦ ✦ ACTIVITY 10.37   Build a Cylinder and Cone
>
> Construct a cylinder and a cone out of stiff cardboard. The base of the cylinder and the base of the cone will be identical. The height of the cylinder will also be the same as the height of the cone.
>
> Have a student fill the pyramid with beans and then pour the beans into the box. The student will find that the beans will fill the box one-third full.
>
> Ask how the volume of the cone is related to the volume of the cylinder.

Measuring Angles

Teaching measurement of angles is easy if sufficient time is spent helping the child to conceptualize the unit of measure for angles. To understand the need for the careful-conceptualization of angle measurement, consider these angles. Although the sides are longer on angle A, we say that angle B is greater. The explanation might be that angle B is "open wider."

Now consider these two angles. Remember, that from previous examples, the student has a sense that the angle that is open wider is the bigger angle. But, even though angle D appears to be open wider, the student is told that angle C is actually the greater angle.

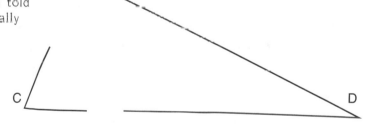

These apparent inconsistencies can be explained in various ways, but the need for such explanations can be reduced or even eliminated by a careful development of what is being measured (Van de Wall, 1998; Wilson & Adams, 1992).

We begin by helping the student to think of an angle as indicating an amount of rotation. One side of the angle represents a beginning position, and the other side represents an ending position. The size of the angle is thought of as the amount of rotation needed to get from the initial position to the terminal position.

The size of angle X is $\frac{1}{4}$ of a turn.

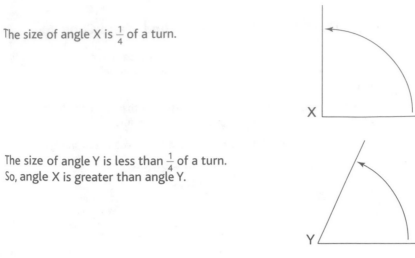

The size of angle Y is less than $\frac{1}{4}$ of a turn.
So, angle X is greater than angle Y.

A folded piece of waxed paper can be used to help students begin to measure angles. Fold the sheet of waxed paper into eighths as pictured below. Then place the paper on top of the angle to measure how many eighths of a rotation are indicated by the angle. The angle shown is about $\frac{3}{8}$ of a rotation. The angle can easily be seen through the waxed paper, and the folds are easy to see. The waxed paper also works well with an overhead projector.

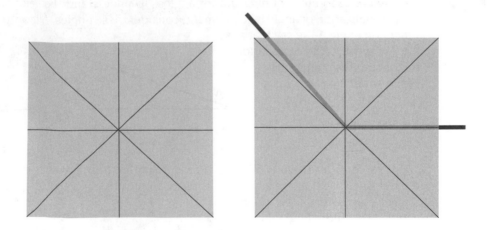

To measure angles with more precision, fold the waxed paper into sixteenths. Angles of about $\frac{3}{16}$ and $\frac{5}{16}$ are shown below.

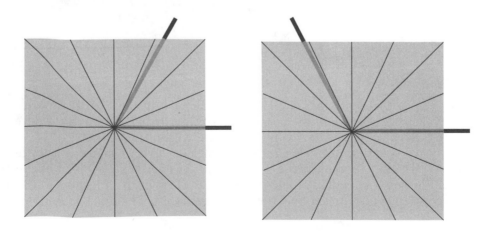

We could fold the paper into smaller parts to gain more precision in our measurement, but there are measuring tools called protractors that let us measure angles to the nearest $\frac{1}{360}$ of a rotation. $\frac{1}{360}$ of a rotation is called a degree. An angle with a measure of 45 degrees shows $\frac{45}{360}$ of a rotation.

The following sequence of activities shows how a teacher might develop the concept of angle measurement.

ACTIVITY 10.38 Rotation

Attach an object to the bulletin board using a single thumbtack in the center.

Draw the students' attention to the object. Turn the object and tell the students that you are rotating it. Tell the students that you are going to do one complete rotation. Then turn the object 360 degrees. Tell them that you are going to do one fourth of a rotation. Then turn the object 90 degrees.

Have students come to the bulletin board and show a full rotation, one half of a rotation, and three fourths of a rotation.

ACTIVITY 10.39 Point and Turn

Call on a student to come to the front and stand with one arm pointing straight out to the side. Tell the class that the student is going to do one complete rotation. Ask where he will be pointing after the rotation. Help the student demonstrate one complete rotation.

Have other students come forward and demonstrate one-fourth, one-half, and three-fourths of a rotation.

ACTIVITY 10.40 Two Strings

Attach a white string and a red string to a thumbtack in the center of the bulletin board. Use a thumbtack to secure the other end of the white string so that it is stretched straight out to the right. Tie the other end of the red string around a push pin and stretch it out on top of the white string.

Show rotation by moving the push pin to a new position to show an angle with one-fourth of a rotation (90°).

Move the white string back to the initial position and then move it to show angles with one-half, and three-fourths of a rotation.

✕ ✦ ᔓ ACTIVITY 10.41 Measuring with Waxed Paper

Fold a sheet of waxed paper into eighths as shown. Draw several angles on transparencies and use the waxed paper on the overhead projector to measure the angles to the nearest eighth of a rotation.

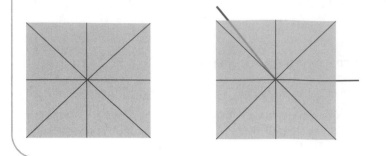

✕ ✦ ᔓ ACTIVITY 10.42 Measuring with More Precision

Fold a sheet of waxed paper into sixteenths as shown. Draw several angles on transparencies and use the waxed paper on the overhead projector to measure the angles to the nearest sixteenth of a rotation.

✕ ✦ ᔓ ACTIVITY 10.43 Measuring with Degrees

Remind the students that they have measured angles to the nearest fourth of a rotation, the nearest eighth of a rotation, and the nearest sixteenth of a rotation. Explain that we normally measure angles to the nearest 360th of a rotation. Explain that one 360th of a rotation is called a degree.

Show the students the degrees on a protractor. Demonstrate how to use the protractor to measure angles.

Assign partners. Have each pair of partners use protractors to measure several angles.

Measuring with Indirect Units

The measurements that we have examined so far have all used direct units of measure. The unit has been a piece of what was being measured. For example, we measured length with pieces of length—inches, centimeters, and so on. We measured area with pieces of area—square inches, square meters, and so on. We measured volume with pieces of volume—cubic centimeters, cubic feet, and so on. We introduced the concept of angles as showing an amount of rotation and then learned to measure angles with parts of rotation, degrees. Some attributes are not measured with direct units, but with indirect units. We examine this kind of measurement next.

Measuring Time

Time is not measured with units that are pieces of time. We use mechanical devices called clocks to measure time. Reading clocks seems a simple task to adults who have had long experience with clocks. But to the child just learning to tell time clocks are complex devices.

They consist of two "hands" (sometimes three) that move at different speeds and point to two different sets of numbers (one set of numbers is usually not there). We tell the children that the hands are moving, but when they look at the clock both hands are obviously not moving, but are standing still. We never let the children see us figure out the time. When we read clocks, we appear to be able to just look and see the time. A typical reaction from the child is, "Wow! How did she do that?" Children often think that they are supposed to memorize all the different positions of the hands and the times that go with those positions.

To teach children to read clocks meaningfully, accurately, and quickly, we need to do two things. First, the clock-reading process must be simplified, so that the child learns to do one thing at a time. Second, the teacher must always model the clock-reading *process* and not just give the time.

The easiest way to simplify the clock-reading process is to *teach one hand at a time* (Thompson & Van de Wall, 1981; Thornton, et al., 1983). First, obtain two inexpensive clocks that are identical and have large, easily read numbers. The numbers for the minutes should be indicated on the clock. The hours should be on the inside circle and the minutes should be on the outside circle. Then carefully remove the minute hand from one clock, and remove the hour hand from the other clock.

Teach the Hours First. Explain that the hour hand is like a spinner that is moving very slowly, so slowly that we cannot see it move. Explain that the number that the hour hand points to is the hour. Sometimes it points right at a number, and that is the hour. Sometimes it does not point directly to a number. It might be a little bit before an hour or a little bit after an hour. Show the hour hand in several different positions. Have the children read the hour that is shown.

When they are comfortable reading the hour from the clock, explain to the children that when the hour hand points between two numbers, we usually are interested in what hour it is after. Show the hour hand in several different positions and have the children tell what hour it is when the hand points directly to a number and what hour it is after when the hand does not point directly to a number.

Second, Teach the Minute Hand. The minute hand is more difficult because the numbers are often missing or partly missing. Create a large spinner with the numbers from 0 to 59. Spin the pointer several times and have the children read the "minutes."

Then paint out the numbers 3, 4, 6, 9, 11, 12, 13, 18, 22, 23, 24, 26, 37, 38, 39, 41, 42, 51, 52, 53, 54, 56, 57, and 58, but leave the marks showing where the numbers were.

Spin the pointer and have the children read the "minutes." When the pointer points to a missing number, have the children figure out what the minute is by counting forward or backward from a number that is given. When the children become comfortable with figuring out the missing numbers, paint out all the numbers but multiples of 5. Next, paint out all the numbers except 0, 15, 30, 45, and have the children practice figuring out the minutes.

Then use the clock with the minute hands. Set the clock with the hand in different positions, and have the children figure out the minutes. Emphasize that if the hand is pointing to a number that is not indicated, start with a number that is indicated and figure it out from there.

Use both clocks to find the time. Explain that we use the hour clock to see "what hour it is after," and use the minute hand to see "how many minutes after the hour." Demonstrate how to write the time.

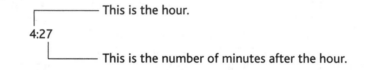

This is the hour.

4:27

This is the number of minutes after the hour.

The time is 27 minutes after 4.

Finally, after the children are able to use the two clocks to find the time, show them a clock with both the hour hand and the minute hand on the same face. Lead them through the process of reading the time from this clock. First, read the hour. Then, read the minutes.

Whenever reading the time from a clock, the teacher should model this same process. First see what hour the hour hand is pointing to. Then see what minute the minute hand is pointing to. If the minute hand is not pointing at a number that you know, go through the process of starting with a minute that you are sure of and figure it out from there. Model the process that the children must use. Have the children help.

Measuring Weight

Weight is not typically measured with direct units. Rather, we usually measure weight using a spring scale. The object being weighed is placed on the scale. Gravity pulls down on the object, causing the spring to stretch. The stretching spring causes a pointer to move along a number line (which is often curved around a circle). We read the number to get the weight in pounds, ounces, kilograms, grams, or some other measurement.

Students need to weigh many things to gain a "sense of heaviness." They need to estimate weights of objects and then weigh those objects to check their estimates. They should experience weight measurement in many situations to learn when and how weight is used.

Note that the mass of an object can be measured using direct units of mass and a balance scale. When the mass of an object is being measured, the object is placed on one side of the scale. Weights are placed on the other side of the scale until the object is balanced. By adding up the weights, we can find the mass of the object.

Measuring Temperature

Temperature is also measured using indirect units. A thermometer consists of a tube of mercury or other substance that reacts to heat and cold by expanding and contracting. As it expands and contracts, the top surface of the mercury reaches higher or falls lower. The numbers beside the tube of mercury indicate how hot or how cold it is.

Students need to measure the temperature of many things to gain a "sense of heat." They need to estimate temperatures and then use thermometers to check their estimates. They should experience temperature measurement in many situations to learn when and how measurement of temperature is used.

Measuring Value

The value of things is also measured using indirect units. When we use money to determine what something is worth, we are measuring the value of that thing. The same 20 pieces of paper ($20) can be traded for bread, for meat, for a taxi ride, for a hair cut, or for any number of things. We can buy things with money because we agree with others to let money represent the value of those things.

The concept that money has certain value because we have agreed to let it have that value must be developed. Without an acceptance of this agreement about the value of money, many things do not make sense to a child. Why are five pennies worth the same amount as one nickel? Only because we have agreed that they should. Why is a nickel worth less than a dime even though it is much bigger than the dime? Only because we have agreed that it is. Why is one dollar bill worth more than three nice shiny quarters? Only because we have agreed that it should be.

Help the child to accept this agreement about the value of coins. Then the value of coins and of different denominations of paper money, and the use of money as a measurement of the value of things are easy concepts for the child to grasp.

Adapting a Lesson on Volume

The following lesson plan is similar to one that might be taken from the third-grade teachers' book of a published elementary school mathematics textbook series.

LESSON OBJECTIVE

The student will find volume by counting cubes.

Lesson Opener

Have the children find the area of these figures.

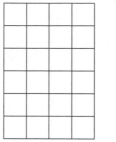 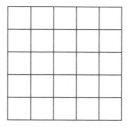

Development

Direct the attention of the children to the picture on the first page of the lesson in the student book. Point out that the child in the picture is filling the box with cubes. Explain that the number of cubic units something holds is called its volume. Ask how many cubes the box in the picture will hold. [8] Ask what the volume of the box is. [8 cubic units.]

Monitor Learning

Direct the attention of the class to the second example on the page. Have everyone find the number of cubes needed to fill the box. Ask how many cubes are needed. [9] Ask what the volume of the box is. [9 cubic units.] Observe to identify children who do not understand.

Practice

Have children who had difficulties with the teaching examples complete the *Extra Practice Worksheet*. Have the rest of the children complete Exercises 1–20.

Closure

At the end of the lesson, remind the children that the volume of a figure is the number of cubes needed to fill the figure.

This lesson focuses on completion of the textbook pages. There is very little development—only two examples. The nature of the lesson requires the children to be still, listen to the teacher, and do "seatwork." There is little active involvement in learning.

We adapt the lesson by increasing the amount of developmental work and reducing the amount of practice. We increase the visual input in the lesson and include a substantial amount of kinesthetic learning activity. We have the children communicate about the lesson, and we monitor learning throughout every part of the lesson.

LESSON OBJECTIVE

The student will find volume by counting cubes.

Lesson Opener

Prepare pairs of cards like these.

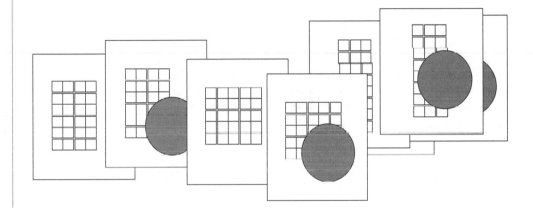

Shuffle the cards and give one to each child. Point out that some of the rectangles have part of the squares hidden. Have the children find partners whose rectangles are the same as theirs. One partner will have a rectangle with some squares hidden. The other partner will have an identical rectangle with no squares hidden. **Monitor understanding.** Pay particular attention to children who might have difficulty with this activity. Provide assistance as needed.

When everyone has found a partner, have the partners figure out how many squares are in their rectangles. Ask them how they could have figured out how many squares if they only had the rectangle with some squares hidden. Choose one of the cards that has some of the squares hidden. With the class telling you how to do it, figure out how many squares are in the rectangle. Emphasize that every row of squares has the same number. They can multiply the number of squares in one row times the number of rows.

Development

Have the partners from the previous activity stay together. Give each pair of partners a small box and some centimeter cubes. Tell them to fill the boxes completely full of cubes and figure out how many cubes their boxes will hold. **Monitor understanding.** Observe to be sure that all the partners are stacking the cubes into the boxes so that there are no spaces between the cubes.

When everyone is finished, ask two or three students how many cubes fit in their boxes. Explain that the amount that a box can hold is called the *volume* of the box. The centimeter cubes are the units used to measure volume. Choose one of the boxes. Ask how many cubes fit in that box. Write the volume of the box on the chalkboard. [For example, the volume might be 12 cubic centimeters.] Have each pair of partners write the volume of their box. **Monitor understanding.** Observe to be sure that all the students are writing the volume correctly. If any students are having difficulty, provide assistance as needed.

Ask which box has the greatest volume. Which has the least? Choose four boxes. Have the class help you line them up in order from least to greatest volume. **Monitor understanding.** Observe to be sure that all the students correctly understand volume.

Direct the attention of the children to the picture on the first page of the lesson in the student book. Point out that the child in the picture is filling the box with cubes. Remind the class that the child in the picture is doing exactly what they were doing, except that the cubes are bigger. Ask how many cubes the box in the picture will hold. [8] Ask what the volume of the box is. [8 cubic units.] Write the volume on the chalkboard.

Direct the attention of the class to the second example on the page. Have everyone find the number of cubes needed to fill the box. Ask how many cubes are needed. [9] Have all the students write down the volume of the box. [9 cubic units.] **Monitor understanding.** Check what the students have written to be sure they understand how to write the volume.

Practice

Have the students work with their partners to complete Exercises 1–5 in the student book. Tell them to do one exercise at a time. Each student is to find the answer, then they are to check with their partner to see if they agree. If their answers are not the same, they should do the exercise together. **Monitor understanding.** Move around the room, observing the students' work. Identify students who are having difficulty and provide assistance where needed.

Closure

After everyone is finished, ask the class what they learned today. Ask how to find the number of cubes that a box will hold. Ask what volume is.

Follow Up

Tell the class that they are to take their books home and explain to their parents what volume is. Then they are to show their parents how to find the volume in Exercise 6 on the practice page.

Using Measurement to Solve Problems

Remember that measurement is simply a process by which we assign a number to a quantity. When measurement is used in problem solving, computation is usually performed on those numbers (measurements). When teaching problem solving using measurements, the same basic principles should be applied as when teaching problem solving using other kinds of numbers. The teacher should emphasize that the choice of operation depends on what is happening to the quantities in the problem. If quantities are being combined, then addition of the measurements can probably be used. If the measurements in the problem are being separated into equal parts, then division can probably be used.

In chapter 8 we saw that a current instructional emphasis for problem solving in mathematics is to develop a wide variety of problem-solving strategies and provide experience using those strategies. We have already seen examples using the following strategies:

Solve part of the problem.
Separate the problem into easier parts.
Work backward.
Use a picture or diagram.
Use a table.
Solve a simpler problem.
Try and check.
List the possibilities.

We now examine a problem, appropriate for children at about the sixth-grade level. The solution employs separating the problem into easier parts, but it also uses a new strategy, *use a formula*.

Anna works for a hardware store where she cuts glass into the sizes and shapes needed by customers. One day, a customer requested a circular piece of glass with a 10-inch diameter.
   The store manager had told Anna that she should always try to have the smallest possible amount of wasted glass. So, Anna began by cutting a circular piece of cardboard with a diameter of 10 inches. She compared the cardboard circle with several pieces of glass and found that she could cut the requested glass from any of the three pieces shown here.
   Which piece should she use in order to have the smallest amount of waste?

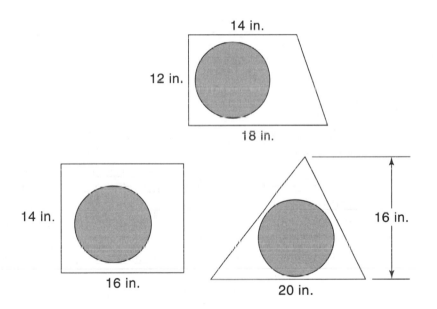

We want to choose the option that leaves us with the smallest amount of wasted glass. To do this we *solve three easier parts* to the overall problem. We find the amount of waste for each of the three options.
   First, we consider the piece of glass that is shaped like a trapezoid. We need to find the amount of glass in the trapezoid and the amount of glass that we will use in the circular piece. To do this we *use the formulas* for area of circles and trapezoids. Then we subtract to find the amount of wasted glass.

The formula for area of a trapezoid is $A = \frac{1}{2}(b_1 + b_2)h$. The two bases of the trapezoid have lengths of 14 inches and 18 inches. The height of the trapezoid is 12 inches. When we use these values in the formula, we find that the area of the trapezoid is 192 square inches.

The formula for area of a circle is $A = \pi r^2$. Since the diameter of the circle is 10 inches, the radius is 5 inches. When we use this value in the formula, we find that the area of the circle is 78.5 square inches.

When we subtract, we find that if we use the trapezoid shaped piece of glass, we will waste 113.5 square inches of glass.

Second, we follow the same procedures with the rectangular piece of glass.

The formula for area of a rectangle is $A = bh$. The base of the rectangle is 16 inches and the height of the rectangle is 14 inches. Using the formula, we find that the area of the rectangle is 224 square inches.

When we subtract the area of the circle, we find that we would waste 145.5 square inches of glass if we use this piece.

Third, we follow these procedures with the triangular piece of glass.

The formula for area of a triangle is $A = \frac{1}{2}bh$. The base of the triangle is 20 inches and its height is 16 inches. Using the formula, we find that the area of the triangle is 160 square inches.

When we subtract the area of the circle, we find that we would waste 81.5 square inches of glass if we use the triangular piece.

Finally, we compare these three results and discover that we have the smallest amount of waste if we use the triangular piece of glass.

Exercises and Activities

1. Adapt Activity 10.06 for a child with blindness.
2. Adapt Activity 10.28 for a child with blindness.
3. Develop an activity to be used between Activities 10.26 and 10.27 for a child with low cognitive abilities.
4. Consider Activity 10.28. How would you choose examples, and in what order would you use those examples so that the sequence would be effective for a child with low cognitive abilities?
5. Develop a learning activity that develops the *concept of area* by having the students make gross comparisons of the areas of different shapes.
6. Develop a learning activity that develops the *concept of a unit of area* as a piece of area. Use units of area that are not squares.
7. Develop a learning activity that develops the *concept of measurement of area* as the number of units it takes to cover the area being measured. Use square units.
8. Develop a learning activity that develops the *ability to estimate areas* using some standard unit. For example, you might use square centimeters or square inches.
9. Write a sequence of developmental activities that can be used to teach the *area formula for rectangles*.
10. Write a sequence of developmental activities that can be used to teach the *area formula for parallelograms*.
11. Write a sequence of developmental activities that can be used to teach the *area formula for triangles*.
12. Write a sequence of developmental activities that can be used to teach the *area formula for trapezoids*.
13. Write a sequence of developmental activities that can be used to teach that the *circumference of a circle is π times its diameter*.

14. Write a sequence of developmental activities that can be used to teach the *area formula for circles.*

15. Choose a lesson on measurement from a published elementary school mathematics textbook series.
    a. Write a lesson plan that follows the teaching suggestions in the teacher's guide.
    b. Identify parts of the lesson that provide visual imagery for the concept(s) or skill(s) taught in the lesson.
    c. Add more activities to the lesson which will develop visual imagery for the concept(s) or skill(s) taught in the lesson.

16. Choose a lesson on measurement from a published elementary school mathematics textbook series.
    a. Write a lesson plan that follows the teaching suggestions in the teacher's guide.
    b. Identify the parts of the lesson that develop the concept(s) or skill(s) taught in the lesson.
    c. Add more developmental activity to the lesson plan.

17. Study the adapted lesson plan on pages 321–322. Make further changes in the lesson plan to make it more appropriate for a child with blindness.

18. Study the adapted lesson plan on pages 321–322. Make further changes in the lesson plan to make it more appropriate for a child who has a history of aggressive classroom behavior including throwing objects.

19. Study the adapted lesson plan on pages 321–322. Make further changes in the lesson plan to make it more appropriate for a child who is cognitively limited.

20. Read "Standard 10: Measurement," on pages 51–53 of *Curriculum and Evaluation Standards for School Mathematics,* published by the National Council of Teachers of Mathematics. In what ways are the suggestions for teaching problem solving presented in this text consistent with or inconsistent with those presented in *The Standards?*

21. Read the discussions related to "The Measurement Standard" on pages 44–47, 102–106,170–175, and 240–247 of *Principles and Standards for School Mathematics,* published by the National Council of Teachers of Mathematics. In what ways are the suggestions for teaching measurement presented in this text consistent with or inconsistent with those presented in *Principles and Standards?*

22. The following subtraction results illustrate an error pattern like those related by Robert Ashlock in his book, *Error Patterns in Computation: A Semi-programmed Approach.*

$$\begin{array}{r} \overset{7}{8}\text{ yards,}{}^{1}\text{1 foot} \\ -5\text{ yards, 2 feet} \\ \hline 2\text{ yards, 9 feet} \end{array} \qquad \begin{array}{r} \overset{8}{9}\text{ meters,}{}^{1}\text{4 decimeters} \\ -4\text{ meters, 8 decimeters} \\ \hline 4\text{ meters, 6 decimeters} \end{array}$$

$$\begin{array}{r} \overset{5}{6}\text{ feet,}{}^{1}\text{7 inches} \\ -2\text{ feet, 9 inches} \\ \hline 3\text{ feet, 8 inches} \end{array} \qquad \begin{array}{r} \overset{5}{6}\text{ gallons,}{}^{1}\text{2 quarts} \\ -2\text{ gallons, 3 quarts} \\ \hline 3\text{ gallons, 9 quarts} \end{array}$$

    a. What is this student's error pattern? What is the student doing to produce the incorrect answers?
    b. Plan a mini-lesson to correct this student's error pattern.

References and Related Readings

Ashlock, R. B. (1976). *Error patterns in computation: A semi-programmed approach* (2nd ed.). Upper Saddle River, NJ: Merrill/Prentice Hall.

Gerver, R. (1990). Discovering pi: Two approaches. *Arithmetic Teacher, 37*(8), 18–22.

National Council of Teachers of Mathematics. (1989). *Curriculum and evaluation standards for school mathematics.* Reston, VA: NCTM.

National Council of Teachers of Mathematics. (2000). *Principles and standards for school mathematics.* Reston, VA: NCTM.

Shaw, J. M. (1983). Student-made measuring tools. *Arithmetic Teacher, 31*(3), 12–15.

Thompson, C. S., & Van de Wall, J. A. (1981). A single-handed approach to telling time, *Arithmetic Teacher, 28*(8), 4–9.

Thornton, C. A., Tucker, B. F., Dossey, J. A., & Bazik, E. F. (1983). *Teaching mathematics to children with special needs.* Menlo Park, CA: Addison-Wesley.

Van de Wall, J. A. (1998). *Elementary and middle school mathematics: Teaching developmentally.* New York: Addison Wesley Longman.

Wilson, P .S., & Adams, V. M. (1992). A dynamic way to teach angle and angle measure. *Arithmetic Teacher, 39*, 6–13.

Web Sites

http://www.proteacher.com/100023.shtml
(Activities and lesson plans on measurement.)

http://www.sasked.gov.sk.ca/docs/elemath/measure.html
(A scope and sequence chart for measurement topics.)

http://www.iit.edu/~smile/ma9705.html
(Measurement activities.)

CHAPTER 11

GEOMETRY:

Learning the Names and Characteristics of Shapes

THE GEOMETRY STANDARD

"Identifying shapes is important…but the focus on properties and their relationships should be strong" (National Council of Teachers of Mathematics, 2000, pp. 41–42).

"Pre-K–2 geometry begins with describing and naming shapes. Young students begin by using their own vocabulary to describe objects, talking about how they are alike and how they are different" (NCTM, 2000, p. 97).

"In grades 3–5, they should develop more-precise ways to describe shapes, focusing on identifying and describing the shape's properties and learning specialized vocabulary associated with these shapes and properties" (NCTM, 2000, p. 165).

"In middle-grades geometry…students investigate relationships by drawing, measuring, visualizing, comparing, transforming, and classifying geometric objects" (NCTM, 2000, p. 233).

For purposes of our discussion in this chapter, we consider geometry to be the naming of shapes and the study of their characteristics. This view of geometry is fairly limited. It departs somewhat from the more mathematical approach, which might be a study of points in space, or perhaps a logical development of a system of theorems from a beginning set of assumptions. However, the naming of shapes and the study of their characteristics is, more or less, what is done in elementary school geometry. As noted at the beginning of Chapter 10, geometry is closely related to measurement. The study of characteristics of geometric shapes frequently calls for the application of skills that were developed in measurement lessons.

The Big Ideas of Elementary School Geometry

The ability to identify and name shapes depends almost entirely on having a working understanding of some combination of geometric relationships (Clements & Sarama, 2000). When studying a geometric shape, we find that each of these relationships either exists or does not exist in that shape. Therefore, these relationships can be thought of as the big ideas of elementary school geometry (Lerch, 1981; Thornton, et al., 1983). If we teach children to look for these big ideas, it is easier for them to classify, name, and use geometric shapes.

Straightness

The first big idea is the notion of *straightness*. It is important to know whether lines or line segments, or edges, or surfaces are straight when studying geometric shapes. For example, one of these shapes is not a triangle. Why not? Figure C is not a triangle because all the sides of a triangle must be straight.

Knowing whether an object is straight is important and children need simple methods for testing straightness. One simple way to check is to pick up the shape and look along the edge to see if the edge is straight. Another way to test straightness is to use a straightedge. Rather than using a ruler, children can be taught to fold a sheet of paper and use the folded edge as a straightedge. Chapter 4 includes a more complete discussion of straightness, along with examples of activities that can be used to develop this concept.

The notion of straightness has a three-dimensional extension—flatness. A surface is flat if and only if it is "straight in all directions." The simplest way to test a surface to see if it is flat is to lay a straightedge on the surface in a lot of directions. If the straightedge always coincides with the surface, then the surface is flat.

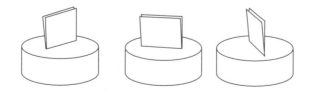

Congruence

The second of the big ideas of elementary school geometry is *congruence*. Two geometric figures are congruent if and only if they are exactly the same size and shape. In elementary school geometry, we study congruence of simple figures such as line segments and angles. We also consider congruence of more complex figures such as triangles and prisms. When classifying geometric figures, congruence is always important. For example, why is one of these figures not a rectangle? Figure K is not a rectangle because the opposite sides of rectangles are always congruent.

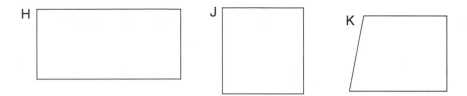

Consider the following two figures. Figure M is a prism but figure P is not. How can you tell? The two bases of a prism are always congruent.

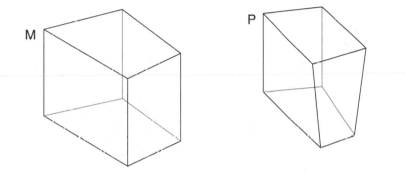

One of the figures below is a circle and one is not. How can you tell? Figure Y is not a circle. Every line segment from the center to the circle (all the radii) must be congruent.

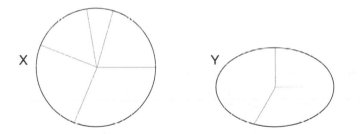

The easiest method for testing two plane figures for congruence arises from the fact that congruence is a transitive relation. Children can easily use the following procedure. The child traces one figure and then moves the tracing onto the second figure. If the tracing is an exact match for the second figure, then the two original figures are congruent. Children can understand that the two figures are congruent because they are both congruent to the tracing.

Similarity

The third of the big ideas for elementary school geometry is the notion of *similarity*. Two figures are similar if they are the same shape. Whenever two figures are the same shape, two important relationships will be present. First, every angle of one shape is congruent to the corresponding angle of the second shape. Second, the lengths of one figure are proportional to the corresponding lengths of the second figure. Another description of proportionality is that the ratio of a length in the first figure to the corresponding length in the second figure is always the same. For example, the two figures that follow are similar.

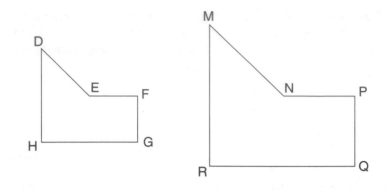

Corresponding angles of the two figures are congruent. For example, angle D is congruent to angle M. Angle G is congruent to angle Q. Angle E is congruent to angle N. Corresponding sides are proportional. For example, the length DE divided by the length MN is $\frac{2}{3}$. HG divided by RQ is also $\frac{2}{3}$ and EF divided by NP is also $\frac{2}{3}$.

Two examples of how the concept of similarity is used in classifying geometric figures are, first, all circles are similar and, second, all squares are similar. In a more complex setting, consider the truncated pentagonal pyramid pictured at the right. If the top of the pyramid is cut off parallel to the base, the top surface of the remaining figure is similar to the base. (A pyramid is the same shape from the bottom to the top, but not the same size.)

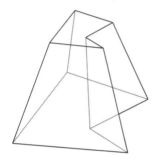

A simple, easy-to-use method for testing plane figures for similarity is illustrated below. Note that a fairly complex shape is used in this example. Children need to be introduced to this method, using simpler shapes such as triangles and rectangles.

Place the two shapes so they are oriented in the same direction. Begin by drawing a line through any point of the first figure and the corresponding point of the second figure.

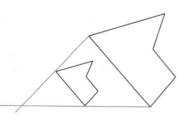

Then draw a line through another pair of corresponding points. Notice that these two lines intersect.

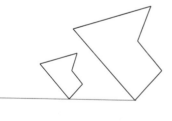

Draw lines through other pairs of corresponding points. All the lines intersect in the same point if the figures are similar.

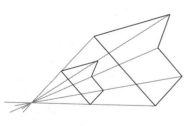

Parallelism

The fourth big idea of elementary school geometry is *parallelism*. If two lines are parallel, we know that the lines do not intersect, no matter how far they are extended. We also know that the lines go in the same direction. The two lines are the same distance apart, no matter where we measure the distance. The first of these characteristics of parallel lines is not helpful, because we cannot extend them forever. However, the other two notions provide ways to test for parallelism.

For example, parallel lines go in the same direction. Consider lines *a* and *b*, shown below. To determine the direction of the two lines, we draw a third line that crosses both of them.

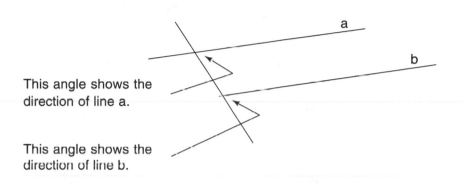

This angle shows the direction of line a.

This angle shows the direction of line b.

We can make a tracing of one of these angles and move it on top of the other angle to see if they are congruent. If the angles are congruent, then the direction of both lines is the same. The lines are parallel.

Parallel lines are also equidistant—the same distance apart wherever they are measured. Consider lines *j* and *k* in the following illustration. If we place a sheet of paper with its edge on line *j*, we can use a pencil to mark the distance between the two lines. By sliding the paper along the line, we can check to see if the distance is the same everywhere.

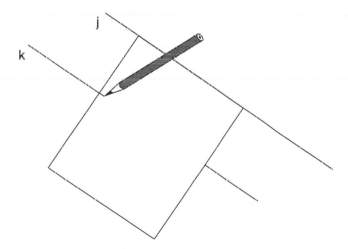

Whether lines are parallel can be used to identify and classify many figures. For example, one pair of opposite sides of a trapezoid is always parallel, but the other pair of opposite sides is not. On the other hand, both pairs of opposite sides of a parallelogram are parallel.

Perpendicularity

The fifth big idea of elementary school geometry is *perpendicularity* (square corners). Children are able to look for square corners to help them recognize certain shapes. For example, a square has four square corners. Every vertical edge of a right prism is perpendicular to the bases. For children, the simplest test of perpendicularity is to create a square corner by folding a sheet of paper and then laying that square corner on top of other corners that are being checked.

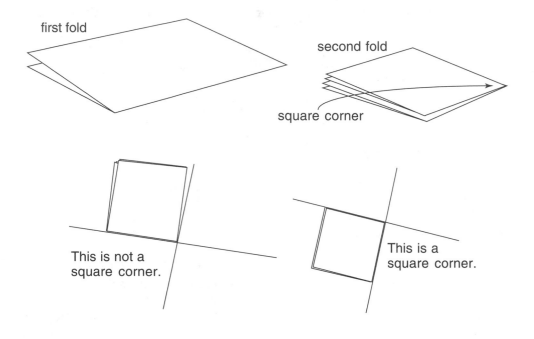

first fold

second fold

square corner

This is not a square corner.

This is a square corner.

Symmetry

The sixth big idea of elementary school geometry is the notion of *symmetry*. There are actually several kinds of symmetry (line symmetry, slide symmetry, and rotational symmetry), but in elementary school geometry, we are primarily concerned with line symmetry. Therefore, we limit the discussion here to line symmetry.

Many shapes studied by elementary children are symmetric. Many important characteristics of those shapes arise from that symmetry. Children need to be able to check figures to see if they are symmetric. The simplest test for line symmetry and the easiest for children to use is to fold the figure along the line of symmetry to see if the two halves are an exact match.

Using the Big Ideas to Study Geometric Shapes

We now trace four geometric shapes as they might be developed in grades K–8 within an elementary textbook series. The four shapes that we examine are rectangles, circles, angles, and prisms. As we look at the development of these four shapes, take note of how the six big ideas identified earlier are used, either informally or formally, to characterize or classify the shapes. Keep in mind also, that other geometric shapes are being developed at the same time.

Rectangles in Elementary School

Rectangles in Kindergarten. Typically, children are first exposed to rectangles in kindergarten. They learn that rectangles have four sides that are *straight*. They are asked to identify examples of rectangles and recognize that other shapes are not rectangles (that they are nonexamples). Usually, the variety of shapes from which they must choose include circles, triangles, squares, and rectangles. They are asked to explain informally why examples are rectangles and why nonexamples are not rectangles.

Often, during the treatment of rectangles in kindergarten, a serious misconception develops that must be corrected later (Fuys & Lebov, 1997). The children are often taught that squares and rectangles are different shapes, when in fact, a square is a special kind of rectangle, in which all the sides are the same length (they are *congruent*). Certainly, it is true that rectangles are not necessarily squares. However, it is absolutely false to say that a square is not a rectangle.

The following sequence of activities illustrates how a kindergarten teacher could develop the concept of rectangles. Notice how the examples and nonexamples are limited so that the child can focus on one necessary attribute of rectangles at a time.

⨉ + ◁ ACTIVITY 11.01   Straight Lines

For this activity, it may be necessary to place some things around the room that have straight lines and some other things that have lines that are not quite straight.

Show the class an oddly shaped piece of paper. Fold the paper and point out to the children that the folded edge is straight. Explain that this paper can be used to check if lines are straight. Show two lines, one straight and the other slightly curved, on the overhead projector. Use the folded paper to check each line for straightness. Use the folded paper to show something in the room that has a straight line. Then find something that has a line that is not quite straight. Use the folded paper to show that it is not straight. Ask the class to identify another straight line somewhere in the room. Have a child use the folded paper to check the line for straightness. Repeat with other lines around the room.

Form groups of 2 or 3 children. Give each group an oddly shaped piece of paper. Have them fold the paper to make a straight edge. Have them use their folded papers to find some straight lines and some lines that are not straight.

⨉ + ◁ ACTIVITY 11.02   Straight Sides

Cut out several large shapes from construction paper. Some of the shapes should have only straight sides and some should have at least one side that is not quite straight. Place these shapes on the walls around the room where they will be within the children's reach.

Show the class two shapes on the overhead projector. One of the shapes should have all straight sides and the other should have one side that is slightly curved. Use a folded paper to show that one shape has all straight sides while the other one does not. Point out the construction-paper shapes. Use the folded paper to check all the sides of one shape to see if they are straight.

Form groups of 2 or 3 children. Have each group use their folded paper to identify a shape that has all straight sides and another shape that has a side that is not straight.

✕+ᐟ ACTIVITY 11.03   Rectangles Have Straight Sides

Cut out several large shapes from construction paper like the ones pictured.

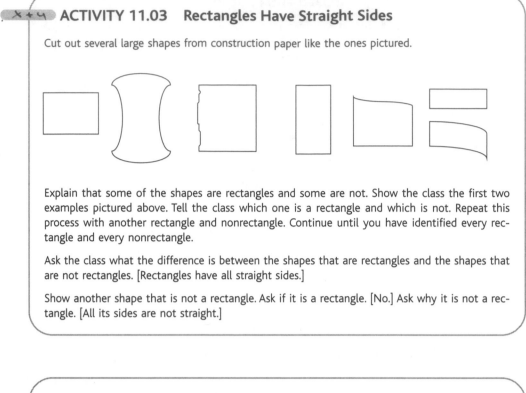

Explain that some of the shapes are rectangles and some are not. Show the class the first two examples pictured above. Tell the class which one is a rectangle and which is not. Repeat this process with another rectangle and nonrectangle. Continue until you have identified every rectangle and every nonrectangle.

Ask the class what the difference is between the shapes that are rectangles and the shapes that are not rectangles. [Rectangles have all straight sides.]

Show another shape that is not a rectangle. Ask if it is a rectangle. [No.] Ask why it is not a rectangle. [All its sides are not straight.]

✕+ᐟ ACTIVITY 11.04   Rectangles Have Four Sides

Cut out several large shapes from construction paper like the ones pictured.

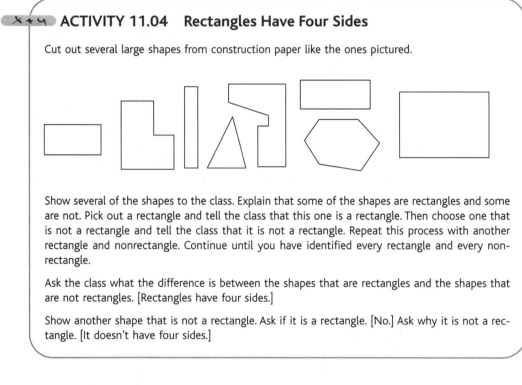

Show several of the shapes to the class. Explain that some of the shapes are rectangles and some are not. Pick out a rectangle and tell the class that this one is a rectangle. Then choose one that is not a rectangle and tell the class that it is not a rectangle. Repeat this process with another rectangle and nonrectangle. Continue until you have identified every rectangle and every nonrectangle.

Ask the class what the difference is between the shapes that are rectangles and the shapes that are not rectangles. [Rectangles have four sides.]

Show another shape that is not a rectangle. Ask if it is a rectangle. [No.] Ask why it is not a rectangle. [It doesn't have four sides.]

✕+ᐟ ACTIVITY 11.05   Rectangle Search

Point to the door, and say "Look! The door is a rectangle!" Ask the class to look around the room and find other things that are shaped like rectangles.

ACTIVITY 11.06   Shape Sort

After the children have been introduced to circles and triangles, prepare cutouts of different sized circles, different shaped rectangles, and different shaped triangles. Tape a rectangle to the front of one box, a circle to the front of the second box, and a triangle to the front of the third box. Place the shapes in a pile on the table in front of the three boxes.

Have children take turns coming to the front, and placing the top shape in the pile into the correct box. When all the shapes have been sorted, ask the children how you can tell if a shape is a rectangle, or a circle, or a triangle.

Rectangles in First Grade.   Children also identify rectangles in grade 1. However, a broader range of nonexamples can be used. That is, the shapes that are not examples of rectangles should be more varied.

This shape is not a rectangle because rectangles must have four sides.

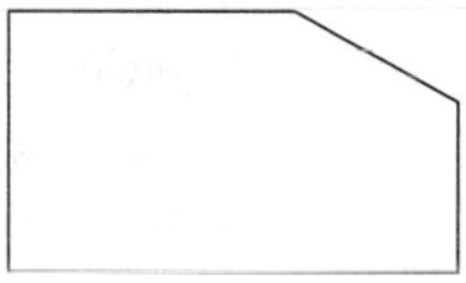

This shape is not a rectangle because rectangles must have *straight* sides.

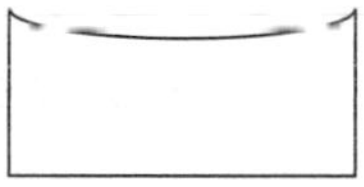

This shape is not a rectangle because rectangles must have square corners (adjacent sides must be *perpendicular*.)

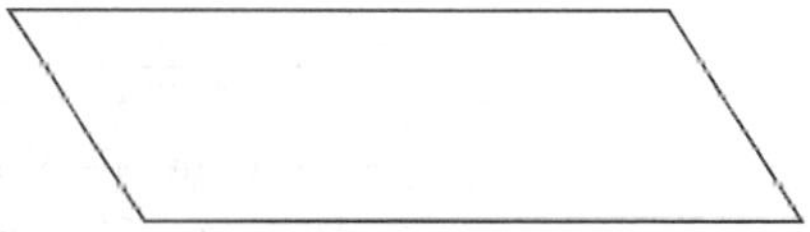

Consideration of these nonexamples, as shown in the following sequence of instructional activities, allows children to focus on the essential characteristics of rectangles and begins to formalize their understanding.

ACTIVITY 11.07   Finding Square Corners

Show the children an oddly shaped piece of paper. Show them how to fold it twice to make a square corner. Explain that you can use the folded paper to check to see if a corner is a square corner. Place the folded paper on the corner of the chalkboard to show that it is a square corner. Use the folded paper to show that a window has a square corner.

Show a figure like the one pictured at the right on the overhead projector. Use the folded paper to show that it has two square corners and two corners that are not square.

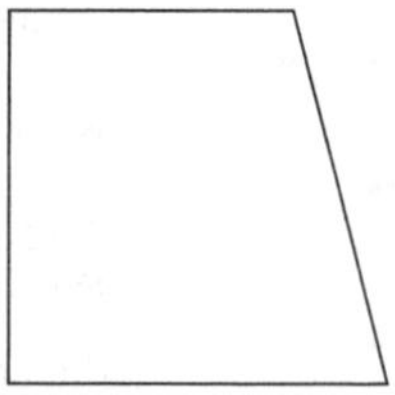

Show the class several shapes with straight sides. Some corners should be square corners and some should not be square corners. Have children come to the front and use the folded paper to check the corners to see if they are square.

×÷◁ ACTIVITY 11.08 Rectangles Have Square Corners

From construction paper cut out several large shapes with four sides like the ones pictured.

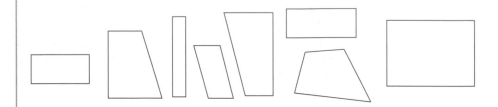

Show some of the shapes to the class. Explain that some of the shapes are rectangles and some are not. Pick out a rectangle and tell the class that this one is a rectangle. Then choose one that is not a rectangle and tell the class that it is not a rectangle. Repeat this process with another rectangle and nonrectangle. Continue until you have identified every rectangle and every non-rectangle.

Ask the class what the difference is between the shapes that are rectangles and the shapes that are not rectangles. [Rectangles have square corners.]

Show another shape that is not a rectangle. Ask if it is a rectangle. [No.] Ask why it is not a rectangle. [It does not have square corners.]

×÷◁ ACTIVITY 11.09 Rectangles: Why or Why Not

Cut out several large shapes from construction paper. Some of the shapes should be rectangles, some should have more than or fewer than four sides, some should have at least one side that is not straight, some should have corners that are not square. Place these shapes on the walls around the room where they will be within the children's reach.

Point out one of the shapes to the children. Ask if it is a rectangle. If it is a rectangle, ask why it is. [It has four straight sides and square corners.] If it is not a rectangle, ask why it is not. [The children should identify the required attribute that the shape does not have.]

Form groups of 2 or 3 children. Have each group choose one of the shapes and stand by it. Have each group tell why their shape is a rectangle or why their shape is not a rectangle.

×÷◁ ACTIVITY 11.10 Rubber Rectangles

Pair the children with partners. Give each pair a geoboard.

Stretch a rubber band on a geoboard to form a parallelogram that does not have square corners. Show it to the children. Ask if it is a rectangle. Ask why not. [Rectangles must have square corners.] Have a child come to the front and change the shape to make it a rectangle.

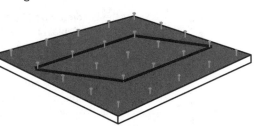

Have every pair of children make a shape on their geoboard that is not a rectangle. Have each pair explain why their shape is not a rectangle.

Then have them form a shape that is a rectangle.

Rectangles in Second Grade. In second grade, children review that rectangles have four sides, and they recognize that rectangles have four corners (an informal reference to the angles). They also learn that rectangles always have two lines of *symmetry*. Square rectangles (squares) have four lines of symmetry. Children are also asked to recognize the faces of some three-dimensional objects as rectangles.

The instructional activities that follow illustrate how a teacher could build understanding of the symmetry that exists in rectangles.

ACTIVITY 11.11   All Rectangles Have Two Lines of Symmetry

From construction paper, cut out many rectangles with different shapes. Form groups of 2 or 3 children and give each group three rectangles that are different.

With one rectangle, show the class how to fold the shape to find the two lines of symmetry. Show them that when the shape is folded along a line of symmetry the two halves are a perfect match. Emphasize that the two creases are called lines of symmetry.

Have each of the groups fold one of their rectangles to find a line of symmetry. Monitor their work to be sure that they find a line of symmetry. Then have them fold the same rectangle to find the other line of symmetry. When you are sure that all the groups are able to find the lines of symmetry, have them find the lines of symmetry in the other rectangle.

Ask one of the groups how many lines of symmetry they found in their rectangles. [Each rectangle has two lines of symmetry.] Ask if everyone found the same thing. Emphasize that all rectangles have two lines of symmetry.

Fold a sheet of paper twice to form a square corner. Using any of the rectangles, show the class that the two lines of symmetry make four square corners where they cross. Check two other rectangles to show that the lines of symmetry of those rectangles also form square corners where they cross.

ACTIVITY 11.12   Rectangles Are Symmetric

From waxed paper, cut out two different rectangles, a parallelogram, and an isosceles trapezoid (a trapezoid with base angles that are equal).

Show the shapes to the class. Ask which of the shapes are rectangles and which are not rectangles. Ask how they can tell. [Rectangles have four straight sides and square corners.] Take one of the rectangles and fold it in half vertically. Run your thumbnail down the fold so that the crease can be seen.

Show the class how the two sides of the rectangle are a perfect match. Open the rectangle and show them the crease. Explain that when you can fold a shape so that the two sides are a perfect match, we say that the shape is symmetric, and the fold line is called the line of symmetry.

Show that the rectangle has a second line of symmetry by folding the rectangle along a horizontal fold. Show the class that the top half folds down onto the bottom half so that the two halves are a perfect match. Fold the other rectangle to show that it also has two lines of symmetry.

Hold up the parallelogram and ask the children if they think it is symmetric. Demonstrate that the parallelogram cannot be folded so that the two halves match. Hold up the trapezoid and ask the children if they think it is symmetric. Demonstrate that this shape can be folded along a vertical line so that the two halves match. It is symmetric. The fold line is the line of symmetry. Show that the trapezoid does not have another line of symmetry.

Rectangles in Third Grade. By third grade, children can be asked to recognize rectangles in a variety of "real-life" settings—in flags, in the classroom (walls, doors, ceiling tiles, sections of the chalkboard, bulletin boards), in the sides of a box, in the pages of a book, in picture frames, in table tops, and so on. They learn that the corners of rectangles are angles. They might also learn that the square corners are called right angles. (Adjacent sides are *perpendicular*.) They could also learn that rectangles are parallelograms. The opposite sides are *parallel*.

The following activities illustrate how a teacher could lead an exploration of the parallelism of the opposite sides of a rectangle.

✕ + ◁ ACTIVITY 11.13   Parallel Lines Go the Same Direction

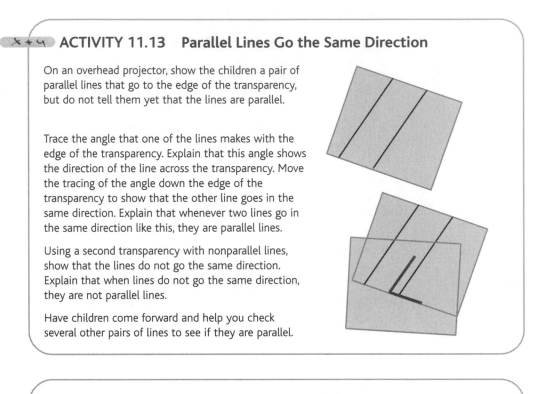

On an overhead projector, show the children a pair of parallel lines that go to the edge of the transparency, but do not tell them yet that the lines are parallel.

Trace the angle that one of the lines makes with the edge of the transparency. Explain that this angle shows the direction of the line across the transparency. Move the tracing of the angle down the edge of the transparency to show that the other line goes in the same direction. Explain that whenever two lines go in the same direction like this, they are parallel lines.

Using a second transparency with nonparallel lines, show that the lines do not go the same direction. Explain that when lines do not go the same direction, they are not parallel lines.

Have children come forward and help you check several other pairs of lines to see if they are parallel.

✕ + ◁ ACTIVITY 11.14   Opposite Sides Parallel

On an overhead projector, show the children a parallelogram.

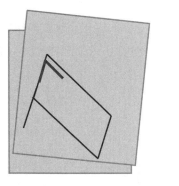

Extend one of the sides as illustrated. Trace one of the angles on the extended side onto another transparency sheet. Move the tracing of the angle down the extended side to show that the two opposite sides are parallel. Follow the same procedures to show that the opposite sides are also parallel.

With another transparency, show that the opposite sides of a second parallelogram are parallel. Explain that when both pairs of opposite sides of a four-sided shape are parallel, that shape is called a parallelogram.

✕ + ◁ ACTIVITY 11.15   Parallelograms or Not?

Form groups of 2 or 3 children. Give each group a sheet of paper with two shapes drawn on it. One shape should be a parallelogram. In the second shape, one pair of opposite sides should be parallel and the other pair should be almost, but not quite, parallel.

Have the groups test the opposite sides of both figures to see if they are parallelograms.

ACTIVITY 11.16   Rectangles Are Parallelograms

Tape a rectangle cut from construction paper to the chalkboard. Be sure that it has straight sides and square corners. Ask the class what they know about rectangles. [Four straight sides, square corners, two lines of symmetry.]

Extend one of the horizontal sides of the rectangle as illustrated. Check these two angles to show that the two vertical sides go in the same direction. Point out that those sides are parallel.

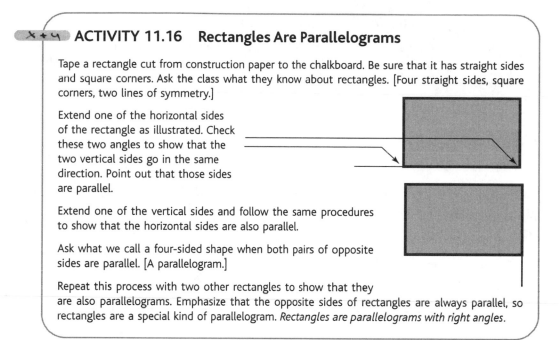

Extend one of the vertical sides and follow the same procedures to show that the horizontal sides are also parallel.

Ask what we call a four-sided shape when both pairs of opposite sides are parallel. [A parallelogram.]

Repeat this process with two other rectangles to show that they are also parallelograms. Emphasize that the opposite sides of rectangles are always parallel, so rectangles are a special kind of parallelogram. *Rectangles are parallelograms with right angles.*

Rectangles in Fourth Grade and Beyond. In the fourth through eighth grades, children use more formal mathematical terminology to describe rectangles, but they continue to use the big ideas of geometry to describe and classify them. They learn that closed figures with straight sides are called polygons. (*Poly* means "many" and *gon* means "side.") They learn that polygons with four sides are called quadrilaterals. (*Quad* means "four" and *lateral* means "side.") They learn that trapezoids and parallelograms are special kinds of quadrilaterals and that rhombi (rhombuses) and rectangles are two special kinds of parallelograms. They also learn that squares are special rhombi and also special rectangles.

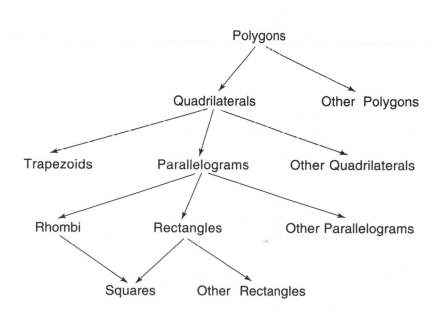

Circles in Elementary School

Circles in Kindergarten. At the kindergarten level, children are introduced to circles informally. They identify shapes that are the same as circles (shapes that match). These shapes are *similar*. They identify shapes that are not the same as circles (for example, the shape that does not belong). They might identify the biggest circle, the smallest circle, and the circle that is the same size.

They typically learn the name for circles. They learn to recognize circles in everyday objects like bicycle wheels, the shape of a clock, jar lids, and coins. They make and talk about patterns that use circles and other shapes. They use informal ways of describing circles, such as: circles are round, circles are smooth, circles are curved (there is no *straight* side), and circles are the same size in all directions (all diameters are *congruent*).

The following activities illustrate how a kindergarten teacher can develop the children's informal understanding of circles.

✕✛✓ ACTIVITY 11.17   Same Shape or Not

Cut out two copies of a triangle, a square, and a nonstandard shape like the one pictured. Also, cut out four copies of a circle.

Place three of the circles in a paper bag with a copy of two other shapes. Show the children the fourth circle and tell them that you want them to help you choose the shapes that are the same. Remove the shapes from the bag, one at a time. As each shape is removed from the bag, have the children decide if it is the same as the shape that you started with. If the children say that a shape is not the same, ask them why it is not.

Repeat the activity using a different combination of shapes. Be sure to include at least two circles in the bag. Repeat the activity, but this time ask them to choose shapes that are the same as one of the noncircle shapes. Include the second copy of the noncircle shape in the bag so there will be one match.

✕✛✓ ACTIVITY 11.18   Which Doesn't Belong?

Cut out three circles of different sizes, each less than 2 inches across. Also cut out a square, a triangle, an oval, and an irregular shape, each less than 2 inches across.

Arrange the three circles and one of the other shapes on the overhead projector. Ask the children which shape does not belong. Whether or not you get the expected answer, ask why that one does not belong.

Repeat the activity using the three circles and a different noncircle shape.

ACTIVITY 11.19 Fitting Shapes in Holes

Cut several large shapes from the middle of full sheets of construction paper. The shapes should be different, but nearly the same size. They should be cut out carefully so that the remaining paper in each sheet remains intact. Place the sheets of construction paper from which the shapes have been cut on a wall of the classroom at a height that the children can easily reach.

Give the shapes to children and have them find the "holes" that their shapes fit into.

Repeat the activity by collecting the shapes, mixing them up, handing them out to other children, and having them find the holes where their shapes fit.

ACTIVITY 11.20 All About Circles

Display several circles in front of the class. Explain that shapes like these are called circles. Ask the children to tell about the circles in their own words. Accept all descriptions that are offered by the children. However, if a description is obviously not correct, ask the child to explain why he or she thinks the circles are like that. Ask what the other children think.

ACTIVITY 11.21 Circles, Circles, Everywhere

If necessary, place a variety of circular objects in sight around the room. Examples of objects that you might have in the room are: a hula hoop, a frisbee, a bicycle (for its wheels), a round-faced clock, a paper plate, a waste basket (for its top and bottom), an oatmeal box, a drinking glass, a round picture frame, a pencil sharpener (circular holes for the pencils), a computer CD, or assorted circles cut from colored paper.

Point out one of those objects, for example, a clock with a circular face. Ask the children to tell you the shape of the clock. Do the same with a second round object. Then have the children look around and identify other objects that have the shape of a circle.

Circles in First and Second Grades. During the first-grade and second-grade years, children continue to learn about circles informally. They choose circles from among other shapes like rectangles, squares, and triangles (from shapes that are not *similar*). They continue to use informal language to describe circles and to explain why other shapes are not circles. The following activity illustrates how a teacher can continue the development of the children's understanding of circles.

×+4 ACTIVITY 11.22   Why and Why Not?

Point out a circle. Ask the children what the shape is. Then ask how they can tell. Get a variety of responses and discuss them. Let the children decide what makes a circle a circle. Point out another shape. If it is a circle, ask again how they can tell. If it is not a circle, ask how they can tell it is not a circle. Continue this process, including several examples and several nonexamples.

Circles in Third and Fourth Grades. During these grades, children will typically identify circles in three-dimensional shapes like cylinders, cones, and spheres. They also learn that circles are *symmetric*. The activity that follows illustrates how the symmetry of circles can be taught.

×+4 ACTIVITY 11.23   The Halves Match

Cut several symmetric shapes (including at least one circle) in half along their lines of symmetry. Show the two halves of one shape to the children. Explain that they are the two halves of a shape. Put them together so the children can see what the whole shape looks like.

Pass out the shape halves to the children. Have them each find a partner so that together, they have both halves of the shape. Have each pair of partners hold their shape halves together to show what the whole shape looks like.

Explain that shapes like these, in which the two halves are a perfect match, are called symmetric shapes. Write the word "symmetric" on the board.

Show other shapes, including circles, and have the children decide if they are symmetric shapes. Show them how to fold the shapes to see if they are symmetric.

Circles in Grades Five Through Eight. In the middle grades the study of circles becomes more formal, with greater emphasis on mathematical terminology. During these years, children are able to identify and use mathematical terminology to name the center, radius, diameter, and circumference of circles. They learn that all the radii are the same length (*congruent*), as are all the diameters. They learn about chords (*straight* lines with both endpoints on the circle), and central angles of circles, as well as angles inscribed in circles. They learn to use mathematical symbols and notation to write about these circle concepts.

Angles in Elementary School

Angles in Kindergarten Through Second Grade. In the early primary grades, angles are encountered and used for the classification of shapes. However, in these grades the treatment of angles is informal. They are usually called corners by the children and by the teachers. The children recognize that some shapes have corners and some do not. They recognize that shapes with *straight* sides have corners and shapes without straight sides do not have corners.

The children recognize that squares and other rectangles have four corners, and triangles have three. They notice that some corners are more "pointed" than other corners. This information (the number of corners and the "sharpness" of the corners) helps them to classify shapes.

The following activities illustrate how teachers in these grades can help children develop an informal understanding of angles.

×+÷ ACTIVITY 11.24   Corners or Not?

Display several different shapes like the ones pictured below.

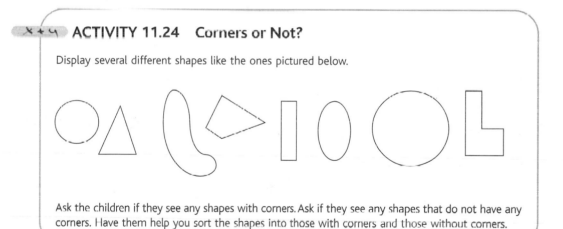

Ask the children if they see any shapes with corners. Ask if they see any shapes that do not have any corners. Have them help you sort the shapes into those with corners and those without corners.

×+÷ ACTIVITY 11.25   I Have a Shape...

Cut out several circles, squares, and triangles. Place a cardboard box on its side on the teacher's desk with the open side facing away from the children. Mix up the cut-out shapes and place them inside the box where you can see them, but the children cannot.

Look at one of the shapes (for example, a triangle) and say, "I have a shape that has three corners. What is it?" After the children decide what they think the shape is, hold it up so they can see it.

Repeat this procedure until you have used each shape in the box.

ACTIVITY 11.26   Corners and Sharper Corners

Cut out several shapes like those shown below.

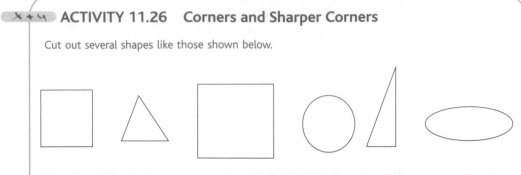

Have the children look at a square and a triangle. Point to one corner of the square and one corner of the triangle. Ask which corner is the "sharpest."

Ask if all the shapes have corners. Have someone identify a shape without a corner. Have someone else identify a shape that has corners. Point to a corner of that shape. Ask if any shape has a corner that is not this sharp. If the children identify such a shape, have someone come forward and point to that corner.

Have someone else choose a shape that has corners. Point to a corner of that shape and ask if any shape has a corner that is sharper than that corner. If the children identify such a shape, have someone come forward and point to that corner.

Repeat the activity until all the children have been included.

Angles in Third and Fourth Grades.   In these grades the study of angles continues as before, except corners of shapes begin to be referred to as angles. Square corners are called right angles (they are formed by *perpendicular* lines). Angles and right angles are identified as attributes of shapes. For example, rectangles, including square rectangles, have four angles, and all four of those angles are right angles. Triangles have three angles, and all three of them might be less than right angles. Triangles might have one right angle, but the other two angles must then be less than right angles.

In these grades we expect the children to draw angles. They should be able to compare angles and identify the one that is greater or the one that is less. They learn about perpendicular lines and become aware that the sides of a right angle are perpendicular. The children classify angles as right angles, greater than right angles, or less than right angles.

The following activities illustrate how some of these concepts might be developed.

ACTIVITY 11.27   Make It Right

Have all the children fold a sheet of paper in half. Then show them how to fold it again to form a square corner. Explain that the angle in a square corner is called a right angle.

Have the children compare their right angles with those of several other children by laying one directly on top of the other. Ask them what they found out. [They are all the same size.]

Have two children place their right angles together as pictured. Ask them what they see. [The sides of the angle make a straight line.]

Have them unfold their papers and look at the folds. How many right angles do they see? [There are four right angles.]

Have the children refold their papers to show right angles. Tell them to hold up their right angles.

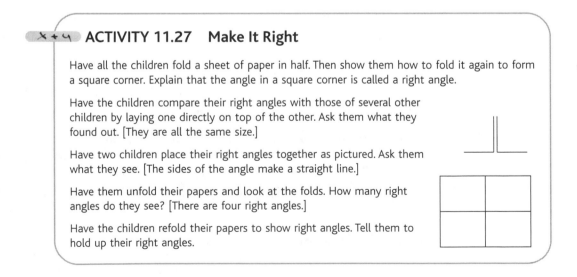

x + y ACTIVITY 11.28   Right Angle Search

Cut sheets of paper into fourths and draw angles on them. There should be 20 right angles, 8 angles that are very close to, but are not quite right angles, 10 angles that are obviously less than right angles, and 10 angles that are obviously more than right angles. Mix up the angles and tape them to the walls around the room.

Separate the children into four teams. Have each team find 5 angles that are right angles and find 5 angles that are not right angles. They are to use the right angles that they made by folding a sheet of paper to decide whether or not the angles are right angles. Each team is to take their 10 angles back to their tables. Every team member is to check every angle to be sure that they have 5 right angles and 5 angles that are not right angles.

x + y ACTIVITY 11.29   Angle Sort

Prepare one-fourth sheets of paper with angles drawn on them. Some should be right angles, some should be greater than right angles, and some less than right angles. Some of the nonright angles should be very close to right angles. Tape the angles to the front wall of the classroom. Place three boxes on the desk. Label them "right angles," "more than right angles," and "less than right angles."

Choose two children to come to the front of the room. One child should choose an angle and indicate which box it should go into. The second child should use his right angle (made from folded paper) to see if the first child was correct. When they agree, the should remove the angle from the wall and place it in the correct box.

Repeat this procedure with other pairs of children until all the angles are sorted into the correct boxes.

Angles in Fifth Through Eighth Grades.   In grades 5 and 6, we expect the children to use mathematical language as they describe and classify angles as right angles, acute angles, and obtuse angles. They learn to use a protractor to measure angles and discover that right angles have 90 degrees, acute angles have less than 90 degrees, and obtuse angles have more than 90 degrees. At this time, they also begin to develop the ability to estimate the measure of angles.

They use more formal mathematical language for angles (for example, angles are two rays with a common endpoint), and use more formal mathematical notation as they write about angles. They learn about *congruent* angles and angle bisectors (separating an angle into two *congruent* angles). They understand how to use a compass and a *straight*edge to construct an angle *congruent* to a given angle and to construct the bisector of a given angle. They learn about complementary and supplementary angles, as well as central angles of circles.

By seventh grade or eighth grade, children learn that the point of an angle is called the vertex. They learn that vertical angles are formed when two lines intersect and that vertical angles have the same measure (they are congruent), and that adjacent angles are two angles with a common side. They learn that the sum of the measures of the angles of a triangle is 180 degrees, and that an angle with a measure of 180 degrees is called a *straight* angle. They study central angles of circles, angles inscribed in circles, and how their measures are related.

They discover the relationships among angles formed when parallel lines are cut by a transversal. They learn about interior angles, exterior angles, alternate interior and alternate exterior angles, corresponding angles, and vertical angles and which of those angles are *congruent* and which of them are supplementary.

Prisms in Elementary School

Prisms in Kindergarten, First Grade, and Second Grade.   The study of prisms begins in kindergarten where informal, nonmathematical language is used to describe them. Children at this age usually identify and describe prisms as box-shaped objects. They might notice that the corners of the box are square corners (they are formed by *perpendicular* edges and *perpendicular* faces). They notice that the opposite sides of the box are the same size and shape (they are *congruent*). They distinguish the prism-shaped (box-shaped) objects from other everyday three-dimensional objects like balls, ice cream cones, and cans. Even though boxes actually come in a wide variety of other shapes, curriculum materials generally assume that those other box shapes do not exist, and this assumption seldom conflicts with children's personal experiences.

By first grade, we expect the children to develop more formal mathematical language for prisms. They learn that certain box shapes (those with all edges *congruent*) are called cubes. By the end of second grade, the children learn the name for rectangular prisms.

Boxes are PRISMS

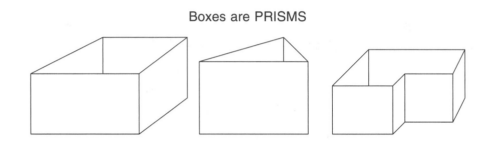

Unfortunately, the treatment of cubes and rectangular prisms often develops into the misconception that cubes are not rectangular prisms. Furthermore, from the limited variety of examples of rectangular prisms that they see in these early grades, children often think incorrectly that all rectangular prisms are right rectangular prisms, and that every face of a rectangular prism must be a rectangle.

The activities that follow are examples of the ways that teachers in kindergarten through second grade can develop the rectangular-prism concepts.

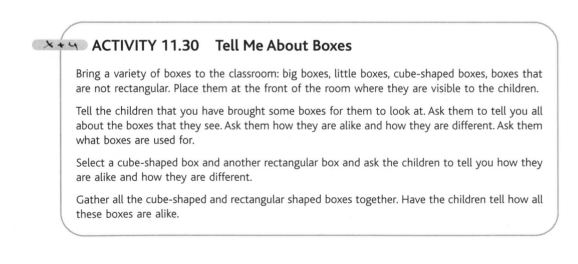

✗ + ⑨   ACTIVITY 11.30   Tell Me About Boxes

Bring a variety of boxes to the classroom: big boxes, little boxes, cube-shaped boxes, boxes that are not rectangular. Place them at the front of the room where they are visible to the children.

Tell the children that you have brought some boxes for them to look at. Ask them to tell you all about the boxes that they see. Ask them how they are alike and how they are different. Ask them what boxes are used for.

Select a cube-shaped box and another rectangular box and ask the children to tell you how they are alike and how they are different.

Gather all the cube-shaped and rectangular shaped boxes together. Have the children tell how all these boxes are alike.

✕ + ◹ ACTIVITY 11.31   Cubes, Cubes, Everywhere

Arrange to have several cube-shaped objects placed in sight in the classroom, in the hallway, in the library or resource center, on the playground, and other places in the school.

Review cubes. Ask the children what cubes are and what they look like. Have them find a picture of a cube on their math page.

Tell the class that you are going to take them on a "cube walk." Tell them to look for cubes when they are on the cube walk. Then lead the class around the room, out into the hallway, around the school, and around the playground. If you pass a cube without anyone seeing it, go back to it and stop. Look directly at the cube and say, "I see a cube. Who else can see it?"

✕ + ◹ ACTIVITY 11.32   All About Rectangular Prisms

Bring a variety of rectangular prisms to the classroom: big boxes, little boxes, cube-shaped boxes, wooden shapes that are rectangular prisms. Also bring some nonrectangular-prism shapes: boxes that are not rectangular, cans, cones, balls. Mix them up and place them at the front of the room where they are visible to the children.

Pick up one of the shapes that is a rectangular prism and show it to the children. Explain that a shape like this is called a rectangular prism. Explain the attributes of rectangular prisms as you point them out in the shape that you are holding. Then pick up another rectangular prism. Explain that it is also a rectangular prism. Point out the attributes that make it a rectangular prism.

Tell the children that you have brought some shapes for them to look at. Explain that some of the shapes are rectangular prisms and some are not. Select another rectangular prism and ask the children if it is a rectangular prism. Have them tell you why it is.

Select other shapes and ask if they are rectangular prisms. If they are rectangular prisms, ask why they are. If they are not rectangular prisms, ask why they are not.

Prisms in Third, Fourth, and Fifth Grades.   In third and fourth grades, the children learn the mathematical names for the faces and edges of cubes and other rectangular prisms, and by fifth grade, they have learned that a corner of a rectangular prism is called a vertex. They can also identify everyday objects that are in the shape of cubes or rectangular prisms.

At this time, the children could also likely develop the misconception that right angles are formed by the edges of rectangular prisms (that *all* the corners are square corners). This misconception arises out of the fact that most curriculum materials picture only rectangular prisms that are right rectangular prisms. Limiting the variety of rectangular prisms also results in the misconception that all faces of rectangular prisms are rectangles. In a right rectangular prism, all angles are right angles and all faces are rectangles. However, in general, the bases of a rectangular prism are rectangles and the rest of the faces are *parallelo*grams. Angles formed by the edges of a rectangular prism may or may not be right angles, and the faces may or may not be rectangles.

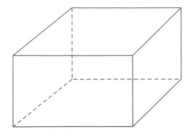

A Right Rectangular Prism

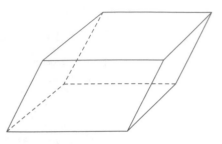

A Nonright Rectangular Prism

In these grades, the children learn to find the volume of rectangular prisms by counting cubes, and later they compute the volume by multiplying length times width times height. They create rectangular prisms by cutting out and folding paper patterns. They learn that the "top" and "bottom" faces of rectangular prisms are the same (they are *congruent*). They learn to recognize and name prisms by the shape of their bases and discover, therefore, that prisms are rectangular prisms when their bases are rectangles. They learn that prisms—cubes, rectangular prisms, and nonrectangular prisms—are all polyhedrons.

The following activity can be used by a teacher in grades 3–5 when the children are learning about rectangular prisms.

---

x + y   ACTIVITY 11.33   Describe These Shapes

Assign children to work with one or two partners. Have one set of partners complete the activity at a time.

Give the partners three shapes: a cube, a rectangular prism that is not a cube, and a triangular prism. Tell them to find out everything that they can about the three shapes and write down everything that they discover. Allow them to use any measurement tools that are appropriate.

After all sets of partners have completed the activity, have the class discuss what they found out about the three shapes. Compile a list for each shape.

Prisms in Sixth Grade Through Eighth Grade.   In these grades, students continue to use mathematical terminology related to rectangular prisms. They recognize that prisms are polyhedrons, and they name the parts of prisms as faces, edges, vertices, and bases. They use mathematical notation as they write about prisms. They learn the formula for volume of prisms, and they compute the volume and surface area of prisms.

Adapting a Geometry Lesson

Earlier, in Chapter 3, we adapted a lesson on symmetry. We now adapt another geometry lesson, one that would likely be found in grade 1. The lesson plan uses teaching procedures typical of those suggested in current first-grade teacher's guides. The lesson is an acceptable one. However, as is all too common, there is a minimal amount of concept development before the practice.

LESSON OBJECTIVE

Children will learn to classify shapes using the attributes of circles, squares, rectangles, and triangles.

Lesson Opener

Display everyday objects in the classroom that are shaped like circles, squares, rectangles, and triangles. Draw a rectangle, a circle, a triangle, and a square on the board and ask the children to name each shape. Then ask the children to find something in the room that has the shape of a square, the shape of a triangle, the shape of a circle, and the shape of a rectangle.

Development

Direct the attention of the class to the picture at the top of the first student page. Explain that, in this picture, there is a circle and a square. Point out the square and explain that a square has four square corners and four straight sides that are all the same length. Then point out the circle and explain that circles are round and do not have any straight sides.

Then direct attention to the second picture on the first student page. Tell the children that this picture has a rectangle and a triangle. Point out the rectangle and explain that rectangles have four square corners and four straight sides, but the sides do not have to be the same length. Point out the triangle and explain that all triangles have three straight sides.

Monitor Learning

Direct the children's attention to the shapes in the *Check Understanding* part of the lesson. Tell them to color the circles red. Then tell them to color the squares green. Then tell them to color the rectangles blue. Finally, tell them to color the triangles yellow. Move around the room while the children are working to check their understanding. Provide additional explanations to any children who need them.

Practice

Explain to the children how to identify the circles, squares, rectangles, and triangles on the practice page by coloring the shapes. Have the children complete the practice page of the lesson.

Closure

Remind the children that today they have learned to identify circles, squares, rectangles, and triangles.

We now adapt this lesson as we have adapted other lessons. We increase the amount of time spent developing the concepts and make it more complete. Although, by the very nature of the concepts being developed, the lesson is essentially visual, we increase the amount of visual information. We make the lesson much more kinesthetic and plan for increased communication about the lesson concepts from and among the children. And, we plan for more constant monitoring of learning throughout the lesson. These adaptations make the lesson appropriate for almost all students. But remember that some students with severe needs may require further instructional adaptations.

LESSON OBJECTIVE

Children will learn to classify shapes using the attributes of circles, squares, rectangles, and triangles.

Lesson Opener

Cut out a variety of circles, squares, rectangles, and triangles, being sure that there are more shapes than children. Mix up the shapes and lay them in a circle on the floor with the shapes about two feet apart. Have the children march around the outside of the circle of shapes. Have the children stop and stand by a shape. Have the children who are by triangles raise their hands. Then have the children who are by squares raise their hands. Have the children who are by circles raise their hands. And, finally, have the children who are by rectangles raise their hands.

Have the children move around the circle of shapes and stop at a different shape. **Monitor understanding.** Observe carefully to see if any children are confused about these shapes. Remember that it is correct if a child standing by a square identifies it as a rectangle. Use this activity as an opportunity to identify children who may need extra help during the lesson, but do not call undue attention to those who do not identify every shape correctly.

Development

Cut out several triangles, all different, from colored paper. Also cut out several rectangles, squares, and circles, all different. There needs to be enough of each shape for all sets of partners to have one during a partner activity.

Form sets of partners. Give each set of partners a triangle. Ask them what the shape is. Explain that each set of partners has a triangle that is different from all the others. Call on someone to tell the class something that is true about the triangle that he or she has. Ask if that is true about all the other triangles. For example, the child might say that his or her triangle has three corners. This is true of all triangles. Or, the child might say that his or her triangle is blue. That is *not* true of all triangles. **Monitor understanding.** Pay particular attention to any child who had difficulty during the opening activity. Make a special effort to include those children in the discussion and give them confidence by praising correct responses.

Continue until the children have identified these attributes of triangles.

> All triangles have   three corners.
>   three sides.
>   straight sides.

Next draw the first of these shapes on the board.

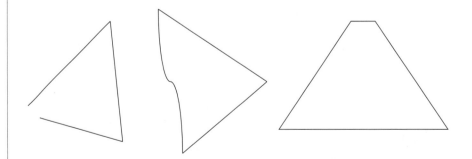

Ask if it is a triangle. [No.] Ask why not. [All triangles have three corners. The sides of triangles are connected to make those corners.] **Monitor understanding.** Direct questions to children who do not participate.

Draw the second of the shapes pictured above. Ask if it is a triangle. [No.] Ask why not. [All triangles have straight sides.] **Monitor understanding.** Watch for difficulties among children who have a history of poor achievement.

Draw the third of the shapes pictured above. Ask if it is a triangle. [No.] Ask why not. [All triangles have three corners. All triangles have three sides.] **Monitor understanding.** Watch the eyes of children who do not respond for unspoken questions or indications of confusion.

Give each set of partners a rectangle. Be sure that some of the rectangles are squares. Ask them what the shape is. Explain that each set of partners has a rectangle that is different from all the others. Call on someone to tell the class something that is true about the rectangle that he or she has. Ask if that is true about all the other rectangles. Continue like this until the children have identified these attributes of rectangles.

All rectangles have   four corners.
                       four sides.
                       square corners.
                       straight sides.

Next draw the first of these shapes on the board.

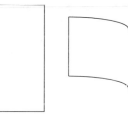

Ask if it is a rectangle. [No.] Ask why not. [All rectangles have four corners. All rectangles have four sides.]

Draw the second of the shapes pictured above. Ask if it is a rectangle. [No.] Ask why not. [All rectangles have straight sides.]

Draw the third of the shapes pictured above. Ask if it is a rectangle. [No.] Ask why not. [All rectangles have square corners.] **Monitor understanding.** Throughout the entire development of rectangle attributes, watch for children who do not understand.

Repeat this same process with the circles and then with the squares. Lead the children to identify that all circles are curved, are the same size in all directions, and have no straight sides. Use the following nonexamples to reinforce those attributes.

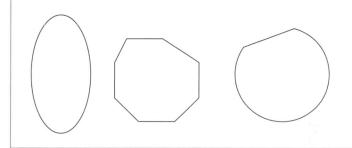

Lead the children to identify that all squares have four sides, four corners, straight sides, square corners, and sides that are equal. Use the following nonexamples to reinforce those attributes. **Monitor understanding.** Ask further questions of children who do not understand. Provide additional explanations as needed.

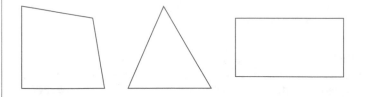

Direct the attention of the class to the picture at the top of the first student page. Explain that, in this picture, there is a circle and a square. Have the children place a finger on top of the square. **Monitor understanding.** Move around the room, checking that all the children have correctly identified the square.

Ask for someone to tell the class what he or she knows about squares. Ask for further help until all the necessary attributes of squares have been described. Repeat this process with the circle. Have the children place a finger on the circle and then have the children tell about circles. **Monitor understanding.** Listen carefully to assure that all the children correctly understand the attributes of squares and circles.

Direct attention to the second picture on the first student page. Have the children identify and then give the characteristics of rectangles and triangles. **Monitor understanding.** Listen carefully to assure that all the children correctly understand the attributes of rectangles and triangles.

Practice

Direct the children's attention to the shapes in the *Check Understanding* part of the lesson. Tell them to color the circles red. Then tell them to color the squares green. Then tell them to color the rectangles blue. Finally, tell them to color the triangles yellow. **Monitor understanding.** Move around the room while the children are working to check their understanding. Provide additional explanations to any children who need them.

Closure

Ask the children to tell you what they have learned about circles, squares, rectangles, and triangles.

Follow Up

Have the children take the practice page home with them and use it to explain to their parents what they know about circles, squares, rectangles, and triangles.

Using Geometry to Solve Problems

Most problems involving geometry are really measurement problems. Although there are geometry concepts that must be considered, the solution frequently requires the application of measurement concepts, such as the problem on pages 323–324 of Chapter 10. The problem that follows is another example of a geometry problem that involves measurement.

> George wants to build a rectangular corral for his horses beside a barn that is 50-feet long. He has 90 feet of fence, but because he wants the corral to have as large an area as possible, George decides to use the side of the barn as one side of the corral. In order to make the area of the corral as large as possible, what should its dimensions be?

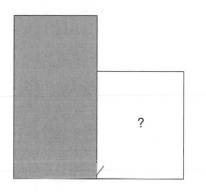

To solve this problem, we use two strategies that we used before, *try and check* and *use a formula*. First we try a couple of possibilities to see what the results are.

> Suppose the corral used the barn for a 20-foot side and the fence for the other three sides. The corral would be 20 feet by 35 feet and would have an area of 700 square feet. Or, suppose the corral were square, with each side 30-feet long, the area would then be 30 × 30 = 900 square feet.

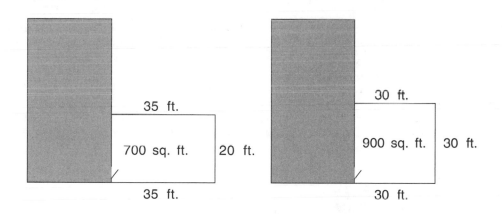

These two possibilities suggest that we can increase the size of the corral by making the barn side of the corral longer. We try other examples to see if this pattern holds.

> By making the barn side of the corral 40-feet long, the corral would be 40 feet by 25 feet, and would have an area of 1000 square feet. By making the barn side of the corral 46-feet long, the corral would be 46 feet by 22 feet, and would have an area of 1012 square feet.

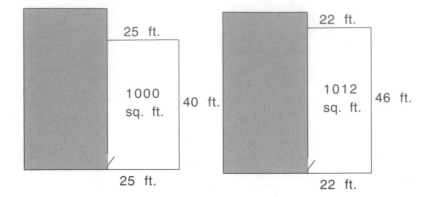

These two examples suggest that the pattern continues and that we can increase the area of the corral by making the barn side of the corral longer. So, it would make sense to use the full length of the barn as a side of the corral. We try that possibility and check to see if we are correct.

But, if we use the full length of the barn for one side, the corral is 50 feet by 20 feet, and the area is 1000 square feet.

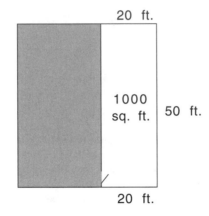

So, we can see that the area would be 1000 square feet if the dimensions are 40 feet by 25 feet or if they are 50 feet by 20 feet. But the area is greater when the length is between 40 feet and 50 feet. We next try a corral with a length halfway between 40 feet and 50 feet.

If the barn side of the corral is 45-feet long, then the corral would be 45 feet by 22.5 feet, and its area would be 1012.5 square feet. If we try other lengths between 40 feet and 50 feet, we would find the areas to be less than 1012.5 square feet. George has the greatest area in his corral if he makes the barn side 45 feet long.

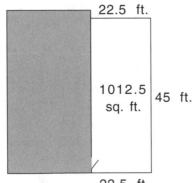

Exercises and Activities

1. Consider the topic, *parallelograms*. Create a list of the ways that each of the six big ideas of geometry (straightness, congruency, similarity, parallelism, perpendicularity, and symmetry) relate to parallelograms.

2. Consider the capital letter, W:

W

Create a list of the ways that each of the six big ideas of geometry (straightness, congruency, similarity, parallelism, perpendicularity, and symmetry) relate to the letter.

3. Choose a lesson on geometry from a published elementary school mathematics textbook series.

   a. Write a lesson plan that follows the teaching suggestions in the teacher's guide.

   b. Identify the parts of the lesson that develop the concept(s) of the lesson.

   c. Expand the lesson by adding more development of the concepts being taught. Use the big ideas of geometry and the ways that those big ideas relate to the lesson concepts to build understanding of those concepts.

4. Choose a lesson on geometry from a published elementary school mathematics textbook series.

   a. Write a lesson plan that follows the teaching suggestions in the teacher's guide.

   b. Identify kinesthetic activity that is included in the lesson.

   c. Add more kinesthetic activity to the lesson.

5. Choose a lesson on geometry from a published elementary school mathematics textbook series.

   a. Write a lesson plan that follows the teaching suggestions in the teacher's guide.

   b. Identify parts of the lesson that include student communication about the concept(s) taught in the lesson.

   c. Plan more opportunities for communication about the lesson concepts from or among the children.

6. Choose a lesson on geometry from a published elementary school mathematics textbook series.

   a. Write a lesson plan that follows the teaching suggestions in the teacher's guide.

   b. Identify the parts of the lesson designed to monitor the learning of the students.

   c. Add more continual monitoring of learning to the lesson plan.

7. Study the adapted lesson plan on pages 350-352. Make further changes in the lesson plan to make it more appropriate for a child who functions at a low cognitive level.

8. Study the adapted lesson plan on pages 350–352. Make further changes in the lesson plan to make it more appropriate for a child whose learning disability includes memory difficulties.

9. Study the adapted lesson plan on pages 350–352. Make further changes in the lesson plan to make it more appropriate for a child who has visual perception difficulties, including difficulty seeing small objects.

10. Read "Standard 9: Geometry and Spatial Sense," on pages 48–50 of *Curriculum and Evaluation Standards for School Mathematics*, published by the National Council of Teachers of Mathematics. Then read the discussions of "The Geometry Standard" on pages 41–43, 96–101, 164–169, and 232–239 of *Principles and Standards for School*

Mathematics, published by the National Council of Teachers of Mathematics. Identify what you believe to be the most important and useful information provided in the standards documents about the teaching of geometry.

References and Related Readings

Clements, D. H., & Sarama, J. (2000). Young children's ideas about geometric shapes. *Teaching Children Mathematics, 6*, 482–487.

Fuys, D. J., & Lebov, A. K. (1997). Concept learning in geometry. *Teaching Children Mathematics, 3*, 248–251.

Lerch, H. H. (1981). *Teaching elementary school mathematics: An active learning approach.* Boston: Houghton Mifflin.

National Council of Teachers of Mathematics. (1989). *Curriculum and evaluation standards for school mathematics.* Reston, VA: NCTM.

National Council of Teachers of Mathematics. (2000). *Principles and standards for school mathematics.* Reston, VA: NCTM.

Thornton, C. A., Tucker, B. F., Dossey, J. A., & Bazik, E. F. (1983). *Teaching mathematics to children with special needs.* Menlo Park, CA: Addison-Wesley.

Web Sites

http://www.proteacher.com/100021.shtml
(Activities and lesson plans on geometry.)

http://www.earthmeasure.com/
(Geometry in Native American art.)

http://mathcentral.uregina.ca/RR/database/RR.09.96 /archamb1.html
(Lessons and activities on tesselations.)

http://www.sasked.gov.sk.ca/docs/elemath/geom.html
(A scope and sequence chart for geometry topics.)

http://www.sedl.org/scimath/compass/v01n03/geometry.html#geo1
(Standards-based activity. Which container holds the most?)

CHAPTER

EFFECTIVE PRACTICE:

Games and Activities for Practice and Fun

THE TEACHING PRINCIPLE

"Teachers establish and nurture an environment conducive to learning mathematics through the decisions they make, the conversations they orchestrate, and the physical setting they create" (National Council of Teachers of Mathematics, 2000, p. 18).

THE LEARNING PRINCIPLE

"The kinds of experiences teachers provide clearly play a role in determining the extent and quality of students' learning" (NCTM, 2000, p. 21)

Because of the importance of the developmental phase of lessons—that part of the lessons during which the children are learning things that they do not already know and developing skills that they do not already have—the learning activities found in the earlier chapters are predominantly developmental activities.

The purpose of practice activities is to help students to become proficient in the use of concepts and skills that have already been developed. Where the emphasis of developmental activities is on comprehension and understanding, the emphasis of practice activities is to develop greater proficiency with what the children have learned. As a general rule, students do not learn new things from practice. However, through practice, they develop higher levels of skill in what they have already learned. Practice also may help that learning to be more permanent.

Think-time practice is preferred over other practice activities. Students have enough time to carefully think about concepts and connections, enough time to think carefully through each step of a procedure, and enough time to look up things they do not fully understand. In think-time practice, the emphasis is on accuracy, not on speed.

In this chapter, we see activities that by their very nature can make practice interesting and even fun. We show activities that provide a lot of practice, even more than the children get by completing a practice page from the textbook. In addition, there are practice activities that require children to cooperate with each other as they consider, discuss, question, and explain mathematical concepts and skills. There are also practice activities that fully engage the children's attention by requiring physical (kinesthetic) involvement.

The reader should be cautious, though. Remember that a practice activity, even one that is really neat, cute, exciting, and engaging, cannot be truly effective until after the children have achieved understanding. *No practice activity can take the place of good, solid concept and skill development.*

We begin with a class of activities that require the children to match two or more things. They might match because they are equal; they might match because they have the same answer; they might match because they share some geometric characteristic; they might match for any number of different reasons. The important thing to remember is that, regardless of what is being matched and regardless of the matching criterion, the activity can easily be adapted to any other things that match. So, if children enjoy a particular matching activity, that activity can be used repeatedly with other content.

Matching Activities

One effective matching activity is *Match Me*. The basic procedure for this activity is illustrated in the following two activities. The procedures for Activities 12.01 and 12.02 are identical but the level of content is different.

× + ꝗ ACTIVITY 12.01   Match Me (variation 1)

Prepare pairs of cards like the ones illustrated. Both cards in each pair should have the same number of dots, but the dots should be arranged differently.

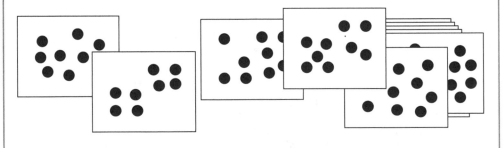

Mix the cards and pass them out to the children. Have the children find partners so that the partners have the same number of dots. If there is an odd number of children, the teacher should take a card and participate so everyone has a partner.

When all the children have found a partner, have the partners show their cards to the class and tell how many dots they have.

ACTIVITY 12.02   Match Me (variation 2)

Prepare pairs of cards like the ones illustrated. The cards in each pair should picture different rectangles with the same area.

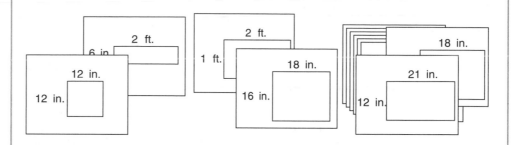

Mix the cards and pass them out to the children. Have the children find partners so that the partners have rectangles with the same area. If there is an odd number of children, include one set of three cards with the same area and tell the children that there will be either two or three partners.

When all the children have found their partners, have the partners show their cards to the class and tell what their area is.

Match Me has an excellent level of kinesthetic activity. The children must get up and move about the room in order to complete the activity. But, because the movement is purposeful, this activity seldom results in behavior problems. Another advantage of Match Me is that it takes little time. This makes it a good choice for inclusion in a lesson opener, when the children's attention should be focused on particular content without using up time that needs to be spent on developing concepts or skills being taught in the lesson.

Another nice use of Match Me is to form pairs of children for a partner activity. This activity can be used if random pairings of children is acceptable. A variation of Match Me also can be used to form small groups or teams for a group or team activity. To do this, the cards need to be constructed so that groups of children (however many are to be in each group) will have matching cards. Activities 12.03 and 12.04 are examples of activities that would accomplish forming groups.

ACTIVITY 12.03   Match Me (variation 3)

Prepare sets of four cards like the ones illustrated. The cards in each set should show subtraction examples with the same answer.

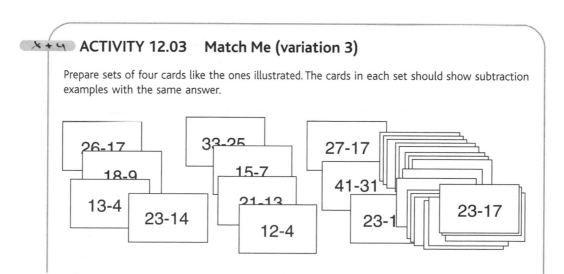

Mix the cards and pass them out to the children. Have the children find others with problems that have the same answer as theirs. Tell them to check the answers for the cards of everyone in the group to be sure that they match.

When all the children have found their groups, have the groups show their cards to the class and tell what their answer is.

ACTIVITY 12.04   Match Me (variation 4)

Place bundles of sticks with unbundled sticks into paper bags so that numbers are represented in several ways. For example, you might include three bundles and one stick, two bundles and eleven sticks, and one bundle with 21 sticks in three of the bags. Prepare enough bags so that each child will have one.

Have the children look in their bags to see what numbers are there. Then have them get into a group with all the other children who the same number represented in different ways.

The preceding examples of Match Me all use equality as the matching criterion, but other matching criteria can easily be used. For example, the children could match money amounts that add up to one dollar, numbers that have a sum of 10, angles that are complimentary, metric lengths that have a sum of 1 meter, or shapes that can be combined to form a rectangle. But, whichever variation of Match Me is used, and whichever matching criterion is used, *remember that Match Me is a practice activity and concepts and skills must be developed before they can be practiced.*

The next matching activity is called *Piles.* Again, we see two variations of the activity demonstrating how it can be used for different content. Note that although the content is different in the two activities, the procedures are identical.

ACTIVITY 12.05   Piles (variation 1)

Prepare cards showing addition examples. Include many sets of examples with the same answers.

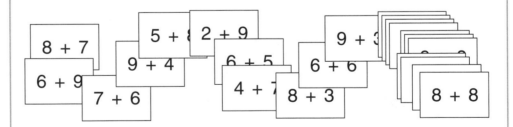

Mix the cards, Place one in the chalk tray, and pass the rest out to the children. Have the children come, one at a time, to place their cards in the chalk tray. If there is already a card in the tray with the same answer as is on a child's card, the card is placed on top of the one with the same answer. If there is not a card in the tray with the same answer as a child's card, the child should start a new pile.

When all the cards have been placed in the chalk tray, go through the cards in each pile with the children to check whether the answers are all the same.

✗ ← ↵ ACTIVITY 12.06   Piles (variation 2)

Prepare cards showing geometric shapes. Include many squares, circles, rectangles, and triangles, all of different sizes.

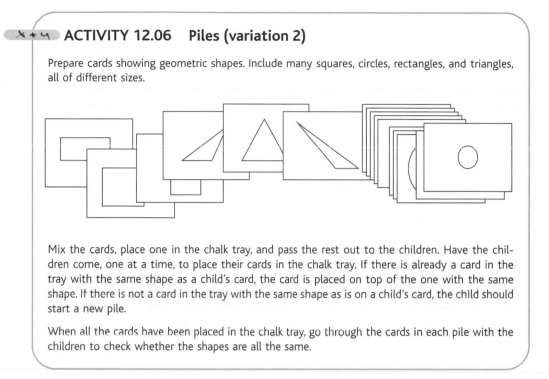

Mix the cards, place one in the chalk tray, and pass the rest out to the children. Have the children come, one at a time, to place their cards in the chalk tray. If there is already a card in the tray with the same shape as a child's card, the card is placed on top of the one with the same shape. If there is not a card in the tray with the same shape as is on a child's card, the child should start a new pile.

When all the cards have been placed in the chalk tray, go through the cards in each pile with the children to check whether the shapes are all the same.

   Piles is another activity that is very kinesthetic, and children usually enjoy it while getting to think about many examples. However, the involvement level is not high in this activity. Only one child is actively involved at a time, while all the rest of the children are either waiting for their turns or they are finished. If the activity is used too often, the children will get tired of it and misbehaviors could occur during the time that they are uninvolved. Piles can be an effective practice activity if it is not over-used. The children will stay mentally involved even when it is not their turn. *Remember, though, that it is practice and should be used only after sufficient concept development has taken place.*
   Around We Go is another excellent matching activity that children invariably enjoy. As was true of earlier activities, Around We Go can easily be adapted for a variety of content topics. Activities 12.07 and 12.08 illustrate Around We Go with two different topics. The children *find things that match what the teacher has.*

✗ ← ↵ ACTIVITY 12.07   Around We Go (variation 1)

Using a broad-tip marker, write addition examples like those illustrated on full sheets of paper. Prepare two examples for most of the answers, and be sure that there are more examples than children. Also prepare large cards with the answers.

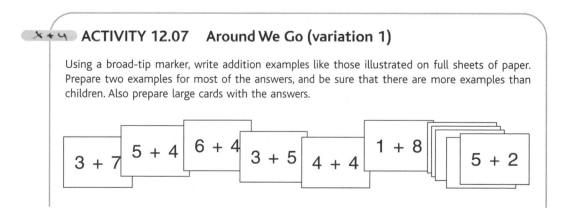

Lay the examples on the floor in a circle. Have the children form a circle outside the addition examples. They should march around the circle while reciting this rhyme.

> Marching, marching, round we go,
> Not too fast and not too slow.
> I won't run and I won't hop.
> I'm almost there. It's time to stop.

On the word stop, they should think about the examples they are standing by. The teacher holds up one of the answer cards, and any child whose addition example has that answer raises a hand.

Repeat the process until all the children have had opportunities to raise their hands.

✕ ✦ ◥ ACTIVITY 12.08   Around We Go (variation 2)

From colored construction paper, cut out shapes like those illustrated. Prepare varied examples of each shape, and be sure that there are more examples than children.

Lay the shapes on the floor in a circle. Have the children form a circle outside the shape examples. They should march around the circle while reciting this rhyme.

> Marching, marching, round we go,
> Not too fast and not too slow.
> I won't run and I won't hop.
> I'm almost there. It's time to stop.

On the word stop, they should think about the shapes they are standing by. The teacher names one of the shapes (triangle, square, circle, or rectangle), and any child who is standing by an example of that shape raises a hand. Remember, a child who is standing by a square should raise a hand if the teacher says "rectangle."

Repeat the process until all the children have had opportunities to raise their hands.

Still another kinesthetic matching activity is *Scavenger Hunt*. This activity also has the advantage of encouraging a lot of student cooperation and communication. In Activities 12.09 and 12.10, we see two variations that demonstrate the variety of content for which it can be used.

×+ч ACTIVITY 12.09   Scavenger Hunt (variation 1)

Prepare four different lists of answers like the ones illustrated. Also prepare large cards with problems on them. Every answer on a list must have a matching problem card. Several problem cards that do not match any answers should also be included.

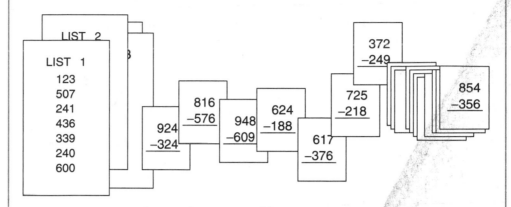

Tape the problem cards to the walls of the classroom.

Form four teams and give each team one of the answer lists. Tell the children that each team is to find a problem that matches each of the answers on their list. They are to collect the problems that match their answers and when they have all of them, bring them to the teacher. The first team to finish correctly wins.

×+ч ACTIVITY 12.10   Scavenger Hunt (variation 2)

Prepare four different lists of name of shapes like the ones illustrated Also prepare large cards with geometric shapes on them. Every shape name on a list must have a matching shape card. Several shape cards that do not match any shape names should also be Included.

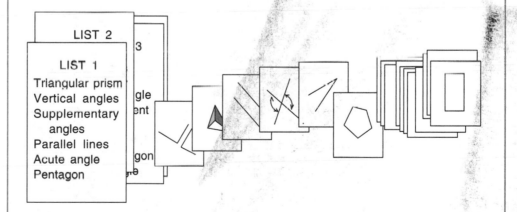

Tape the shape cards to the walls of the classroom.

Form four teams and give each team one of the shape name lists. Tell the children that each team is to find a shape that matches each of the shape names on their list. They are to collect the shapes that match their shape names and when they have all of them, bring them to the teacher. The first team to finish correctly wins.

There are many matching activities using cards that are effective with small groups of two to four children. These small group activities offer opportunities for children to talk about the mathematical concepts or skills that they use when they participate. One such activity is *Concentration*. We include three variations of Concentration to demonstrate how it can be used to practice a wide variety of content.

✗ ✦ ⁴ ACTIVITY 12.11   Concentration (variation 1)

Prepare 12 pairs of matching cards. In each pair of cards, one will show the picture of a shape and the other will show the name of that shape.

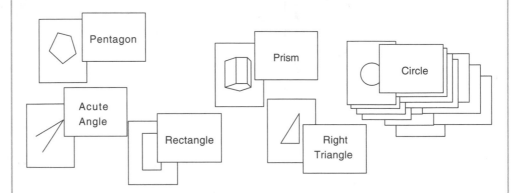

Form a group of two to four players. Shuffle the cards and place them face down in six rows of four cards.

Players take turns. The player turns two cards over. If the cards match, the player takes them and the play is finished. If the cards do not match, the player returns the cards to their face-down positions, and the play is finished. Play continues until all the cards have been taken. The player with the most cards wins.

X + Y ACTIVITY 12.12   Concentration (variation 2)

Prepare 12 pairs of cards. In each pair of cards, both cards will picture coins showing less than 10 cents, and the amounts on the coins in each pair will add up to 10 cents.

Form a group of two to four players. Shuffle the cards and place them face down in six rows of four cards.

Players take turns. The player turns two cards over. If the money on the cards adds up to 10 cents, the player takes them and the play is finished. If the money on the cards does not add up to 10 cents, the player returns the cards to their face-down positions, and the play is finished. Play continues until all the cards have been taken. The player with the most cards wins.

X + Y ACTIVITY 12.13   Concentration (variation 3)

Prepare 30 cards showing one-digit numbers. There should be three cards showing each of the numbers 0 through 9.

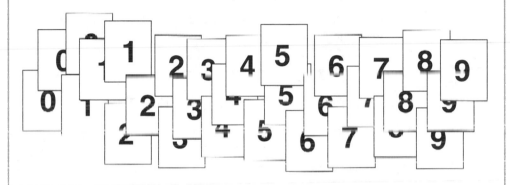

Form a group of two to four players. Shuffle the cards and place them face down in six rows of five cards. Players take turns.

The player turns two cards over. If the cards have a sum of 9, the player takes them and the play is finished. If the cards do not have a sum of 9, the player returns the cards to their face-down positions, and the play is finished. Play continues until all the cards have been taken. The player with the most cards wins.

The procedures described in these concentration activities are different from those that are usually followed (Tucker, 1981). In most concentration games, if a player finds a match he gets to try to find another one and can continue to pick up cards as long as he finds matches. In the procedures recommended here, the player is only allowed to pick up one match in each turn. The reason this is recommended is that we want to reduce the amount of time the other players have to wait for their turns (the time when they are not directly involved). This helps to maintain interest for a longer time and to reduce disruptive off-task behavior.

Another small-group card game that is a matching activity is *Pairs*. This game, has simple procedures that can be quickly taught, as is true of the other activities presented in this chapter. Pairs can be used to provide practice with a great variety of content. Activities 12.14, 12.15, 12.16, 12.17, and 12.18 demonstrate this variety.

✖ ✚ ➗ ACTIVITY 12.14　Pairs (variation 1)

Prepare 50 cards showing one-digit numbers. There should be five cards showing each of the numbers 0 through 9.

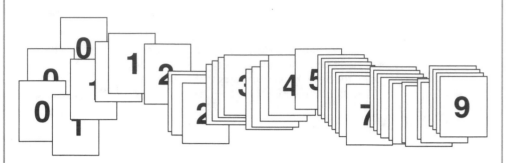

Form a group of two to four players. Shuffle the cards and place them face down on the table. Spread three starter cards face up around the deck.

Players take turns. The player takes one card from the deck and turns it over, placing it with the other starter cards. If the player sees two cards that have a sum of 10, the player takes those cards and the turn is over. If no two cards have a sum of 10, the turn is over.

Play continues until all the cards have been turned face up and all possible sums of 10 have been taken. The player with the most cards wins.

✖ ✚ ➗ ACTIVITY 12.15　Pairs (variation 2)

Prepare 25 pairs of cards showing addition facts without answers. The cards in each pair should have the same answer. You may use the same answer in more than one pair.

Form a group of two to four players. Shuffle the cards and place them face down on the table. Spread three starter cards face up around the deck.

Players take turns. The player takes one card from the deck and turns it over, placing it with the other starter cards. If the player sees two cards that have the same answer, the player takes those cards and the turn is over. If no two cards have the same answer, the turn is over.

Play continues until all the cards have been turned face up and all possible matching pairs have been taken. The player with the most cards wins.

✖ ✚ ➗ ACTIVITY 12.16　Pairs (variation 3)

Prepare 25 pairs of cards showing division examples with one-digit divisors and two-digit dividends. The cards in each pair should have the same remainder. Remember that the remainder could be zero. You may use the same remainder in more than one pair.

Form a group of two to four players. Shuffle the cards and place them face down on the table. Spread three starter cards face up around the deck.

Players take turns. The player takes one card from the deck and turns it over, placing it with the other starter cards. If the player sees two cards that have the same remainder, the player takes those cards and the turn is over. If no two cards have the same remainder, the turn is over.

Play continues until all the cards have been turned face up and all possible matching pairs have been taken. The player with the most cards wins.

ACTIVITY 12.17   Pairs (variation 4)

Prepare 25 pairs of cards showing lengths expressed in standard units. The cards in each pair should have equal lengths (for example, 24 inches and 2 feet).

Form a group of two to four players. Shuffle the cards and place them face down on the table. Spread three starter cards face up around the deck.

Players take turns. The player takes one card from the deck and turns it over, placing it with the other starter cards. If the player sees two cards that have equal lengths, the player takes those cards and the turn is over. If no two cards have equal lengths, the turn is over.

Play continues until all the cards have been turned face up and all possible matching pairs have been taken. The player with the most cards wins.

x + y **ACTIVITY 12.18   Pairs (variation 5)**

Prepare 25 pairs of cards showing pictures of combinations of coins. The cards in each pair should have the same amount of money (for example, 2 nickels and 1 dime, or 1 dime, 1 nickel, and 5 pennies).

Form a group of two to four players. Shuffle the cards and place them face down on the table. Spread three starter cards face up around the deck.

Players take turns. The player takes one card from the deck and turns it over, placing it with the other starter cards. If the player sees two cards that have equal amounts of money, the player takes those cards and the turn is over. If no two cards have equal amounts of money, the turn is over.

Play continues until all the cards have been turned face up and all possible matching pairs have been taken. The player with the most cards wins.

Another small-group card game that can be an effective way to provide practice is a simplified variation of *Rummy*. The procedures for playing rummy are more complex than the ones that we have seen so far. The added complexity means that rummy is probably not appropriate for children below grade 3 or 4. In Activities 12.19 and 12.20 we demonstrate that rummy can be used with a wide variety of content.

x + y **ACTIVITY 12.19   Rummy (variation 1)**

Prepare 48 cards showing multiplication facts without answers. There should be four cards for each answer.

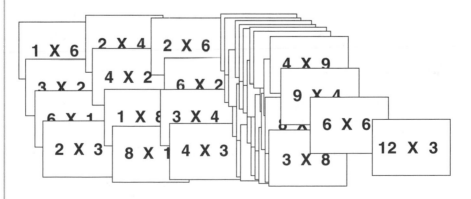

Form a group of two to four players. Shuffle the cards. Deal each player six cards, and place the rest of the deck face down. Turn over the top card and place it next to the deck to start a discard pile.

Players take turns. On each play, the player may either draw the top card from the deck or the top card from the discard pile. If the player holds two or more cards that have the same answer, the matching cards are laid face up on the table. If the player has cards with the same answer as cards that have been laid down by other players, those cards may be laid down with the others having the same answer. When the player is unable to lay down any more cards, he or she places one card on the discard deck, and the play is finished.

Play continues in this fashion until a player has used all the cards in his or her hand. That player is the winner. If no one has won when the deck has been played, then there is no winner.

ACTIVITY 12.20   Rummy (variation 2)

Prepare 48 cards showing metric lengths. There should be four cards for each length.

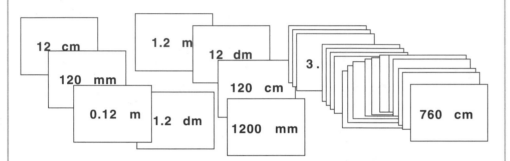

Form a group of two to four players. Shuffle the cards. Deal each player six cards, and place the rest of the deck face down. Turn over the top card and place it next to the deck to start a discard pile.

Players take turns. On each play, the player may either draw the top card from the deck or the top card from the discard pile. If the player holds two or more cards that have equals lengths, the matching cards are laid face up on the table. If the player has cards with the same length as cards that have been laid down by other players, those cards may be laid down with the others having the same length. When the player is unable to lay down any more cards, he or she places one card on the discard deck, and the play is finished.

Play continues in this fashion until a player has used all the cards in his or her hand. That player is the winner. If no one has won when the deck has been played, then there is no winner.

Ordering Activities

Another category of activities requires the participant to make comparisons or to arrange things in order. There are multiple uses for these activities also, since many things that we study in mathematics can be arranged in order. The first activity from this category that we consider is *Line Up* A. It is kinesthetic, requiring the children to get up and move about in order to complete the required tasks. To demonstrate the flexibility of this activity, we show three variations in Activities 12.21, 12.22, and 12.23.

✖ ÷ ◁ ACTIVITY 12.21 Line Up A (variation 1)

Prepare large cards showing lengths using standard units. There should be enough cards for all the participating students to have one. The cards should be big enough so that they can be read from a distance. There should not be cards with equal lengths.

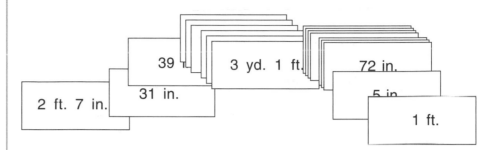

Shuffle the cards, and give one to each child. Separate the class into two teams. Have the teams go to opposite sides of the room.

Tell them to line up along the wall, so that the lengths are in order from shortest to longest. When both teams are lined up, have them hold their cards in front of them so the other team can read them.

Have each team check the other to see if they are lined up exactly right. Discuss the line ups. Why are they correct, or why are they not correct?

✖ ÷ ◁ ACTIVITY 12.22 Line Up A (variation 2)

Prepare large cards showing multiplication facts. There should be enough cards for all the participating students to have one. The cards should be big enough so that they can be read from a distance.

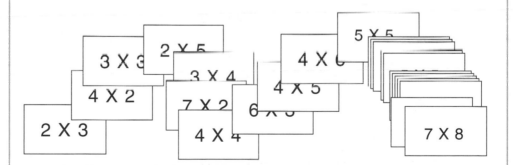

Shuffle the cards, and give one to each child. Separate the class into two teams. Have the teams go to opposite sides of the room.

Tell them to line up along the wall, so that their answers are in order from smallest to largest. When both teams are lined up, have them hold their cards in front of them so the other team can read them.

Have each team check the other to see if they are lined up exactly right. Discuss the line ups. Why are they correct, or why are they not correct?

ACTIVITY 12.23   Line Up A (variation 3)

Prepare large cards showing mixed computation examples without answers. There should be enough cards for all the participating students to have one. The cards should be big enough so that they can be read from a distance. Avoid having two cards with the same answer.

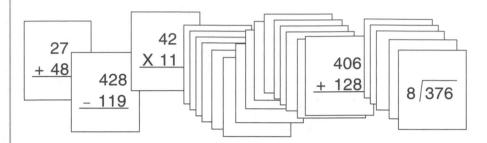

Shuffle the cards, and give one to each child. Separate the class into two teams. Have the teams go to opposite sides of the room.

Tell them to line up along the wall, so that their answers are in order from smallest to largest. When both teams are lined up, have them hold their cards in front of them so the other team can read them.

Have each team check the other to see if they are lined up exactly right. Discuss the line ups. Why are they correct, or why are they not correct?

The second activity in this category, *Line Up B*, is another good kinesthetic activity. It is a version of Line Up A, but uses alternative procedures. Where Line Up A encourages the children to help their team members get lined up correctly, Line Up B minimizes a child's opportunities to get help from the other children. Line Up B is just as flexible as Line Up A, and can be used with a wide variety of content topics.

ACTIVITY 12.24   Line Up B

Prepare large cards like the ones described in Activities 12.21, 12.22, or 12.23.

Shuffle the cards, and give one to each child. Choose two children to come to the front of the room and hold their cards so that the other children can read them.

Have other children come forward, one at a time, and stand in line with the others so that their answers are in order from smallest to largest. If a child has difficulty deciding where to stand, have the other children help.

There are several small-group activities that are based on comparisons or ordering. One of these activities is a game called *Shuffle*. Shuffle emphasizes arranging problems in order quickly. As children play Shuffle, they quickly realize that they do not need to know the exact answers, but rather, just which answers are bigger or smaller. As a result the game naturally becomes an estimation activity. Although only one variation is included here, Shuffle can also be used to provide practice with a variety of content topics.

✗ ✚ ✦ ACTIVITY 12.25   Shuffle

Prepare a deck of 40 cards showing two-digit addition examples. Avoid having two cards with the same answer.

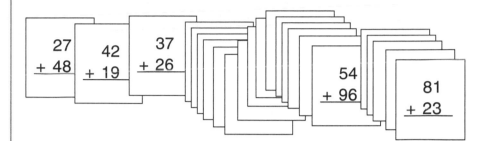

Form a group of 2 to 4 children. The children take turns dealing the cards.

On each play, the dealer shuffles the cards and gives each player four cards face down. When the dealer says, "Go," the players race to arrange their cards in order from smallest answer to largest answer.

The first player to correctly arrange the cards in order scores one point. The first player to get five points is the winner.

Compare is another small-group comparison activity. Activities 12.26, 12.27, and 12.28 are three versions of this game. The content variations that are illustrated can be used in all three versions.

✗ ✚ ✦ ACTIVITY 12.26   Compare: Big Wins

Prepare a deck of 40 cards showing two-digit addition examples. Avoid having two cards with the same answer.

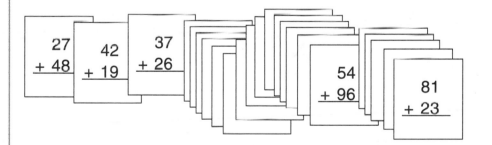

Form a group of 2 to 4 children. The children take turns dealing the cards.

On each play, the dealer gives one card to each player. The players compare their cards, and the player with the largest answer takes the cards used in that play.

When there are not enough cards for another play, the player with the most cards is the winner.

✕ ÷ ⊣ ACTIVITY 12.27 Compare: Small Wins

Prepare a deck of 40 cards showing rectangles labeled with their dimensions. Avoid having two cards with the same area.

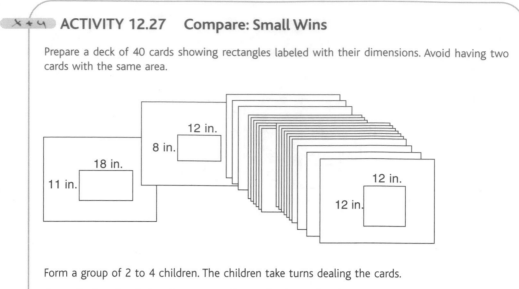

Form a group of 2 to 4 children. The children take turns dealing the cards.

On each play, the dealer gives one card to each player. The players compare their cards, and the player with the smallest area takes the cards used in that play.

When there are not enough cards for another play, the player with the most cards is the winner.

✕ ÷ ⊣ ACTIVITY 12.28 Compare: Dealer's Choice

Prepare a deck of 40 cards showing multiplication facts without answers. Avoid having two cards with the same area.

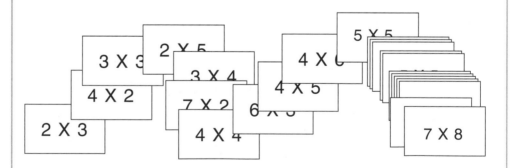

Form a group of 2 to 4 children. The children take turns dealing the cards.

On each play, the dealer gives one card to each player face down. Before anyone looks at their cards, the dealer indicates whether the big answer or the small answer will win. Then, the players compare their cards, and the player with the winning card takes the cards used in that play. If there is a tie, all the cards from that play stay on the table, and the winner of the next play takes them also.

When there are not enough cards for another play, the player with the most cards wins the game.

Answer/Example Construction Activities

Many excellent practice activities require the children to construct their own examples or answers, rather than select from examples or answers that are given to them. We now show a selection of activities of this type. The answer/example construction activities range from small-group to whole-class activities. Some are very kinesthetic and some are minimally kinesthetic. Many of them are flexible and can be used for a wide variety of content.

The first answer/example construction activity that we consider is *Take the 5 Path*. Note that even though the children enjoy this activity enough to stay focused, the level of active involvement is low. So, if the activity is used too long or too often, children begin to lose interest. We include two variations of Take the 5 Path in Activities 12.29 and 12.30, which show different content levels. Notice that although the layout of the game court and the numbers that are available to the children are different, the procedures of these activities are identical.

ACTIVITY 12.29 Take the 5 path (variation 1)

On the floor, sidewalk, or playground, prepare a game court like the one illustrated. The spaces should be about 20 inches across. The game court can be made using masking tape or chalk, or a permanent one can be painted on a concrete or asphalt surface.

Have the children line up at the game court. You say, "Take the 5 path," and the first child hops across the game court landing on the numbers that add up to 5 (1 and 4). If you say, "Take the 11 path," the next child in line must cross the game court by hopping on 1, 8, and 2.

Using this game court, unless you allow children to use numbers more than once, there is a unique path for each number from 1 to 31.

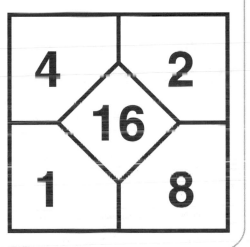

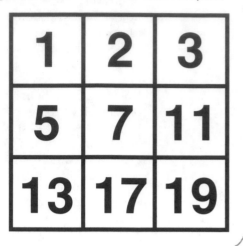

✕ ✦ ✦ ACTIVITY 12.30 Take the 5 path (variation 2)

On the floor, sidewalk, or playground, prepare a game court like the one illustrated. The spaces should be about 20 inches across. The game court can be made using masking tape or chalk, or a permanent one can be painted on a concrete or asphalt surface.

Have the children line up at the game court. You say, "Take the 5 path," and the first child hops across the game court landing on the numbers that add up to 5. If you say, "Take the 11 path," the next child in line must cross the game court by hopping on numbers that add up to 11.

With this game court, *children must be allowed to use numbers more than once,* otherwise, some paths will not be possible.

The next activity, *Bounce* 10, is really a version of Take the 5 Path. We show two variations of this activity. Activity 12.31 is appropriate for kindergarten and first-grade children. Activity 12.32 is appropriate for second- and third-grade children.

✕ ✦ ✦ ACTIVITY 12.31 Bounce 10 (variation 1)

On the floor, sidewalk, or playground, prepare a game court like the one illustrated. The spaces should be about 20 inches across. The game court can be made using masking tape or chalk, or a permanent one can be painted on a concrete or asphalt surface.

Have two children face each other across the game court. You hand an inflated playground ball to one of the children and say, "Bounce 10." That child bounces the ball on a number and to the other child. The second child then bounces the ball on a number and back to the first child. The numbers should add up to 10. For example, if the first child hits 7, the second child must hit 3. Also have children bounce 2, 3, 4, 5, 6, 7, 8 and 9. The first child must bounce on a number

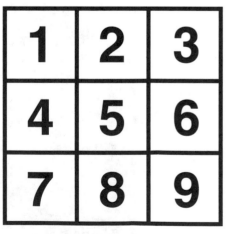

less than the target sum. Otherwise, it will not be possible to complete the sum.

ACTIVITY 12.32   Bounce 10 (variation 2)

On the floor, sidewalk, or playground, prepare a game court like the one illustrated. The spaces should be about 20 inches across. The game court can be made using masking tape or chalk, or a permanent one can be painted on a concrete or asphalt surface.

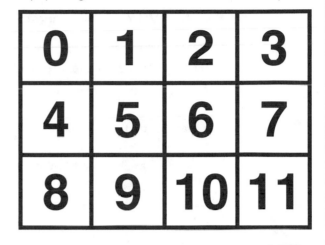

Have two children face each other across the game court. Hand an inflated playground ball to one of the children and say, "Bounce 10." That child says a number and bounces the ball on that number. The other child catches the ball and bounces it on a another number then gives the sum of the numbers. The first child then bounces the ball on another number and gives the sum so far. They continue until the numbers add up to 10. For example, if the first child hits 7, and the second child hits 2, then the first child must hit 1 to complete a sum of 10. The children must be careful not to go over 10. Also have children bounce 11, 12, 13, 14, 15, 16, 17 and 18.

Century Mark is an interesting small-group game that provides practice with two-digit addition and subtraction. Activity 12.33 is appropriate for grades 3 through 5.

ACTIVITY 12.33   Century Mark

Prepare a deck of 50 cards showing the digits, 0 through 9. There should be five cards for each digit.

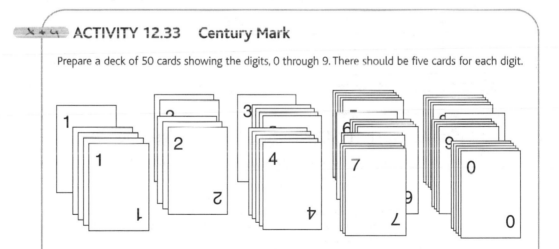

Form a group of 2 to 4 children. Shuffle the cards and place the deck face down on the table. All players write a beginning score of zero on a sheet of paper. On each play, each player takes two cards from the deck and forms a two-digit number. (For example, if a player draws 7 and 4, that player could form either 74 or 47. If a player draws 3 and 0, the player could form 30 or 03.) The players then either add their numbers to their current score, or they may subtract their numbers from their current score.

Play continues until a player's score is exactly 100. That player wins the game. If play continues without a winner until there are not enough cards for another play, the game ends, and the player whose score is closest to 100 is the winner.

Another excellent small-group practice activity is *Target Practice*. Activities 12.34 through 12.39 illustrate the flexibility of this activity.

× + ◁ ACTIVITY 12.34 Target Practice (variation 1)

Prepare a deck of 50 cards like those illustrated in Activity 12.33, showing the digits 0 through 9.

Form a group of 2 to 4 children. The children take turns dealing the cards.

On each play, the dealer shuffles the cards and gives each player two cards. The players add the numbers on their cards. The player with the sum closest to 10 takes all the cards used in that play.

If there is a tie, the cards from that play are left on the table. The winner of the next play gets those cards also.

When there are not enough cards for another play, the player who has taken the most cards is the winner.

× + ◁ ACTIVITY 12.35 Target Practice (variation 2)

Prepare a deck of 50 cards like those illustrated in Activity 12.33, showing the digits 0 through 9.

Form a group of 2 to 4 children. The children take turns dealing the cards.

On each play, the dealer shuffles the cards and gives each player two cards. The players use their cards to form two-digit numbers. The player whose two-digit number is closest to 50 takes all the cards used in that play.

If there is a tie, cards from that play are left on the table. The winner of the next play gets those cards also.

When there are not enough cards for another play, the player who has taken the most cards is the winner.

× + ◁ ACTIVITY 12.36 Target Practice (variation 3)

Prepare a deck of 50 cards like those illustrated in Activity 12.33, showing the digits 0 through 9.

Form a group of 2 to 4 children. The children take turns dealing the cards.

On each play, the dealer shuffles the cards and gives each player three cards. Each player uses two of the three cards to form a two-digit number. The player whose two-digit number is closest to 50 takes all the cards used in that play.

If there is a tie, the cards from that play are left on the table. The winner of the next play gets those cards also.

When there are not enough cards for another play, the player who has taken the most cards is the winner.

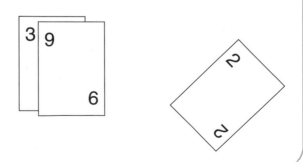

×+⁴ ACTIVITY 12.37   Target Practice (variation 4)

Prepare a deck of 50 cards like those illustrated in Activity 12.33, showing the digits 0 through 9. Form a group of 2 to 4 children. The children take turns dealing the cards.

On each play, the dealer shuffles the cards and gives each player four cards. Each player uses the cards to form two two-digit numbers whose sum is as close to 100 as possible. The player whose sum is closest to 100 takes all the cards used in that play.

If there is a tie, the cards from that play are left on the table. The winner of the next play gets those cards also.

When there are not enough cards for another play, the player who has taken the most cards is the winner.

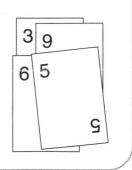

×+⁴ ACTIVITY 12.38   Target Practice (variation 5)

Prepare a deck of 50 cards like those illustrated in Activity 12.33, showing the digits 0 through 9. Form a group of 2 to 4 children. The children take turns dealing the cards.

On each play, the dealer shuffles the cards and gives each player three cards. Each player uses the cards to form a two-digit number and a one-digit number whose product is as close to 200 as possible. The player whose product is closest to 200 takes all the cards used in that play.

If there is a tie, the cards from that play are left on the table. The winner of the next play gets those cards also.

When there are not enough cards for another play, the player who has taken the most cards is the winner.

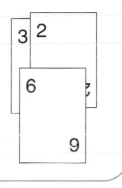

×+⁴ ACTIVITY 12.39   Target Practice (variation 6)

Prepare a check of 50 cards like those illustrated in Activity 12.33, showing the digits 0 through 9. Form a group of 2 to 4 children. The children take turns dealing the cards.

On each play, the dealer shuffles the cards and gives each player five cards. Each player uses the cards to form a three-digit number and a two-digit number whose difference is as close to 500 as possible. The player who difference is closest to 500 takes all the cards used in that play.

If there is a tie, the cards from that play are left on the table. The winner of the next play gets those cards also.

When there are not enough cards for another play, the player who has taken the most cards is the winner.

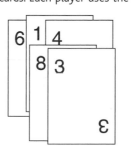

The final answer/example construction activity that we present in this chapter is *Shape Makers*. In this activity children create shapes by stretching a loop of rope.

✕ ＋ ◁ ACTIVITY 12.40   Shape Makers

Make a loop of rope by tying the ends of a rope that is about 25-feet long.

Give the rope to a group of four children. Have them stretch the rope loop out to make a rectangle. Have them also make a square. Have them try to make a circle. Ask why this is not possible.

Form a group of three children. Have then stretch the rope into the shape of a triangle. Have them make a triangle with all three sides equal. Have them make a right triangle. Have them try to make a rectangle. Ask why this is not possible.

Have six children try to make a circle. Have ten children try to make a circle. Can 20 people make a circle?

Summary

There are many activities that provide interesting—even fun—practice. Good practice activities are widely varied. Some of these activities are games, where there are winners. Others can be just as engaging even though they are not games. Good practice activities have varying levels of active involvement. They range from small-group to whole-class activities. Good practice activities range from very kinesthetic to moderately kinesthetic to fairly sedate. Good practice activities nearly always allow interaction among the children about the concepts or skills being practiced.

Most effective teachers of elementary school mathematics develop and use a wide repertoire of nonpencil-and-paper practice activities. But even though those activities are neat and lots of fun, the effective teacher must remember that *practice activities can only be effective after the concepts and skills have been adequately developed.* They know that *mathematical concepts and skills must be learned before they can be practiced.* And, of course, they know that *before we can expect those concepts and skills to be learned, they must be taught.*

References and Related Readings

Smith, S. E., Jr., & Backman, C. A. (Eds.). (1975). *Games and puzzles for elementary and middle school mathematics: Readings from the Arithmetic Teacher.* Reston, VA: NCTM.

Tucker, B. F. (1971). Parallelograms: A simple answer to drill motivation and individualized instruction. *The Arithmetic Teacher,* 18(7), 489–493.

Tucker, B. (1978). Match games. *The Illinois Mathematics Teacher,* 29(1), 24–28.

Tucker, B. F. (1981). Variations on concentration. *The Arithmetic Teacher,* 29(3), 22–23.

INDEX

Activities are in *italics*